Game Theory

Game theory is concerned with strategic interaction among several decision-makers. In such strategic encounters, all players are aware of the fact that their actions affect the other players. Game theory analyzes how these strategic, interactive considerations may affect the players' decisions and influence the final outcome. This textbook focuses on applications of complete-information games in economics and management, as well as in other fields such as political science, law, and biology. It guides students through the fundamentals of game theory by letting examples lead the way to the concepts needed to solve them. It provides opportunities for self-study and self-testing through an extensive pedagogical apparatus of examples, questions, and answers. The book also includes more advanced material suitable as a basis for seminar papers or elective topics, including rationalizability, stability of equilibria (with discrete-time dynamics), games and evolution, equilibrium selection, and global games.

Aviad Heifetz is Professor of Economics at the Open University of Israel, where he served as chair of the Economics and Management Department from 2006–2009. He was previously Visiting Professor of Managerial Economics at Kellogg School of Management, Northwestern University (2009–2011).

Game Theory

Interactive Strategies in Economics and Management

Aviad Heifetz

CAMBRIDGE
UNIVERSITY PRESS

University Printing House, Cambridge CB2 8BS, United Kingdom

One Liberty Plaza, 20th Floor, New York, NY 10006, USA

477 Williamstown Road, Port Melbourne, VIC 3207, Australia

314-321, 3rd Floor, Plot 3, Splendor Forum, Jasola District Centre, New Delhi - 110025, India

79 Anson Road, #06-04/06, Singapore 079906

Cambridge University Press is part of the University of Cambridge.

It furthers the University's mission by disseminating knowledge in the pursuit of education, learning and research at the highest international levels of excellence.

www.cambridge.org
Information on this title: www.cambridge.org/9780521176040

First published in Hebrew by Open University of Israel Press 2008
First published in English by Cambridge University Press 2012

Translation: Judith Yalon Fortus

A catalogue record for this publication is available from the British Library

Library of Congress Cataloging in Publication data
Heifetz, Aviad, 1965–
Game theory : interactive strategies in economics and management / Aviad Heifetz.
    pages   cm
ISBN 978-0-521-76449-0
1. Game theory.   2. Economics.   3. Management.   I. Title.
HB144.H455   2012
330.01´5193–dc23   2012000086

ISBN 978-0-521-76449-0 Hardback
ISBN 978-0-521-17604-0 Paperback

In loving memory of my father
Gutman Heifetz, 1933–2010

CONTENTS

FOREWORD

Game theory is concerned with strategic interaction among several decision-makers. In a strategic encounter of this kind, each player is aware of the fact that her actions affect the well-being of the other players, just as their actions affect hers. Game theory analyzes how these mutual influences channel the players' decisions and lead to the ultimate outcome. Since the basic theoretical foundations of game theory were laid in the mid twentieth-century, numerous applications have been found for it in economics and management, as well as in political science, anthropology, sociology, biology and computer science.

It is important to realize that game-theoretic tools do not provide off-the-shelf solutions for predicting players' behavior in a complex, real-life situation. In the social sciences, *y compris* in game theory, every model distils only a small number of critical aspects out of the vast plethora of dimensions characterizing a given situation. And it is exclusively in light of those aspects that it proceeds to analyze the situation, using highly stylized hypotheses regarding a whole host of other aspects. The purpose of the model is to provide a framework for *systematic thinking* about the complicated situation. Insights gained while analyzing the model may enable one to think more intelligently and profoundly about an actual, realistic situation. In this way, game theoretic models have shed light on the *modus operandi* of many economic and political mechanisms; and insights gained from such models have made a substantial contribution towards a more intelligent design of such mechanisms – incentives for workers in firms, financial markets and auctions for a large variety of assets, policies for diminishing air pollution, voting and election systems, and numerous other types of mechanisms, institutions and organizations.

Acknowledging the importance and salience of game theory, the Nobel Prize for Economics was awarded in 1994 to three of the founding fathers of game theory – John Nash, John Harsanyi, and Reinhard Selten, and in 2005 to another two of these founding fathers, Robert (Yisrael) Aumann and Thomas Schelling. In 2007, the Nobel Prize in Economics was dedicated to the domain of mechanism design with tools from information economics and game theory, and the prize was awarded to Leonid Hurwicz, Roger Myerson and Eric Maskin.

This textbook sets forth key notions in the analysis of non-cooperative games, with an emphasis on its applications for analyzing and designing economic institutions and markets. Special emphasis is placed on realistic examples and the results of laboratory experiments of games, which are conducted on a progressively larger scale in recent years. Especially interesting are those instances in which the results of the experiments do not align perfectly with the theoretical predictions. In such instances, the experiment results may provide a pointer to new directions for enhancing and improving the model. I have tried to indicate such innovative directions insofar as possible.

The textbook is suited for a one-semester elective course for Economics or Management undergraduates, as well as for MBA students. The book assumes minimal mathematical pre-requisites – mainly acquaintance with very basic concepts in probability and the technique for finding the maximum of a function. In fact, the book elaborates the requisite mathematical tools while making use of them. It is written in a style allowing for self study, with detailed solutions to many of the problems and questions that appear in the text.

Most chapters deal with classical themes of non-cooperative game theory: normal-form games, dominant and dominated strategies, Nash equilibrium, pure and mixed strategies, the minimax theorem, extensive-form games, subgame perfect equilibrium, and repeated games.

A small number of chapters address more advanced topics that can serve as enrichment and as the basis for seminar papers. Chapter 14 deals with rationalizable strategies. Chapter 15 addresses the stability of equilibria – a topic of particular importance in analyzing real-life problems. The chapter provides a definition of a discrete-time dynamical system; and for a number of games, it offers an analysis of the stability of their equilibria under the best-reply dynamics. This chapter prepares readers for the consecutive chapter on games and evolution. The chapter starts with a discussion of the discrete-time replicator dynamics, modeling directly a process of natural selection in which the survivors are the fittest types of players. The second part of Chapter 15 presents the static notion of an evolutionary stable strategy (ESS), and analyzes the link between ESS and the notion of stability under the replicator dynamics.

Chapter 17 delves into global games, with the focus on an example of currency exchange-rates attack. The discussion opens with a case in which there is a finite number of investor types, and only later proceeds to analyze the continuous case. The fact that the game between investor types is solvable by dominance considerations makes it possible to analyze the game, which is, in fact, a game with asymmetric information, using the tools provided in the book. Chapter 19, too, brings an example of a game with asymmetric information, addressing the issue of buyer types' screening by an uninformed seller. This example allows for the analysis of basic concepts in information economics, even though a general presentation of games with asymmetric information and an analysis of their solution concepts are beyond the scope of this book.

The book was originally published in Hebrew by the Open University of Israel. Since its publication in 2008 it served as a textbook for hundreds of students. I'm grateful to Chen Cohen who has vigorously coordinated the course at the Open University since its inception. I'm also grateful to colleagues in other Israeli universities, from whom I was delighted to hear comments based on their use of the book. Special warm thanks go to Zvika Neeman, Shmuel Nitzan, Motty Perry and Ella Segev, who took part in reviewing the book when it was still in draft form, and provided so many invaluable suggestions.

I'm deeply indebted to Judith Yalon Fortus, who translated the book into English with remarkable lucidity and rigor. Working along with Judith was a particularly pleasant experience. During much of the preparation of the English edition I was on a two-year visit to the MEDS department at Kellogg School of Management, Northwestern University. I'm grateful to my colleagues there for the very warm hospitality and the energetic spirit which made the visit so enjoyable. Burkhard Schipper from UC Davis deserves special thanks for reviewing the final draft of the English edition and providing additional very helpful suggestions.

I'm grateful for the excellent support I have received from the entire team at Cambridge University Press. I'm particularly indebted to the social sciences publishing director, Chris Harrison, with whom it was a splendid experience to work right from the very start. Always encouraging and attentive, this project would not have materialized without his genuine engagement. My gratitude goes also to the senior production editor, Daniel Dunlavey, who was so helpful with skillfully overcoming last-stage formatting issues and finalizing the project.

I was very happy that Noa Dar permitted us to use for the cover the photo from her choreography "Children's Games," inspired by Pieter Breughel's painting. May this be a tribute to Noa Dar's thrilling creations and to the vibrant Israeli dance scene at large.

And, of course, warm hugs to the ladies with whom I'm blessed to share my life – my wife Dana and our daughters Inbal and Maayan – for being so supportive along the entire journey of writing this book, and for making life playful as it should be.

Aviad Heifetz
The Open University of Israel
February 2012

PART I

Strategic interactions as games

Social interaction is essential to human life. How do people choose what to do when they encounter one another? And how do organizations, firms or countries interact? Game theory is a modeling tool designed to represent and analyze such strategic interaction.

The first part of this book is devoted to introducing the basic building blocks of game theory. The parties to the interaction are called *players*, the courses of actions available to them are their *strategies*, and the *payoffs* of each player from the various profiles of strategies (of *all* players) represent the way each player ranks the possible outcomes of the interaction from her own individual point of view.

Chapter 1 will be devoted to the definition of these concepts, and their illustration with a preliminary example. Chapter 2 will expand on these modeling considerations in concrete real-world examples. The first of these will be a historical military episode in the Middle East. Additional examples will concern competition over promotion in the workplace, and the design of incentives for teamwork. The considerations elaborated in the modeling process will set the stage for analyzing and predicting the outcomes of such strategic encounters in the chapters that follow.

1 Strategic form games

Man is a social animal. Our notions about the world and ourselves are indissolubly linked with the way we acquired those notions and experienced them together with our family and friends in kindergarten and at school and work. Some of our social encounters get us into confrontations with others as we seek to secure some gain for ourselves or improve our standing. Other encounters find us primarily cooperating with others in an effort to achieve a common goal. But all social encounters share one salient and important attribute: the action chosen by each of the participants in the encounter affects the other participants. That is what **game theory** is about.

Game theory deals with the behavior of individuals in a social environment where the actions of each individual affect the others. Game theory analyzes the considerations that rational participants entertain when deciding on their moves, and how such considerations affect the moves they choose to make.

The participants may be, for example, individual employees on the job, commercial firms in the economic market, or nations in the international arena. In order not to restrict the context of the study *ab initio*, such individuals are habitually referred to as "players" and the interaction between them is called a "game."

In everyday usage, the word "game" typically refers to children's games or sporting and social games such as football, chess or Monopoly. We derive direct enjoyment and entertainment value from the game and sometimes other added values, too. In game theory, the term "game" is assigned a more general meaning, to describe interactive encounters between several participants.

The borrowed use of the game concept in this context is based on the fact that every game has its predetermined rules. These rules define a permanent and built-in connection between causes and effects. In modeling a social situation in game theory, one seeks to single out such built-in connections from the vast plethora of the details of the event. As in a game in the everyday meaning of the word, the motivating forces are the actions or the **strategies** that participants can employ, and the results are the effects of the action of each of the participating **players** on each and every one of them.

In reality, this influence is of course multifaceted and highly diversified: it may take the form of the material resources at the participant's disposal, her emotional sense, her social status, what she expects of herself and what others expect from her, and so forth.

Despite this complexity, we will assume that each participant is able to rate the outcome of the encounter (which depends on the actions of *all* participants) in accordance with her own order of priorities. We will express this scale of preferences with the aid of numbers, which we will call **payoffs** or levels of **utility**. Thus the highest payoff will be ascribed to the outcome that is the most desirable for that individual, and the lowest payoff will be ascribed to the result that is worst for her.

Consider the following example.

1.1   Representation in negotiations over a business partnership

A manufacturing firm and a marketing firm are negotiating the formation of a business partnership. They estimate that the partnership will yield a joint profit of $1 million. If the companies' chief executive officers (CEOs) negotiate directly with one another, they will agree to share the anticipated profit equally between the two companies – $500,000 for each. However, a CEO hiring a lawyer to support her in the negotiations will be able to increase her share in the joint profit by $100,000 at the expense of the second company (by virtue of a more painstaking and sophisticated wording of the clauses of the contract). The cost of such legal representation is $50,000. If both directors hire lawyers, the profit formulated in the contract will be divided equally between the two companies.

In this example, the players are the company CEOs.

Each CEO has two possible negotiation strategies: to hire legal representation or to conduct the negotiations herself. The following matrix describes each company's financial profit (in thousands of dollars) in accordance with the strategies chosen by the CEOs.

		Marketing firm CEO	
		Negotiating directly	Hiring legal representation
Manufacturing firm CEO	Negotiating directly	500, 500	400, 550
	Hiring legal representation	550, 400	450, 450

Each entry in the matrix shows the financial profit (net of the expenses of legal representation, if any) of each of the companies for the combination of strategies corresponding to that entry. The left-hand figure is the profit of the manufacturing company, and the right-hand figure is the profit of the marketing company. Let us assume, for example, that the director of the manufacturing company chooses to hire legal representation (her strategy is shown in the second row), while the marketing company director chooses to conduct the negotiations herself (her strategy appears in the left-hand column). In the resulting contract, the manufacturing company will earn $600,000 so that its profit, net of legal representation, will amount to $550,000. Correspondingly, the marketing company's profit will be $400,000 (the right-hand figure in that entry).

We note that the figures appearing in the matrix of this game are the corporate profits, while the players in the game we have described are not the firms themselves but rather the firm CEOs. The CEOs do not pocket the entire profit that they obtained for the firm, and therefore the figures in the matrix do not reflect the monetary payments received by the players. The figures do, however, aptly describe the players' preferences, since each CEO shows preference for that combination of strategies that will yield a higher profit for her firm, over some other combination of strategies that will yield it a lower profit. This preference may derive from the CEO's sense of identification with her role, from incentives in the form of monetary rewards that may accrue to her if she succeeds in improving the firm's profitability, from a personal valuation she may obtain from the company's shareholders and from her colleagues, and so forth. The figures appearing in the matrix are accordingly called "payoffs" because the order in which they are arranged faithfully reflects preferences: if a particular combination of strategies leads to a particular outcome that a player deems preferable over some other result obtainable from a different combination of strategies, the payoff to the player in the game matrix from the first outcome is higher than the payoff to that player from the second result.

1.2 Definition of a strategic form game

Definition A **strategic form game** is defined by means of the following three components:

1. **The players** who take part in the game.
2. The set of **strategies** of each player.
3. The **payoff** to each player from every possible strategy profile of the players.

Let N be the number of players in the game, and denote by I the set of players. For player k in the set I of players, we will denote by X_k the set of strategies available to player k. A strategy x_k of player k is therefore an element in the set X_k of strategies.

In the example shown in section 1.1 above, the set of players consists of the two CEOs:

$I = \{$manufacturing firm CEO, marketing firm CEO$\}$

The set of strategies of the CEO of the manufacturing firm is:

$X_{\text{manufacturing firm CEO}} = \{$negotiating independently,

hiring legal representation$\}$

Similarly, the set of strategies of the CEO of the marketing firm is:

$X_{\text{marketing firm CEO}} = \{$*negotiating independently, hiring legal representation*$\}$

A profile of strategies of the players has the form $x = (x_1, \ldots, x_k, \ldots, x_N)$. That is, for every player k, $k \in I$, the profile of strategies specifies the strategy x_k of player k.
We will denote by X the set of all strategy profiles of the players:[1]

$$X = \Pi_{k \in I} X_k$$

Likewise, we will denote by

$$X_{-i} = \Pi_{j \neq i} X_j$$

the set of strategy profiles of all the players other than player i. Thus a strategy profile of all the players other than i takes the form

$$x_{-i} = (x_1, \ldots, x_{i-1}, x_{i+1}, \ldots, x_N) \in X_{-i} = \Pi_{j \neq i} X_j$$

and a strategy profile of all the players takes the form

$$x = (x_1, \ldots, x_{i-1}, x_i, x_{i+1}, \ldots, x_N) = (x_i, x_{-i}) \in X_i \times X_{-i}$$
$$= \Pi_{k \in I} X_k = X$$

In this form of writing, we have presented the strategy profile x in two different ways. At first we presented it explicitly as the combination $(\ldots x_k, \ldots)_{k \in I}$ of the strategies x_k chosen by the players k in the set I of players. Next, we presented it as the combination (x_i, x_{-i}) of the choice x_i of player i and the profile of choices x_{-i} of the other players. We will use the latter presentation whenever we wish to emphasize that a profile x of strategies is a combination of the choice x_i of player i, which depends solely on her own will, and of the choice profile x_{-i} of the other players, which does not depend on the will of player i. If i and j are the only two players in the game, then $X_{-i} = X_j$, i.e. the set of strategy profiles of all the players other than i is simply the set of strategies of the second player, j, and there is no difference between the two presentations.

---

[1] The symbol Π, the "Cartesian product" (after the French philosopher and mathematician Descartes), signifies "the set of all the possible combinations of elements from the sets."

It now remains to define the players' payoffs. As we have explained, a key feature of a game is that the payoff of each player depends on the strategic choices of all the players. Therefore, the payoff to each player is a function that associates a number to each strategy profile of the players. We will call this function the player's payoff function or utility function. Formally, the payoff function u_i of player i,

$$u_i : X \to \mathbb{R}$$

profile x the real number $u_i(x)$. (The letter $\mathbb{R}$ represents the set of real numbers.)

The payoff function u_i represents the player's preferences. That is,

$$u_i(x) > u_i(x')$$

if and only if i prefers the outcome obtained from the strategy profile x over the outcome obtained from the strategy profile x'.

In the particular case in which there are only two players, $I = \{1,2\}$, each of whom has a finite set of strategies, the payoff function may be described by means of a game matrix, as in the example in section 1.1 above. In this matrix, each row corresponds to one of the strategies of player 1 and each column corresponds to one of the strategies of player 2. In each entry of the matrix there appear two payoffs – the payoff of player 1 (the left-hand figure) and the payoff of player 2 (the right-hand figure). The payoffs in the entry of the matrix in row m and column n are:

$$u_1(m, n), u_2(m, n)$$

These are the payoffs to the players when player 1 chooses the strategy corresponding to row m and player 2 chooses the strategy corresponding to column n.

> Game theory is not the only domain that has borrowed the term "game" from its day-to-day usage. The philosopher Ludwig Wittgenstein coined the notion "language-game" in his book *Philosophical Investigations* (1953). Wittgenstein rejects the view whereby every word in a language is a name or representation of something in the real world, and the understanding of the meaning of a word consists of knowing what object the word represents. Wittgenstein maintains that "to imagine a language is to imagine a form of life." According to him, the meaning of a word is the way it is used in the language, and the meaning of a name is clarified by pointing at its subject. Accordingly, it is the social "game" that establishes the meaning of words. Thus Wittgenstein too adopts the term "game" to describe a basic and fundamental phenomenon in human society.

2 Representing strategic interactions with games

In this chapter we will examine several examples that can be analyzed using game-theoretic tools. These examples will help to illustrate the considerations involved when social interactions or confrontations are represented by **strategic form games**. We will also discover what aspects cannot be represented by a strategic form game, and find out in what ways the game concept needs to be extended so as to realize more appropriate representations.

2.1 The background to the Six Day War

The Six Day War of June 5–10, 1967, between Israel and its neighboring Arab states Egypt, Jordan and Syria, was a key event in the evolution of the conflict in the Middle East. The strategic dilemmas faced by the belligerents constitute a prime example for game-theoretic analysis.

After Israel declared its independence on May 14, 1948, in accordance with the United Nations resolution from November 1947, its borders with Egypt, Jordan, Syria, and Lebanon were established via a war which lasted until March 1949. In 1956, in response to terrorist infiltrations from the Sinai Peninsula, Israel captured it from Egypt, but withdrew under international pressure and guarantees for shipping rights in the Red Sea, from the port of Eilat via the Straits of Tiran.

2.1.1 The circumstances on the eve of the war

In the year preceding the Six Day War, tension between Israel and Syria was on the rise, sparked by three principal causes. First, Syria was claiming additional rights over the Jordan River source waters, while planning to divert the Yarmuk River in such a way that a smaller share of its water would reach territory under Israeli control. Second, Israel and Syria had a dispute about the cultivation rights of the agricultural land in the demilitarized zone established between the two armies at the end of Israel's War of Independence. The third factor was the terror attacks initiated and perpetrated by Palestinian terrorist organizations (primarily the Fatah) under Syrian auspices, by infiltrating Israel from within Syrian territory.

This tension would sporadically erupt in the form of military skirmishes such as that in July 1966 when Israel launched an attack on the Yarmuk River waters diversion project, using aircraft and artillery. On April 7, 1967, an incident between Israel and Syria escalated into a day of combat when the Syrians fired on an Israeli tractor that had entered the demilitarized zone. Israel's refusal to withdraw the tractor prompted an exchange of fire between amored, artillery and aerial forces, culminating in the silencing of the Syrian positions and the downing by the Israel Air Force of six Syrian MiG airplanes. Two of the airplanes were shot down over the outskirts of Damascus, in full view of Syrian citizens attending the Baath Party anniversary celebrations that were taking place that day.

Yet the frequency of incursions from Syrian territory into Israel kept mounting. In the first half of May 1967, Israel sent Damascus some severe warnings. Speaking publicly, Prime Minister Levi Eshkol stated that Israel might resort to measures no less harsh than those taken on April 7, 1967. News agencies cited a senior Israeli source as saying that Israel might take restricted military action with the aim of overthrowing the military regime in Damascus if the incursions from Syrian territory into Israel were to continue.

Syria responded by appealing to Egypt for support, as part of the mutual defense pact the two countries had formed on November 4, 1966. In addition, Egypt was receiving (erroneous) intelligence reports from the Soviet Union to the effect that Israel was massing forces on her border with Syria. Egypt, which under President Gamal Abdel Nasser aspired to leadership of the Arab world, therefore decided to take action. On May 15, Egyptian troops ostentatiously passed through Cairo *en route* for the Sinai Peninsula. The next day, the Egyptian Chief of Staff notified the Officer in Command of the UN Forces in Sinai (which had been positioned there in 1957 as a barrier between the armies of Israel and Egypt) that they must vacate their positions immediately. On May 18, Egyptian forces took over the UN positions in Sharm-el-Sheikh that controlled the Straits of Tiran. On May 22, Nasser accused Israel of threatening to go to war, and announced that the Straits would henceforth be closed to Israeli ships making their way to the port of Eilat. On May 26, Nasser, in a public speech, alleged that the problem was not just Israel but also the United States and the western nations that supported Israel. He declared that if Israel attacked Syria and Egypt, the conflict would not be confined to the frontier regions only but would be an all-out war, in which Egypt's aim would be to destroy Israel. The Voice of Cairo radio station then started airing broadcasts featuring calls to wipe Israel off the face of the earth.

The opening of the Straits of Tiran to Israeli vessels under the supervision of the United Nations had been one of Israel's most important achievements in the 1956 Sinai Campaign, and Israel's traditional position was that the closure of the Straits by Egypt would constitute a *casus belli*. Nevertheless, Egypt was hoping that Israel would be afraid to open war simultaneously on two fronts.

2.1.2   Presentation of the circumstances as a game

Following the closure of the Straits, both countries had to simultaneously reach a decision as to how to act.

Thus, Israel faced two principal alternatives:

1. To fulfill its commitment to war following the closure of the Straits.
2. To threaten to go to war, but not to launch hostilities on its own initiative.

Egypt had three principal alternatives:

1. To launch a war on its own initiative.
2. To leave the situation unchanged.
3. To respond to international mediation efforts, to withdraw its troops from Sinai, and to restore the status quo ante.[1]

Question 2.1   Describe this historical situation as a game. Who are the players? What strategies do they have at their disposal? What are the payoffs in this game?

Answer   According to the description, the players are Israel and Egypt, and the strategies available to each player are the alternatives outlined above.

What are the payoffs to the players? The payoffs represent the ranking, from the point of view of each player, of the six combinations of choices that are possible. We will now propose certain considerations that will lead to such a ranking.

We must not, however, lose sight of the fact that this is not necessarily the only ranking that is consistent with the historical data on the parties' positions. This is therefore an example of the manner in which using game theory to analyze a historical situation can sharpen the discussion on how to **interpret** historical events.

To our understanding, the leading considerations for describing the parties' preferences are as follows.

Israel's preferences
1. Had Egypt indeed intended to launch an all-out war, it would have been preferable for Israel to initiate the war itself, thus gaining whatever military advantages might be had from taking the initiative. Of all the strategy combinations leading to war, this is the one that is best for Israel, since the justification for

---

[1] In 1960, Egypt had put troops in Sinai without ordering the UN forces out, and had withdrawn them after a certain period.

launching war is the strongest and its military outcomes are optimal from Israel's point of view. Were Israel to wait while Egypt initiated a war it would be the worst combination from Israel's point of view.

2. Had Egypt intended leaving things as they were, and, in particular, leaving the Straits of Tiran closed to Israeli shipping but not launching an all-out war, it would still have been preferable for Israel to initiate a war. Had it not done so, Israel would have damaged its power of deterrence by putting up indefinitely with the closure of the Straits of Tiran, a contingency it had already declared would constitute a *casus belli*. Renouncing this threat might have avoided the war at that juncture, but the damage to the image of Israel's resoluteness might have led Egypt or Syria to take further aggressive measures against Israel.

3. Had Egypt intended lifting the blockade on the Straits of Tiran following a short period of muscle flexing, it would have been preferable for Israel to avoid the war and its repercussions. The Israeli threat of going to war would, in this case, have appeared effective, and Israeli deterrence would not have been injured. Of all the strategy combinations, this one, in which diplomacy achieves effective results without bloodshed, would have been best for Israel.

4. The "erroneous war" combination, in which Israel goes to war whereas it could in fact have safeguarded its interests without doing so, would have been the worst for Israel. Likewise, a situation in which Israel merely threatened war (without actually initiating one) while Egypt kept blockading the Straits of Tiran would have been bad for Israel.

Egypt's preferences

1. The reason why Egypt took aggressive measures against Israel in the first place, by bringing troops into Sinai and blockading the Straits, was that Syria saw itself threatened by Israel, and Egypt felt called upon to act by virtue of their mutual defense pact, and with an eye to maintaining a position of leadership in the Arab world. At that point in time, however, Egypt was not militarily prepared for a war with Israel. Therefore, all strategy combinations that were going to lead to the outbreak of full-scale hostilities were inferior from the Egyptian point of view to those in which war could be avoided.

2. War was avoidable only if both countries individually elected not to be the first to launch hostilities. Assuming this to be the case, Egypt's position would have been optimal if it had continued to demonstrate its strength and block the Straits of Tiran to Israeli shipping. It would have been in not quite as advantageous a position if, as a response to international mediation efforts, it had consented to reopen the Straits after a certain interval.

3. Of all the strategy combinations leading to the outbreak of war, Egypt's position would have been optimal if it had been the one to initiate war while Israel were to wait. Its position would not have been as good if Israel, too, had

simultaneously decided to go to war. Egypt's position would have been worst if it had had no intention of launching a war itself, while Israel took the initiative in opening fire.

These considerations lead to a description of the payoffs in the following game matrix:

		Egypt	
	Launch hostilities	Leave the Straits of Tiran closed	Retreat from Sinai in response to mediation efforts
Israel Go to war	4,2	3,1	2,1
Threaten war	1,3	2,5	5,4

Work out for yourself why this payoff matrix reflects the considerations outlined above.[2]

2.2   Competing for promotion

The managers of two departments in a major firm are both candidates for promotion at the end of the year to the job of managing the division. Given that both have, to date, won considerable esteem, their achievements in the current year will largely determine which of them will gain the promotion, which both are keen to get.

Ann manages the sales department in the northern region, while Beth manages the sales department in the southern region. Each needs to decide, at the very beginning of the year, which of the firm's products she is going to promote that year, what specials she should offer her customers, what incentives to propose to retail outlets, and how much money to invest in purchasing shelf space, having products conspicuously displayed, etc.

Who are the players in this example? What are their strategies? What are the payoff functions?

---

[2] Note that we need at least five different numbers to represent the preferences outlined, in order for the result that is preferable in the eyes of a particular country to be represented by a higher payoff. The absolute size of the numbers and the differences between them are irrelevant in representing preferences.

2.2.1   Analyzing the game

In this example, the set of players consists of the two managers. For the purpose of the notation below, Ann will be called "Player 1" and Beth will be called "Player 2."

What is the set of strategies of each manager? Every strategy is a complex description of the actions she chooses along the year as described above – the products the manager decides to emphasize, her marketing strategy, and so forth. At the same time, we will not insist on such a highly involved description of strategies, since we prefer to focus, instead, on the **competition** between the two managers – that being the **strategic** aspect we wish to analyze.

One way of bypassing the complexity of the managers' strategies is to assume that the description of any marketing and sales tactics can be **summed up** in terms of the amount of money the manager chooses to spend on the marketing campaign. This is a reasonable assumption if the managers are talented and experienced, so that for any given sum of money that either of them decides to spend on marketing in that year, the use she will make of the money will be efficient (which is to say, no better alternative can be found for utilizing the money for marketing purposes, such that for any profit level P that may be realized, the prospect of earning at least P will be higher by using the alternative marketing tactic). In this way, the strategy set of each manager is the segment $[0,M]$ of the numbers describing the amount of money (in dollars, for example) that the manager can choose to spend on marketing. M is the maximum amount available to her for this purpose. Manager i ($i = 1,2$) can therefore choose to spend any amount x_i satisfying $0 \leq x_i \leq M$.

Presented in this way, each player has a continuum of strategies to choose from, and hence this is not a situation that can be presented by means of a game matrix. In reality, of course, the number of strategies is finite because the budget the manager chooses will be denominated in whole dollars (or at least in whole cents). Even so, as we will see, by presenting the set of strategies as a continuum, we may make the payoffs easier to define.

What, then, are the payoffs of the players? The data relevant to this question are not detailed enough to provide an explicit description of the payoffs. In later chapters we will address similar questions while filling in the missing details. We can even now, however, describe some of the qualitative features of the payoffs.

Each manager realizes that a relatively moderate selling strategy will result in a better prospect of moderate achievements. The more aggressive the selling strategy, the greater the likelihood of a more significant increase in sales; but there will be a correspondingly greater likelihood that increase will fail to compensate for the heavy investment in marketing. The current year is one in which it is most important for each manager to present higher net profits than her rival.

We understand, therefore, that the prospects of each manager to be chosen for promotion depend both on the selling strategy she chooses and on the selling strategy the other manager chooses. Whatever strategy Ann chooses, Beth's prospects will be somewhat dim if she herself picks a radical strategy:

1. A very low-key selling strategy will almost certainly lead Beth to a low volume of sales and lower profits than those attained by her rival.
2. At the other extreme, a highly aggressive selling strategy may increase Beth's prospects of outperforming Ann in terms of volume of sales, but at the same time will also greatly increase the likelihood that the net profit presented by the department will be lower, due to the high marketing expenses incurred.

Accordingly, in the "low" range of very moderate selling strategies, Beth's chances to be promoted increase with the investment she makes in sales promotion. But in the "high" range of very aggressive selling strategies, Beth finds herself less likely to be promoted as her investment in sales promotion increases further.

The selling strategy that will maximize Beth's promotion prospects is therefore to be found somewhere in the middle range, between the extremes. This optimal strategy, however, also depends on the strategy Ann chooses.

Ann obviously faces a similar dilemma. The optimal selling strategy, from her point of view, that will maximize her shot at promotion depends on the strategy chosen by Beth. For example, payoff functions of the form:

$$u_1(x_1, x_2) = \left(x_1 - \frac{M}{2}\right)(x_2 - x_1)$$

$$u_2(x_1, x_2) = \left(x_2 - \frac{M}{2}\right)(x_1 - x_2)$$

have the qualitative properties we have described above.

2.3   Teamwork incentives

A start-up company employs five engineers who are engaged in the challenging development of an innovative technology. The company is being traded on the New York Stock Exchange at a per-share price of $10. A key component of the monetary compensation to each engineer is given in the form of options for the purchase of 10,000 shares of the company in two years' time, at a price of $15 per share. Hence, if the value S of the company's share two years hence proves to be lower than or equal to $15, then the options conferred on the engineers will be worthless. If, however, in two years' time the company's share S is valued at more than $15, then each engineer will receive a bonus of $10,000(S-15)$ dollars. This reward mechanism is designed to encourage the engineers to invest a special effort in developing the company's technology, in such a way that its market value two years hence will be at least 50 percent higher than its current value.

An engineer's investment takes the form of the number of weekly hours he spends at work, and the degree of attention, concentration, and will he invests in each work-hour.

Comprehension check

What is the set of players in this example? (Does it consist exclusively of the company's engineers, or also, perhaps, of investors in the stock exchange and analysts reviewing the company's share and the shares of companies in related fields? Might it also include national leaders, whose decisions may affect money markets worldwide? How should we select the set of players if we want to focus on the teamwork of the engineers?)

What is each player's set of strategies? Is each player's payoff function reflected solely in the monetary payment that will accrue to him, or are any other aspects involved? To answer this question, consider, for example, the following:

1. Is it reasonable to assume that every engineer prefers a high monetary payment over a lower payment in two years' time?
2. Is it reasonable to assume that every engineer prefers to work ten hours per week rather than thirty hours per week? Sixty work-hours as against eighty work-hours per week? (Factor in considerations such as fatigue, attrition, work interest and challenge, gaining proficiency and the fulfillment of one's personal potential, a sense of obligation toward the team members, leisure time for spending with the family and caring for children, and so forth.)

2.4   Discussion

In the first and second examples above, all players act simultaneously.[3] They must decide how to proceed while uninformed as to the decisions of the other players. As stated, games of this type are called **strategic form games**. Parts I–V of this book focus on games of this type.

However, in the third, last example, each engineer may decide afresh, every day, how many work-hours he wishes to dedicate to the corporate development effort.

---

[3] In the example in section 2.2 we have assumed that the two managers must reach a decision at the beginning of the year as to marketing policy for the entire year.

This decision may be contingent on the effort he and his fellow team members have invested to date, on the company's stock exchange value, on global economic developments, and so forth. Games of this type, in which the players do not necessarily make their choices simultaneously or on a one-off basis, are called **extensive form games**, addressed in parts VI–VII of this book. Extensive form games have an additional description component, namely the **order** in which the players are called to play. The identity of the players who must act at each and every stage, and the set of actions available to them at each stage, may depend on actions chosen by the players at earlier stages of the game. This dependency makes it much more complicated to describe the game as a whole.

This book will deal only with **games with complete information**. In a such game, the payoffs to the players (describing how each player rates the game results) are public: all players know everybody else's payoffs; moreover, all players are also aware that the payoffs are known to all players; everybody knows that all of them know everybody else's payoffs; and so on. In a situation of this kind we say that the players have **common knowledge** of the payoffs.

The assumption that players have **common knowledge** of the payoffs is never literally fulfilled. The players' payoffs, after all, reflect the individual preferences of the players, and human beings are not mind readers. Therefore, it is difficult to imagine a situation in which every player knows with certainty what the other players' preferences are, not to mention having common knowledge of those preferences.

This applies *a fortiori* where a culture gap yawns between the players. In the illustration in section 2.1, for example, it is highly doubtful whether Israel correctly understood the considerations weighing with the Egyptians, or whether Egypt correctly assessed Israel's interests.

In order to describe **games with incomplete information** – which is to say, without common knowledge of the payoffs – we must describe not only what each player's true payoffs (i.e. real preferences) are but also what each player believes about the other player's payoffs, what he believes about the beliefs of the other players, and so forth, a topic that is beyond the scope of this book.

Notwithstanding all qualifications, there are many cases that reasonably well approximate the description of games with complete information. For example, in the case outlined in section 2.2 above, it is entirely possible that the two managers share common information to the effect that both of them are very keen to be promoted to the division management job. It is also possible that both possess many years of experience in their jobs, and therefore reach very similar assessments of the economic implications of various selling tactics. They may also be aware that they are both using the same models and the same data, and that, accordingly, each may be aware of the promotion prospects of them both, as a function of the strategies they choose. Thus, in this example, the assumption that the players have common knowledge of the payoffs is a reasonable one for analyzing the competition between them.

However, over and above the issue of how reasonable it is to assume complete information, there are important methodological reasons for developing the study of game theory by analyzing games with complete information. Further on, we will encounter several general phenomena that are characteristics of games, and that do not feature in decision-making problems of a single individual. It is therefore important to diagnose such phenomena before we proceed to the study of more complex games with incomplete information. In that way, we can differentiate between phenomena arising from the very fact of strategic mutuality and other, more complicated, phenomena that arise from a lack of symmetry in the information available to the participating players.

PART II

Basic solution concepts for strategic form games

INTRODUCTION

In Part II we will explore the basic solution concepts for strategic form games. The strongest solution concept of all, introduced in Chapter 3, is that of strongly dominant strategies. A strongly dominant strategy is one which is strictly preferable for the player irrespective of the choices of the other players.

We will see, though, that – somewhat surprisingly – even when all players have strongly dominant strategies, the outcome of the strategic interaction might be inefficient, and all players wish they could have coordinated to play a different strategy profile. The prime examples of this phenomenon are the two-player games of the Prisoner's Dilemma type, called also "social dilemma" games.

A somewhat weaker solution concept, also discussed in Chapter 2, is that of weakly dominant strategies. A strategy is weakly dominant if, irrespective of the choices of the other players, the strategy is never inferior to any other strategy the player could have chosen, and for some strategy profile of the other players it is strictly better than all the alternative strategies available to the player. When each player has a weakly dominant strategy, the game is said to be solvable by weak domination.

A second price auction, which is akin (though not identical) to the one carried out in eBay and other online auctions, is an example of a game in which each bidder has a weakly dominant strategy – namely to bid the maximum amount she is willing to pay for the auctioned good. Upon winning, she will be paying only the second-highest bid, and hence any other bidding strategy is weakly dominated: bidding more than one's maximum willingness to pay might lead to winning but paying more than this maximum, while bidding less than this maximum might lead to losing an opportunity to win the auction at a profitable price.

Another prime example of a game with weakly dominant strategies is that of a competition between two political candidates, in which each voter votes for the candidate with the platform closest to his opinion. The median voter theorem asserts that in order to maximize the chances of winning the election, it is a weakly dominant strategy for each candidate to run with a platform identical to the opinion of the median voter – i.e. the voter for whom there are as many voters with more right-inclining opinions than his own as there are voters with more left-inclining opinions. This theorem may provide an insight regarding the tendency of political competitors to present moderate opinions in two-party regimes.

Not all games, though, have strongly or weakly dominant strategies, which the players would naturally choose. Nevertheless, some games have strategies which the players would *not* be inclined to choose, namely strategies that are strongly dominated by some other strategy. One strategy is said to be strongly dominated by another if, irrespective of the choices of the other players, the first strategy would yield a strictly lower payoff than the second.

This does not necessarily mean that the second strategy will actually be chosen – it could very well be the case that once strictly dominated strategies of the other players are eliminated, the second strategy becomes strictly dominated by yet another, third strategy. If this process of iterative elimination of strongly dominated strategies eventually leaves a unique strategy for each player, the game is said to be solvable by iterative elimination of strictly dominated strategies. This solution concept is discussed in Chapter 4.

An example of a game solvable by iterative elimination of strictly dominated strategies is that of the choice of location of newsstands along a street by two competitors, assuming that residents would only buy newspapers from a newsstand closest to them. Iterative elimination of strongly dominated strategies would drive both competitors to position their newsstands in the middle of the street.

A related solution is that of iterative elimination of weakly dominated strategies, also called iterated admissibility. This solution concept is presented and analyzed in Chapter 5. A strategy is weakly dominated by another strategy if, irrespective of the choices of the other players, the first strategy is not better than the second strategy, and for some strategy profile of the other player the first strategy is strictly worse than the second. A strategy which is not weakly dominated by any other strategy is called admissible.

This second strategy may itself become weakly dominated by a third strategy once the weakly dominated strategies of the opponents are eliminated. The process of iteratively eliminating strategies that become weakly dominated given the strategies of the opponents which survived the previous round leads, eventually, to the set of iteratively admissible strategies. If each player has a unique strategy which survives this process, the game is said to be solvable by iterated admissibility.

Several interesting games are solvable in this way. One is that of price competition between two firms selling the same product. Another game is that of a "beauty contest," in which each student in a class is asked to name a number between 0 and 100, and the winner is the one whose number is closest to 2/3 of the average guess but does not exceed 2/3 of this average. The only iteratively admissible strategy in this game is to name the number "0."

Yet another example is the "traveler's dilemma," in which two travelers have to claim, simultaneously and independently, a monetary compensation from an airline for identical lost objects, but if there is a discrepancy between the claims the traveler with the lower claim gets a bonus compensation at the expense of the other. The logic behind the solution to this game is similar to that of the beauty contest. Interestingly enough, in laboratory experiments of both games, subjects manifest behavior which deviates from the game-theoretic prediction, and we discuss the potential sources for this deviation.

A voting paradox is another example of a game amenable to solution with iterative admissibility. In a three-member committee which has to choose among three alternatives, it is shown how the chairperson, having the privilege of choosing the alternative in case no alternative gets a majority, ends up having the alternative he likes most being chosen!

Lastly, we return to the example from the Six Day War discussed in Chapter 2 and solve it using iterative elimination of weakly dominated strategies. The historical events do not match the game-theoretic prediction, and we discuss the possible reasons for the discrepancy.

The elimination procedures we defined call for eliminating simultaneously, in each round, the dominated strategies for each player. In the case of strong domination, the outcome would be the same if at each round only one of the player's strongly dominated strategies were eliminated, alternating between the players. In contrast, for the case of weak domination, setting such an arbitrary alternating order may make a difference in some games, and we show the possibility of such order-dependence in an example.

But some games don't even have weakly dominated strategies. How should such games be solved? The conceptual breakthrough of John Nash was his notion of equilibrium, which is the topic of Chapter 6. A Nash equilibrium is a profile of strategies, one for each player, in which each player's strategy is a **best reply** to the strategy profile of her rivals. We provide several conceptual justifications for this equilibrium concept – a self-sustaining, stable agreement, a mutually consistent profile of forecasts, or an equilibrium of choices and forecasts.

Some games have more than one Nash equilibrium. One example is the Battle of the Sexes, in which each party in a couple has a different taste regarding the preferred venue for spending the evening, but each prefers spending the evening together over going alone to their preferred show. In this game, coordinating on either one of the shows would be a Nash equilibrium.

We show the general procedure to find out the Nash equilibria in a game with finitely many strategies, as well as in games with a one-dimensional continuum of strategies. The latter case involves the important notion of the best-reply curve, depicting for each strategy profile of the rivals the strategy or strategies which yield the best payoff to the player. Each intersection of the players' best-reply curves constitutes a Nash equilibrium.

In some games with several Nash equilibria there are natural procedures to screen some of these equilibria. For example, in some games there are Nash equilibria in which some or all of the players employ weakly dominated strategies, and therefore such equilibria may be deemed less plausible as predictions for the outcome of the game. Some games may have a focal equilibrium, which stands out due to its symmetry. We show both ideas via the game of "Divvying up the Jackpot."

3

Dominant strategies

The simplest games to analyze are those in which each of the players has a **strongly dominant strategy**. A strongly dominant strategy is one that is preferred by the player to any other strategy available to her, for every possible profile of strategies the other players may adopt.

3.1   Strongly dominant strategies

Definition

A strategy $x_i \in X_i$ of player i is called a **strongly dominant strategy** if for every other strategy of hers $x_i' \neq x_i$ and every strategy profile $x_{-i} \in X_{-i}$ of the other players, it is the case that

$$u_i(x_i, x_{-i}) > u_i(x_i', x_{-i}).$$

If x_i is a strongly dominant strategy of player i, this player may say to herself: It is true that I don't know what strategies x_{-i} the other players will choose, and I am therefore not sure what my payoff $u_i(x_i, x_{-i})$ will be. However, I have noticed that in any event, for any profile of strategies x_{-i} that the other players can choose, the choice of x_i is strictly preferable for me than any other strategy x_i' I could choose.

Let us examine the game:

Player 2

		L	R
	T	3, 3	1, 2
Player 1			
	B	2, 0	0, 0

In this game, strategy T of player 1 is a strongly dominant strategy: whether player 2 chooses the strategy L or the strategy R, the choice of T is strictly preferable for player 1 over the choice of B.

Let's verify this:

- If player 2 chooses L, then player 1's choice of T will yield her the payoff 3, which is higher than the payoff 2 that she will get if she chooses B.
- If player 2 chooses R, then player 1's choice of T will yield her the payoff 1, which is higher than the payoff 0 she will get by choosing B.

Question 3.1

Is strategy L of player 2 a strongly dominant strategy?

Answer

No. Of course, strategy L always yields player 2 a payoff that is at least as high as that which strategy R yields him. But if player 1 chooses strategy B, then the payoff to player 2 from strategy L will be equal to the one he could obtain from strategy R – in both cases, the payoff will be 0. Therefore, L is not strongly dominant. (NB: when checking whether L is strongly dominant, it makes no difference that T is a strongly dominant strategy for player 1, and that therefore – if player 1 is rational – she will never choose B. For a strategy of a player to be strongly dominant, the player should strictly prefer it regardless of any considerations of common sense, absence of confusion or any other aspect of the other players. No such strong and unconditional preference figures in respect of strategy L of player 2, and for this reason L is not strongly dominant for him.)

In practice, when the payoffs in a game are presented in the form of a matrix, it is easy to ascertain whether a particular strategy is a strongly dominant strategy. In the present example, the payoffs $\begin{matrix} L & R \\ 3 & 1 \end{matrix}$ of player 1 in the first row are higher than the payoffs $\begin{matrix} L & R \\ 2 & 0 \end{matrix}$ of player 1 in the second row (when compared for each column separately!). Since, in this example, player 1 has only two strategies, one may conclude that the strategy T – the strategy of choosing the first row – is a strongly dominant strategy.

Generally speaking, if the payoffs of the game are represented in matrix form, and the payoffs to player 1 in a particular row are higher than the payoffs to player 1 in any other row (when compared for each column separately), then the strategy associated with that particular row is a strongly dominant strategy for player 1.

Similarly, if the payoffs to player 2 in a particular column are higher than the payoffs to that player in any other column (when compared for each row separately), then the strategy associated with that particular column is a strongly dominant strategy for player 2.

> **Comprehension check**
>
> Show that a player cannot have two different strategies both of which are strongly dominant.

3.2   Solution of the game with strongly dominant strategies

Definition If each of the players in the game has a strongly dominant strategy, the combination of these strategies is called **the solution of the game with strongly dominant strategies**.

A solution of a game with strongly dominant strategies is the strongest solution concept in game theory, since the assumptions leading to it are the weakest. In effect, the sole assumption needed here regarding the behavior of the players is that each player does what is best from her point of view. To that end, the players are not required to assess or to guess how the other players will behave. Whether or not all or any of the other players conduct themselves rationally, whether or not they get confused, whether their beliefs concerning the probable behavior of the players in the game are correct or incorrect – all this has no effect on which strategy, from the viewpoint of each player, is the optimal one. This optimal strategy is the strongly dominant strategy.

But will the players in fact always choose this strategy?

3.2.1   A social dilemma

Let's take a look at the following game:

		Player 2	
		C	D
Player 1	C	2, 2	0, 3
	D	3, 0	1, 1

This game could be descriptive of many social situations. Each player's strategy C corresponds to "social" behavior, while strategy D corresponds to "selfish" behavior. Let us imagine, for example, two neighboring families who share a common backyard. Either family's strategy C may be "keeping the backyard clean during the holiday" while D may be "not keeping the backyard clean." The description of the game payoffs indicates that both families prefer a clean backyard (with a payoff of 2 for each family) over a very dirty backyard (when both families fail to preserve cleanliness, with a payoff of 1 to each family). However, the effort involved in keeping the backyard clean makes strategy D (of not keeping it clean) a strongly dominant strategy: whether or not the other family contributes its share of effort, failure to maintain cleanliness will get the family a higher payoff (3 compared with 2 if the other family contributes, and 1 compared with 0 if the other family fails to do so).

Accordingly, a solution to this game can be found in strongly dominant strategies: both families will choose strategy D. However, even though each family chooses an action that is optimal from its point of view for any possible choice the other family may make, the outcome obtained is not the optimal outcome from a social point of view: both families would prefer that the combination of actions be (C,C) with a payoff of 2 to each family, rather than the payoff of 1 that each family obtains in the solution (D,D) of the game.

In other words, individual rationality – in which each player seeks its own best interest – might lead to a socially undesirable outcome.

On the face of it, this conclusion may provide the rational basis for ethics. The following argument could have been advanced:

> When all behave selfishly, the outcome is bad for all. Therefore, it is logical and rational for each to contribute her share to the common effort. This is because if everyone does so, all will be better off.

Unfortunately, this is not a valid argument. In the "social dilemma" game, if one of the players acts in a socially responsible manner (which is to say, chooses strategy C), it is not worthwhile for the other player to emulate her by choosing strategy C; rather, it is preferable for him to act selfishly (i.e. to choose strategy D). This is because strategy D is a strongly dominant strategy which is always preferable for the player than strategy C.

The players are therefore trapped: they understand perfectly well, from the outset, that if they act rationally (that is, if each of them aspires to achieve the outcome that is best for them) then the combination of their moves will produce an outcome that is bad for both. Nevertheless, there is no way they can coordinate among themselves a successful combination of actions as long as both are rational.

Kant's categorical imperative

The German philosopher Immanuel Kant (1724–1804), in his book *Groundwork of the Metaphysics of Morals* (1785), coined the following "categorical imperative": "Act only according to that maxim by which you can at the same time will that it would become a universal law."

Kant maintained that the categorical imperative derives from reason, meaning that the categorical imperative is imposed upon man by virtue of his possessing the faculty of reasoning. Yet he never fully defined the concept of reason. According to Kant, reason is a broad concept and more nearly approximates "what distinguishes man from beast" than rationality in the narrow sense of "payoff maximization."

The notion of rationality underlying game theory possibly could have been thought to be identical with Kant's notion of reason. However, an analysis of the "social dilemma" game shows us that Kant's categorical imperative cannot in fact arise from reason or rationality in the sense we are dealing with in game theory. In the "social dilemma" game, the action that each player would have liked to become a general law is action C: given that the two players make the same choice ("obey the general rule"), the general rule "Choose C" is preferable for both players than the general rule "Choose D." Nevertheless, a rational player – one who always chooses whichever action is optimal from his point of view – will choose action D, which he would not have liked to become a general rule.

3.2.1.1　The Prisoner's Dilemma

Two partners in an accounting firm are suspected of having double-billed various clients. The police already have sufficient incriminating evidence to send them both to jail for a year. The police, in an effort to ferret out the truth of the matter, are trying to extract a confession. Each suspect is promised that if he confesses, he will become a state witness and will go free, while his collaborator will incur the maximum, five-year penalty for this offence. If both confess, each will get a three-year prison term – five for committing the offence, less two years for having confessed.

Question 3.2　What, in your opinion, should each of the partners do?

Answer　Each partner obviously prefers a shorter rather than a longer prison term. Therefore, the following payoffs matrix, in which the payoff to each player is minus the number of years he will spend in jail, faithfully represents the players' preferences.

Player 2

	Do not confess	Confess
Do not confess	−1,−1	−5,0
Confess	0,−5	−3,−3

(Player 1 labels rows)

From the point of view of player 1, therefore, the "confess" strategy is strongly dominant. If player 2 confesses and so does he, he will get −3 (which is to say, a three-year prison term); but if he does not confess, he will get −5 (a five-year prison term). If player 2 does not confess, and he himself does confess, he will get 0 (go free), but if he himself does not confess he will get −1 (a one-year prison term). Player 1, then, will obviously choose to confess. On the basis of precisely the same considerations, player 2 will also choose to confess, and the inevitable outcome of the game is that both confess, with each spending three years in prison. If, however, they could confabulate ahead of time and arrive at a binding agreement as to what strategies to adopt, they would prefer not to confess and to spend just one year each in prison.

Question 3.3

What is the connection between the games in the examples in sections 3.1, 3.2.1, and 3.2.1.1?

Answer

Player 2

	"Social move"	"Selfish move"
"Social move"	b,b	d,a
"Selfish move"	a,d	c,c

(Player 1 labels rows)

All these games have a payoff configuration where the numbers a, b, c, d satisfy $a > b > c > d$. In other words, in the various games in sections 3.1, 3.2.1 and 3.2.1.1, the players' strategies do, of course, have different names, but they can be associated to strategies of "selfish move" or "social move," and once so associated, the players in all these games have the same preferences. (A reminder: a player prefers strategy profile A over strategy profile B if and only if the payoff she gets from strategy profile A is greater than the payoff she gets from strategy profile B. The absolute size of the payoffs, the difference between them, or the question of whether the payoffs are positive or negative are all immaterial in this context.) Quite frequently, each of these games is called a "social dilemma" game, or a Prisoner's Dilemma-type game because the Prisoner's Dilemma was one of the first examples of a game with such preferences. (Ironically enough, the rational players in this example happen to be criminals, and the "social action" of either one of them is an attempt to disrupt the action of the forces of social order.)

Yet we know that in real situations matching the "social dilemma" game, people do not always choose the strongly dominant strategy D – the selfish strategy. In game-theoretic terms, the choice of the social strategy C rather than the selfish strategy D can be understood as part of a more complicated game. We shall now describe three ways of doing this.

1. The payoffs in the "social dilemma" game may not give full expression to the preferences of the players. For example, if a player who has chosen D is subject to a monetary fine after the game, or is socially ostracized in such a way as to cause him material damage, such fine or damage should be expressed beforehand by means of the payoffs in the game itself. Thereupon, the game will change and strategy D may no longer be strongly dominant.

2. Payoffs in the "social dilemma" game, while they may give full expression to the material payoffs of the players, still may not correctly reflect the players' preferences. For example, if a player has a good feeling when she chooses social action C that is useful to her colleague, or if social ostracism resulting from the choice of D, while not causing her material damage, is a source of anguish for her, these emotional aspects should be taken into account in the payoffs of the original game. Recall that numerical payoffs do not necessarily reflect material payoffs only, but rather the result from the overall comparison the players make between the outcomes.

3. Even if the payoffs in the "social dilemma" game faithfully express the players' preferences, the players may be aware that they are about to play the game over and over again, without knowing beforehand exactly how many times. In this case, the social interaction is properly expressed only by means of a description of the repeated game as a whole, and not by the isolated game at any given moment. A description of the repeated game and the players' strategies therein must take into account how the players will act over time, and how a particular behavior at any given moment will be influenced by behavior at previous stages. In Chapter 23 we shall see how, in a repeated game of this kind, the recurrent choice of C may not, in fact, run counter to the concept of rationality.

3.3   Weakly dominant strategies

We now turn to discuss a weaker notion than that of strong dominance.

Definition

A strategy $x_i \in X_i$ of player i is called a **weakly dominant strategy** if for any other strategy of hers, $x_i' \neq x_i$ and any other strategy profile $x_{-i} \in X_{-i}$ of the other players, it is the case that:

$$u_i(x_i, x_{-i}) \geq u_i(x_i', x_{-i})$$

and there exists at least one strategy profile $\hat{x}_{-i} \in X_{-i}$ of the other players for which the inequality is strict:

$$u_i(x_i, \hat{x}_{-i}) > u_i(x_i', \hat{x}_{-i}).$$

When x_i is a weakly dominant strategy, player i will never regret having chosen it. But if there exists a strategy x_i of player i and a strategy profile x_{-i} of the other players, for which the equation:

$$u_i(x_i, x_{-i}) = u_i(x_i', x_{-i})$$

is satisfied, then player i will not be worse off if she chooses x_i' while the other players choose x_{-i}.

Question 3.4

In the example shown in section 3.1, is the strategy L of player 2 a weakly dominant strategy?

Answer

Yes. The payoffs $\begin{pmatrix} 3 \\ 0 \end{pmatrix}$ to player 2 from the strategy L are greater than or equal to the payoffs $\begin{pmatrix} 2 \\ 0 \end{pmatrix}$ of player 2 from the strategy R. In addition, if player 1 chooses T, then the payoff of player 2 if he chooses L (payoff 3) is strictly greater than his payoff if he chooses R (payoff 2). Therefore strategy L is weakly dominant for player 2.

Question 3.5

Can player i possibly have two different strategies, $x_i, \tilde{x}_i$, both being weakly dominant?

Answer

No. If x_i is weakly dominant for player i, then the other players have a strategy profile $\hat{x}_{-i} \in X_{-i}$ for which:

$$u_i(x_i, \hat{x}_{-i}) > u_i(\tilde{x}_i, \hat{x}_{-i})$$

Hence $\tilde{x}_i$ is not weakly dominant for player i.

Question 3.6

In the following game, is player 1's strategy T a weakly dominant strategy?

Player 2

		L	R
	T	1,1	1,1
Player 1	M	1,0	0,1
	B	0,1	1,0

Answer

Yes. For player 1, T, of course, is strictly preferred over M when player 2 plays R, while T is strictly preferred over B when player 2 chooses L. However, we note that the definition of weak dominance does not require the existence of **one particular** strategy profile $\hat{x}_{-i} \in X_{-i}$ of the other players (in this instance, player 2) against which the weakly dominant strategy is strictly preferred. The requirements in the definition follow the opposite order – for every strategy x_i' of player i that differs from her weakly dominant strategy x_i, there must be a strategy profile $\hat{x}_{-i}$ for the other players, for which:

$$u_i(x_i, \hat{x}_{-i}) > u_i(x_i', \hat{x}_{-i})$$

However, the associated profile $\hat{x}_{-i}$ may be different for different strategies x_i'.

> **Comprehension check**
>
> Find an argument supporting the following claim: If a player's strategy is strongly dominant, then it is also weakly dominant.

Definition   If each of the players in the game has a weakly dominant strategy, then this strategy profile is called the solution of the game in weakly dominant strategies.

3.3.1 Second price auction

A single object is being auctioned by invitation to tender. The number of bidders participating is n, where $n > 1$. Each participant submits a (one and only one) price offer. Bids are tendered in sealed envelopes (which is to say, none of the participants knows what her competitors have bid). The value of the object to player i is v_i, i.e. she is willing to pay for the object any sum lower than or equal to the amount v_i.

The auction rules are as follows: the bidder winning the auctioned object is the one whose bid is the highest; but the price she pays is the second highest offer. For example, if the highest bid is posted by player 1, who offered the price 1,000, and the second highest bid is 900, then the winning bidder is player 1, and she pays 900.

If the two highest bids are identical, the winner is determined by a lottery, with equal chances to each of them, and the winner pays the amount of the bid (which is also the second highest bid).

A player's profit is zero if she is not awarded the object; and if she does win the object and pays r for it, then her profit is $v_i - r$: she is getting the object whose value to her is v_i whereas she is paying r for it.

What will player i's bid b_i be? We will show that it is a weakly dominant strategy for player i to submit the bid $b_i = v_i$. This bid, equal to the value v_i she ascribes to the object, is "truthful" in the sense that the player is not "misreporting" her valuation of the object in her bid.

In order to see that bidding $b_i = v_i$ is weakly dominant, we will denote by r the highest of all the other players' bids. We will compare the various possible strategies of player i vis-à-vis the strategy $b_i = v_i$.

1. We shall first examine strategies in which player i submits a bid b_i which is higher than the value she ascribes to the object: $b_i > v_i$.

   Let's examine the various possible cases:

   1.1 If $r < v_i$

   then the player wins the object, since $r < b_i$ and her profit is $v_i - r$. Had she tendered $b_i = v_i$, then, too, she would have won the object and her profit would have been identical.

   1.2 If $r = v_i$

   then she would win the object, since $r < b_i$ and her profit is zero: $v_i - r = 0$.

   If she had tendered $b_i = v_i$, then the winner would have been determined by a lottery between herself and whoever posted the identical bid $r = v_i$. Whether or not she wins the object, her profit would have been zero.

   1.3 If $v_i < r$, then one of the three following possibilities obtains:

   1.3.1 She wins the object (which is to say, her bid is higher than r: $v_i < r < b_i$) at a price higher than the value she ascribes to it.

   Therefore, her profit is negative: $v_i - r < 0$.

   1.3.2 She fails to win the object (which is to say, her bid is lower than r: $v_i < b_i < r$).

   And her profit is zero.

   1.3.3 She draws lots with the player who bid r (which is to say, whose bid is equal to r).

And then, if she wins the object, her profit is negative, and if she doesn't, her profit is zero.

Whenever $v_i < r$, then the bid $b_i = v_i$ would have yielded the player a zero profit, since the player's bid would not have been successful. Hence, $b_i = v_i$ is a strategy that weakly dominates any strategy $b_i > v_i$ which in any event yields a profit that is smaller than or equal to the profit yielded by the strategy $b_i = v_i$ (and is sometimes strictly smaller).

2. We shall now proceed to examine strategies in which player i posts a bid b_i which is smaller than the value she ascribes to the object: $b_i < v_i$.
   We shall examine the various possibilities:

   2.1 If $r < v_i$, then one of the following three possibilities obtains:

   2.1.1 She wins the object (which is to say, her bid is higher than r: $r < b_i < v_i$) and her profit is positive: $v_i - r$.

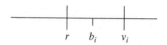

   2.1.2 She does not win the object (i.e. her bid is smaller than r: $b_i < r < v_i$) and her profit is zero.

   2.1.3 She draws lots with the players who also posted bid r.

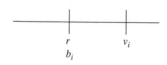

   And then, if she wins the object, her profit is $v_i - r$, and otherwise, her profit is zero.

If she had posted the bid $b_i = v_i$, she would have made sure of winning the object and securing a profit of $v_i - r$ and would not have risked losing the object to another player.

2.2 If $r = v_i$, then the player loses the object and her profit is zero. If she had offered $b_i = v_i$ she would have drawn lots with the player offering r, and in any event, her profit would have been zero (whether or not she won the object).

2.3 If $v_i < r$,

b_i v_i r

she does not win the object and, accordingly, her profit is zero. Even if she were to submit the bid $b_i = v_i$, she would not have won the object in this case, and would have remained with a zero profit.

Thus we see that any bid $b_i < v_i$ always yields a profit equal or smaller (and sometimes strictly smaller) than the bid $b_i = v_i$.

We have thus found that the strategy $b_i = v_i$ is weakly dominant: it will always yield a profit that is greater than or equal to the profit yielded by any other strategy. This conclusion is valid no matter how the other competing bidders choose to behave, and whether or not each of them likewise tenders a bid that matches the value he ascribes to the object. The reason is that the player is influenced only by the bids tendered by the other participants (and particularly by the highest of those bids, namely r) and not by how the other participants value the object.

3.3.1.1   Example: eBay

Do such auctions actually take place? They certainly do. Several Internet sites conducting public auctions operate by this method. A good example is www.ebay. com. It auctions off all sorts of objects (from handbags, furniture, and books to *objets d'art* and even automobiles). Some of the vendors are private individuals selling stuff they own, and some are actual shops that also use the site as a retail outlet. In 2010, the eBay site, with 94.4 million registered users, had a gross merchandise volume (GMV) of more than US$115 billion.

Each auction has a precise closing date and time, and the auction typically starts several days beforehand. If you want to purchase something on the site, you are invited to submit a bid – the highest price you are willing to pay. The system then takes over and handles the bids for you. Let's assume, for example, that you want to purchase a book, for which you are willing to pay at most $40. If the highest bid tendered prior to yours was $25, then the system will record your bid as $26 (meaning that it raises the price by preset intervals that are determined based on the value of the object – in the present case at intervals of $1).[1]

---

[1] For cheap items valued less than $1, the bid increment is $0.05, while for costly objects, valued at $5,000 and more, the bid increments will be as much as $100.

If another bid is posted some time later at $27, the system will update and record your bid as $28, and so on. Only if the second highest offer is $39 will the system record your actual $40 bid. If bids higher than $40 have been entered by closing time, you won't get the book.

How does this auction resemble the one we have analyzed? If you win the book, you will pay the the second highest bid (plus a small increment of $1) and not necessarily the amount you tendered. Accordingly, our analysis indicates that the strategy whereby one tenders a bid that equals the value she ascribes to the object is a weakly dominant strategy. Some people may first try to post a lower bid, which they will gradually ratchet up when it is not the leading offer. If the eBay rules were identical to a second price auction, it would have been worthwhile to tender from the outset a bid that equals the value you ascribe to the object.[2]

Yet another type of multi-billion online auction which has features in common with second price auctions is run by the Google search engine. Advertisers compete for appearing in one of the first places within the list of sponsored links when Google searches contain particular keywords. For example, in response to a search containing the word "hotel" and a city name, hotels in that city may like to bid for appearing high in the list of sponsored links so as to attract attention and hence customers.[3]

3.3.2   Political contest and the median voter theorem

We shall now present a political contest game in which two candidates are vying for the role of Prime Minister. Before we proceed, we should emphasize that the story underlying the game is especially simplistic.

---

[2] In practice, the eBay auctioning method does not completely coincide with the rules of the second price auction, and the difference in method also results in a difference in participants' behavior. Every eBay auction has a rigid closing time. Therefore, bids tendered by surfers in the last seconds of the invitation to tender (a practice dubbed "sniping") may well fail to get into the system. Quite a lot of participants in eBay auctions take advantage of this rule for a tacit form of collusion: they tender very low bids throughout the auction, posting "serious" price offers, which are usually lower than the value they ascribe to the object, only in the closing seconds. Thus, the successful bidder is not necessarily the one who is prepared to pay the most for the object (in the event that the system failed to record his bid); but on average, over a large number of auctions, the winners pay a price that is lower than they would have paid if all the participants (and particularly the one whose willingness to pay is the second highest) had tendered offers being identical to the value they ascribe to the object. By contrast, there are other Internet auction sites in which bidding ends at a specific closing time, unless bids are also tendered during the final ten minutes. If that happens, closing is postponed until ten minutes have elapsed from the time the latest bid is tendered. This alternative rule forestalls tacit collusion of the kind described above, and sniping is by and large eliminated. For more on this subject see Roth, A. E. and A. Ockenfels (2002), "Last-Minute Bidding and the Rules for Ending Second-Price Auctions: Evidence from eBay and Amazon Auctions on the Internet," *American Economic Review* 92 (4), 1093–1103.

[3] For the similarities and differerences between the Google auctions and second price auctions see e.g. Edelman, B., M. Ostrovsky, and M. Schwartz (2007), "Internet Advertising and the Generalized Second-Price Auction: Selling Billions of Dollars' Worth of Keywords," *American Economic Review* 97 (1), 242–259.

First, the model will present extremely opportunistic candidates, seeking nothing but to win the election. Both will accordingly adopt any position that will boost their chances of winning. Second, the potential political positions in this game will be assumed to be one-dimensional, reflecting a situation in which only a single item is on the agenda, and that one item is represented by a single variable. We shall call the straight line representing the various positions the *political positions line*. Finally, we will be assuming that the possible number of positions is finite.

In reality, things are obviously more complicated: the candidates will have positions on a broad range of topics, usually represented by several variables. A candidate may, for example, take a left-wing position on economic affairs but a right-wing stance on security.

For instance, let us first posit three views concerning the topic under discussion: right-wing, left-wing, and centrist.

Each candidate chooses a position for its platform in the elections, and the voters then cast their ballots. We will assume that each voter votes for the candidate closest to his position. If both candidates are equally close to his position (for example, if the voter is a centrist while the candidates are left-wing and right-wing), then the voter tosses a fair coin to decide which candidate to choose. The candidate obtaining the highest number of votes wins the elections. If both candidates poll the same number of votes, the winner is determined by a lottery.

As a first example, assume a 4 million electorate of whom 1 million are right-wing, 1 million are left-wing and 2 million are centrists. What positions will the candidates choose to present?

It turns out that presenting a centrist position is a strongly dominant strategy. For example, if one candidate chooses to present a right-leaning position while the other presents a centrist position, the first candidate will obtain 1 million votes from right-wing voters, while the second candidate will poll 3 million votes from left-wing and centrist voters, and will therefore emerge as the winner. Alternatively, if one candidate chooses to present a right-wing position while the other opts for the left, the first candidate will get 1 million votes from rightists and, on average, a million votes from centrist voters (all of whom will toss a coin), which is to say 2 million voters on average, while the second candidate will get 1 million votes from the left and, on average, half the votes of centrists, which is to say, likewise, 2 million votes on average. In this case both candidates have the same prospect of gaining the premiership.

The following matrix illustrates how the voting will go in the different instances (the figures in the table stand for average number of votes, in millions, polled by candidates 1 and 2).

		Candidate 2		
		Left-wing	Centrist	Right-wing
Candidate 1	Left-wing	2,2	1,3	2,2
	Centrist	3,1	2,2	3,1
	Right-wing	2,2	1,3	2,2

We shall translate this into a table of payoffs. If a candidate wins, then her payoff is 1; if she loses, then her payoff is 0; and if a candidate polls on average the same number of votes as her rival, then her payoff is 0.5 (representing her chance of getting elected). Accordingly, the payoff matrix is as follows:

		Candidate 2		
		Left-wing	Centrist	Right-wing
Candidate 1	Left-wing	0.5,0.5	0,1	0.5,0.5
	Centrist	1,0	0.5,0.5	1,0
	Right-wing	0.5,0.5	0,1	0.5,0.5

Thus we see that choosing a centrist position is a strongly dominant strategy (compare the first candidate's payoffs in the middle row to her payoffs in the first and third rows). If both candidates do indeed choose a centrist position, the election results will be determined by a lottery.

This example, in all its simplicity, may explain why we frequently observe candidates tending to obfuscate their real positions in the run-up to the elections, and opt to make their appeal to the centrist voter.

What will happen if the voter breakdown does not arrange itself symmetrically around the center? As a second example, let us now assume that the electorate consists of 1 million left-wingers, half a million centrists, and 2.5 million right-wingers. The **median voter** is now no longer in the center.

Definition

- **Median position** – a point on the political positions line such that at least half the voters are positioned to the right of it or identify with it, and at least half the voters are positioned to the left of it or identify with it.
- **Median voter** – a voter holding a median position.

What, then, is the median position in our second example? The median position is the right-wing position, since it satisfies the definition – 2.5 million voters are positioned to the right of it or identify with it on the political positions line, and 4 million voters are positioned to the left of it or identify with it on the political positions line (work out for yourself that none of the other positions fits the definition of a median position).

In that case, what political position will the candidates choose? The voting table in the different instances will appear as follows:

		Candidate 2		
		Left-wing	Centrist	Right-wing
Candidate 1	Left-wing	2,2	1,3	1.25, 2.75
	Centrist	3,1	2,2	1.5,2.5
	Right-wing	2.75,1.75	2.5,1.5	2,2

For example, if candidate 1 presents a left-wing position and candidate 2 a right-wing position, then candidate 2 will take all the votes of the right-wingers and half the votes of the centrists – meaning 2.75 million votes – and candidate 1 will get all the votes of the left-wing voters and half the votes of the centrists – amounting to 1.25 million votes. The corresponding payoff matrix is:

		Candidate 2		
		Left-wing	Centrist	Right-wing
Candidate 1	Left-wing	0.5,0.5	0,1	0,1
	Centrist	1,0	0.5,0.5	0,1
	Right-wing	1,0	1,0	0.5,0.5

We see that the strategy of choosing a right-wing position is now weakly dominant. Both candidates will accordingly choose to present a right-wing position, and the winner will be determined by lottery.

Thus, the two examples demonstrate how, in a two-candidate election, it is preferable for each candidate to run with the median position – whether centrist or radical. This is an instance of the **median voter theorem**.

We shall now devise a precise formulation of one version of this theorem.

Theorem 3.1: The median voter theorem

Let us assume that two candidates are up for election and the winner is whoever polls a majority of votes. There is just one item on the agenda in these elections, and the various existing positions concerning it are represented by points along the political positions line. Each voter has a position that is represented on this line, and he votes for the candidate representing the position closest to his own. If the two positions represented by the candidates are equidistant from the voter's position, he tosses a coin as to who to vote for. The number of possible positions is finite, and each voter holds one of them. If there is one single median position, then the strategy of running with the median position is a weakly dominant strategy for each of the candidates.

Proof

We shall denote the median position by M, the nearest position to the left of M by L, and the nearest position to the right of M by R.

Total votes to the right of or coinciding with L constitute at least half the votes (since some of these votes, those positioned to the right of M or coinciding with it, amount to at least half the votes). Therefore, since L is not in the median position (M being the only median position), the total votes to the left of or coinciding with L amount to less than half the votes. Thus, the complementary set of votes, which is to say, those to the right of or coinciding with M, consists of *more* than half the votes.

A symmetric argument entails that the set of votes to the left of M or coinciding with it consists of *more* than half the votes.

Hence, if one of the candidates picks M, she will win the elections unless her rival also chooses M, in which case the elections result in a draw.

Let us now examine the various alternatives to M:

- Suppose the candidate is considering for her platform a position r which is to the right of M. If her rival presents a position even further to the right of r (if there exists such a position on the political positions line), then either position – M or r – will secure electoral victory for the candidate. (Note that in the model we are using, the fact that r will result in victory with a greater majority is inconsequential, since winning the elections is all that matters.) However, if the rival chooses r, then the choice of M will ensure victory for the candidate, whereas choosing r will result in a draw; and if the rival chooses a position to the left of r, then choosing r will cause the candidate to lose, whereas choosing M will lead her to victory (if the rival's position is anything other than M) or at least to a draw (if the rival chooses M).

Therefore, choosing to run with M will ensure the candidate at least as good an outcome as choosing r, and will sometimes yield her a strictly better outcome.

- By a symmetric argument, the choice of M will ensure the candidate at least as good an outcome as choosing a position l which is to the left of M, and will sometimes yield the candidate a strictly better outcome.

Therefore, the choice of the position M is a weakly dominant strategy for each of the candidates.

QED

4 Strongly dominated strategies

4.1 ## The definition of a strongly dominated strategy

In the preceding chapter, we analyzed games in which each of the players had a dominant strategy. In such cases, it was easy to predict the behavior of the players (even if, as we saw, the players' choice profile need not necessarily be the profile they deem most efficient). But there are many games in which none of the players has a dominant strategy. In such cases, the best strategy for any player depends on the choices made by the other players: if the other players modify their profile of choices, the most worthwhile strategy for a player could very well change, too. How, then, can we determine how each player will act?

The problem seems circular: the most worthwhile strategy for player A depends on the choice of player B, while the most worthwhile strategy for player B depends on the choice of player A. But when the players are required to choose and act simultaneously, what expectations may they develop concerning the behavior of their fellow players?

When the straight road to solving the problem proves to be a dead end, there are indirect access routes that may be worth trying. In the present case, instead of asking "What strategy is optimal for the player?" we will prefer another question: "What strategies are bad for the player?"

Definition
A strategy x_i is called a **strongly dominated strategy** of player i if she has another strategy, x_i', which is always better than x_i; that is, if for every strategy profile x_{-i} of the other players:

$$u_i(x_i, x_{-i}) < u_i(x_i', x_{-i}).$$

If player i is rational, she will never choose a strongly dominated strategy x_i. When considering whether playing x_i is worthwhile for her, she will try to determine against what strategy profile x_{-i} of the other players the strategy x_i is optimal in her view. In this process, she will discover that x_i is always inferior relative to x_i'. That is, for every combination of actions x_{-i} of the other players, the choice of x_i' will always yield her a preferable outcome. Player i will therefore conclude that if x_i is at all worthwhile (possibly because it yields a high payoff as against certain action combinations x_i of the other players, which player i believes to be reasonable), then x_i' is strictly even more so. This does not necessarily mean that at the end of the day player i will choose x_i' (rather than some third strategy – x_i''). What it does mean, however, is that the choice of x_i is not optimal for player i. And therefore, assuming the player to be rational, we may conclude that she will not choose x_i.

Two numerical examples

Example A

Player 2

		L	M	R
Player 1	T	0,0	0,2	2,1
	B	1,2	1,1	0,0

In this game, no player has a strongly or a weakly dominant strategy.

Question 4.1

Verify that the above is true.

Answer

A. Strategy T is not dominant for player 1 – if player 2 plays L or M, then strategy B is preferable.
B. Strategy B is not dominant for player 1 – if player 2 plays R, then strategy T is preferable.
C. Strategy L is not dominant for player 2 – if player 1 plays T, then strategies M and R are preferable.
D. Strategy M is not dominant for player 2 – if player 1 plays B, then strategy L is preferable.
E. Strategy R is not dominant for player 2 – if player 1 plays T, then strategy M is preferable.

Note, however, that strategy R of player 2 is strongly dominated by strategy M: whether player 1 chooses T or B, strategy M will give player 2 a higher payoff than strategy L (a payoff of 2 rather than 1 in the event that player 1 chooses T, and a payoff of 1 rather than 0 in the event that player 1 chooses B).

Example B

Let's examine the following game:

Player 2

		L	M	R
	T	0,0	0,3	2,2
Player 1				
	B	1,3	1,0	0,2

Question 4.2

In this game, is strategy R of player 2 a strongly dominated strategy?

Answer

No. Of course, if player 1 chooses T, then strategy M of player 2 is to be preferred over R; but if player 1 chooses B, then strategy L of player 2 is preferable to R. But player 2 has no particular single strategy that is always preferable to R. Therefore, strategy R is not strongly dominated. (To recapitulate – a player's strategy x_i is strongly dominated if there is some other particular strategy x_i' that is always better than x_i for the player.) In the present example, if player 2 is not sure how player 1 will act, and considers either of his two strategies to be equally likely, then the choice of R represents a sort of "insurance policy," ensuring a relatively high payoff of 2 for certain, compared with the risk of getting a low payoff of 0 in any of the other choices (along with a chance of obtaining the higher payoff of 3). Therefore, the choice of R is not "irrational" for player 2.

Comprehension check

If a player has a strongly dominant strategy, does she have a strongly dominated strategy as well?

4.2   Iterative elimination of strongly dominated strategies

We assume that rational players will not choose strongly dominated strategies. This criterion may well exclude some of the strategies of certain players (in Example A above, strategy R of player 2 may be so excluded). Can this approach be extended to cover the exclusion of additional strategies?

Let us assume that a player believes her fellow players are rational. In light of such an assumption, she believes that they will never choose strongly dominated strategies. Therefore, if all the players are:

1. themselves rational, and also
2. believe that all the players are rational,

then strongly dominated strategies may be eliminated from the game, since no player will choose such strategies, and the other players, too, will be convinced that such strategies will not be chosen. Post-elimination, the game remaining to be analyzed is smaller, with fewer strategies for some of the players. We may then check whether there are players who have strongly dominated strategies in the reduced game. Since the players are rational, they will not adopt such strategies.

For example, in the game in Example A, following elimination of the strongly dominated strategy R,

Player 2

	L	M	R
T	0,0	0,2	2,1
B	1,2	1,1	0,0

Player 1

The remaining game is:

Player 2

	L	M
T	0,0	0,2
B	1,2	1,1

Player 1

In the reduced game, strategy T of player 1 is strongly dominated by B (while B is a strongly dominant strategy). Therefore, we may assume that player 1 will not choose strategy T. Let us explicitly reexamine the relevant considerations:

1. Strategy R of player 2 is a strongly dominated strategy. Player 2, if he is rational, will not choose it.
2. Player 1 believes that player 2 is rational. Therefore, player 1 believes that player 2 will not choose R, but will confine himself to choosing between L and M only; such that effectively, the game to be analyzed is the one shown above.
3. In the remaining game, T is a strongly dominated strategy of player 1, and he will therefore not choose it.

Elimination of strategy T in the game:

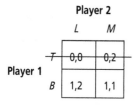

will accordingly leave us with the game:

Player 2

	L	M
Player 1 B	1,2	1,1

In this game, strategy M of player 2 is strongly dominated by strategy L of player 1. Once we eliminate it

Player 2

	L	M
Player 1 B	1,2	1 1

we are left with the game:

Player 2

	L
Player 1 B	1,2

In the remaining game, each player has a single strategy, and therefore the elimination process cannot continue. Thus we have obtained that $Y_1 = \{B\}$, $Y_2 = \{L\}$. Accordingly, in this example, the elimination process has provided us with an unequivocal prediction as to the players' behavior. As explained above, this prediction is compatible with the assumption that the two players share common knowledge that both are rational.

4.2.1   Iterative elimination – the general case

As seen in the example, we can repeat the elimination process in a similar manner over and over again. Accordingly, we will denote by D_i^1 the strongly dominated strategies of player i in the first round. Likewise, we will denote by Y_i^1 the remaining strategies of player i – those that are not strongly dominated. That is, $X_i = D_i^1 \cup Y_i^1$. As usual, we will denote by:

$$Y^1 = \Pi_{j \in I} Y_j^1$$

those strategy profiles of the players that are not strongly dominated. These strategy profiles and the payoffs associated with them describe the game that remains following the elimination of strongly dominated strategies. Likewise, we will denote by:

$$Y_{-i}^1 = \Pi_{j \neq i} Y_j^1$$

the remaining strategy profiles of all the players other than player i.

We say that $x_i \in Y_i^1$ is a strongly dominated strategy of player i in the second round if it is a strongly dominated strategy in the remaining game with the strategy profiles Y^1, i.e. if player i has a strategy $x_i' \in Y_i^1$ such that for every strategy profile $x_{-i} \in Y_{-i}^1$ it is the case that:

$$u_i(x_i, x_{-i}) < u_i(x_i', x_{-i}).$$

We will now denote by D_i^2 the strongly dominated strategies of player i up till the second round, which is to say, those strategies that were eliminated in the first round (D_i^1) and those that are strongly dominated in the second round. Likewise, we will denote by Y_i^2 the rest of player i's strategies, namely those that have not been eliminated up to and including the second round. Similarly, we will denote by:

$$Y^2 = \Pi_{j \in I} Y_j^2$$

those strategy profiles of the players that were not eliminated by the second round, and by:

$$Y_{-i}^2 = \Pi_{j \neq i} Y_j^2$$

the remaining strategy profiles of all the players other than player i after the second round.

In this way we will be able to generalize the definition, by induction on the elimination rounds, n. That is to say, if D_i^n are the strategies of player i that were eliminated by round n, and Y_i^n are the rest of her strategies – those that survived the first n elimination rounds – we will denote by:

$$Y^n = \Pi_{j \in I} Y_j^n$$

those strategy profiles of the players that survived the first n elimination rounds, and by:

$$Y_{-i}^n = \Pi_{j \neq i} Y_j^n$$

those strategy profiles of all the players other than player i that survived those n rounds.

We now say that $x_i \in Y_i^n$ is a strongly dominated strategy of player i in round n if it is a strongly dominated strategy in the remaining game with strategy profiles Y^n, i.e. if player i has a strategy $x_i' \in Y_i^n$ such that for every strategy profile $x_{-i} \in Y_{-i}^n$ it is the case that:

$$u_i(x_i, x_{-i}) < u_i(x_i', x_{-i}).$$

Definition

A strategy $\hat{x}_i$ of player i survives **iterative elimination of strongly dominated strategies** if it is in every Y_i^n, $n = 1, 2, \ldots$, i.e. if $\hat{x}_i \in Y_i = \cap_{n=1}^{\infty} Y_i^n$.

Induction. According to a well-known saying attributed to the nineteenth-century mathematician Leopold Kronecker, men's knowledge of the natural numbers 1,2,3 … is God-given; the rest of mathematics is man-made: "God made the integers; all else is the work of man." In fact, however, the set of natural numbers is also amenable to a methodical definition, as follows:

1. 1 is a natural number.
2. For every natural number there is a successive natural number.

The set of natural numbers is the minimal set containing all the numbers defined by this pair of rules. By this definition, the set of natural numbers is also known as the **Peano system**.

Therefore, if we wish to define a series of objects X_k for $k = 1, 2, \ldots$, we must first define the object X_1, and then the rule by means of which the objects X_{n+1} are to be defined with the aid of the previously defined objects $X_1, \ldots, X_n$. This is a **definition by induction**.

Similarly, if we wish to prove that all the objects $X_1, X_2, \ldots$ in the series satisfy a particular property, we must prove that:

1. X_1 satisfies that property.
2. If $X_1, \ldots X_n$ satisfy the property, then X_{n+1} likewise satisfies the property.

Such a proof is called a **proof by induction**.

In light of this discussion, each player choosing only strategies that survive iterative elimination of strongly dominated strategies is compatible with the players sharing *common knowledge of rationality*, as defined below.

Definition   The players share **common knowledge of rationality** if:

1. All the players are rational.
2. All the players believe that all the players are rational.
3. All the players believe that all the players believe that all the players are rational, and so forth.

We note, however, that it is not in every game that the elimination process of strongly dominated strategies will provide us with an unequivocal prediction as to the players' behavior. For example, in the game in section 2.1 (Israel and Egypt on the eve of the Six Day War), neither player has strongly dominated strategies, and considerations of this type will therefore not help us predict the players' behavior in this game. In such games, we will need ideas of a different kind so as to arrive at a solution, a matter that will be dealt with in the following chapters.

Comprehension check

Give an example of a game in which iterative elimination of strongly dominated strategies leads to the elimination of some of each player's strategies, but leaves some (or all) of the players with more than one strategy.

According to the definition of the elimination process of strongly dominated strategies, in each round we simultaneously eliminate all of the players' strategies that are strongly dominated in the game remaining from the previous round.[1] Does the outcome of the process depend on the order of elimination? For example, if we were to subdivide each round into secondary rounds arranged in order of the players (a secondary round for player 1, a secondary round for player 2, and so forth), and in each secondary round we were only to eliminate strongly dominated strategies of the player associated with that secondary round, would the final outcome be different?

---

[1] This does not necessarily mean that in each round every player does in fact have strictly dominated strategies that can be eliminated. For example, in the game we analyzed in Example A above, in each elimination round only one of the players had a strongly dominated strategy.

The answer is that the order of elimination would not modify the final outcome. This is because if strategy x_i of player i is strongly dominated by her strategy x_i', which is to say if:

$$u_i(x_i, x_{-i}) < u_i(x_i', x_{-i})$$

is satisfied for every strategy profile x_{-i} of the other players in the (remaining) given game, then this strict inequality will persist even if some of the strategy profiles x_{-i} of the other players in that game have already been eliminated due to the order of elimination being modified. Therefore, the combination of remaining strategies will be identical for whatever order of elimination "visiting" each player infinitely often (which is to say, if for every elimination stage n and for every player i there exists a later stage m, $m > n$, in which strongly dominated strategies of player i are eliminated in the game remaining at stage m).

Comprehension check

Assume that two newspaper vendors seek to position their stands alongside a long street. The street has nine buildings, at the entrance to any of which a stand may be set up, and these buildings, numbered from 1 to 9, stand at equal intervals along the street.

Each building is occupied by 100 newspaper-reading tenants. The newspaper stand holders know that each of the tenants on the street will purchase the newspaper at the newspaper stand nearest his building. If two stands are equidistant from the tenant, he will patronize each stand on alternate days.

For example, if the first vendor chooses to position her stand at the entrance to Building 4, and the second vendor places hers at the entrance to Building 8, then all the tenants of Buildings 1–5, and on average half the tenants of Building 6, will purchase from the first vendor – i.e. 550 tenants on average – and all the other tenants will purchase from the second vendor – i.e. 350 tenants on average.

Where will the newspaper vendors choose to position their stands? Solve the problem with the aid of iterative elimination of strongly dominated strategies.

5 Weakly dominated strategies

Definition A strategy x_i is called a **weakly dominated strategy** of player i if she has another strategy x_i' that is at least as good as and sometimes strictly better than x_i. That is, if for every strategy profile x_{-i} of the other players it is the case that:

$$u_i(x_i, x_{-i}) \leq u_i(x_i', x_{-i})$$

and there also exists at least one strategy profile $\hat{x}_{-i}$ of the other players for which:

$$u_i(x_i, \hat{x}_{-i}) < u_i(x_i', \hat{x}_{-i}).$$

If the strategy x_i is weakly dominated by the strategy x_i', player i will never lose if she ignores the strategy x_i and makes her choice out of her other strategies. This is because one of these other strategies is the strategy x_i', which will guarantee the player a payoff that is at least as good as the one she will obtain by choosing x_i, and sometimes the payoff will be even (strictly) higher.

However, one cannot argue that a rational player will never choose a weakly dominated strategy, since if x_i is weakly dominated by x_i' but:

$$u_i(x_i, x_{-i}) = u_i(x_i', x_{-i})$$

and in addition, player i is convinced that the other players will choose the strategy profile x_{-i} (for example, if these are strongly dominant strategies of theirs), then the choice of x_i may be optimal in her view.

The elimination of weakly dominated strategies may nonetheless be relevant, assuming that the players are always in doubt – even if only slightly – as to the expected behavior of the other players. If a player ascribes a positive probability, no matter how low, to all of the other players' strategy profiles, she will not choose her weakly dominated strategies.

Comprehension check

1. If the strategy x_i of player i is strongly dominated by her strategy x_i', is x_i also weakly dominated by x_i'?
2. If strategy x_i of player i is weakly dominated by her strategy x_i', is x_i also strongly dominated by x_i'?
3. If the player has a weakly dominant strategy, does she also have a weakly dominated strategy?

5.1 Iterative elimination of weakly dominated strategies

In many applications the players do not have strongly dominated strategies, but they do have weakly dominated strategies. It is therefore reasonable to consider the process whereby weakly dominated strategies are repeatedly eliminated, in exactly the same way as we defined the iterative elimination of strongly dominated strategies. We will consider the outcome of this process in the following examples.

5.1.1 Price competition

Two firms manufacture the same product, and they compete with one another in the market by means of the prices they set. Assume that the demand curve for the product in this market is given by:

$$Q = 130 - P$$

where P is the per-unit product price and Q is the total quantity of units that will be demanded by consumers at that price. Note that the demand curve is a descending one: the higher the price, the lower the quantity of units demanded at that price.

If firm 1 sells its product at the price p_1, but the manufacturing cost per unit is only c, then for every unit it sells, the firm earns the mark-up:

$$p_1 - c$$

The quantity of units the firm will be able to sell at the price p_1 depends, of course, also on the price p_2 that is set by the rival firm. We will denote this quantity by $x_1(p_1, p_2)$.

In the price profile (p_1, p_2), the profit of firm 1 will therefore be:

$$u_1(p) = (p_1 - c)x_1(p_1, p_2)$$

Similarly (and with corresponding subscripts), the profit of firm 2 will be given by:

$$u_2(p) = (p_2 - c)x_2(p_1, p_2)$$

Note that we assume here that the per-unit production cost c is identical for both firms.

Assume henceforth in this example that $c = 25$. How will the demand for the product of the first firm, $x_1(p_1, p_2)$, be determined?

The quantity sold by firm 1 depends both on the price it sets and the price its competitor sets. Let's assume that each of the firms can set one of the following prices per unit: $20, $40, $50 or $70. If firm 1 sets a lower price, i.e. $p_1 < p_2$, then it corners the entire market (since no consumer will want to purchase at a higher price), and accordingly, in this case:

$$x_1(p_1, p_2) = 130 - p_1$$
$$x_2(p_1, p_2) = 0$$

If firm 2 sets a lower price, $p_2 < p_1$, then firm 2 corners the entire market and firm 1 sells nothing, i.e.:

$$x_1(p_1, p_2) = 0$$
$$x_2(p_1, p_2) = 130 - p_2$$

Finally, if both firms set the same price, $p_2 = p_1$, then they share the market equally. In that case:

$$x_1(p_1, p_2) = x_2(p_1, p_2) = \frac{(130 - p_1)}{2}$$

We will now present the firms' payoff matrix (the first number in each cell is the profit of firm 1, and the second is the profit of firm 2).

		Firm 2			
		$P_2 = 20$	$P_2 = 40$	$P_2 = 50$	$P_2 = 70$
Firm 1	$P_1 = 20$	-275, -275	-550, 0	-550, 0	-550, 0
	$P_1 = 40$	0, -550	675, 675	1350, 0	1350, 0
	$P_1 = 50$	0, -550	0, 1350	1000, 1000	2000, 0
	$P_1 = 70$	0, -550	0, 1350	0, 2000	1350, 1350

For example, if both firms set a price of $p_1 = p_2 = 50$, then the number of units that each of them will produce is:

$$x_1(50, 50) = x_2(50, 50) = \frac{(130 - 50)}{2} = 40$$

and accordingly, the profit of each one of them will be:

$$u_1(p) = u_2(p) = (50 - 25) \times 40 = 1000$$

Verify that you know how to calculate the profits in the other cases, too.

What prices will the firms set? Notice that for firm 1, the strategies $p_1 = 20$ and $p_1 = 70$ are weakly dominated by the strategy $p_1 = 50$ (the payoffs in the third row are greater than or equal to those in the first or fourth row for every possible price choice of firm 2, and they are strictly greater for some of the prices that firm 2 can choose). Therefore, they can be eliminated. In fact, the strategy $p_1 = 20$ is strongly dominated by the strategy $p_1 = 50$.

Similarly, for firm 2, the strategies $p_2 = 20$ and $p_2 = 70$ are weakly dominated by the strategy $p_2 = 50$, and therefore they, too, can be eliminated (work out for yourself which of them is weakly dominated and which is strongly dominated). Following these eliminations, we remain with the following game:

	Firm 2	
	$P_2 = 40$	$P_2 = 50$
$P_1 = 40$	675, 675	1350, 0
$P_1 = 50$	0, 1350	1000, 1000

(Firm 1 labels the rows)

In this game, we see that for firm 1, the strategy $p_1 = 50$ is strongly dominated by the strategy $p_1 = 40$ (the payoffs in the second row are strictly lower than those in the first row for any choice of firm 2), and therefore it may be eliminated. Similarly, for firm 2, the strategy $p_2 = 50$ is strongly dominated by the strategy $p_2 = 40$, and it, too, can be eliminated.

Note that in the original game, the strategy $p_1 = 50$ is neither strongly nor weakly dominated by the strategy $p_1 = 40$ (if firm 2 chooses the strategy $p_2 = 70$, then the strategy $p_1 = 50$ gives a higher profit than the strategy $p_1 = 40$). Therefore, the strategy $p_1 = 50$ cannot be eliminated immediately, but only at the second stage of the process.

Accordingly, the solution of the game obtained by iterative elimination of weakly dominated strategies is $(p_1, p_2) = (40,40)$.

Definition When iterative elimination of weakly dominated strategies leaves each player with a single strategy, we say that the game is *solvable by iterated admissibility*.

5.1.2   "Beauty contest"

Let's assume that there are twenty students in your class. Every student is asked to choose a whole number between 0 and 100, and to write it on a slip of paper. Once all the folded slips are opened, the student whose guess most nearly approximates but does not exceed two-thirds of the average of all guesses will win a prize of $50. If more than one student comes up with a winning guess, then those having guessed correctly will draw lots, and each will win the prize with the same probability.

For example, if the table of guesses is

Guess	1	5	10	14	17	25	30
No. of students	1	2	4	2	3	5	3

then the four students guessing 10 will draw lots for the prize (verify this).

The economist John Maynard Keynes compared the stock market to a beauty contest, in which it is important for each investor to guess which investment portfolios the other investors will choose, and not necessarily to properly understand the objective economic data.[1] If an investor today correctly anticipates that tomorrow a large number of investors are going to buy a particular stock, causing its price to rise, he will be in good time to snap up the stock cheaply, and realize a profit. This will not necessarily have to be related to the real economic soundness of the firm that issued the stock. The game we have just described has similar attributes – winning the prize depends solely on guessing the behavior of the other players; the guess has no objective value for the player beyond its value relative to the choices of the other players. The literature therefore dubs this game a "beauty contest."

We shall show that the only strategy to survive iterative elimination of weakly dominated strategies is "to guess 0." First, any guess of a number greater than 66 will never win. Even in the extreme case that all the other students guess 100 while your guess is higher than 66, it is the case that two-thirds of the average of the guesses is lower than your guess. Accordingly, you will not win in this instance, and you will certainly not win in any other instance (in which some or all of the guesses are lower than 100). We conclude that guesses which are higher than 66 are weakly dominated

---

[1] Keynes, J. M. (1936), *The General Theory of Interest, Employment and Money*, London: Macmillan.

strategies, e.g. by the strategy of guessing 1 (which will enable winning in certain instances – for example, if all the others guess 2).

We remain with the game in which every player chooses a guess between 0 and 66. With a similar consideration in mind, in the remaining game any guess of a number higher than 44 will never win. Even if all the others guess 66 and your guess is higher than 44, it is the case that two-thirds of the average guess is lower than your guess, and therefore you will not win, and you will certainly not win in any other instance (in which some or all of the guesses are lower than 66). Hence, in the remaining game, these strategies are weakly dominated strategies (for example, by the strategy of guessing 1) and can be eliminated – both for you and for the other players. We therefore remain with the game in which every player makes her choice from the range of strategies between 0 and 44.

Similarly, one could go on eliminating weakly dominated strategies until ultimately remaining with the strategy of guessing 0.

Comprehension check

Verify that you understand why this outcome does not depend on the amount of the prize or the number of students, as long as there are at least three students in the class.

5.1.2.1   **"Beauty contest" in laboratory experiments**

How do people actually choose in a game of this type? Do most people actually guess 0? It is worth a player's while to guess "0" only if she believes that a large number of players are also about to guess either "0" or "1" and that only a negligible minority of them will guess slightly higher numbers. In other words, a player may guess low numbers if she believes that everybody or almost everybody follows in their mind the process of iterative elimination of weakly dominated strategies.

It may naturally be assumed, however, that a not inconsiderable proportion of players will mentally process only some of the strategy-elimination rounds. If a player believes that this is how things are, she will choose a guess that is higher than "0" even if she herself has entertained in her mind all the elimination rounds. It follows that even if a large proportion of participants are capable of mentally going through all the elimination rounds, a considerable percentage of them may nevertheless choose guesses that are substantially greater than "0." This fact even further reinforces the conclusion that the "0" guess is unlikely to be the winning guess.

The game was tested in laboratory experiments[2] and also in wide-ranging experiments in which readers of broad-circulation newspapers were invited to participate.[3] It was found that while some of the participants guess "0", the great majority do not. Most participants choose a guess that is consistent with one, two or at most three rounds of elimination of weakly dominated strategies: a participant implementing one elimination round, and who believes that the other participants' guesses will be uniformly distributed between 0 and 100, with an average of 50, would rather guess 33; a participant implementing two elimination rounds, and who believes that all the others will implement one elimination round (and will hence guess 33), himself guesses 22; and so on. In practice, the winning guess in these experiments is typically around 25. Some participants who gave a verbal description of their rationale for choosing "0" actually guessed higher numbers because, in their opinion, most participants do not implement all the elimination rounds.

5.1.3   The Traveler's Dilemma

Two friends travel abroad together on vacation. During the vacation, each of them purchases a ski equipment kit. Each kit costs $250. When they land back at their home airport, they find that the airline has lost both the kits. Unfortunately, neither of the friends has receipts proving the value of the lost equipment. Absent any receipts, it transpires, the airline is obliged to compensate each of them to the tune of at least $80, but the compensation will not, in any case, exceed $200.

Since the two lost kits were identical, one of the friends proposes to the airline representative that each of them go into a different room and write the price of her kit on a scrap of paper. If the two claims are identical, the friend argues, the airline representative may be convinced that the reported price is in fact what each of them paid for the equipment. The airline representative agrees, promising to pay each of the friends the amount specified if that amount is in the range of $80–200, and provided that both claims are identical. But, the representative warns, if the two claims are not identical, the airline will compensate each of them in the amount of the lower of the two claims. Moreover, in that event, the airline will also deduct a token "fine" of $10 from the compensation paid to the friend submitting the higher claim, while adding the $10 "fine" to the compensation paid to the friend submitting the lower claim. The claims must be denominated in whole dollars only.[4]

[2] Nagel, R. (1995), "Unraveling in Guessing Games: An Experimental Study," *American Economic Review* 85 (5), 1313–1326.
[3] Bosch-Domenech, A., J. G. Montalvo, R. Nagel, and A. Satorra (2002), "One, Two, (Three) Infinity, ...: Newspaper and Lab Beauty-Contest Experiments," *American Economic Review* 92 (5), 1687–1701.
[4] The game in this example was presented by Basu, K. (1994), "The Traveler's Dilemma: Paradoxes of Rationality in Game Theory," *American Economic Review* 84 (2), 391–395.

Comprehension check

What will each of the friends do? What amount will each decide to claim?

To obtain the answers to these questions, try to focus on the following points:

A. Show that in this game "claiming $200" is a weakly dominated strategy.
B. What strategies survive iterative elimination of weakly dominated strategies?
C. If the "fine" imposed on the friend submitting the higher claim (which is added to the compensation paid to the friend submitting the lower claim) is less than $5, will your answer be different, and if so, how? How will your answer change if the "fine" is increased to $50? To $80?
D. This game was tried out in an experiment[5] (in which the actual payments to the participants were denominated in cents rather than dollars). It was found that when the fine was low, at a level of 5 or 10, most of the claims submitted by the participants in the experiment were close to 200. However, when the fine was high, at a level of 50 or 80, most claims submitted by the participants were close to 80. When the fine was of medium size, at a level of 20 or 25, most claims were in a medium range of between 100 and 160. Thus, the higher the fine, the lower were most of the claims.

Are the results of the experiment consistent with the prediction you obtained by applying iterative elimination of weakly dominated strategies? If not, how do you explain the discrepancies?[6]

5.1.4   A voting paradox

A committee has three members who must choose one of three projects, A, B, or C. If one of the projects gets a majority of votes, that project will be implemented; otherwise, the project will be picked by the committee president, player 1. Assume that the committee members' preferences are as follows:

Player 1's most preferred project is A, B is less preferred, and C is least preferred.
Player 2's most preferred project is C, A is less preferred, and B is least preferred.
Player 3's most preferred project is B, C is less preferred, and A is least preferred.

---

[5] Capra, C. M., J. K. Goeree, and C. A. Holt (1999), "Anomalous Behavior in a Traveler's Dilemma?" *American Economic Review* 89 (3), 678–690.
[6] For the results of an additional experiment with a small "fine," see Rubinstein, A. (2006), "Dilemmas of an Economic Theorist," *Econometrica* 74 (4), 865–883.

There preferences can be represented by the following utilities from the projects:

Player 1 – the utility from A: 3, the utility from B: 2, and the utility from C: 1.
Player 2 – the utility from A: 2, the utility from B: 1, and the utility from C: 3.
Player 3 – the utility from A: 1, the utility from B: 3, and the utility from C: 2.

The three committee members simultaneously cast a single ballot each (i.e. they must choose whether to vote for A, B, or C). What will be the outcome of the vote?

We will present the payoff matrices of the game. First, if player 1 votes for project A, the players' payoffs in accordance with the votes cast by players 2 and 3 will be as follows:

		Player 3	
	A	B	C
A	3,2,1 A	3,2,1 A	3,2,1 A
Player 2 B	3,2,1 A	2,1,3 B	3,2,1 A
C	3,2,1 A	3,2,1 A	1,3,2 C

(The left-hand number in each entry is the payoff to player 1, the middle number is the payoff to player 2, and the right-hand number is the payoff to player 3. The project that is chosen in each instance appears in the second row of the entry.)

If player 1 votes for project B, the players' payoffs and the chosen project in accordance with the votes of players 2 and 3 will be as follows:

		Player 3	
	A	B	C
A	3,2,1 A	2,1,3 B	2,1,3 B
Player 2 B	2,1,3 B	2,1,3 B	2,1,3 B
C	2,1,3 B	2,1,3 B	1,3,2 C

If player 1 votes for proposal C, the players' payoffs and the chosen project in accordance with the votes of players 2 and 3 will be as follows:

Player 3

	A	B	C
A	3,2,1 A	1,3,2 C	1,3,2 C
B	1,3,2 C	2,1,3 B	1,3,2 C
C	1,3,2 C	1,3,2 C	1,3,2 C

Player 2

It can now be seen that for player 1, the strategy of choosing B is weakly dominated by the strategy of choosing A (if you compare the first number in the first and second tables for any given choice profiles of players 2 and 3, you will notice that the number in the first table is always greater than or equal to the corresponding number in the second table, and sometimes strictly larger). Similarly, the strategy of choosing C is weakly dominated by the strategy of choosing A (when the first and second tables are subjected to a similar comparison). Therefore, these strategies may be eliminated for player 1.

Moreover, it can be seen that for player 2, the strategy of choosing B is weakly dominated by the strategy of choosing C (in every matrix, compare the payoffs of player 2 resulting from the two strategies, i.e. the middle number in the second and third rows) and therefore it, too, can be eliminated.

Finally, for player 3, the strategy of choosing A is weakly dominated by the strategy of choosing B, and therefore it, too, can be eliminated. (Note that in this example we need not eliminate all the dominated strategies of all players in one stage. We could have contented ourselves with eliminating the dominated strategies of player 1 while continuing with the reduced game, and we would have arrived at the same outcome.)

After all these eliminations, we remain with the game in which player 1 votes A and the matrix of payoffs to the players is as follows:

Player 3

	B	C
A	3,2,1	3,2,1
C	3,2,1	1,3,2

Player 2

Player 1 now has only one strategy, and dominated strategies can no longer be eliminated for that player. For player 2, the strategy of choosing A in this game is weakly dominated by the strategy of choosing C (compare the middle numbers in the first row to those in the second row). Likewise, for player 3, the strategy of choosing B is weakly dominated by the strategy of choosing C and therefore it, too, can be eliminated.

The outcome that is obtained by iterative elimination of weakly dominated strategies is therefore as follows: player 1 will vote A, player 2 will vote C, and player 3 will vote C. The choice will therefore fall on project C.

Note that the chosen outcome is the worst for the committee president, player 1. The committee president would prefer that not he but one of the other players be the president and have the casting vote. The casting vote, in this instance, is not an advantage but rather a drawback.

Question 5.1

Solve the game in section 2.1.2 by iterative elimination of weakly dominated strategies.

Answer

The payoffs table in this game is as follows:

		Egypt		
		Initiate war	Straits of Tiran left closed	Retreat from Sinai after a short interval
Israel	Initiate war	4,2	3,1	2,1
	Threat of war	1,3	2,5	5,4

Hence the Egyptian strategy of "Retreat from Sinai after a short interval" is weakly dominated by the strategy of "Straits of Tiran left closed."

The remaining game, following this elimination, is:

		Egypt	
		Initiate war	Straits of Tiran left closed
Israel	Initiate war	4,2	3,1
	Threat of war	1,3	2,5

Here, Israel's strategy of "threat of war" is strongly dominated by the strategy "initiate war" (i.e. "initiate war" is a strongly dominant strategy of Israel in the remaining game).

Following the appropriate elimination, the remaining game is now:

Egypt

	Initiate war	Straits of Tiran left closed
Israel Initiate war	4,2	3,1

Now the Egyptian strategy of "Straits of Tiran left closed" is strongly dominated by the strategy of "initiate war." Accordingly, in this game, the process of iterative elimination of weakly dominated strategies leads to the conclusion that both countries will initiate the war.

What did actually happen? Israel opened fire on June 5, 1967, thereby surprising the Egyptian armed forces, which were not prepared for war and had not intended to open fire on their own initiative at that stage. How are we to understand the discrepancy between this choice on the part of Egypt and the prediction we obtained by iterative elimination of weakly dominated strategies? We will now present some possible explanations.

1. We have seen that in order to reach the conclusion that it was worthwhile for Egypt to go to war, we needed three rounds of elimination of (weakly or strongly) dominated strategies. In order to justify three elimination rounds, Egypt would have had to believe that:
   1.1 Israel believes that Egypt will act rationally and will not retreat from Sinai after a short interval.
   1.2 Israel will thence derive the obvious conclusion whereby it is worth her while to take the initiative in opening fire.
   It is definitely possible that, absent any reliable communication between the leaders of the two countries, Egypt cannot be assumed to have held such complex beliefs regarding Israel.
2. Egypt may have erred in assessing the Israeli order of priorities as reflected by its payoffs in the game. In particular, Nasser may well have assessed that even if Egypt left the Straits of Tiran closed to Israeli shipping, Israel would prefer not to go to war on two fronts simultaneously. Nasser was, in fact, giving vent to thoughts along those lines until a few hours before the launch of hostilities. Likewise, in a speech he delivered about a month after the war, he claimed that

when he had taken the decision to close the Straits, he had assessed, at the time, that the probability of war was only 50 percent.[7] Indeed, had Israel's payoff from initiating war when the Straits remained closed been 2 rather then 3, this would have been compatible with Nasser's assumption that Israel would initiate war with a 50 percent probability.

Furthermore, had the payoff to Israel been 1, this would have meant that Israel preferred to refrain from war in the event that Egypt left the Straits of Tiran closed. Such a profile of interests conforms to the Egyptian assessment on the eve of the war that Israel would not take the initiative in opening fire.

How, therefore, are we to model a situation in which one of the players errs or is unsure of what the other player's payoffs are? This state of affairs falls within the domain of **games with incomplete information**. This book will not deal with games of that kind, since their definition and analysis is an advanced topic beyond the scope of our present discussion. The analysis of games with incomplete information is at the research forefront of modern game theory.

5.2   Changes in the order of elimination of weakly dominated strategies

In contrast with the elimination process of strongly dominated strategies, changes in the order of elimination of weakly dominated strategies might bring about a change in the composition of the surviving strategy set. This is because if a strategy x_i is weakly dominated by the strategy x_i', early elimination of some of the strategy profiles x_{-i} of the other players might make x_i just as good as x_i' for player i and thereby prevent the elimination of x_i. We shall see this in the following example.

Consider the game:

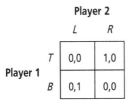

[7] See, for example, Cohen, R. (1990), *Culture and Conflict in Egyptian–Israeli Relations*, Indiana University Press, p. 108.

In this game, strategy B of player 1 is weakly dominated by strategy T, and strategy R of player 2 is weakly dominated by strategy L. Therefore, the process of iterative elimination of weakly dominated strategies (in which, in each round, we simultaneously eliminate dominated strategies of all the players in the remaining game at the beginning of the round) will even after round one give us the outcome (T,L). But if we were first to eliminate the weakly dominated strategy B of player 1, we would still have with the following game:

Player 2

		L	R
Player 1	T	0,0	1,0

In this game, R is not weakly dominated by L (since both strategies always ensure the same payoff to player 2). Therefore, in this remaining game, we will not get an unequivocal prediction of the outcome of the game.

Similarly, if we were to first eliminate the weakly dominated strategy R of player 2, we would remain with the game:

Player 2

	L
T	0,0
B	0,1

Player 1 (label positioned at left of rows T and B)

in which B is not weakly dominated by T. Thus, in this order of elimination, we obtain another reduced set of strategies, which is different from the two preceding sets.

Thus we have shown that the possible sensitivity to the order of elimination of weakly dominated strategies prevents us from adopting this process as a general principle for predicting the outcome of the strategic encounter. Yet in many applications, as demonstrated in the examples we have analyzed in this chapter, the outcome of the elimination process of weakly dominated strategies does not actually depend on the order of elimination. For such games, iterative elimination of weakly dominated strategies is a useful solution procedure.

6 Nash equilibrium

In previous chapters, we discussed solution concepts that relied on rationality or on common knowledge of rationality. Not for all games, however, can a solution be found solely with the aid of these concepts. Let's examine, for example, the following game.

6.1 Battle of the Sexes

Iris and Ben have agreed to spend the evening out together. Iris prefers to watch a movie while Ben would rather go to the theatre, but in any event, both prefer one another's company to spending the evening alone. Their preferences, therefore, can be represented by the payoffs in the following game:

		Ben	
		Cinema	Theatre
Iris	Cinema	2,1	0,0
	Theatre	0,0	1,2

Iris and Ben work at different locations, and both typically come straight from work to wherever they have arranged to spend the evening.

In this game each player has only two strategies. Moreover, neither player has a (strongly or weakly) dominant strategy. It follows that neither of them has a (strongly or weakly) dominated strategy. In particular, in a process of elimination of dominated strategies, not a single strategy can be eliminated. So this is not a process that can help us predict how the players will behave.

Even so, we note that if Iris and Ben agree beforehand to go to the theatre together, then Iris can say to herself, at the end of her work day: "It's true that I prefer to watch a movie with Ben rather than go to the theatre with him. But if Ben does as we agreed and turns up at the theatre, then I, too, will prefer to go to the theatre rather than make my way to the cinema and watch a movie alone."

Correspondingly, Ben can tell himself: "It's true that Iris would prefer that we go together to the cinema, but we agreed that, this evening, we would go to a theatre performance together. If Iris does as we agreed and turns up at the theatre, it's also worthwhile for me to go to the theatre and not go to the cinema."

Accordingly, we may say that in this game the agreement "to go to the theatre together" is a **self-enforcing agreement**. If each player believes that the other player will perform their role in the agreement, then they, too, will prefer to abide by the agreement.

In order to arrive at a formal description of this concept, we will first define the notion of a **best reply**.

Definition If $x_{-i} = (\ldots, x_j, \ldots)_{j \neq i}$ is a given strategy profile of all the players other than player i, we say that the strategy x_i^* is a **best reply** of player i against x_{-i}, if i has no other strategy that will yield her a higher payoff, i.e. if it is the case that:

$$u_i(x_i^*, x_{-i}) \geq u_i(x_i', x_{-i})$$

for every strategy x_i' of player i.

6.2   Definition of Nash equilibrium

We can now proceed to define **Nash equilibrium**. This solution concept was defined by John F. Nash, who won the Nobel prize for Economics in 1994 for his important contributions to the foundations of game theory.[1]

Definition The profile of strategies $x^* = (\ldots, x_i^*, \ldots)$ is a **Nash equilibrium** if for every player $i \in I$, the strategy x_i^* is a best reply to the strategy profile $x_{-i}^* = (\ldots, x_j^*, \ldots)_{j \neq i}$ of the other players.

In other words, $x^* = (\ldots, x_i^*, \ldots)$ is a Nash equilibrium if, for every player i, the strategy x_i^* yields the player a payoff at least as high as any other

[1] Nash won the Nobel prize after about thirty years in which he suffered from the schizophrenia that cut short his academic career. S. Nasar, in the biography *A Beautiful Mind* (Simon & Schuster, 1998), immortalized Nash's dramatic life story, as did a movie by that name in 2001. The scenario of this fictional movie coincides only partially with Nash's life.

strategy of hers, assuming that the other players adopt their own equilibrium strategies:

$$u_i(x_i^*, x_{-i}^*) \geq u_i(x_i', x_{-i}^*)$$

for every strategy x_i' of player i.

In such a state of affairs, no player has any reason to deviate from their equilibrium strategy, if they believe that the other players will adhere to their equilibrium strategies.

In the Battle of the Sexes game, the strategy profile "theatre, theatre" is a Nash equilibrium (work out for yourself how this emerges from the discussion). Similarly, the strategy profile "cinema, cinema" is also a Nash equilibrium: if Iris and Ben agree beforehand to meet at the cinema, then when the time comes for them to begin their evening, each will, in fact, opt on their own account to turn up at the cinema, on the assumption that the other will also abide by their agreement of going to the cinema.

In the Battle of the Sexes game, we have presented the Nash equilibrium as a **stable agreement**. An agreement is stable if, at the moment each of the players must make their own choice of how to act, it is worth their while to abide by the arrangement on the assumption that the other players will do the same. This interpretation of the equilibrium concept presumes the existence of such a prior agreement, which the players have somehow reached by themselves or which a third party has proposed to them.

Another interpretation of the notion of a Nash equilibrium is also possible, whereby it is not necessary to assume that the players have reached prior agreement as to how to act. This interpretation pertains to the players' **predictions**. For example, in the Battle of the Sexes game, Iris may say to herself: "Today, we talked about spending the evening at the cinema or the theatre, but ultimately, we forgot to decide where to meet. I've already left work, and I have no way of contacting Ben. When we spoke, Ben was very keen to see the show today, and he always thinks that if he is enthusiastic about something, then everyone else must concur with his opinion there and then. So I believe he will be going to the theatre."

Correspondingly, Ben may say to himself: "Of course, we didn't make any definite arrangement about where to spend the evening, but I think Iris expressed willingness to see the play, so I believe she will go to the theatre."

In this interpretation of Nash equilibrium, the players' predictions are consistent with and confirm one another. For every player i, the strategy the other players expect her to choose is a best reply to the strategies that i expects them to choose.

Finally, we may combine these two interpretations, and describe the Nash equilibrium as an equilibrium of choices and predictions. Every player is called upon to choose a strategy, and to substantiate their choice with a prediction regarding the strategies the other players will choose. At a Nash equilibrium:

1. Each player chooses a strategy that is optimal given her prediction.
2. The prediction of each player does, in fact, coincide with the strategies chosen by the other players.

Question 6.1

Assume that in a certain game, each player $i \in I$ has a weakly dominant strategy x_i^*. Demonstrate that the strategy profile $(\ldots x_i^*, \ldots)$ is a Nash equilibrium.

Answer

Since x_i^* is a weakly dominant strategy of player i, then it is the case that:

$$u_i(x_i^*, x_{-i}) \geq u_i(x_i', x_{-i})$$

for every strategy x_i' of player i, and for every strategy profile x_{-i} of the other players. This is particularly true for the strategy profile $x_{-i} = x_{-i}^*$ of the other players, in which each of them adopts their weakly dominant strategy. That is to say, it is the case that:

$$u_i(x_i^*, x_{-i}^*) \geq u_i(x_i', x_{-i}^*)$$

for every strategy x_i' of player i in the set of players. Accordingly, $(\ldots x_i^*, \ldots)$ is a Nash equilibrium.

Question 6.2

Assume that in a certain game, every player i has a unique strategy x_i^* that survives iterative elimination of weakly dominated strategies. Demonstrate that $(\ldots x_i^*, \ldots)$ is a Nash equilibrium.

Answer

Let x_i' be a strategy of player i that is different from x_i^*. By assumption, there exists an elimination round n in which it is the case that:

$$u_i(x_i^*, x_{-i}) \geq u_i(x_i', x_{-i})$$

for every strategy profile x_{-i} that survived the first n elimination rounds. By assumption, the strategies in x_{-i}^* survived all the elimination rounds, and in particular the round n. Therefore it is the case that:

$$u_i(x_i^*, x_{-i}^*) \geq u_i(x_i', x_{-i}^*)$$

for every strategy x_i' of player i, for every player i in the set of players. Therefore, $(\ldots x_i^*, \ldots)$ is a Nash equilibrium.

6.3   Focal point equilibrium

In the Battle of the Sexes example, we saw that Nash equilibrium is not necessarily unique. Therefore, the Nash equilibrium concept cannot always determine and provide an unambiguous prediction as to how the players will act. Moreover, in the sequel we will encounter games in which some Nash equilibria are "improbable" or "dubious" in various senses.

Therefore, when a particular strategy profile x^* is a Nash equilibrium, this does not mean that x^* may justifiably be adopted as "The Solution" of the game. The importance of the concept derives from the fact that this is a necessary condition that must be met by any possible candidate for serving as "The Solution." In other words, if a particular strategy profile is not a Nash equilibrium, we cannot deem it a proper, unique prediction as to how rational and intelligent players will behave in the game.

In the Battle of the Sexes game, the two equilibria "theatre, theatre" and "cinema, cinema" were perfectly symmetric. But there are games in which no such symmetry exists, and one equilibrium is distinctive in some sense. This distinctiveness may cause the players to focus on that equilibrium, and to choose it out of the set of equilibria. In this case, we would say that the equilibrium is a **focal point**. We will demonstrate this idea in the following game.

6.3.1   Divvying up the Jackpot

A cash box containing four gold coins falls into the hands of a chief of a tribe. Two of the tribe's families claim ownership of the cash box. In order to resolve the dispute, the tribal chief announces that each family must inform him, simultaneously and separately, how many of the gold coins in the box it claims for itself. If the total claimed is not more than four coins, each family will receive the share it claims, and the tribal chief will keep any remainder. If, however, the total claimed is more than four coins, the tribal chief takes all.

In the situation we have described, each family has five strategies – it can claim any number of coins from zero to four. The following game matrix describes the number of coins each family will receive in accordance with the claims submitted by the families.

		Family B				
		0	1	2	3	4
	0	0,0	0,1	0,2	0,3	0,4
	1	1,0	1,1	1,2	1,3	0,0
Family A	2	2,0	2,1	2,2	0,0	0,0
	3	3,0	3,1	0,0	0,0	0,0
	4	4,0	0,0	0,0	0,0	0,0

How do we find the Nash equilibrium in this game? According to the definition, a pair of the families' strategies is a Nash equilibrium if the strategy of each family at equilibrium is a best reply to the other family's strategy. Therefore, in order to find the equilibria, we will adopt the following procedure:

1. For every strategy x_b of family B, i.e. for every column in the matrix, we will find the optimal strategy (or optimal strategies) of family A against x_b. For this optimal strategy (or strategies) we will underline the payoff of family A, i.e. the left-hand figure in the entry (or entries) that corresponds to that optimal strategy (or strategies) in the strategy column x_b.
2. For every strategy x_a of family A, i.e. for each row of the matrix, we will find the optimal strategy (or optimal strategies) of family B against x_a. For this optimal strategy (or strategies) we will underline the payoff of family B, i.e. the right-hand number in the entry (or entries) that corresponds to that optimal strategy (or strategies) in the strategy row x_a.
3. At the end of the process, all entries in the matrix in which we have underlined the two payoffs correspond to a Nash equilibrium: in every such strategy profile, the strategy of family A is optimal as against the strategy of family B, and the strategy of family B is optimal against the strategy of family A.

In the present game, the outcome of this process is as follows:

Family B

	0	1	2	3	4
0	0,0	0,1	0,2	0,3	0,4
1	1,0	1,1	1,2	1,3	0,0
Family A 2	2,0	2,1	2,2	0,0	0,0
3	3,0	3,1	0,0	0,0	0,0
4	4,0	0,0	0,0	0,0	0,0

Thus, we have found six Nash equilibria in this game. In five of them, one family demands and gets x of the coins, and the other family demands and gets the rest, $4 - x$ of the coins. In the sixth equilibrium, each of the families claims all four coins for itself and neither gets anything.

How can we reduce the set of predictions in this game? First, we note that the strategy of "demanding zero coins" is a weakly dominated strategy (verify this!) for each of the families. If we eliminate these strategies from

Family B

	0	1	2	3	4
0	0,0	0,1	0,2	0,3	0,4
1	1,0	1,1	1,2	1,3	0,0
Family A 2	2,0	2,1	2,2	0,0	0,0
3	3,0	3,1	0,0	0,0	0,0
4	4,0	0,0	0,0	0,0	0,0

we obtain the reduced game:

Family B

	1	2	3	4
1	1,1	1,2	1,3	0,0
2	2,1	2,2	0,0	0,0
Family A				
3	3,1	0,0	0,0	0,0
4	0,0	0,0	0,0	0,0

Here the strategy of "demanding four coins" is weakly dominated for each family. (Explain why!) After it is eliminated from

Family B

	1	2	3	4
1	1,1	1,2	1,3	0,0
2	2,1	2,2	0,0	0,0
3	3,1	0,0	0,0	0,0
4	0,0	0,0	0,0	0,0

Family A

we remain with the game

Family B

	1	2	3
1	1,1	1,2	1,3
Family A 2	2,1	2,2	0,0
3	3,1	0,0	0,0

in which there are three equilibria.

Now, if it is common knowledge that the two families are similar in terms of their tribal standing, then the egalitarian equilibrium in which each family demands and gets half the coins promptly comes into focus as a "natural" solution. Of course, considerations of rationality cannot here rule out the other two remaining equilibria, but the symmetry of the egalitarian solution renders it conspicuous by comparison. In this case we say that the egalitarian equilibrium is a **focal point**. Thus, even though the families are not in communication with one another and are unable to agree on a coordinated course of action, absent any history of similar instances which could provide a basis for one family's pre-dictions regarding the behavior of the other, it is probable that each family will assume that the symmetric equilibrium is a focal point also in the eyes of the other family. In this way, the expectation of each family that the other family will choose a strategy of 'demanding two coins' becomes a self-fulfilling expectation, even though it is neither based on a prior agreement nor deduced from the families' past behavior.

6.4   Finding a Nash equilibrium

In the preceding example, we illustrated a general method of finding a Nash equilibrium in a two-player game, in which each player has a finite number of strategies.

1. For player 1, the one who has to choose the row in the payoff matrix, we must find in each column the entry (or entries) in which her payoff (the left-hand number in the entry) is the highest and underline that payoff. This payoff is the highest that player 1 can obtain if player 2 chooses that column.
2. Similarly, for player 2, the one who has to choose the column in the payoff matrix, we must find in each row the entry (or entries) in which his payoff (the right-hand number in the entry) is the highest and underline this payoff. This payoff is the highest that player 2 can obtain if player 1 chooses that row.
3. Every entry in which the two payoffs are underlined corresponds to a strategy profile which is a Nash equilibrium.

Why does this method lead to finding all the Nash equilibria?

In step 1 above, we found player 1's best reply to any possible strategy of player 2: given a column of the matrix corresponding to a strategy x_2 that player 2 can choose, we found the row or rows x_1 that are best replies for player 1 against the strategy x_2. We will denote by $BR_1(x_2)$ the set containing the best reply (or best replies) x_1.

Similarly, in step 2 we found the best reply of player 2 to any possible strategy of player 1: given a row of the matrix corresponding to a strategy x_1 that player 1 may choose, we found the column or columns x_2 that are best replies for player 2 against the strategy x_1. We will therefore denote by $BR_2(x_1)$ the set containing the best reply (or best replies) x_2.

Thus, if in the strategy profile (x_1, x_2) (which is described by an entry in the matrix) the payoffs of both players were underlined, then this profile satisfies $x_1 \in BR_1(x_2)$ and $x_2 \in BR_2(x_1)$. This means that the strategy of each player in this profile is a best reply to the strategy of the other player and therefore it is a Nash equilibrium.

However, in many examples the strategy set of each player is not a finite set. How, then, do we find the Nash equilibrium? In games of this type we must find the strategy profiles (x_1, x_2) that satisfy $x_1 \in BR_1(x_2)$ and $x_2 \in BR_2(x_1)$. In order to do so, for each of the infinitely many strategies x_2 of player 2, we must find the best replies $BR_1(x_2)$ of player 1, and for each of the infinitely many strategies x_1 of player 1, we must find the best replies $BR_2(x_1)$ of player 2.

On the face of it, this is a highly complicated task. But we will immediately see that in many examples the task is in fact fairly easy.

6.4.1   Partnership

Two partners run a company jointly. At the beginning of each quarter, they agree about the projects to be handled by the company over the coming three months, and how to share the handling of these projects between them. This distribution will dictate the level of effort that each of them will have to invest. This effort finds expression in parameters of which some – such as the number of work hours – are observable, while others – such as concentration, intensity, and level of motivation on the job – are not directly observable. We will denote the partners' effort levels by x_1, x_2. We will assume that the company's profit (in thousands of dollars) is $P(x_1, x_2) = 4x_1 + 4x_2 + x_1x_2$.

The profit is an increasing function of effort levels – the greater the effort exerted by the partners, the greater will be the profit. Moreover, the partners have mutually complementary talents, and this fact is expressed in the term x_1x_2 in the profit function. If the first partner invests more effort and increases x_1, then the effort of the second partner will become more effective: if partner 2 increases her effort by one unit, the company's profit will increase by $4 + x_1$ thousands of dollars. Therefore, the higher the effort x_1 the first partner exerts to begin with, the more productive for the company will be the incremental effort of the second partner.

However, investing in work exacts a price. That price takes the form of fatigue, physical or mental stress, and fewer hours remaining for spending time with family and friends. It seems reasonable to assume that the "cost" of every unit of additional effort is higher than that of its predecessor. For example, the day's first hour of work will probably take place at a time when the rest of the family is also either at work or in school. Therefore, for a partner to renounce time with the family during this hour is less painful than the renunciation represented by the tenth hour of work, by which time at least some family members are at home, the partner's level of fatigue is higher, and so forth.

In this example, we assume that the "cost" of the effort x_i for each of the partners $i = 1,2$ is a given of the function $C(x_i) = x_i^2$. Thus, the first unit of effort "costs" 1, but the second unit of effort already "costs" 3 (since the "cost" of two units of effort is altogether $C(2) = 2^2 = 4$), the third unit "costs" 5, and so forth; thus each additional unit of effort "costs" more than its predecessor.

In this state of affairs, and assuming that the partners share the profit equally, the payoff of partner i, as a function of her level of effort x_i and of the level of effort x_j exerted by the other partner, is given by:

$$u_i(x_i, x_j) = \frac{1}{2}P(x_i, x_j) - C(x_i) = \frac{1}{2}(4x_i + 4x_j + x_ix_j) - x_i^2$$

$$= 2x_i + 2x_j + \frac{1}{2}x_ix_j - x_i^2$$

In particular, the payoff function lends precise meaning to the "price" of the effort $C(x_i)$. Given the effort level x_j of the other partner, partner i will want to increase her effort from x_i to x_i' if, and only if, it is the case that:

$$u_1(x_i', x_j) > u_1(x_i, x_j)$$

i.e. if and only if, as a result of the increased effort, her incremental share in the profit,

$$\frac{1}{2} P(x_i', x_j) - \frac{1}{2} P(x_i, x_j)$$

is greater than the additional "cost" of the effort:

$$C(x_i') - C(x_i)$$

Hence, the "cost" of the effort is a **subjective index** of **monetary equivalence** to effort.

What is the optimal level of effort for partner i when the other partner chooses the effort level x_j? In other words, what is the best reply $x_i \in BR_i(x_j)$? In order to answer this question, we must find an x_i that will maximize:

$$u_i(x_i, x_j) = 2x_i + 2x_j + \frac{1}{2}x_i x_j - x_i^2$$

as a function of x_i only, i.e. for a given and fixed effort level x_j. This is a quadratic function of x_i, and the shape of its graph is a reverse parabola. For example, if $x_j = 1$, then the graph of the function $u_i(x_i, 1) = 2x_i + 2 + \frac{1}{2}x_i - x_i^2$ is as shown in Figure 6.1.

If j increases her effort level to $x_j = 2$, the graph of the function will shift and will now be described by the gray parabola in Figure 6.2.

How will we find the value x_i^* at which the maximum of each such parabola is obtained, i.e. the value x_i^* which will maximize $u_i(x_i, x_j)$ for a given x_j? The function $u_i(x_i, x_j)$ increases on the left of this value x_i^*, descends on the right of it, and at the value x_i^* itself it levels out. In other words, the derivative of the function u_i with respect to the variable x_i vanishes at $x_i = x_i^*$:

$$\frac{\partial u_i(x_i^*, x_j)}{\partial x_i} = 0$$

or, more explicitly:

$$0 = \frac{\partial u_i(x_i^*, x_j)}{\partial x_i} = 2 + \frac{1}{2}x_j - 2x_i^*$$

Hence we find that:

$$x_i^* = BR_i(x_j) = 1 + \frac{1}{4}x_j$$

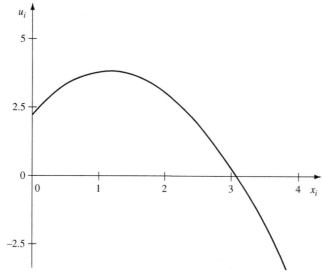

Figure 6.1

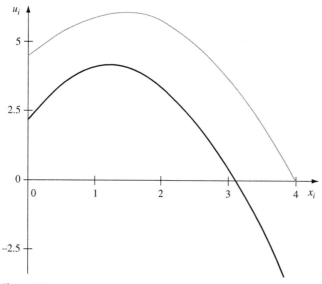

Figure 6.2

This is therefore the best reply for partner i if she expects that j will choose the effort level x_j. The graph of the best-reply function looks like that shown in Figure 6.3. This is also called the **reaction curve**. In the particular case before us, this curve is a straight line.

We find, therefore, that to the extent that partner j increases her investment of effort x_j, the optimal level of effort $x_i^* = BR_i(x_j)$ for i will likewise increase, albeit

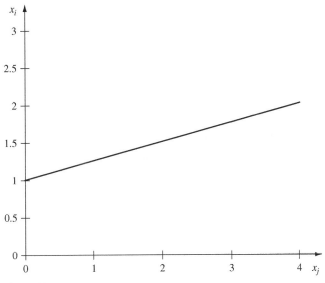

Figure 6.3

moderately: the slope of the function $x_i^* = BR_i(x_j)$ is $\frac{1}{4}$, and therefore the addition of one unit of effort by j will lead i to increase her effort only by $\frac{1}{4}$ of a unit of effort.

For example, if $x_j = 1$, the best reply of i is $BR_i(1) = 1.25$ (the effort level $x_i = 1.25$ maximizes the utility function of i, which is described by the black parabola). If j increases her effort level to $x_j = 2$ (whereupon the utility function of i will be described by the gray parabola), then the best reply of i will increase to $BR_i(2) = 1.5$. We can see this explicitly in Figure 6.4.

We have now reached the stage at which we must find a Nash equilibrium with the aid of the best-reply functions. At a Nash equilibrium (x_i^*, x_j^*), the strategy of each partner is a best reply to the other partner's strategy. That is:

$$x_i^* = BR_i(x_j^*) = 1 + \frac{1}{4}x_j^*$$
$$x_j^* = BR_j(x_i^*) = 1 + \frac{1}{4}x_i^*$$

This is a system of two equations with the two unknowns, x_i^*, x_j^*, the unique solution to which is:

$$x_i^* = \frac{4}{3}$$
$$x_j^* = \frac{4}{3}$$

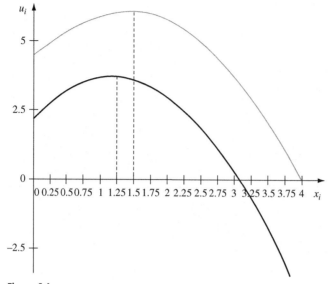

Figure 6.4

Thus, the strategy profile $(x_i^*, x_j^*) = \left(\frac{4}{3}, \frac{4}{3}\right)$ is the only Nash equilibrium in this game. The payoff of each partner in this equilibrium is:

$$u_i\left(\frac{4}{3}, \frac{4}{3}\right) = \frac{1}{2}P\left(\frac{4}{3}, \frac{4}{3}\right) - C\left(\frac{4}{3}\right) = \frac{40}{9}$$

We can also illustrate the procedure to find the equilibrium graphically, by presenting together the graphs of both best-reply functions, BR_i and BR_j. We need to remember only that BR_i is a function whose domain is the values of x_j and whose range is the values of x_i, whereas BR_j is a function whose domain is the values of x_i and whose range is the values of x_j. In outlining the best reply BR_i above, we drew the values of x_j on the horizontal axis and the values of x_i on the vertical axis. If we now wish to add to that figure the graph of BR_j, then the domain of BR_j will, in contrast, be the vertical axis, and the range will be the horizontal – see Figure 6.5.

The intersection of the two reaction curves is at the unique Nash equilibrium:

$$(x_i^*, x_j^*) = \left(\frac{4}{3}, \frac{4}{3}\right)$$

The equilibrium is symmetric because the partners' payoff functions are symmetric.

Question 6.3

From among all the symmetric effort profiles $(x_i, x_j) = (x, x)$, does the equilibrium $\left(\frac{4}{3}, \frac{4}{3}\right)$ maximize the payoff of each player?

Nash equilibrium

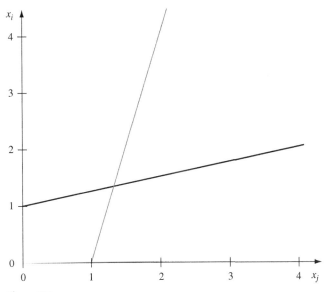

Figure 6.5

Answer

If each partner invests the effort x, the payoff of each partner will be:

$$u_i(x, x) = \frac{1}{2}P(x, x) - C(x) = \frac{1}{2}(4x + 4x + x^2) - x^2 = 4x - \frac{1}{2}x^2$$

This payoff will be optimal for an effort level of $x = 4$ (verify this!) by each partner, which is far higher than the effort level $\frac{4}{3}$ at the Nash equilibrium. Accordingly, the payoff of each partner will be $u_i(4,4) = 8$, which is much higher than the payoff $\frac{40}{9}$ at a Nash equilibrium.

What is the reason for this state of affairs? Why, at a Nash equilibrium, do the partners not choose a strategy that will maximize the payoff of both? Why is it that if one of the partners, j, nevertheless chooses an effort level 4, the other partner, i, will prefer to choose the effort level $BR_i(4) = 2$, instead of choosing the effort level 4 as well?

When considering whether to increase her effort level, partner i is aware that she will herself pay the "cost" of additional effort, but will pocket only half the increase in profit. The utility which the second partner will derive from the increase in profit is not a part of the payoff function of i. If each partner wished to maximize the total payoffs of the partnership or the average thereof, then each partner would choose the effort level 4. But if each partner contemplates only her own narrow interest, and does not "internalize" the external effect of her own effort on the other partner, she will choose a lower level of effort.

Since both partners reach their decisions in this manner, at a Nash equilibrium they act symmetrically, but not with that extent of symmetric effort that would yield both of them the highest payoff.

This state of affairs is reminiscent of that in the Prisoner's Dilemma, albeit in a less extreme version. In the problem before us, each partner has a broad range of strategies and not just two. Accordingly, at a Nash equilibrium, the partners do not choose the extreme strategy of zero effort level, but rather a positive one. However, as in the Prisoner's Dilemma, it is a different symmetric strategy profile, which is *not* a Nash equilibrium, that would yield both partners the highest payoff.

6.4.2   Finding a Nash equilibrium in games with a continuum of strategies

In the solution of the partnership game, we demonstrated a general method for finding a Nash equilibrium in a game between two players, when the strategy of each player is a continuous variable. In this method, we must:

1. Find the best-reply functions:

$$BR_1 : X_2 \to X_1$$
$$BR_2 : X_1 \to X_2$$

   BR_1 associates to any strategy $x_2 \in X_2$ of player 2 the best reply $x_1^* = BR_1(x_2)$ of player 1. Similarly, BR_2 associates to any strategy $x_1 \in X_1$ of player 1 the best reply $x_2^* = BR_2(x_1)$ of player 2.
2. To solve the system of two equations:

$$x_1^* = BR_1(x_2^*)$$
$$x_2^* = BR_2(x_1^*)$$

   with the two unknowns x_1^*, x_2^*. Each solution (x_1^*, x_2^*) of this system of equations is a Nash equilibrium of the game.

In order to find the best-reply function BR_i of player i, we must identify, from among all the strategies $x_i \in X_i$ of player i, the strategy x_i^* that will maximize her payoff $u_i(x_i, x_j)$ for each given strategy $x_j \in X_j$ of the other player, j. If the function u_i is differentiable at the point (x_i, x_j) with respect to the first variable, then the maximum we are seeking will be obtained at the point at which the derivative $\frac{\partial u_i(x_i, x_j)}{\partial x_i}$ of $u_i(x_i, x_j)$ with respect to the variable x_i equals zero, or at a boundary point of the strategy set X_i.[2]

Note: the boundary points of X_i and also the strategies X_i in which the derivative $\frac{\partial u_i(x_i, x_j)}{\partial x_i}$ vanishes are only candidates for being the maximum $x_i^* = BR_i(x_j)$ that we are

---

[2] A boundary point of X_i is a strategy x_i to the right or to the left of which we cannot find additional strategies in X_i that are as close as we wish to x_i.

seeking. Why? Because the derivative $\frac{\partial u_i(x_i,x_j)}{\partial x_i}$ vanishes also at minimum or local minimum points x_i of the function $u_i(x_i, x_j)$, and also at its local maximum points, as well as at its inflection point, if any. Similarly, a boundary point x_i of the range of strategies X_i is not necessarily the one in which u_i is maximized when player j chooses x_j. Therefore, we must consider all these points one by one and find at which of them the maximum is obtained.

If the maximum is obtained at more than one of these points, BR_i is not a function but rather a **correspondence**; it associates to the strategy x_j of player j all the best replies of player i. In this case, we will not have a system of two equations, the solution of which will give us the Nash equilibrium. Nevertheless, we can in any event continue to employ the geometric procedure that we illustrated in the example in section 6.4.1, and we can present the reaction curves of the two players in that figure.

In the space of the strategy profiles $X_1 \times X_2$ we will use a particular color – black, for example – to draw the reaction curve of player 2: for every strategy x_1 of player 1, we will denote in black all the points (x_1, x_2) for which x_2 is a best reply of player 2 to x_1. (If player 2 has several best replies to x_1 we will depict them all!) If possible, we will connect the dots we have denoted and obtain a curve.[3] We will then repeat the process for player 1: for every strategy x_2 of player 2, we will denote with another color – gray, for example – all the points (x_1, x_2) for which x_1 is a best reply of player 1 to x_2. If possible, we will connect the points we have denoted to form a curve. Finally, all the points that are marked with both black and gray – i.e. all the points of intersection between the two reaction curves – are Nash equilibria.

Question 6.4

Assume that in the partnership game of section 6.4.1, the possible levels of effort for each partner are in the range of $[0,4]$. Show that the game is solvable by iterative elimination of strongly dominated strategies.

Answer

Consider the reaction curve in Figure 6.3. For effort levels in the range $[0,4]$, the best reply is in the range $[1,2]$. In other words, when $x_j \in [0,4]$, the maximum of the parabola $u_i(x_i, x_j)$ is located between 1 and 2. Therefore the payoff function $u_i(x_i, x_j)$ is **increasing** in the range $x_i < 1$ and **decreasing** in the range $x_i > 2$, for every $x_j \in [0,4]$. That is to say, any strategy of player i that satisfies $x_i < 1$ is strongly dominated by her strategy $x_i = 1$:

For every $x_i < 1$ and for every $x_j \in [0,4]$, $u_i(1,x_j) > u_i(x_i, x_j)$

---

[3] Or part of the plane if, for a continuum of strategies x_1 of player 1, player 2 has a continuum of best replies. For example, in the degenerate game in which player 2 is indifferent among the possible game outcomes, her "reaction curve" will consist of all the strategy profiles $X_1 \times X_2$.

Similarly, every strategy of player i that satisfies $x_i > 2$ is strongly dominated by her strategy $x_i = 2$:

For every $x_i > 2$ and for every $x_j \in [0,4]$, u_i $(2, x_j) > u_i$ (x_i, x_j)

Therefore, all the strategies x_i that satisfy $x_i < 1$ or $x_i > 2$ are eliminated in the first elimination round of strongly dominated strategies. In contrast, the strategies $x_i \in [1,2]$ survive the first elimination round for each of the partners $i = 1,2$, since every strategy $x_i \in [1,2]$ is optimal against some strategy $x_j \in [0,4]$ of the other partner.

We can now repeat the argument for the effort levels $[1,2]$ that survived the first elimination round. For these effort levels, the best reply is in the range $\left[\frac{5}{4}, \frac{6}{4}\right]$. In other words, when $x_j \in [1,2]$, the maximum of the parabola u_i (x_i, x_j) lies between 5/4 and 6/4. Therefore, the payoff function u_i (x_i, x_j) is **increasing** in the range $x_i < \frac{5}{4}$ and **decreasing** in the range $x_i > \frac{6}{4}$, for every $x_j \in [1,2]$. That is, in the second round every strategy $x_i < \frac{5}{4}$ of partner i is strongly dominated by her strategy $x_i = \frac{5}{4}$; and similarly, every strategy $x_i > \frac{6}{4}$ of partner i is strongly dominated by her strategy $x_i = \frac{6}{4}$. Therefore, all the strategies that satisfy $x_i < \frac{5}{4}$ or $x_i > \frac{6}{4}$ are eliminated in the second elimination round of strongly dominated strategies.

The strategies x_i that satisfy $x_i \in \left[\frac{5}{4}, \frac{6}{4}\right]$ survive the second elimination round for each of the partners $i = 1,2$, since every strategy $x_i \in \left[\frac{5}{4}, \frac{6}{4}\right]$ is optimal against some strategy $x_j \in [1,2]$ of the other partner that has survived the first elimination round. In this way, the range of surviving strategies diminishes progressively with each round of elimination. The strategies that survived the first elimination round were:

$$BR_i([0,4]) = [1,2]$$

The strategies that survived the second elimination round were:

$$BR_i\left(BR_j([0,4])\right) = BR_i([1,2]) = \left[1 + \frac{1}{4} \times 1, 1 + \frac{1}{4} \times 2\right] = \left[\frac{5}{4}, \frac{6}{4}\right]$$

The strategies surviving the third elimination round will be:

$$BR_i\left(BR_j(BR_i([0,4]))\right) = BR_i\left(BR_j([1,2])\right)$$

$$= BR_i\left(\left[1 + \frac{1}{4} \times 1 , 1 + \frac{1}{4} \times 2\right]\right)$$

$$= \left[1 + \frac{1}{4} \times \left(1 + \frac{1}{4} \times 1\right) , 1 + \frac{1}{4} \times \left(1 + \frac{1}{4} \times 2\right)\right]$$

$$= \left[1 + \frac{1}{4} + \frac{1}{16} , 1 + \frac{1}{4} + \frac{2}{16}\right] = \left[\frac{21}{16}, \frac{22}{16}\right]$$

and so forth. By induction, the strategies surviving the round n will be those in the interval:

$$\left[1 + \frac{1}{4} + \frac{1}{16} + \ldots + \frac{1}{4^{n-1}} \quad , \quad \left(1 + \frac{1}{4} + \frac{1}{16} + \ldots + \frac{1}{4^{n-1}}\right) + \frac{1}{4^{n-1}}\right]$$

Therefore, any effort level that is lower than $1 + \frac{1}{4} + \frac{1}{16} + \ldots + \frac{1}{4^{n-1}}$ will not survive one of the elimination rounds up to n, and similarly any effort level higher than $\left(1 + \frac{1}{4} + \frac{1}{16} + \ldots + \frac{1}{4^{n-1}}\right) + \frac{1}{4^{n-1}}$ will not survive one of the elimination rounds up to n.

Thus, we have obtained a geometric series:[4]

$$1 + \frac{1}{4} + \frac{1}{16} + \ldots + \frac{1}{4^{n-1}} + \ldots$$

the sum of which is $\frac{1}{1 - \frac{1}{4}} = \frac{4}{3}$. Therefore, all effort levels that are lower than $\frac{4}{3}$ will be eliminated sooner or later in one of the elimination rounds. Similarly, the series $\left(1 + \frac{1}{4} + \frac{1}{16} + \ldots + \frac{1}{4^{n-1}}\right) + \frac{1}{4^{n-1}}$ likewise converges to $\frac{4}{3}$ and therefore all effort levels that are higher than $\frac{4}{3}$ will be eliminated sooner or later in one of the elimination rounds. Thus, the strategy $\frac{4}{3}$, which is the strategy that each player chooses at a Nash equilibrium, is, in this example, also the only strategy that survives iterative elimination of strongly dominated strategies.

---

[4] Reminder: the sum of the n first terms in the geometric series $a, ak, ak^2 \ldots$ is

$$a + ak + ak^2 + \ldots + ak^{n-1} = \frac{a(1 - k^n)}{1 - k}$$

If $0 < k < 1$, this sum converges to $\frac{a}{1-k}$ when $n \to \infty$. In this case we say that the sum of the infinite geometric series is:

$$a + ak + ak^2 + \ldots = \frac{a}{1 - k}$$

PART III

Prominent classes of strategic form games

─── INTRODUCTION ───────────────────────────

In the previous chapters we defined the basic solution concepts for strategic form games – from those relying on considerations of dominance to the notion of Nash equilibrium which hinges on a concept of stability. It is now time to explore important classes of strategic form games and to analyze their properties.

Chapter 7 addresses a twofold classification: games of cooperation vs. games of conflict, and games with strategic complements vs. games with strategic substitutes. The first distinction asks whether each player would have preferred her rivals to increase the intensity of their action (games of cooperation) or decrease it (games of conflict). The second distinction asks whether, upon an increase in the intensity of the rivals' action, the player herself would have preferred to increase the intensity of her own action (strategic complements) or decrease it (strategic substitutes); or, in other words, whether the reaction function of the player is increasing (the case of strategic substitutes) or decreasing (strategic complements).

Somewhat surprisingly, these two dimensions of classification are independent of one another, and each of the four combinations of cooperation/conflict and strategic complements/substitutes is possible. The partnership game, presented already in Chapter 6, is an example of a game of cooperation with strategic complements. The first example in that chapter, that of a public good game, is of cooperation with strategic substitutes. This game is analyzed in detail, showing, first, that its Nash equilibrium is inefficient – i.e. that all players would have preferred to play a profile of strategies in which they all invest more than at the Nash equilibrium. Unfortunately, such a unanimously preferable investment profile is not a Nash equilibrium and hence does not constitute a stable, self-sustaining agreement. Furthermore, we show that the larger the group of players, the more inefficient the Nash equilibrium becomes.

A related game is that of the tragedy of the commons, in which a similar inefficiency arises, this time in the form of over-congestion. In both games each player's strategy imposes an externality on its peers, and the inefficiency arises due to the fact that the player does not take into account this external influence when choosing its best reply to others' choices. In the public good investment game this is a positive externality, and the game is thus of strategic complements; in the tragedy of the commons the externality is negative, and the game is of strategic substitutes.

An essential difference between the two games is that while enjoying the public good (e.g. a safe, green, clean neighborhood) does not limit the extent of benefit others can make of the good, a common pasture land or a highway is a limited resource, the usage of which by some creates congestion which decreases the benefit accrued to others. We therefore discuss various ways in which communities or governments can overcome, at least partially, the inefficiency due to the externality. These range from limiting access to the congested resource, to imposing a tax on its usage, privatizing it or creating a market for its yields, such as the recently evolving markets for pollution permits.

A game modeling a patent race is the next interesting example. In this example the reaction functions of the competitors are first increasing and then decreasing as a function of the rival's investment level, while the game is one of conflict for each level of investment. Interestingly, the Nash equilibrium investment levels are precisely at the point where the best-reply functions level up, thus passing from a regime of strategic complements to one of strategic substitutes.

The last example of Chapter 7 has to do with a law enforcement game between a criminal and the authorities. The game is definitely one of conflict – the government would have liked the criminal to moderate his unlawful activities, and the criminal would have liked the government to decrease its policing efforts. However, the reaction function of the criminal is decreasing – he moderates his activity in reply to increasing law-enforcing activities, while the government increases these efforts when crime levels rise.

In Chapter 8 we turn to an important application of game theory for the study of oligopolistic behavior. This is the middle case in which the same product, or close variants thereof, are produced by a small number of competing producers. None of these producers is therefore a monopolist with absolute market power for setting the price or the quantity, but neither is it the case that every producer is so small that they can practically ignore the influence of their supply or pricing strategy on consumers' behavior. In other words, each of these competitors has limited but non-negligible market power. How should we expect them to behave?

Chapter 8 studies the basic models of oligopoly – that of competition in quantities, due originally to Cournot, and that of price competition, due to Bertrand. Both models are studied first under the assumption that the different firms produce identical products, and then for the case in which their products are somewhat differentiated from each other. In particular, we show how an increase in the number of competing firms decreases the market power of each competitor, tending in the limit to the classical economic model of perfect competition. This limiting behavior of the oligopoly models is an important contribution of game theory for providing a foundation of the perfect competition equilibrium in Economics. In the last part of Chapter 8 we show how seemingly competitive pricing strategies of sellers may in fact hide a collusive, anti-competitive motive, arising at the Nash equilibrium of the game between them.

Chapter 9 discusses the important class of coordination games, the archetype of which is the Stug-hunt game described by Jean-Jacques Rousseau in his essay on the source of inequality among men. A coordination game is one possessing several Nash equilibria which can be unanimously ranked by the players – from the least efficient to the most efficient. In the Stug-hunt game, focusing on the efficient equilibrium is hindered by the fact that the efficient equilibrium embodies a higher **strategic uncertainty** – if the other players deviate from their strategies at the efficient equilibrium, the player adhering to his efficient equilibrium strategy would suffer more than if he were to play his part in the inefficient equilibrium.

After analyzing the Stag Hunt game we provide a real-world example of such a game between whale hunters in Indonesia, as well as other examples of coordination games such as the origin of the QWERTY keyboard and video-recording standards. We discuss also the outcome of coordination game experiments in the lab, and discuss the potential sources for discrepancies that sometimes arise between lab findings and theoretical predictions.

Two further important examples are analyzed in detail in this chapter. The first is that of network externalities, in which the utility of each user of the network increases with the number of users (as in the case of a communication network or a social online network); the second is that of job search and unemployment, in which entrepreneurial initiatives which *inter alia* create jobs enjoy higher incentives the greater the purchasing means workers have.

7 Cooperation and conflict, strategic complements and substitutes

In the preceding chapters, we described a variety of games possessing various attributes, yet some of those games resembled one another in various ways. In Chapters 1 and 2 we described three different games of the "social dilemma" type, and we explained in what sense the three games are equivalent. More generally, finding common attributes for various games will enable us to catalog the games into categories, and to identify the forces and tensions that affect the equilibrium in a given category of games.

In this chapter, we take our first step in this cataloging process, by identifying two game attributes. The first attribute for differentiating between games is natural and simple. This attribute will answer the question: is the strategic interaction between the players one of cooperation or of conflict? We say that the strategic interaction is one of **cooperation** if every player always prefers that the other player or players **intensify** their actions. We will say that the strategic interaction is one of **conflict** if every player always prefers that the other player or players **moderate** their actions. The distinction between games of cooperation and games of conflict is accordingly relevant when the strategies of each player are completely ordered by their intensity or strength, from the most moderate to the most intensive strategy. An order relation of this kind is, in fact, definable in each of the examples we have encountered so far.

The second attribute we will present in this chapter, for the purpose of distinguishing between games, is more complex. It, too, is applicable only in games in which the strategies of each player can be ordered by their intensity. It will answer the question: will the player wish to intensify her actions when the other players intensify their actions? If every player will wish to **intensify** her action in response to the **intensification** of the activity of the other players or of at least some of them, we say that the game is one of **strategic complements**. If every player will wish to **moderate** her action in response to the **intensification** of the activity of the other players or of at least some of them, we say that the game is one of **strategic substitutes**. In other words, if the best-reply function of every player is an increasing function, the game is one of strategic complements; and if the best-reply function of every player is a decreasing function, then the game is one of strategic substitutes.[1]

Is there a link between this game attribute and the question of whether the game is one of cooperation or of conflict? For example, in a case in which the players in a game cooperate, is it not natural for every player to want to make more of an effort when the other players intensify their efforts?

In the partnership game in section 6.4.1, that is indeed how things are; each partner in this game benefits when the other partner steps up her efforts (the game is one of cooperation), and in this case, it is as if she wishes to "reward" her and to make more of an effort on her own part (the game is one of strategic complements).

In fact, however, there is no "reward" component when the best-reply function of each partner is increasing; each partner wishes to intensify her efforts in response to the stepped-up efforts of the other partner because it is worth her while to do so. When partner B intensifies her efforts, the effort exerted by partner A becomes more effective. This heightened effectiveness causes partner A to want to boost her own efforts, too, because in that way her share of the profit will increase to an amount over and above the "cost" of the additional effort she will have to invest to that end.

This discussion hints that there may also be games of cooperation that are not games of strategic complements but rather of strategic substitutes. We will now examine one such example.

7.1   Investing in a public good

A set of players must decide how much to invest in a public good from which all will benefit. For example, pollutant industrial plants must decide how much to invest in pollution-reducing means, given that all local residents benefit from the improved air quality, and the region as a whole becomes more attractive for residential, commercial, and tourism purposes; storekeepers must decide how much to invest in their window displays, given that nearby stores will also benefit from the potential customers who will be drawn to the pleasant environment; and so forth.

Assume therefore that we have n players. Each player i, $i = 1, \ldots n$, has a sum of money e_i that is available for investment. Each of the players must decide how much

---

[1] The notions of "strategic complements" and "strategic substitutes" were first presented by Bulow, J. I., J. D. Geanakoplos, and P. D. Klemperer (1985), "Multimarket Oligopoly: Strategic Substitutes and Complements," *Journal of Political Economy*, 93, 488–511, in a context in which the strategies are the quantities of products that firms are able to manufacture, and in comparison with the classical concepts in economics of substitute and complementary products. Today, the notions "strategic complements" and "strategic substitutes" are also used in more general contexts, in which the strategies are not necessarily the quantities of products.

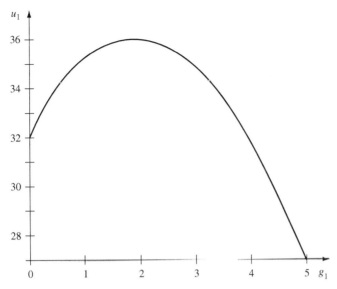

Figure 7.1

of that sum she will invest in the public good. We will denote by g_i the investment of player i, $0 \leq g_i \leq e_i$. The payoff function of player i is:

$$u_i(g_i, g_{-i}) = (e_i - g_i) + (e_i - g_i) \sum_{k=1}^{n} g_k$$

First, the player directly benefits from the post-investment sum of money $e_i - g_i$ remaining in her possession, which she uses for investing in personal interests, of which she is the sole beneficiary. The second element in the payoff function reflects the increase in utility that every player i derives from the investment $e_i - g_i$ in her personal interest as a result of the total investment $\sum_{k=1}^{n} g_k$ of all the players in the public good.

What, then, will be each player's investment in the public good at a Nash equilibrium?

We will first solve the problem for two players. The payoff functions of the two players are:

$$u_1(g_1, g_2) = e_1 - g_1 + (e_1 - g_1)(g_1 + g_2)$$
$$u_2(g_1, g_2) = e_2 - g_2 + (e_2 - g_2)(g_1 + g_2)$$

Assume, for example, that $e_1 = 8$ and $e_2 = 10$. If player 2 chooses to invest $g_2 = 3$, then the utility of player 1 as a function of her investment g_1 is depicted in Figure 7.1. That is to say, she will obtain her maximum utility if she chooses the investment level $g_1 = 2$, and the maximal utility obtained will be 36.

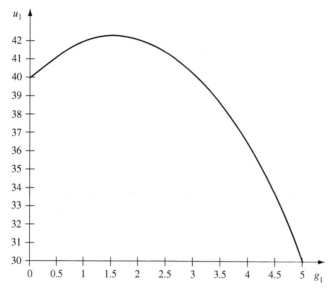

Figure 7.2

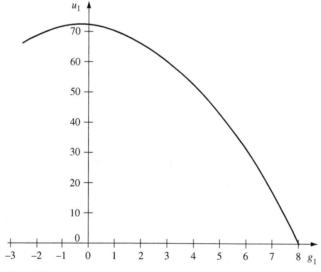

Figure 7.3

However, if player 2 chooses to invest $g_2 = 4$, then the situation of player 1 will improve. Her payoff as a function of her investment will be as described in Figure 7.2. Now she will obtain her maximal utility if she invests only $g_1 = 1.5$ and this maximal utility will be 42.25. If player 2 ratchets up her investment even higher to $g_2 = 8$, then the payoff function of player 1 will be as depicted in Figure 7.3. In this situation, the optimal investment for player 1 will be $g_1 = 0$, which is to say, she will choose not to make any contribution whatsoever to the public good. (The maximum of the parabola is obtained at the point $g_1 = -0.5$, but the player cannot invest a negative amount of money in the public good.)

What, then, is the investment level which each player will choose at a Nash equilibrium? In order to answer this question, we must first find the best-reply function of each of the players $i = 1,2$. If player j chooses to invest g_j, then the payoff to the other player, i, from an investment g_i will be:

$$u_i(g_i, g_j) = (e_i - g_i)(1 + g_i + g_j)$$

As a function of g_i, this is a parabola whose maximum is obtained at the point at which it is the case that:

$$0 = \frac{\partial u_i(g_i, g_j)}{\partial g_i} = -(1 + g_i + g_j) + (e_i - g_i) = e_i - 2g_i - 1 - g_j$$

i.e. at the point:

$$g_i = \frac{1}{2}(e_i - 1 - g_j)$$

In such a case, $\frac{1}{2}(e_i - 1 - g_j)$ will be the optimal investment level for player i. The size of the investment will be positive (or zero) when $g_j \leq e_i - 1$. This is the investment level that player i can actually choose, because it is smaller than the total resources e_i at her disposal.

On the other hand, when $g_j > e_i - 1$, the term $\frac{1}{2}(e_i - 1 - g_j)$ is negative. But player i cannot choose a negative level of investment. In such case, as a function of g_i, the parabola:

$$u_i(g_i, g_j) = (e_i - g_i)(1 + g_i + g_j)$$

is a decreasing function throughout the possible investment range $g_i \in [0, e_i]$ and therefore the maximal payoff to player i will be obtained at the point $g_i = 0$.

To sum up, the best-reply function of player i is:

$$BR_i(g_j) = \begin{cases} \frac{1}{2}(e_i - 1 - g_j) & g_j \leq e_i - 1 \\ \\ 0 & \text{otherwise} \end{cases}$$

This best-reply function is a **decreasing function** of the investment level g_j of the other player, j. Hence, the public good game is a game of **strategic substitutes**.

For example, for $e_1 = 8$ and $e_2 = 10$, the best-reply functions of player 1 (in gray) and of player 2 (in black) look like those shown in Figure 7.4. (In order to draw the reaction curve (in black) of player 2, g_1 must be extracted from the equation $g_2 = BR_2(g_1) = \frac{1}{2}(e_2 - 1 - g_1)$ thus obtaining, for $e_2 = 10$:

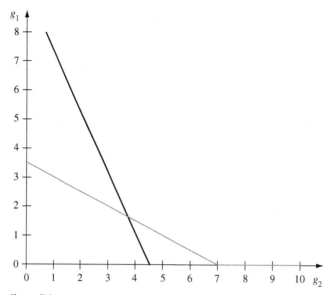

Figure 7.4

$$g_1 = 9 - 2g_2$$

in the range of $g_i \in [0,e_1] = [0,8]$, i.e. $0.5 \le g_2 \le 4.5$.)

Now, a Nash equilibrium is obtained in this example at the point of intersection of the two reaction curves. We find it with the following computation:

$$g_2 = \frac{1}{2}\left(e_2 - 1 - \frac{1}{2}(e_1 - 1 - g_2)\right) \Rightarrow g_2 = \frac{1}{3}(2e_2 - e_1 - 1) = \frac{11}{3}$$

and:

$$g_1 = \frac{1}{2}(e_1 - 1 - g_2) = \frac{5}{3}$$

Hence at a Nash equilibrium player 1 will invest 5/3 and player 2 will invest 11/3 – way below the maximum that they are able to invest. The payoff of player 1 at the equilibrium will be:

$$u_1(g_1) = e_1 - g_1 + (e_1 - g_1)(g_1 + g_2) = \frac{361}{9} = 40.11$$

and the payoff of player 2 at equilibrium will be:

$$u_2(g_2) = e_2 - g_2 + (e_2 - g_2)(g_1 + g_2) = \frac{361}{9} = 40.11$$

If the players could sign, ahead of time, a binding agreement whereby player 1 invests 3 and player 2 invests 5, then the utility of player 1 would be 45 and the utility of player 2 would also be 45 (verify this). Both of them would prefer such an agreement over the actions profile in the Nash equilibrium. The problem is that an agreement of this kind is not "self-enforcing;" if player 1 believes that player 2 will in fact honor the agreement and invest 5, then she will prefer to invest 1 rather than 3, and thereby increase her payoff to 49.

What happens when more than two players take part in the game? In such a case, we cannot plot the reaction curves in a two-dimensional coordinate system, but we can calculate the point of equilibrium. Assume, for the sake of simplicity, that all the players have the same sum of money:

$$e_1 = e_2 = \ldots = e_n \equiv e > 1$$

Now, in order to find the best-reply function of player j to the investments of the other players, we will find the derivative of her utility function with respect to her own investment in the public good, and equate the derivative to zero. To keep things simple, we will first do this for player 1:

$$0 = \frac{\partial}{\partial g_1} u_1(g_1, g_{-1}) = -1 - \sum_{i=1}^{n} g_i + e - g_1$$

Hence we obtain that:

$$g_1 = BR_1(g_2, \ldots g_n) = \frac{1}{2}(e - 1 - (g_2 + g_3 + \ldots + g_n))$$

as long as it is the case that:

$$e - 1 - (g_2 + g_3 + \ldots + g_n) \geq 0$$

and otherwise:

$$g_1 = BR_1(g_2, \ldots g_n) = 0$$

Similarly, for player j we obtain that:

$$g_j = BR_j(g_{-j}) = \frac{1}{2}(e - 1 - (g_1 + g_2 + \ldots + g_{j-1} + g_{j+1} + \ldots + g_n))$$

as long as:

$$e - 1 - (g_1 + g_2 + \ldots + g_{j-1} + g_{j+1} + \ldots + g_n) \geq 0$$

and otherwise:

$$g_j = BR_j(g_{-j}) = 0$$

Or, in short:

$$BR_j(g_{-j}) = \max\left\{0, \frac{1}{2}\left(e - 1 - \sum_{i \neq j} g_i\right)\right\}$$

We will now try to find a Nash equilibrium, i.e. an investment profile in which all the equations $g_j = BR_j(g_{-j})$ are simultaneously satisfied for $j = 1, \ldots, n$. We will restrict attention to seeking a Nash equilibrium in which each of the players makes a strictly positive investment $g_j > 0$ in the public good. In order to find a Nash equilibrium of this kind, we must solve the system of equations:

$$g_j = \frac{1}{2}\left(e - 1 - (g_1 + \ldots + g_{j-1} + g_{j+1} + \ldots + g_n)\right) \qquad j = 1, \ldots, n$$

The solution is:

$$g_1^* = g_2^* = \ldots = g_n^* = \frac{1}{(n+1)}(e - 1)$$

Why? We have the following system of equations:

$$g_1 = \frac{1}{2}(e - 1 - (g_2 + g_3 + \ldots + g_n))$$

$$g_2 = \frac{1}{2}(e - 1 - (g_1 + g_3 + \ldots + g_n))$$

•

•

•

$$g_n = \frac{1}{2}(e - 1 - (g_1 + g_2 + \ldots + g_{n-1}))$$

If we add up all the equations (note that on the right-hand side each of the elements g_i appears $(n - 1)$ times), we will obtain:

$$\sum_{i=1}^{n} g_i = \frac{1}{2}\left(n(e - 1) - (n - 1)\sum_{i=1}^{n} g_i\right)$$

After simplifying we obtain:

$$(n + 1)\sum_{i=1}^{n} g_i = n(e - 1)$$

or

$$\sum_{i=1}^{n} g_i = \frac{n}{(n+1)}(e - 1)$$

Now we can substitute this expression in the equation for g_j:

$$g_j = \frac{1}{2}\left(e - 1 - \left(\frac{n}{(n+1)}(e-1) - g_j\right)\right)$$

and we will obtain:

$$g_j^* = \frac{1}{(n+1)}(e-1)$$

Notice that as the number of players gets larger, the investment of each player progressively diminishes (because the denominator in the expression increases). When about to decide how much to invest in the public good, the player takes into account the total number of players. The larger that number, the more surely she is convinced that she "will be able to hide behind" the investment of the other players, and therefore, she invests less at a Nash equilibrium. This phenomenon is known as "**the free-rider problem.**"

Thus, the overall size of the public good:

$$\sum_{i=1}^{n} g_1^* = \frac{n}{(n+1)}(e-1)$$

will always be smaller than $e - 1$. Even if the number of players n increases without bound, the size of the public good will remain smaller than the sum e initially at the disposal of each and every player!

As a result, the utility of each of the players at this equilibrium point will be:

$$u_i(g_i^*, g_{-i}^*) = e - g_i^* + (e - g_i^*)\sum_{k=1}^{n} g_k^* = \frac{(ne+1)^2}{(n+1)^2}$$

As the number of players n gets larger, this utility converges to the finite size e^2. That is, even when the community of players gets larger, with a corresponding increase in the total potential resources that can be channeled to the public good to the benefit of all, it is still the case that at a Nash equilibrium the utility of each player will not exceed e^2.

If the players could sign an egalitarian binding contract by which each one of them invests g in the public good, the overall size of the public good would amount to ng. The investment g^{**} in such a contract would maximize the utility:

$$u_i(g) = (e - g)(1 + ng)$$

of every player $i = 1, \ldots n$. This level of investment g^{**} is obtained by finding the derivative of the function $u_i(g)$ and calculating the investment g^{**} for which this derivative vanishes:

$$0 = \frac{du_i(g^{**})}{dg} = ne - 2ng^{**} - 1$$

that is:

$$g^{**} = \frac{e}{2} - \frac{1}{2n}$$

Hence the investment g^{**} in a binding contract of this kind would, in contrast, increase as the number of players became larger. The overall size of the public resource:

$$ng^{**} = \frac{(ne - 1)}{2}$$

would accordingly increase without bound with the increase in the size of the community of players, and along with it the utility of each player would increase without bound as well:

$$u_i(g^{**}) = (e - g^{**})(1 + ng^{**}) = \frac{(ne + 1)^2}{4n} \xrightarrow[n \to \infty]{} \infty$$

Unfortunately, however, a contract of this type is not a stable agreement, and it is not self-enforcing. If such a contract were to be signed, and player 1, for example, had the opportunity to get away with breaching the contract, she would choose to invest:

$$g_1 = BR_1(g_2 = g^{**}, \ldots g_n = g^{**}) = \max\left\{0, \frac{1}{2}(e - 1 - (n - 1)g^{**})\right\}$$

This investment vanishes when the number of players n exceeds 2. (Verify this.) In this example, with three or more players, if a player believed that all the others would honor their undertakings per the agreement, she would prefer not to invest anything in the public good.

Therefore, the contract whereby every player is to contribute g^{**} to the public good is not a self-enforcing agreement. Only a Nash equilibrium is a self-enforcing agreement, and, as we have seen, the entire community of players derives no more than a limited utility from it.

From this analysis it emerges that a player will wish to deviate from an agreement whereby every player contributes g^{**} to the public good, if she believes that the other players will continue to contribute g^{**} even after she herself deviates from the agreement. But even if the player who has ceased to contribute cannot be identified or punished, one might advance the *prima facie* argument that all the players will see that the public good has decreased from ng^{**} to $(n - 1)g^{**}$ and therefore no player can be forced any longer to contribute more than her relative share $\frac{(n-1)}{n}g^{**}$. As a result, the level of the public good will continue to deteriorate progressively until reaching $(n-1)\frac{(n-1)}{n}g^{**}$ because only $n-1$ players will continue to contribute $\frac{(n-1)}{n}g^{**}$ to the public good. Thus, a player's breach of contract will, it emerges, indirectly boomerang against her as a result of the "weakening of the social norm concerning each player's proper contribution to society."

But for a sufficiently large number n of players, an individual player will still prefer not to make any contribution to the public good even if every other player contributes $\frac{(n-1)}{n}g^{**}$ rather than g^{**}. (Verify this!) Therefore, not even an indirect influence of this kind on the actions of the other players will cause the player to contribute g^{**} of her own free will. Only at a Nash equilibrium, when every player is doing her best given the choices of all the other players, will none of the players wish to further reduce their contribution, since they are liable to disadvantage themselves by doing so.

From our discussion so far we may conclude that all the players will be better satisfied if an enforcement apparatus exists enabling them to sign a binding agreement whereby each of them will contribute g^{**} to the public good. But in order for such an enforcement apparatus – police, law courts and so forth – to be able to find and punish the violators of the agreement, resources must first be invested in the set-up and maintenance of the enforcement apparatus. Hence, the enforcement apparatus is, itself, a public good. Therefore, the reasoning that led us to conclude that the size of the public good at a Nash equilibrium will be smaller than is desirable will also lead us to expect that the resources invested by the community in the maintenance of the enforcement apparatus itself will be less than required for full enforcement.

7.1.1   Investment in a public good in laboratory experiments

The behavior of individuals in games of public good contribution has been examined in a large number of laboratory experiments.[2] In most cases, the game in the experiment was an extreme version of the game in example 7.1, with a payoff function of the form:

$$u_i(g_i, g_{-1}) = (e - g_i) + \alpha \sum_{k=1}^{n} g_k$$

---

[2] Surveys of the results of these experiments appear in Ledyard, J. O. (1995), "Public Goods: A Survey of Experimental Research," in J. Kagel and A. Roth (eds.), *The Handbook of Experimental Economics*, Princeton University Press, pp. 111–194; Holt, C. A. (2006), *Markets, Games and Strategic Behavior*, New York: Addison-Wesley, Chapter 26.

in which all players have the same amount e available for investment, and α is a constant satisfying:

$$\frac{1}{n} < \alpha < 1$$

In this game, every additional dollar a player invests in the public good yields her an incremental utility of $\alpha < 1$. However, if the player channels this dollar to her personal interests, her payoff increases by 1. Therefore, the dominant strategy of any player i is to choose $g_i = 0$, i.e. not to make any investment whatsoever in the public good. In the resulting equilibrium, the size of the public good is 0, and the utility of each player is e. Yet if the players were able to sign a binding agreement whereby each of them would contribute the entirety of their available assets to the public good, $g_i = e$, the utility of each of them would be higher:

$$\alpha \sum_{k=1}^{n} e = \alpha n e > e$$

By and large, the participants in these experiments did not adhere to their dominant strategy. In a large set of experiments, the average contribution to the public good was in a range of 40–60 percent of the amount e available for investment. This percentage tended to increase both when the constant α was higher and when the number of players n increased. However, there was considerable variance in the choices of the different participants.

When the game was replicated about ten times with the same group of players, the average contribution to the public good tended to decrease in the final rounds of the game, whereas in the initial rounds, the players' behavior was often diversified and not necessarily monotonic. Some players contributed all or most of the entire amount at their disposal in the initial rounds of the game, apparently with the object of signaling to other participants their willingness to go on contributing large sums of money in subsequent rounds. However, if this signal did not meet with a like response, in the form of higher contributions on the part of their fellow players, those participants sometimes greatly reduced their contributions in the following game rounds, apparently out of frustration, or with the aim of punishing those who failed to cooperate with them. Some of the experiments enabled participants to communicate in the course of the game. In general, verbal communication led to an increase in the average contribution throughout the game.

Similar qualitative results were obtained in the laboratory experiments of games with a payoff structure similar to the one we analyzed in the example in section 7.1, i.e. games in which absolute abstention from contributing is not a dominant strategy.[3]

---

[3] Laury, S. K. and C. A. Holt (2008), "Voluntary Provision of Public Goods: Experimental Results with Interior Nash Equilibria," in C. R. Plott and V. L. Smith (eds.), *Handbook of Experimental Economics Results*, New York: Elsevier.

The tragedy of the commons

Commencing in the sixteenth century, English villages had shared grazing pastures called commons. Not only the aristocracy and the landowners but all the villagers (commoners) could use these pastures. Due to these pastures suffering over-utilization, this example came to symbolize the archetype of a shared resource that is not utilized efficiently when it is accessible to all. We will now show how the analysis of the problem with the use of game-theoretic tools explains the origin of this inefficiency.

Assume that two players share a common resource of size y, from which they may consume over two periods of time. In the first period, player 1 can consume the quantity c_1 of the resource, and player 2 can consume c_2 of it, on condition that $c_1 + c_2 \leq y$. If both jointly attempt to consume more than the overall quantity, we will assume that the overall quantity will be distributed equally between them, such that each will consume $\frac{y}{2}$ of the resource. If they jointly consume less than the overall quantity, then the remaining quantity $y - (c_1 + c_2)$ constitutes the common quantity remaining for consumption in the second period. In the second period, the two players share the remaining quantity equally, each of them then obtaining $\frac{y-(c_1+c_2)}{2}$.

If a player consumes a quantity x during a particular period, her utility thereof will be $\log x$. That is to say, her utility from consumption as a function of the quantity consumed is graphically described as in Figure 7.5.

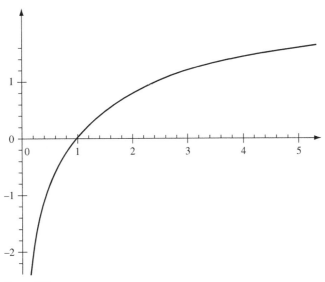

Figure 7.5

In particular, if a player consumes a in the first period and b in the second period, her overall utility from consumption is:

$$\log a + \log b$$

Player 1 must determine what quantity c_1 she will wish to consume in the first period out of the available quantity of the resource. If player 2 chooses to consume c_2 in the first period, then the overall utility of player 1 from consumption in the two periods will be:

$$U_1(c_1, c_2) = \log c_1 + \log \frac{y - (c_1 + c_2)}{2}$$

Similarly, the overall utility of player 2 will be:

$$U_2(c_1, c_2) = \log c_2 + \log \frac{y - (c_1 + c_2)}{2}$$

Question 7.1

A. Is this a game of cooperation or of conflict? Is this a game of strategic complements or strategic substitutes?

B. How much will each player consume in the first period at a Nash equilibrium? What will be her overall utility in the two periods?

C. If a social planner were able to dictate a quantity c that each of the players is to consume during the first period, what quantity would she stipulate in order to maximize the total utility of each player? What would such utility then be equal to?

D. Answer questions B and C when n players share the common resource. What happens when n progressively increases in size?

Answer

A. In this game, the players compete over their share in the common resource, and therefore this is a game of conflict. Each player would prefer the other player to reduce her consumption in the first period, because in such a case the overall portion remaining for the second period would increase, and the player would then benefit from half that increase.

To determine whether this is a game of strategic complements or of strategic substitutes, we will first find the best-reply function of each player. If player 2 consumes c_2 of the resource in the first period, player 1 will choose c_1 so as to maximize her overall utility:

$$U_1(c_1, c_2) = \log c_1 + \log \frac{y - (c_1 + c_2)}{2}$$

We will find the derivative of this function with respect to c_1 and equate the derivative to zero in order to find the best-reply function of player 1:

$$\frac{\partial}{\partial c_1} U_1(c_1, c_2) = \frac{1}{c_1} - \frac{1}{y - (c_1 + c_2)} = 0$$

from which we deduce:

$$BR_1(c_2) = \frac{y - c_2}{2}$$

(Verify that this solution does, in fact, constitute a maximum point by verifying that the second derivative of U_1 with respect to c_1 is negative.[4])

The function $BR_1(c_2)$ is a descending function: the more player 2 increases her consumption in the first period, the greater is the tendency of player 1 to cut back her consumption.

Similarly, the best-reply function of player 2 is:

$$BR_2(c_1) = \frac{y - c_1}{2}$$

Therefore, this is a game of strategic substitutes.

B. We will draw the reaction curves in Figure 7.6.

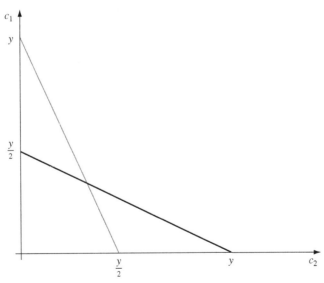

Figure 7.6

---

[4] If the function f is differentiable and obtains its maximum value only at the point x which is in the interior of the domain of f, then the function f is increasing in some interval $(\underline{x}, x)$ to the left of x (i.e. the derivative $f' = \frac{df}{dx}$ is positive in this interval), and is decreasing in some interval $(x, \bar{x})$ to the right of x (i.e. the derivative f' is negative there). In other words, at the point x the derivative f' tends downwards (from the

A Nash equilibrium is obtained at the intersection point of the reaction curves. We find it thus:

$$c_1 = \frac{y - \left(\frac{y-c_1}{2}\right)}{2}$$

and hence:

$$c_1 = \frac{y}{3}$$

Similarly:

$$c_2 = \frac{y}{3}$$

Which is to say, in the first period, each of the two players consumes 1/3 of the resource, leaving 1/3 of it for future consumption. The utility of each of them at equilibrium is $\log\frac{y}{3} + \log\frac{y}{6}$.

C. If each player consumes c in the first period, the total resource remaining for the second period will be $y - 2c$, and each player will benefit from half that amount, namely $\frac{y}{2} - c$. In this case, the utility of each player will be:

$$U_i(c, c) = \log c + \log\left(\frac{y}{2} - c\right)$$

This utility will be maximal for the consumption level c^* satisfying:

$$0 = \frac{d}{dc} U_i(c^*, c^*) = \frac{1}{c^*} - \frac{1}{\frac{y}{2} - c^*} = 0$$

i.e.:

$$c^* = \frac{y}{4}$$

With such a first-period consumption, each player will consume the same quantity in both periods, thus preventing over-consumption by the players in the first period at the expense of the over-dilution of the resource in the second period. The player's utility will be greater than her utility at a Nash equilibrium:

$$\log\frac{y}{4} + \log\frac{y}{4} > \log\frac{y}{3} + \log\frac{y}{6}$$

At a Nash equilibrium, player 1 knows that if she waives one consumption unit in the first period, she can obtain only half of it in the second period (because at that time, the remaining quantity will be divided equally between her and player 2). Therefore, player 1 (and, similarly, also player 2) tends to over-consume in the first period.

---

range $(\underline{x}, x)$ in which it is positive to the range $(x, \bar{x})$ in which it is negative). Therefore, if the derivative f' is in itself differentiable, then its derivative $f'' = \frac{df'}{dx} = \frac{d^2 f}{dx^2}$ is negative at the point x.

D. What happens in this example when the number of players increases? Intuitively, when the number of players increases, the phenomenon of first-period over-consumption will become even more severe, because each player now knows that if she waives a consumption unit in the first period, she will get only a small portion of it in the second period. We will see that this is in fact the case.

Assume that we are dealing with a society of n players. Player 1 is seeking c_1 which will maximize her utility (given the first-period consumption of all the other players):

$$U_1(c_1, c_{-1}) = \log c_1 + \log \frac{y - \sum_{i=1}^n c_i}{n}$$

We will find the best-reply function of player 1:

$$\frac{\partial}{\partial c_1} U_1(c_1, c_{-1}) = \frac{1}{c_1} - \frac{1}{y - \sum_{i=1}^n c_i} = 0$$

from which we deduce:

$$c_1 = \frac{1}{2}(y - (c_2 + c_3 + \ldots + c_n))$$

Similarly, the best-reply function of player j is:

$$c_j = \frac{1}{2}(y - (c_1 + \ldots + c_{j-1} + c_{j+1} + \ldots + c_n))$$

The intersection point of these best-reply functions is:

$$c_1 = c_2 = \ldots = c_n = \frac{1}{n+1}y$$

and this is a Nash equilibrium.

The overall consumption in the first period is therefore $\frac{n}{n+1}y$ and the quantity remaining for consumption in the second period is $\frac{1}{n+1}y$. The greater n is, the smaller is the quantity remaining for the second period. In other words, the larger the society, the more the tragedy of the commons is exacerbated.

By contrast, the optimal symmetric solution in the view of each of the players is the one in which consumption is evenly divided between the two periods, i.e.:

$$c_1 = c_2 = \ldots = c_n = \frac{1}{2n}y$$

(Verify this!)

Thus, we have found a high degree of similarity between the inefficiency in the problem of investing in a public good and the inefficiency that comes to light in the tragedy of the commons. In both cases, each player "internalizes" the effect of her action on herself alone, without taking into account the **externality** of her action on the other player or players. In the first case, this is a **positive externality**: all the players – and not just the player herself – benefit from her investment in the public good. In the second case, it is a **negative externality**: all the players – and not just the player herself – suffer from the dwindling of the commons due to over-consumption in the first period.

The similarity between the two examples will be enhanced if we also formulate the problem of the tragedy of the commons in "positive" terms. We can define a new strategic variable, $x_i = y - c_1$, which is the quantity of the shared resource which the player i refrains from consuming in the first period. (Obviously, the choice of c_i in the original formulation of the problem uniquely defines the choice of x_i in the new formulation, and vice versa.) The greater x_i, the greater the contribution of player i to the commons remaining in the second period. After formulating the problem in these "positive" terms, we see that in both examples, the commons are jointly built up by the players (**jointly provided resource**). Likewise, in both examples, the common resource is a **non-excludable**: no player can be prevented from using the common resource, even if her contribution to the resource was small or non-existent.

Nevertheless, there remains an important difference between the two examples. In the tragedy of the commons in section 7.2, the use of the common resource is limited and the players share it. If the number of players increases but the size of the resource remains as is, then each player's share in the resource diminishes. For example, an increase in the number of herders in the English village reduced the ability of any one of them to benefit from the common pastures. Generally speaking, an increase in the number of participants in a resource increases the **congestion** and this congestion is detrimental to all.

This aspect is different in the example in section 7.1. There, the joining of an additional player to the society of players will never be injurious to the old-timers. In the worst case, the additional player will not contribute anything to the public good, but this fact will in no way prejudice the ability of the long-standing players to benefit from the common resource to the same extent as they enjoyed hitherto. The very fact of the existence of the resource upgrades the efficiency of the personal action of each of the players in the society, and those newly joining the society do not prejudice that upgrade.

In other words, the use of the public resource does not create **rivalry** among the players (the resource is a **non-rivaled good**). For example, a computer software program being jointly developed by a large number of participants[5] does not create rivalry: every user can use it for her benefit on her personal computer,

[5] As in the case of the development of the Linux operating system and software programs based on it.

whether or not she has contributed to its development. Yet using the Internet gives rise to congestion: massive use of the network will increase the delays in network data traffic, which will be experienced by every surfer.

7.2.1 The greenhouse effect

An important example of the tragedy of the commons is the problem of global warming. Most of the energy generated for heating our homes, driving our cars, and manufacturing our consumption goods comes from carbonaceous sources. We get this energy from burning coal, from fuel, or from natural gas. In the process of producing it, we release carbon dioxide into the atmosphere – some of it is absorbed by plants but the greater part remains in the atmosphere. Carbon dioxide, along with certain other gases, traps heat and wraps the atmosphere in a kind of greenhouse, thus affecting the earth's global climate. The utility derived from energy consumption is experienced only by those who use it, but the cost – higher temperatures and climatic problems – is exacted from everybody. The average temperature on the global surface has risen by 0.5–1.2°C in the past 200 years, and is liable to rise another 2–4.5°C over the next few years if the current trend of accumulation of carbon dioxide in the atmosphere persists.

7.2.2 Coping with the tragedy of the commons

How is the tragedy of the commons to be overcome? The privatization of the resource is one possible solution. This solution has been extensively applied on real estate, and today there is scarcely any public land in city centers. Privatization solves the problematic aspects of common ownership of the resource while at the same time depriving the public of access to that resource. Moreover, privatization is not a realistic solution for many commons (such as the atmosphere).

Another solution is to impose a limit on the number of people who can use the resource. This number is calculated in such a way as to enable the resource to renew itself. In the United States, for example, many national parks restrict the number of people allowed to visit simultaneously. This solution, however, is inapplicable to many public resources.

Still another solution is that of imposing a tax on the use of the resource. This is the most widely used approach for solving problems of pollution of water or air by industrial plants. The problem with this type of solution is that it isn't always efficient, and many industrial plants would rather risk being detected as polluters and be forced to pay the fine than invest millions of dollars in solving the pollution problem. The public authority that determines how much to fine offenders and what means of enforcement to use cannot know the precise costs these enterprises will actually incur if they try to reduce the pollution they generate.

7.2.2.1 Pollution Permits Exchange

In an effort to overcome the dearth of information available to the central planner, California in the 1990s established a Pollution Permits Exchange, with the approach called "cap and trade." Every polluting plant received quarterly pollution permits from the state for several years in advance, in accordance with an overall descending curve of pollution that the state had decided to impose. Plants for which pollution reduction would entail high costs could use that exchange to purchase pollution permits from other plants, which could then finance their own pollution reduction from the proceeds they received from selling their permits.

7.3 Patent race

In the example in section 7.1, we saw how a game of cooperation, in which every player benefits from increased investment by the other players, can at the same time be a game with strategic substitutes, in which every player will tend to decrease her investment in response to her co-players increasing their investment. This is in contrast to the partnership game in section 6.4.1, which was a game of cooperation with strategic complements, in which the increased effort of one of the partners triggered an increase in effort by the other partner. In other words, we learned that the reaction curves in games of cooperation may be increasing or decreasing. Accordingly, we will not be surprised to find that some games of conflict may be games with strategic substitutes and other games of conflict may exhibit strategic complements. We will now demonstrate this in a game that models competition in research and development (R&D).

The growth engine of modern economies is technological development. Many sectors that currently enjoy the highest economic growth rate, such as high-tech and biotechnology, are actually the fields in which the technological growth rate is very fast. It is therefore especially important to understand what drives the growth of new technologies, and what institutional structures and government policy will encourage such growth.

Key features of any new technology are that it can be utilized by anyone having access to it, and that it is non-perishable. These attributes raise the question as to why a commercial firm would even want to invest in developing a new technology. And it is here that the concept of a **patent** comes into the picture. The patent secures the company exclusivity in the manufacture, use, or sale of a new idea, and constitutes a way of rewarding the company that conceived the idea. Patents provide private companies with incentives for investing in research and development. The patent is of limited duration. After a specific period of time determined by law, the special know-how that served to create the product or the service becomes available to all, and any other company may use it.

In most modern economies, R&D is carried out by private companies in sectors with a small number of competitors. The international pharmaceutical industry, for example, which spends billions of dollars annually on R&D, comprises a small number of giant companies,[6] along with a small number of medium-size firms.

We will now present a model to illustrate the issues faced by firms that decide to invest in R&D.[7] Our model will be one of conflict between a small number n of companies. The firms are working on a new technological development. Whichever is the first to succeed will be awarded a patent on the invention, while for the others the development process will yield no revenue.

The firms $i = 1, 2, \ldots, n$ must simultaneously choose how much money $x_i \geq 0$ to invest in R&D. Given the financial investment of all the firms, firm i's prospects of being the first to achieve a patent is $\frac{x_i}{x_1 + x_2 + \ldots + x_n}$. The larger is its investment relative to the companies' overall investment in R&D, the better is its chance of being the first to achieve the patent. The value of the patent will be denoted by a V. The value may express, for example, the increase in profits resulting from the sales of the new product.

Accordingly, the expected profit to firm i is:

$$u_i(x_1, \ldots x_n) = \frac{x_i V}{x_1 + x_2 + \ldots + x_n} - x_i$$

(The first term $\frac{x_i V}{x_1 + x_2 + \ldots + x_n}$ is the firm's expected revenue – the probability $\frac{x_i}{x_1 + x_2 + \ldots + x_n}$ of winning the patent is multiplied by the value of the patent V. In order to obtain the expected profit, development costs x_i are subtracted from the expected income.)

This game, therefore, is one of **conflict** between the firms. Every firm would have liked its competitors to reduce their investment in R&D because this would boost its own chances of winning the patent.

We will now ascertain the Nash equilibrium in this game.

In order to find the best-reply function of firm 1, we will compute the derivative of its expected profit function and equate the derivative to zero:[8]

---

[6] These giants often outsource parts of their research initiatives to small firms, which eventually sell the developed drug to the giant (and at times the entire small firm is bought by the giant company).

[7] This model was proposed in a more general context by Tullock, G. (1980), "Efficient Rent-Seeking," in J. M. Buchanan, R. D. Tollison, and G. Tullock (eds.), *Toward a Theory of the Rent-Seeking Society*, College Station, TX: A&M Press, pp. 97–112.

[8] Recall that: $\frac{d}{dx}\left(\frac{f(x)}{g(x)}\right) = \frac{f'(x)g(x) - f(x)g'(x)}{(g(x))^2}$

$$\frac{\partial u_1}{\partial x_1} = \frac{V(x_1 + \ldots + x_n) - x_1 V}{(x_1 + \ldots + x_n)^2} - 1 = \frac{(x_2 + \ldots + x_n)V}{(x_1 + \ldots + x_n)^2} - 1 = 0$$

whence:

$$(x_2 + \ldots + x_n)V = (x_1 + \ldots + x_n)^2$$

or:

$$(x_1 + \ldots + x_n) = \sqrt{(x_2 + \ldots + x_n)V}$$

i.e.:

$$x_1 = BR_1(x_2 \ldots x_n) = \sqrt{(x_2 + \ldots + x_n)V} - (x_2 + \ldots + x_n)$$

This calculation is relevant only when $x_2 + \ldots + x_n > 0$. If, in contrast, all the other firms choose not to invest, i.e. if $x_2 = \ldots = x_n = 0$, then the profit function of firm 1 is:

$$u_1(x_1, x_2 = 0, \ldots x_n = 0) = \begin{cases} V - x_1 & x_1 > 0 \\ 0 & x_1 = 0 \end{cases}$$

and therefore firm 1 will choose to make a minimal positive investment in R&D in order to secure itself the patent.

For example, if $n = 2$ and $V = 9$, then the best-reply function of company 1 is:

$$x_1 = BR_1(x_2) = 3\sqrt{x_2} - x_2$$

for $x_2 > 0$.

Similarly, the best-reply function of firm 2 is:

$$x_2 = BR_2(x_1) = 3\sqrt{x_1} - x_1$$

for $x_1 > 0$.

We will draw the reaction curve of firm 1 (in black) and of firm 2 (in gray) in Figure 7.7.

In order to draw the two reaction curves on the same coordinate system, x_1 must be extracted from the function BR_2 and expressed as a function of x_2. This is done as follows:

$$x_2 = BR_2(x_1) = 3\sqrt{x_1} - x_1$$

i.e.:

$$3\sqrt{x_1} = x_2 + x_1$$

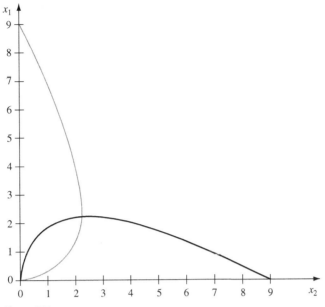

Figure 7.7

or:

$$9x_1 = (x_2 + x_1)^2$$

$$x_1^2 - (9 - 2x_2)x_1 + x_2^2 = 0$$

$$x_1 = \frac{9 - 2x_2 \pm 3\sqrt{9 - 4x_2}}{2}$$

In Figure 7.7, we have drawn the two solution branches that we obtained.

Why is each firm's reaction curve first increasing and then decreasing? If the investment x_2 of firm 2 in R&D is very low, firm 1 can obtain chances of winning that are greater than $\frac{1}{2}$ by making a larger investment, $x_2 > x_1$, which is at the same time still low relative to the value of the invention V. Therefore, if firm 2 slightly increases its investment, it will still be worthwhile for firm 1 to go some way toward bypassing that investment, and thereby maintain good prospects of winning.

However, if the investment x_2 of firm 2 continues to increase, then from a certain stage onwards the increase required in firm 1's investment x_1 for maintaining preferable winning prospects (greater than $\frac{1}{2}$) will no longer be worth the cost, because the overall investment amount x_1 will start to approach the value V of the patent. Thenceforth, firm 1 will choose an investment level with which its prospects of winning are smaller than $\frac{1}{2}$. Finally, if the investment x_2 of firm 2 continues to increase yet further, and approaches the value of the investment V, then firm 1 will prefer to invest a progressively decreasing amount x_1 in R&D,

sufficing to give it very small prospects of winning but still yielding it a positive expected profit.

Since the reaction curve of each firm is first increasing and then decreasing, the game is not a game of strategic complements, nor is it a game of strategic substitutes.

The reaction curves have a single point of intersection, in which the strategy profile is $(x_1, x_2) = \left(\frac{9}{4}, \frac{9}{4}\right)$. (Recall that the reaction curves are relevant only for $x_1 > 0$ and $x_2 > 0$, and therefore the intersection point at the origin does not constitute an equilibrium.) This is the Nash equilibrium of the game.[9]

In general, for n firms we have to solve the following system of equations:

$$x_1 = \sqrt{(x_2 + \ldots + x_n)V} - (x_2 + \ldots + x_n)$$
$$x_2 = \sqrt{(x_1 + x_3 + \ldots + x_n)V} - (x_1 + x_3 + \ldots + x_n)$$

$\bullet$

$\bullet$

$\bullet$

$$x_n = \sqrt{(x_1 + \ldots + x_{n-1})V} - (x_1 + \ldots + x_{n-1})$$

Since the problem is symmetric across the firms, we will look for a symmetric equilibrium in which $x_1 = x_2 = \ldots = x_n = x$. Such a symmetric equilibrium will satisfy the equation:

$$x = \sqrt{(n - 1)xV} - (n - 1)x$$

whence:

$$x = \frac{(n - 1)V}{n^2}$$

The average profit of each of the firms $i = 1, \ldots, n$ in this equilibrium will accordingly be:

$$u_i(x, \ldots x) = \frac{V}{n^2}$$

We can see that when the number of firms n progressively increases, the symmetric equilibrium investment x progressively decreases, and so, correspondingly, does the average profit of each firm. This is a possible explanation for the fact that in sectors

---

[9] In a laboratory experiment of this game – Shogren, J. F. and K. H. Baik (1991), "Reexamining Efficient Rent-Seeking in Laboratory Markets," *Public Choice* 69 (1), 69–79 – the participants' choices were consistent with this equilibrium.

with a very large number of competing firms we find little investment in R&D. Despite the small investment per firm in such sectors, the total investment of the firms in the race to obtain the patent:

$$nx = n\frac{(n-1)V}{n^2} = \frac{n-1}{n}V \xrightarrow[n\to\infty]{} V$$

tends toward the entire value of the patent, V, as the number of competing firms increases. From the social point of view this investment dissipates almost the entire economic rent accrued by the invention.

Comprehension check

Two world powers have to decide what quantity of resources to invest in arming their military forces. The greater the relative strength of one of the powers, the stronger is that power's regional hegemony. At the same time, the larger the resources it invests in arming its military, the fewer resources remain to it for the well-being of its residents.

Use ideas employed in the previous example to describe a game that expresses this tension, and find its Nash equilibrium.

7.4   Crime and enforcement policy

To conclude this chapter we will examine an example of a conflict in which one of the players has an increasing reaction curve and the other has a decreasing reaction curve.

Nowhere, unfortunately, is there a country that is not infected with some level of criminality. Crime is destructive to society because in most cases, the profit the criminal derives from his loot is smaller than the damage he causes. This damage is reflected not only in material loss and the victim's anguish; the spread of criminality is detrimental to the willingness of individuals in society to take commercial or other initiatives, since only a reasonable measure of personal and public security can render them worthwhile. The following game, which is based on a model of Gary Becker, gives expression to these aspects.[10]

---

[10]   Becker, G. (1968), "Crime and Punishment," *Journal of Political Economy* 76 (2), 169–217. Our description of the game is also based on Watson, J. (2001), *Strategy: An Introduction to Game Theory*, New York: W. W. Norton & Company.

The game features two players: a criminal C and a government G. The government chooses the level of resources $x \in [0,A]$ that it invests in law enforcement, A being the total resources at its disposal. Correspondingly, the criminal chooses his level of criminal activity $y \geq 0$. The government's utility function is:

$$u_G(x,y) = (A - x) - \frac{y^2}{x}$$

The first term $(A - x)$ describes the resources remaining to the state following the investment x in enforcement activities. These remaining resources diminish as the investment x increases. The second term, $-\frac{y^2}{x}$, describes the negative effect of criminal activity on society. This negative effect diminishes as enforcement level x increases, and significantly increases as the level of criminality y rises. For a given level of enforcement x, if the level of criminal activity y increases e.g. twofold, then the damage to society $\frac{y^2}{x}$ increases fourfold, as a result of the detrimental effects described above to the level of personal and public security. For a given level of criminal activity $y > 0$, if the enforcement level x declines, becoming vanishingly close to zero, then the damage to society, $\frac{y^2}{x}$, will increase indefinitely.

The criminal's utility function is given by:

$$u_C(x,y) = \left(\frac{1}{1+xy}\right)\sqrt{y}$$

The first factor $\left(\frac{1}{1+xy}\right)$ in the utility function is the probability of the criminal escaping punishment. This probability diminishes as the extent of criminal activity y increases, and as the enforcement level x rises. The second factor $\sqrt{y}$ of the utility function is the material payoff accruing to the criminal from the extent of criminal activity y assuming he is not caught. This payoff does not increase in direct proportion to y. For example, if the level of criminal activity increases fourfold, then the material payoff to the criminal increases only twofold, due to the increasing difficulty the criminal experiences in finding markets for stolen goods, laundering money, and so forth.

If we normalize to 0 the utility to the criminal in case he is caught (the likelihood of this is $1 - \frac{1}{1+xy}$), then we obtain that the expected utility of the criminal is indeed:

$$\left(\frac{1}{1+xy}\right)\sqrt{y} + \left(1 - \frac{1}{1+xy}\right) \times 0 = \left(\frac{1}{1+xy}\right)\sqrt{y} = u_C(x,y)$$

We note that if the criminal chooses to refrain from crime ($y = 0$), his utility will be $u_C(x,0) = 0$, the same utility he will obtain if he perpetrates a crime and is caught. Thus, this model assumes that the criminal's starting point in life is so low that unless he has profits from crime, he might just as well be doing jail time if caught committing a crime (possibly because in jail, he may get special support and benefits from his accomplices in the criminal fraternity).

Thus, in this model, the strategy $y = 0$ is not optimal for the criminal for any level of enforcement x, no matter how high. Abstaining from crime ($y = 0$) will yield him a utility of $u_C(x,0) = 0$, whereas any positive level of crime will yield him a positive expected payoff.

This is, of course, a game of **conflict**: the criminal would rejoice if the government soft-pedaled its enforcement policy, and the government would rejoice if the criminal reduced his volume of criminal activity.

What is the equilibrium in this game? In order to find the equilibrium, we will first find the players' reaction curves. In order to find the government's best-reply function, we will compute the derivative of its utility function $u_G(x, y)$ with respect to its strategy x, and equate the derivative to zero:

$$\frac{\partial u_G(x, y)}{\partial x} = -1 + \frac{y^2}{x^2} = 0$$

whence:

$$x = BR_G(y) = y$$

Does enforcement level $x = y$ in fact maximize $U_G(x, y)$ – rather than minimizing it – for a given y? In order to verify this, we will find out whether at the point $x = y$ the second derivative of U_G with respect to x is indeed negative:

$$\frac{\partial^2 u_G(x, y)}{\partial x^2} = \frac{\partial}{\partial x}\left(-1 + \frac{y^2}{x^2}\right) = -\frac{2y^2}{x^3}$$

and at the point $x = y$ (for a given $y > 0$) we will obtain:

$$\frac{\partial^2 u_G(x, y)}{\partial x^2} = -\frac{2y^2}{y^3} = -\frac{2}{y} < 0$$

(Additionally, for a given $y > 0$, the function $U_G(x, y)$ does not attain its maximum at the boundary point[11] $x = 0$, because $U_G(0,y) = -\infty$.)

We have therefore verified that the best-reply function of the government is:

$$BR_G(y) = y$$

which is an **increasing** function: the government will do well to step up the level of enforcement as the criminal intensifies his volume of activity y.

---

[11] Recall that the points that are candidates for being the maximum points of a differentiable function f are the points at which the derivative f' vanishes, and the boundary points of the domain of f.

We will now proceed to find the criminal's best-reply function. First, we have already seen that the strategy $y = 0$ will yield the criminal a utility of $u_C(x,0) = 0$. This strategy is not optimal for the criminal for any level of enforcement x on the part of the government, no matter how intense, because stepping up criminal activity from $y = 0$ to a positive level $y > 0$ increases the utility of the criminal. We will now try to find the strategy of the criminal at which the derivative of his utility function $u_C(x,y)$ vanishes with respect to his strategy y:

$$\frac{\partial u_C(x,y)}{\partial y} = \frac{\frac{1+xy}{2\sqrt{y}} - x\sqrt{y}}{(1+xy)^2} = \frac{1 - xy}{2(1+xy)^2\sqrt{y}} = 0$$

from which we get:

$$y = BR_C(x) = \frac{1}{x}$$

Thus, for a given enforcement level x, the strategy $y = \frac{1}{x}$ is the only one at which this derivative vanishes. This is in fact a maximum point. (Verify this by computing the derivative with respect to y of the expression

$$\frac{\partial u_C(x,y)}{\partial y} = \frac{1 - xy}{2(1+xy)^2\sqrt{y}}$$

and verify that at the point at which $y = \frac{1}{x}$, the second derivative is negative.)

Thus, we have found that the criminal's reaction function is a **decreasing** function; the higher the government ratchets up the enforcement level x, the more the criminal will tend to reduce his volume of criminal activity.

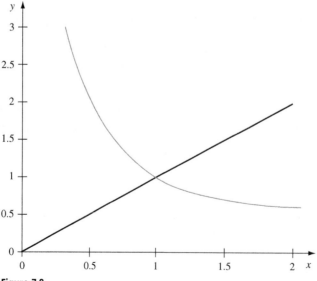

Figure 7.8

We will now draw the reaction curves of the two players in the space of the strategy profiles (x, y) – see Figure 7.8.

The profile of strategies $(x,y) = (1,1)$, which is the intersection point of the two reaction curves, is a Nash equilibrium of the game. This is of course the solution to the system of equations:

$$x = y$$

$$y = \frac{1}{x}$$

8 Concentrated markets

One of the most important applications of game theory in economics is that of analyzing the behavior of commercial firms. When production activity in a particular sector is carried out by a small number of firms, the situation is one of oligopoly or **concentrated markets**.

In some sectors, the prices set by the various firms for their products are either identical or very nearly so. Dairy manufacturers, for example, typically sell a quart of milk at the same or almost the same price. In the dairy market, therefore, firms compete over shelf space in the super-markets and grocery stores, and, consequently, over the quantities sold to consumers. This is a typical example of **quantity competition**.

In other sectors, the quantity of units offered to customers is a constant, and firms compete primarily by means of the prices they charge consumers. For example, the flights operated by the various airlines on each route are scheduled well in advance, and the number of seats per airplane of a particular type is constant. Therefore, on short notice, airlines can neither increase nor decrease the number of seats offered to customers. They can, however, compete with each other by making changes in ticket prices and by launching various sales specials. This, therefore, is a typical example of **price competition**.

The various firms often differentiate products which are by and large similar to one another. For example, dairy manufacturers produce yoghurt treats which are similar but not identical. In this case we say that the firms' products are **differentiated**.

If every firm has already reached agreement with the major supermarket chains as regards the shelf space that it is to be allocated for its yoghurt treats, then it remains only for each firm to quote a price for its product. In this case, we say that the firms are engaged in **price competition with differentiated products**.

But in certain periods, the main decision variable of yoghurt treat manufacturers will not necessarily be that of price. For example, once a new yoghurt treat has been launched, the firm may not wish to make frequent price changes so as not to confuse its customers. The firm may, however, reopen negotiations with the supermarket chains over the quantities of the product they are to purchase and display on their shelves. In this state of affairs, we say the firms engage in **quantity competition with differentiated products**.

Competition over consumers' hearts and pockets often assumes a more sophisticated guise. For example, we are accustomed to reading ads in which a particular firm undertakes to sell us its product at a lower price than the competition, and even give us a refund if we can find a cheaper offer in the market. On the face of it, a marketing strategy of this type is an example of aggressive competition between firms. But is it really as it seems?

In this chapter, we will see how the application of game theory can shed light on questions of this type.

8.1   The Cournot model: competition in quantities

French Professor of Mechanics Antoine Augustine Cournot published his book *Research into the Mathematical Principles of the Theory of Wealth* in 1838. Cournot presents a model describing two firms that compete with one another, each of them repeatedly adjusting the quantity it chooses to produce in response to the actions of its rival. The quantities they produce in this process gradually converge; and had the firms chosen these quantities from the outset, they would have gone on producing them forever. This profile of quantities is the first example in the literature of a Nash equilibrium – even though it was published more than 100 years before Nash explicitly defined his equilibrium concept (which he evidently did without being aware of Cournot's work). We will now present a generalization of Cournot's model for a finite number of competing firms.

Assume there are n firms in the market producing exactly the same commodity (such as whole milk or white sugar), and also that there is no difference in the price to the consumer of the commodity units produced by different firms. Every firm i, $i = 1, \ldots n$, must choose how many units q_i to produce. We will denote by c_i the production cost of a single unit of the commodity by firm i. The price P of the product is determined by market demand. The demand function is given by:

$$Q = A - P$$

where $Q = q_1 + q_2 + \ldots + q_n$ is the total quantity that consumers will purchase from all the firms together, and the size A is a constant characterizing the market. At a given price $P > 0$, some consumers will not want to purchase the product at all, while others will wish to purchase more than one unit. If the product price increases to $P' > P$, some consumers, who would have purchased the product at price P, will now waive the purchase, and other consumers will now purchase fewer units than they would have purchased at the lower price P. Thus, as a result of the price hike, there will be a decrease in the overall number of units Q that consumers will wish to purchase. Firm i's profit, therefore, is given by:

$$\Pi_i(q_i, q_{-i}) = (P - c_i)q_i = \left(A - \sum_{j=1}^{n} q_j - c_i\right)q_i$$

and each firm strives to maximize its profit. What is the equilibrium in this game?

We will first find the best-reply function of firm 1. Assume that the other firms, $2 \le i \le n$, have each chosen to produce q_i units of the commodity, respectively. Firm 1 seeks a quantity q_1 that will maximize its profit. If this optimal quantity is positive, then the derivative of its profit function Π_1 with respect to q_1 will vanish. We will accordingly find this derivative of the profit function and equate it to zero:

$$\frac{\partial}{\partial q_1} \Pi_1(q_1, q_{-1}) = -q_1 + A - \sum_{i=1}^{n} q_i - c_1 = 0$$

whence:

$$q_1 = \frac{1}{2} \left(A - (q_2 + q_3 + \ldots + q_n) - c_1 \right)$$

In order to verify that this is indeed a maximum point of the profit function, we will compute the second derivative of Π_1 with respect to q_1, obtaining:

$$\frac{\partial^2}{\partial q_1^2} \Pi_1(q_1, q_{-1}) = -2$$

This means that we have found a quantity that maximizes the firm's profit.

In contrast, if firm 1 loses for every positive quantity q_1 it chooses to produce, it will prefer not to produce at all and will be driven out of the market. (In this case the expression $q_1 = \frac{1}{2}(A - (q_2 + q_3 + \ldots + q_n) - c_1)$ will be negative – it describes the quantity that would have maximized the profit function of firm 1 had it been able to produce a negative quantity of the commodity, which, of course, is impossible.) To sum up, the best-reply function of firm 1 is:

$$q_1 = \begin{cases} \frac{1}{2}\left(A - (q_2 + q_3 + \ldots q_n) - c_1 \right) & \frac{1}{2}\left(A - (q_2 + q_3 + \ldots q_n) - c_1 \right) > 0 \\ 0 & \text{otherwise} \end{cases}$$

In general, the best-reply function of firm i is:

$$q_i = \begin{cases} \frac{1}{2}\left(A - \sum_{j \neq i} q_j - c_i \right) & \frac{1}{2}\left(A - \sum_{j \neq i} q_j - c_i \right) > 0 \\ 0 & \text{otherwise} \end{cases}$$

For example, if there are only two firms in the market, the best-reply function of firm 1 is:

$$q_1 = \begin{cases} \frac{1}{2}\left(A - q_2 - c_1 \right) & \frac{1}{2}\left(A - q_2 - c_1 \right) > 0 \\ 0 & \text{otherwise} \end{cases}$$

Concentrated markets

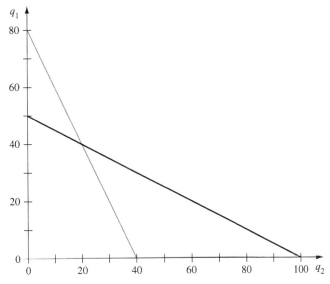

Figure 8.1

and the best-reply function of firm 2 is:

$$q_2 = \begin{cases} \frac{1}{2}(A - q_1 - c_2) & \frac{1}{2}(A - q_1 - c_2) > 0 \\ 0 & \text{otherwise} \end{cases}$$

Assume for example that:

$$c_1 = 30, \quad c_2 = 50, \quad A = 130$$

For these parameters we will now draw the best-reply functions (of firm 1 in black and of firm 2 in gray), shown in Figure 8.1.

The Nash equilibrium is obtained at the intersection point, at which the two firms choose to produce positive quantities of the commodity. We will find the intersection point:

$$q_1 = \frac{1}{2}\left(130 - \frac{1}{2}(130 - q_1 - 50) - 30\right)$$

whence:

$$q_1 = \frac{1}{3}(50 - 2 \times 30 + 130) = 40$$

and also:

$$q_2 = \frac{1}{2}(130 - q_1 - 50) = \frac{1}{2}(130 - 40 - 50) = 20$$

implying that in this example:

$$q_1 = 40, \quad q_2 = 20$$

The market price of the product will accordingly be:

$$P = 130 - (q_1 + q_2) = 130 - (20 + 40) = 70$$

Note that this price leaves each firm with a positive profit (since the price is higher than each firm's per-unit production cost), and that firm 1, which has a lower production cost, attains a larger market share than firm 2, whose production technology is less efficient (its production costs are higher).

In general, for n firms we will want to find the intersection point of the n best-reply functions. As in the example, we will try to find a Nash equilibrium in which all firms produce positive quantities. This equilibrium will be the solution of the following system of equations:

$$q_1 = \frac{1}{2}\left(A - (q_2 + q_3 + \ldots + q_n) - c_1\right)$$

$$q_2 = \frac{1}{2}\left(A - (q_1 + q_3 + \ldots + q_n) - c_2\right)$$

$$\bullet$$
$$\bullet$$
$$\bullet$$

$$q_n = \frac{1}{2}\left(A - (q_1 + q_2 + \ldots + q_{n-1}) - c_n\right)$$

If we add up the n equations we will obtain the following equation:[1]

$$\sum_{j=1}^{n} q_j = \frac{1}{2}\left(nA - (n-1)\sum_{j=1}^{n} q_j - \sum_{j=1}^{n} c_j\right)$$

Isolating $\sum_{j=1}^{n} q_j$ yields:

$$\sum_{j=1}^{n} q_j = \frac{1}{n+1}\left(nA - \sum_{j=1}^{n} c_j\right)$$

---

[1] Note that on the right-hand side every variable q_j appears in all the equations except in the equation j, and therefore, in the sum of all the equations, every variable q_j appears in a right-hand side $n - 1$ times.

Substituting this in the equation for q_i, we obtain:

$$q_i = \frac{1}{2}(A - (q_1 + \ldots q_{i-1} + q_{i+1} \ldots + q_n) - c_i)$$

$$= \frac{1}{2}\left(A - \sum_{j=1}^{n} q_j + q_i - c_i\right) = \frac{1}{2}\left(A - \frac{1}{n+1}\left(nA - \sum_{j=1}^{n} c_j\right) + q_i - c_i\right)$$

and hence the solution is:

$$q_i = \frac{1}{(n+1)}\left(A + \sum_{j=1}^{n} c_j\right) - c_i$$

As in the above two-firm numerical example, we see that also in the n-firm case the more efficient firm i is, i.e. the lower its production costs c_i, the higher will be its market share, i.e. the quantity q_i that it produces at equilibrium.

In the case in which all the firms have identical production costs:

$$c = c_1 = c_2 = \ldots = c_n$$

we will obtain that:

$$q_1 = q_2 = \ldots = q_n = \frac{1}{(n+1)}(A - c)$$

The price at which the product will be sold will be:

$$P = A - \frac{n}{(n+1)}(A - c) = \frac{1}{(n+1)}(A + nc)$$

When $c < A$, this price yields the firms positive profit margins, because it is higher than the per-unit production cost c. (If it were the case that $c \geq A$, no firm could make a profit if a positive quantity $Q < 0$ of the product units was offered for sale. In such a case, no firm would produce at a Nash equilibrium.)

As the number of firms n progressively increases, the quantity that every firm produces at equilibrium diminishes, and the price tends to the per-unit production cost, $P = c$. Those of you who have taken basic courses in economics will certainly recall that this is the price that will prevail in a market in which perfect competition takes place between the firms, with no restriction as to the number of firms that can offer their output on the market. In this model of perfect competition, every firm believes that the quantity it produces and offers for sale will not affect the product price P in the market. This assumption is approximately reasonable if the production volume of each firm is very small relative to the overall quantity manufactured Q. In such a case, a change in the production volume of a single firm will lead to a very small relative change in the overall quantity Q offered for sale, and therefore the price P, at which all the units will be sold on the market, will also remain virtually unchanged.

In the Cournot model, this intuition gets a precise meaning. In this model, every firm i is well aware of the effect it has on the price P. One of the considerations it takes into account is that the price P will decrease when it increases the quantity q_i it produces. A slight increase in the produced quantity q_i will alter the profit:

$$\Pi_i(q_i, q_{-i}) = [P - c]q_i = \left[\left(A - \sum_{j=1}^{n} q_j\right) - c\right]q_i$$

at the rate:

$$\frac{\partial}{\partial q_i} \Pi_i(q_i, q_{-i}) = \left[\left(A - \sum_{j=1}^{n} q_j\right) - c\right] - q_i = [P - c] - q_i \qquad (*)$$

The first term, $P - c$, describes the positive effect on profit resulting from the production of an additional (small) unit that is sold on the market at price P, whose production cost is only c. The second term, $-q_i$, describes the negative effect on the profit (from the sale of all the units) as a result of the decrease in price $P = A - \sum_{j=1}^{n} q_j$.

However, at a Nash equilibrium with a very large number n of firms, the quantity:

$$q_i = \frac{1}{(n + 1)}(A - c)$$

that every firm will produce is very small. Therefore, if every firm were to ignore its effect on the market price (as, in fact, is assumed in a competitive market model), and the second term, $-q_i$, did not appear in the expression $(*)$, then the size of the expression $(*)$ would scarcely change. As a result, the competitive equilibrium that would be obtained would be very close to the Nash equilibrium in the Cournot model.

We will now show this explicitly. At a competitive equilibrium with equilibrium price P, supply equals demand. The overall quantity produced is sold in its entirety, and is equal to the demand:

$$Q = A - P$$

at the price P. If the competitive equilibrium is symmetric, every firm i will produce and sell:

$$q_i = \frac{Q}{n} = \frac{A - P}{n}$$

units, as long as $P \geq c$.

This quantity q_i will be maximal when $P = c$, but even in this case, the quantity q_i will diminish and will tend to 0 as the number of firms n gets larger.[2]

---

[2] If the per-unit cost of production were not constant, but increased along with the number of units, the competitive equilibrium price P would be determined uniquely. And indeed, if the production cost of q

Thus, Cournot's strategic model provides a basis for the competitive model for a large number of firms. In particular, it delivers precise confirmation for the assumption that every firm can (almost) ignore its own effect on the price when a large number of similar firms are operating in the market.

The Cournot model analyzes the strategic interaction among manufacturing firms, but assumes that *consumers* ignore their market power. When we assume in the model that the total demand Q of consumers at price P is given by the expression:

$$Q = A - P$$

we are actually ignoring the ability of every consumer to affect the price P itself by reducing their demand for the product. By seeking to purchase fewer units of the product, the consumer may force the producers to reduce the price, so that the (diminished) purchased quantity becomes cheaper. Furthermore, in the Cournot model there is only one product (and money, which implicitly represents the possibility of purchasing other products).[3]

units is given by the convex function $c(q)$, in a competitive market with price P, every firm i would believe that its profits would amount to:

$$\Pi_i(q_i) = Pq_i - C(q_i)$$

if it produced q_i units, and would choose to produce the quantity q_i which maximizes its profits, for which it is the case that:

$$\frac{d}{dq_i}\Pi_i(q_i) = P - \frac{d}{dq_i}C(q_i) = 0$$

The quantity q_i in a symmetric competitive equilibrium would then be determined by the equation:

$$\frac{d}{dq_i}C(q_i) = P = A - nq_i$$

from which it would be possible to extract the competitive price P. If we denote by:

$$c = \frac{d}{dq_i}C(q_i)$$

the marginal cost of production (i.e. the cost of production of the last small unit) in this equilibrium, we will obtain that:

$$q_i = \frac{A - c}{n}$$

This quantity is small and tends to 0 as the number of firms n increases, similarly to the quantity $\frac{A-c}{n+1}$ that we obtained at the Nash equilibrium in the Cournot model.

[3] In a more general model of a general competitive equilibrium, all participants in the market can produce, sell, and purchase a large range of products, but all disregard their ability to affect market prices by altering the quantities of products that they offer for sale or seek to purchase. Can this disregard of market power be confirmed when the number of participants in the market is very large?

Indeed, just as the Cournot model provides a strategic basis for the partial competitive equilibrium among manufacturing firms, so the *market game* model of Shapley and Shubik, presented in Shapley, L. and M. Shubik (1977), "Trade Using a Commodity as a Means of Payment," *Journal of Political Economy* 85 (5), 937–968, provides a strategic foundation for the general competitive equilibrium model. Since the general equilibrium model is a basic model for describing economic phenomena in the modern world, this is an example of an important contribution of game theory to economic analysis.

8.1.1   Quantity competition with differentiated products

Many firms do whatever they can to differentiate themselves from other firms, for example by creating a brand name. What happens, then, when the firms do not produce exactly the same commodities but rather similar ones (such as Pepsi Cola and Coca-Cola)? In such a case we say that the products of the firms are differentiated, and that the firms compete with **differentiated products**.

In such a competition it may be assumed, on the one hand, that the different consumers will purchase from different firms even if the product prices are not identical, and that each of the products will have its own demand curve. On the other hand, the price of each product will obviously also affect the demand for the other product. As the price of product 1 (Pepsi Cola, say) rises, the demand for product 2 (Coca-Cola in this example) will correspondingly post a certain increase whereas the demand for product 1 will decrease, and vice versa.

Question 8.1

Assume that the demand functions for the two commodities (which are produced by different firms) are given by:

$$q_1 = B + \frac{1}{2}p_2 - p_1$$

$$q_2 = B + \frac{1}{2}p_1 - p_2$$

where $q_i (i = 1,2)$ is the quantity demanded of product i if its price is p_i.

Assume that $B = 100$. Likewise, assume that for firm 1 the per-unit production cost is $c_1 = 40$, and that also for firm 2 the per-unit production cost is $c_2 = 40$. The firms simultaneously choose what quantity of the good to produce.

The profit of firm 1 is given by:

$$\Pi_1(q_1) = (p_1 - c_1)q_1$$

and the profit of firm 2 is given by:

$$\Pi_2(q_2) = (p_2 - c_2)q_2$$

What quantities will the firms choose to produce at a Nash equilibrium?

Answer

In order to present the profit as a function of the quantities q_1, q_2 (as chosen by the firms), we must first extract p_1, p_2 from the demand functions:

$$p_1 = 200 - \frac{2}{3}q_2 - \frac{4}{3}q_1$$

$$p_2 = 200 - \frac{2}{3}q_1 - \frac{4}{3}q_2$$

(Explanation: $q_1 = 100 + \frac{1}{2}p_2 - p_1$ and therefore $p_1 = 100 + \frac{1}{2}p_2 - q_1$ similarly $p_2 = 100 + \frac{1}{2}p_2 - q_2$ is also satisfied. By substituting the second equation into the first and extracting p_1 we get the above result.)

Accordingly, the profit function of firm 1 is:

$$\Pi_1(q_1, q_2) = (p_1 - c_1)q_1 = \left(200 - \frac{2}{3}q_2 - \frac{4}{3}q_1 - c_1\right)q_1$$

In order to find the best-reply function of firm 1, we will compute the derivative of this function and equate to zero:

$$\frac{\partial}{\partial q_1}\Pi_1(q_1, q_2) = -\frac{4}{3}q_1 + 200 - \frac{2}{3}q_2 - \frac{4}{3}q_1 - c_1 = 0$$

Hence:

$$q_1 = 75 - \frac{3}{8}c_1 - \frac{1}{4}q_2$$

(Check that this is indeed a maximum point, by examining the sign of the second derivative.) As explained above, this will in fact be the quantity that will maximize the firm's profit on condition that the quantity q_1 is positive. Thus, the best-reply function is:

$$q_1 = \begin{cases} 75 - \frac{3}{8}c_1 - \frac{1}{4}q_2 & 75 - \frac{3}{8}c_1 - \frac{1}{4}q_2 > 0 \\ 0 & \text{otherwise} \end{cases}$$

Similarly, the best-reply function firm of 2 is:

$$q_2 = \begin{cases} 75 - \frac{3}{8}c_2 - \frac{1}{4}q_1 & 75 - \frac{3}{8}c_2 - \frac{1}{4}q_1 > 0 \\ 0 & \text{otherwise} \end{cases}$$

We will draw the reaction curves – see Figure 8.2.

The equilibrium is obtained at the intersection point of the reaction curves: $q_1 = q_2 = 48$. The prices that will prevail in the market are: $p_1 = p_2 = 104$ (they are higher than the per-unit production cost, leaving the firms with positive profit margins).

8.2 Bertrand's model: price competition

In 1883, French mathematician Joseph Bertrand published a critique of Cournot's book, which until that time had attracted relatively little attention. Bertrand was

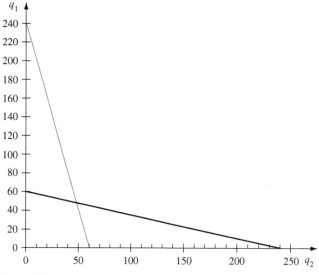

Figure 8.2

under the (mistaken!) impression that in the Cournot model, firms repeatedly revise the prices they charge rather than the quantities they produce. Under that impression, he argued that Cournot's analysis was misleading, and that each of the firms would attempt, turn by turn, to post a lower price than that of its rival, and that there would be no bound to this process.

We will now show that this conclusion on Bertrand's part was erroneous, by finding a Nash equilibrium in a model in which the firms' decision variable is the price they set for the product and not the quantity they produce. Despite Bertrand's errors both in understanding the Cournot model and in analyzing the price competition, the price competition model is designated the **Bertrand Model**. In section 5.1.1, we have already analyzed a particular example of this model, in which each firm could choose one of a finite number of prices. We will now lift this restriction.

In a price competition model, each firm chooses a price for the product it produces and sells the number of units that consumers are prepared to purchase at that price. Firms therefore choose a price and sell as much as they can at that price. Since the product is identical, then if the price set by one of the firms is lower than the price set by the competing firms, all consumers will purchase from that firm only, which will thus corner the entire market. If the lowest price in the market is set by several firms, we will assume that they share the market equally between them.

Assume that in the market n firms produce the same good. The demand function for the product is given by:

$$Q = A - P$$

where:

$$P = \min\{p_1, p_2, \ldots, p_n\}$$

is the lowest of the prices set by the competing firms.

Assume that the production cost of one unit of the good is identical for all firms and is equal to c, and that $c < A$.

The profit of firm i is hence determined as follows:

1. If the price p_i of this firm is strictly lower than the prices of all the other firms, then its profit is:

$$\Pi_i(p_i) = (p_i - c)Q = (p_i - c)(A - p_i)$$

2. If there exist $k - 1$ additional firms whose price is identical to the price p_i of this firm, and this is the lowest price in the market (i.e. $P = p_i$), then the profit is:

$$\Pi_i(p_i) = \frac{1}{k}(p_i - c)(A - p_i)$$

3. If there exists in the market a price that is lower than the price p_i of this firm, its profit is zero.

Let's find the Nash equilibrium in this game. First, we will assume that there are only two firms in the market. We will show that this game has a single equilibrium, in which $p_1 = p_2 = c$. In order to verify this, we will first examine strategy profiles in which $p_1 \neq p_2$.

Can the strategy profile in which $p_1 > p_2 > c$ be a Nash equilibrium? In such a case, firm 1 sells nothing and makes no profit. But if it sets a price $p_1' < A$ that satisfies $p_2 > p_1' > c$, all consumers will switch to purchasing from it and its profit will be positive. Therefore a price profile in which $p_1 > p_2 > c$ is not a Nash equilibrium. Similarly, a price profile in which $p_2 > p_1 > c$ is not a Nash equilibrium.

We will go on to examine a strategy profile in which $p_1 > c \geq p_2$. In such a case, firm 2 attracts all the customers, but does not make a profit (it even loses, if $c > p_2$). But if firm 2 sets a price p_2' which satisfies $p_1 > p_2' > c$, it will still attract all the consumers, and will have a positive profit. Therefore the price profile in which $p_1 > c \geq p_2$ is not a Nash equilibrium. Similarly, a prices profile in which $p_1 > c \geq p_2$ is not a Nash equilibrium.

What about strategy profiles in which $c \geq p_1 > p_2$? In this case, firm 2 attracts all the customers, but loses money. It can improve its position by setting the price $p_2' = c$. In this case, it will not lose even if only some customers patronize it (if $p_1 = c$). Therefore, the price profile in which $c \geq p_1 > p_2$ is not a Nash equilibrium. Similarly, a price profile in which $c \geq p_2 < p_1$ is not a Nash equilibrium.

We will now proceed to examine strategy profiles in which $p_1 = p_2$.

If $p_1 = p_2 > A$, then no firm sells anything at all. In this case, firm 1, for example, can sell and make a profit if it sets a price p'_1 that satisfies $A > p'_1 > c$. Therefore, a price profile in which $p_1 = p_2 > A$ is not a Nash equilibrium.

If $A > p_1 = p_2 > c$, the firms divide the market equally between them. In such a case, firm 1, for example, can increase its profits by very slightly reducing the price it demands. It will, of course, sell each unit at a slightly lower price, but it will corner the entire market, and the number of units it sells will be more than double the number it sold previously. (Check it out: why more than double and not exactly double?) A sufficiently small reduction will, therefore, ensure it a greater profit. Therefore the price profile in which $A > p_1 = p_2 > c$ is not a Nash equilibrium.

If $p_1 = p_2 < c$, then the two firms divide the market equally between them, but they both lose. Firm 1, for example, can improve its position by demanding the price $p'_1 = c$. As a result, it will sell nothing, but neither will it lose money. Therefore the price profile in which $p_1 = p_2 < c$ is not a Nash equilibrium.

It remains for us to examine the case in which $p_1 = p_2 = c$. In this case, the two firms divide the market equally between them but they neither profit nor lose. If one of the firms reduces the price it charges, it will capture the entire market, but will lose money. Therefore, such a change is not worth its while. If one of the firms increases the price it charges, it will sell nothing, and therefore will continue neither to profit nor to lose. Hence, since it does not stand to gain from the change, such a change is not worth its while.

We have hereby shown, therefore, that the profile $p_1 = p_2 = c$ is a Nash equilibrium. It is the only Nash equilibrium in the game, because we have already shown that any other strategy profile is not a Nash equilibrium.

Comprehension check

Assume that firm 1 is more efficient than firm 2 and that therefore $c_1 < c_2$ is satisfied. Find the Nash equilibrium in the Bertrand model for this instance.

On the basis of similar considerations, the equilibrium we obtained is the only equilibrium even when the number of firms in the market is greater than two. In this equilibrium, all the firms $i = 1, \ldots, n$ will set the price $p_i = c$, which will leave them with no profit.

This result is very different, of course, from the result obtained in the Cournot model. There, all firms have a positive profit, and only when the number of firms progressively increases does the profit of each one of them progressively decrease and tend to zero while the price tends to c. This qualitative difference derives from the non-continuity of the Bertrand model, i.e. from the fact that a very small change in the price charged by one of the firms may lead to a sweeping change in consumers' behavior and the firms' profits. This fact follows from the assumption that all the firms are selling exactly the same product. If we assume, more realistically, that even minor differences exist between the products manufactured by the different firms, we will obtain a continuous model, the equilibrium in which resembles, in character, the equilibrium in the Cournot model. This is the model of price competition with differentiated products.

8.2.1   Price competition with differentiated products

In the United States gas stations typically sell three types of gas: octane 87, 89, and 93. For a given gas quality, there are price differences across gas stations of different brands, even when gas stations are adjacent to one another, and some brands charge somewhat higher prices than others. Moreover, there are differences in gas prices even across gas stations of the same brand, located only a short distance apart.

This is an extreme example in which the differentiation among the products of different firms is minimal: all firms supply a product of essentially the same quality, yet enough consumers buy the high-cost gas, thus sustaining the more pricy brands.

In this case, the Bertrand model does not properly reflect reality, and the model we need is one in which only some of the consumers purchasing a product from one firm react to a decrease in price of a similar product of another firm. It may reasonably be assumed that the steeper the decrease in price, the higher the number of consumers who will react to it by switching to another firm and purchasing the product there. This is the assumption in the following model of Bertrand competition with differentiated products.

We will launch our discussion for the case of two firms producing similar goods which are competing in the market. We will denote the different product prices by p_1, p_2 and the average market price by $\bar{p} = \frac{p_1 + p_2}{2}$. We will now assume that the demand curves for the various products (i.e. the desired quantity of a product $i = 1,2$ when the product prices are p_i) are given by

$$q_i(p_1,p_2) = A - p_i - (p_i - \bar{p})$$

for a positive constant $A > 0$.[4] This demand function gives expression to the fact that if the price charged by the firm is higher than the average market price, the firm will lose some of its customers (i.e. demand will decrease) but not all of them – some customers will remain loyal to the brand and will not switch to cheaper competitors.

---

[4] More precisely, the demand function is given by: $q_i(p_1,p_2) = \max[A - p_i - (p_i - \bar{p}), 0]$ since the demand for the product will never be negative.

The demand curves are explicitly given by:

$$q_1(p_1,p_2) = A - p_1 - \left(p_1 - \frac{p_1 + p_2}{2}\right) = A - \frac{3}{2}p_1 + \frac{1}{2}p_2$$

and similarly:

$$q_2(p_1,p_2) = A - \frac{3}{2}p_2 + \frac{1}{2}p_1$$

Assume that firm 1 has a production cost of $c_1 < A$ per product unit, and firm 2 has a production cost of $c_2 < A$ per product unit. The profit of firm 1 (as a function of the prices) is:

$$\Pi_1(p_1,p_2) = (p_1 - c_1)q_1 = (p_1 - c_1)\left(A - \frac{3}{2}p_1 + \frac{1}{2}p_2\right)$$

and the profit of firm 2 is:

$$\Pi_2(p_1,p_2) = (p_2 - c_2)q_2 = (p_2 - c_2)\left(A - \frac{3}{2}p_2 + \frac{1}{2}p_1\right)$$

In order to find the best-reply function, we will find the derivative of the profit function and equate it to zero:

$$\frac{\partial}{\partial p_1}\Pi_1 = A - \frac{3}{2}p_1 + \frac{1}{2}p_2 - \frac{3}{2}p_1 + \frac{3}{2}c_1 = 0$$

And hence:

$$p_1 = \frac{A}{3} + \frac{1}{6}p_2 + \frac{1}{2}c_1$$

Similarly, the best-reply function for firm 2 is:

$$p_2 = \frac{A}{3} + \frac{1}{6}p_1 + \frac{1}{2}c_2$$

The equilibrium is obtained at the intersection point:

$$p_1 = \frac{A}{3} + \frac{1}{6}\left(\frac{A}{3} + \frac{1}{6}p_1 + \frac{1}{2}c_2\right) + \frac{1}{2}c_1$$

Hence:

$$p_1 = \frac{2}{5}A + \frac{18}{35}c_1 + \frac{3}{35}c_2$$
$$p_2 = \frac{2}{5}A + \frac{18}{35}c_2 + \frac{3}{35}c_1$$

The equilibrium quantities will be:

$$q_1(p_1,p_2) = A - \frac{3}{2}p_1 + \frac{1}{2}p_2 = \frac{3}{5}A - \frac{51}{70}c_1 + \frac{9}{70}c_2$$
$$q_2(p_1,p_2) = A - \frac{3}{2}p_2 + \frac{1}{2}p_1 - \frac{3}{5}A - \frac{51}{70}c_2 + \frac{9}{70}c_1$$

If the firms' production costs are equal, i.e. if:

$$c = c_1 = c_2$$

then we will obtain, in contrast to the Bertrand model, that the firms retain a positive profit (on condition, of course, that $c < A$ – otherwise no firm can offer a price that is greater than c at which consumers will wish to purchase the product), since then the mark-up $p_1 - c$ is positive:

$$p_1 - c = p_2 \quad c = \frac{2}{5}A - \frac{2}{5}c > 0$$

Hence brand differentiation enables firms to retain a positive profit (making it worth their while to invest money in marketing and in the differentiation of their product from those of the rival firms – activity that is not included in the model we have described here).

Question 8.2

Extending the discussion to n firms

Assume that there are n firms in the market, and the per-unit production cost of each firm is c. The demand for the product of firm i (as a function of the product prices $p_1, \ldots, p_n$) is given by

$$q_i(p_1,\ldots,p_n) = A \quad p_i - \frac{n}{2}(p_i - \bar{p})$$

where $\bar{p} = \frac{p_1 + \ldots + p_n}{n}$ is the average market price.[5] The coefficient $\frac{n}{2}$ reflects the intensity of competition in the market. The greater the number of firms n, the more closely must the firm's offered price approximate average market price in order to preserve its market share. This is because the greater n is, the greater is also the effect on demand of the gap between the price quoted by the firm and the average market price.

What will the prices be in a symmetric Nash equilibrium in which all firms quote the same price p? What happens to the price of this equilibrium when the number of firms n gets larger?

---

[5] More precisely, the demand for the product is: $q_i(p_1,\ldots,p_n) = \max\left[A - p_i - \frac{n}{2}(p_i - \bar{p}), 0\right]$ since demand for the product is never negative.

Answer

The profit of firm i is given by:

$$\Pi_i(p_i,\ldots p_n) = (p_i - c)q_i = (p_i - c)\left(A - p_i - \frac{n}{2}(p_i - \bar{p})\right)$$

i.e.:

$$\Pi_i(p_i,\ldots,p_n) = (p_i - c)\left(A - p_i - \frac{n}{2}\left(p_i - \frac{p_1 + \ldots + p_i + \ldots + p_n}{n}\right)\right)$$

or:

$$\Pi_i(p_i,\ldots,p_n)$$
$$= (p_i - c)\left(A - \frac{(n+1)}{2}p_i + \frac{1}{2}(p_1 + \ldots + p_{i-1} + p_{i+1} + \ldots + p_n)\right)$$

In order to find the best-reply function, we will find the derivative of the profit function with respect to p_i and equate the derivative to zero. (Note: even though we are seeking a symmetric equilibrium in which all firms quote the same price p, we cannot substitute p into the profit function $\Pi_i(p,\ldots,p)$ and then find its derivative with respect to p. Doing so would have implied that what firm i controls is not the price it quotes, but rather, directly, the equilibrium price p itself – an assumption that is, of course, erroneous.)

$$\frac{\partial}{\partial p_i}\Pi_i = A - \frac{(n+1)}{2}p_i + \frac{1}{2}\left(p_1 + \ldots + p_{i-1} + p_{i+1} + \ldots + p_n\right) - \frac{(n+1)}{2}p_i$$
$$+ \frac{(n+1)}{2}c = 0$$

Hence:

$$p_i = \frac{A}{(n+1)} + \frac{1}{2(n+1)}(p_1 + \ldots + p_{i-1} + p_{i+1} + \ldots + p_n) + \frac{1}{2}c$$

In order to find the equilibrium, we must solve the system of equations:

$$p_1 = \frac{A}{(n+1)} + \frac{1}{2(n+1)}(p_2 + p_3 + \ldots + p_n) + \frac{1}{2}c$$
$$p_2 = \frac{A}{(n+1)} + \frac{1}{2(n+1)}(p_1 + p_3 + \ldots + p_n) + \frac{1}{2}c$$

•
•
•

$$p_n = \frac{A}{(n+1)} + \frac{1}{2(n+1)}(p_1 + p_2 + \ldots + p_{n-1}) + \frac{1}{2}c$$

In this question, we were asked to find a symmetric solution in which $p_1 = p_2 = \ldots = p_n = p$. In such a solution all the equations take the following form:

$$p = \frac{A}{(n+1)} + \frac{(n-1)}{2(n+1)}p + \frac{1}{2}c$$

and the solution is therefore:

$$p = \frac{2A}{(n+3)} + \frac{(n+1)}{(n+3)}c$$

When n progressively increases (tends to infinity), this price tends toward the per-unit production cost c (as we also obtained in the Cournot model).

8.3   Competition or collusion?

We frequently encounter advertisements by a vendor promising that his product is the cheapest in the market, and that if a consumer can prove to him that she has found the product more cheaply priced somewhere else, then he, the vendor, will refund the difference plus additional compensation. This is, on the face of it, bold competitive behavior on the part of the vendor. But is it really so? We will now see how we can check this out by means of a strategic interaction model.[6]

Assume that two chain stores selling HD television sets are competing in the market. The chains purchase TVs from the importer at a price of $250 per unit. We assume that price competition takes place in the market: if one of the chains sets a lower price, it corners the entire market, and if both set the same price, they share the market equally between them.

Suppose that the demand function for HD TVs is given by:

$$Q(P) = 350 - P$$

where P is the dollar price of a television set. Thus, had there been only one chain store operating in the market, selling each television set at price P, it would earn $P - 250$ dollars on every set, and therefore its total profit would be:

$$\Pi(P) = (P - 250)Q(P) = (P - 250)(350 - P)$$

The price $P = 300$ is the price that would maximize this profit (verify this!). This price is higher than the price that would be obtained in a Bertrand competition between the

---

[6] This model appears in Dixit, A. and B. Nalebuff (1991), *Thinking Strategically*, New York: W.W. Norton & Company, which presents accessible basic notions in game theory.

chains, since then the price at a Nash equilibrium would be – as we have seen – identical to the cost of purchase, i.e. $250. That price would leave each of the chains with no profit.

Now assume that one of the chains advertises that its price for a television set is $300, but that if a customer discovers that she could have purchased an identical TV at a lower price from the competing chain, the first chain will compensate her to the tune of twice the difference between the prices. (For example, if the competing chain charges $275 for the TV, the customer will get a $50 refund.) We will now show that at a Nash equilibrium, both chains will collect $300 per TV!

Assuming that one of the chain stores actually publishes such an advertisement, what is its competitor's best reply? If it charges a price lower than $300 (for example, $290), it will lose all its customers because everyone will prefer to obtain the refund from the first chain store, thus actually purchasing the TV at a lower price (i.e. they will purchase at $300 and get a $20 refund, so that they are actually getting the set for $280). Setting a price higher than $300 will certainly not attract customers. Only a price of $300 will enable the firm to share the market and the profits with the first firm, and that is therefore its best reply.

Thus we have in fact obtained that this device of offering to equate the price to the consumer with the price charged by the competitor covertly enables chain stores to coordinate a price that will benefit them both. Our assumption here was that the first firm was able to commit to its advertised pricing policy. We will explore more explicitly the topic of commitment in Chapter 20.

9 Coordination games and strategic uncertainty

In 1753, the Academy of Dijon in France announced an essay contest on the topic of: *"What is the origin of inequality among men, and is it authorized by the natural law?"*

Jean-Jacques Rousseau took up the challenge, and wrote his discourse on "The Origin and the Foundation of Inequality among Men".[1] This essay (together with his later book, *"The Social Contract, or Principles of Political Right,"*[2] published in 1762) became one of the cornerstones of the social sciences and political philosophy.

Rousseau secluded himself for a week in the Forest of St Germain to muse about what human life was like at the dawn of civilization, and completed the discourse upon returning to Paris. In his discourse, Rousseau describes human evolution from the primordial era of the "savage" to the age of the social order of "civilized man."

In the first part of his discourse, Rousseau describes the "savage" or natural man who lived a life of instinct in Nature, innocent of alienation and inequality. In the second part, he goes on to describe the gradual process whereby social and political organization-forming activity took shape, providing man with security and technological progress, but also bringing inequality, wars and alienation in its wake. Rousseau describes the beginning of social cohesion as follows:

> Taught by experience that the love of well-being is the sole motive of human actions, he found himself in a position to distinguish the few cases, in which mutual interest might justify him in relying upon the assistance of his fellows; and also the still fewer cases in which a conflict of interests might give cause to suspect them. In the former case, he joined in the same herd with them, or at most in some kind of loose association, that laid no restraint on its members, and lasted no longer than the transitory occasion that formed it. In the latter case, every one sought his own private advantage, either by open force, if he thought himself strong enough, or by address and cunning, if he felt himself the weaker.

[1] *The Social Contract and Discourses by Jean-Jacques Rousseau*, translated with an Introduction by G. D. H. Cole (London and Toronto: J. M. Dent and Sons, 1923).

[2] Ibid.

In this manner, men may have insensibly acquired some gross ideas of mutual undertakings, and of the advantages of fulfilling them: that is, just so far as their present and apparent interest was concerned: for they were perfect strangers to foresight, and were so far from troubling themselves about the distant future, that they hardly thought of the morrow. If a deer was to be taken, every one saw that, in order to succeed, he must abide faithfully by his post: but if a hare happened to come within the reach of any one of them, it is not to be doubted that he pursued it without scruple, and, having seized his prey, cared very little, if by so doing he caused his companions to miss theirs.[3]

The archetypal scenario Rousseau describes here is particularly appropriate for describing using the tools of game theory. First, man perceives himself as separate from other humans; and social conventions dictating the categories that will help him understand himself and the world around him have yet to come into existence. Wherefore, "the love of well-being is the sole motive of human actions." The extent to which the individual enjoys well-being depends, of course, on the actions he and other people take, but there is no interdependence in the definition of different people's well-being.

Indeed, it is precisely this notion of preferences that we ascribe to players in game theory. We assume that every player can be characterized by the way she ranks the possible action profiles of all the players (including her own). A preferred action profile will procure her a greater measure of well-being, which may accordingly be represented by a higher level of utility according to the utility function that represents her preferences. The utility function is one of the building blocks with the aid of which the game is defined. Thus, in a game, we may replace the utility function of one of the players by another function (which will define the payoff to that player for any action profile) without modifying the definition of the utility function of the other players, and obtain a well-defined new game.

Second, Rousseau describes interactions, each of which is unique, and is perceived and analyzed on its own account. People "were so far from troubling themselves about the distant future, that they hardly thought of the morrow." In other words, Rousseau here describes interactions that are amenable to description with the aid of strategic form games.

To begin with, Rousseau notes the few opportunities that a person encounters "in which mutual interest might justify him in relying upon the assistance of his fellows." In the language of game theory, these are situations in which man perceives that each of those surrounding him has a **dominant strategy**.

Rousseau adds, however, that not all opportunities are of this kind, and promptly cites a pertinent example. The specific game that Rousseau describes has been designated the Stag Hunt game. It may be described as follows.

[3] Ibid.

9.1   The Stag Hunt game

A band of hunters is trying to catch a stag. If the hunting band consists of two hunters, the payoffs in the game can be described as follows:

		Hunter 2	
		Stag	Hare
Hunter 1	Stag	3,3	0,2
	Hare	2,0	2,2

Why does this game reflect Rousseau's description of the situation? The utility from the hunting of the hare is here represented by the payoff 2. It is easier for each hunter to catch a hare on his own. Therefore, if a hunter chooses to set out to catch a hare, he will ensure himself of a payoff of 2, regardless of what the other hunter does. Success in a stag hunt, however, necessitates coordination between the two hunters – they must ambush the stag from two different points in the forest. Given such coordination, the stag hunt will be crowned with success, the hunters will share the kill between them, and each hunter will obtain a larger hunk of meat (represented by the payoff 3) than he would have obtained by hunting a hare on his own. But if one of the hunters should desert his post during the stag hunt in order to catch a hare he has happened to catch sight of, the remaining hunter will be unable to capture the stag on his own, and will be left empty-handed (with a payoff of 0).

There are two Nash equilibria in this game. In one of the equilibria each hunter traps a hare on his own and gets a payoff of 2. In the other, the two hunters collaborate in the hunting of the stag, and get a payoff of 3. For both hunters, the second equilibrium is preferable to the first equilibrium – the stag hunt yields a higher payoff for each one of them.

Definition

When one of two equilibria

1. is deemed at least as preferable as the other equilibrium **by all players**, and
2. is strictly preferred over the other equilibrium by at least one of the players,

we say that it is **more efficient** than the other equilibrium. An equilibrium is called **payoff dominant** if it is more efficient than all other equilibria of the game.

Definition   A game with several Nash equilibria, any two of which are comparable in terms of their efficiency, is called **a coordination game**.

It is not possible to rate the equilibria in terms of efficiency in every game with several equilibria. In other words, not every game is a coordination game. In games such as the Battle of the Sexes (in section 6.1) and Divvying up the Jackpot (in section 6.3.1), for example, if equilibrium A is preferable to equilibrium B in the eyes of a particular player, then in the eyes of the other player, by contrast, equilibrium B is preferable to equilibrium A. Accordingly, in these games, no one equilibrium is more efficient than the other, since the players cannot reach unanimous agreement as to which equilibrium is preferable.

Therefore, in a game such as the Stag Hunt, in which a particular equilibrium can be indicated as being the most efficient of all, one might reasonably assume that the players would naturally focus on the efficient equilibrium as a focal point equilibrium, and that this equilibrium would be the one to be brought into play.

As we have seen, Rousseau does not share this view. In his opinion, "if a hare happened to come within the reach of any one of them, it is not to be doubted that he pursued it without scruple." What negative feature can be found, therefore, in the efficient equilibrium?

When each hunter sets out to bag a hare on his own, he is entirely independent of anyone else's cooperation. Had the hunters reached prior agreement to adhere to the non-efficient equilibrium and set out on a hare hunt, no hunter would have suffered any damage if another hunter had, nevertheless, tried (unsuccessfully!) to catch a stag. In other words, this non-efficient equilibrium is safe for every player, since no player suffers damage if the other player nonetheless deviates from the agreement.

By contrast, the efficient equilibrium, in which the players cooperate in hunting the stag, is risky for every one of them. Of course, being a Nash equilibrium, such cooperation is a stable agreement: if every player believes that the other will play his part in the agreement, he will prefer to adhere to it likewise. However, if the player suspects that for any reason the other player will not do his bit – either because he has decided to hunt a hare as described by Rousseau, or because he has been taken ill in mid-hunt and is unable to continue, or for any other reason – the player will begin to doubt whether it is worth his while to continue in pursuit of the stag. After all, if he withdraws from the agreement and catches himself a hare, he can save himself the uncertainty and the risk of going dinner-less. Thus, every hunter cooperating in the stag hunt faces **strategic uncertainty**.

As we saw in Rousseau's description, the criterion of strategic uncertainty prevails over the criterion of efficiency in the eyes of the hunters. What, in your opinion, is the leading criterion in situations of this sort? What does it depend on?

Actually, Rousseau describes a more complex scenario. The hunter who betrayed his comrades' trust "having seized his prey, cared very little, if by so doing he caused his companions to miss theirs." Which is to say, there are more than two hunters in the "herd," but the withdrawal of even a single hunter suffices for the stag hunt to fail. In other words, the "weakest link" in the band is liable to bring about the failure of the group as a whole.

Let us assume, therefore, that the band consists of n hunters and that, for the stag hunt to succeed, all must cooperate. As before, success in the stag hunt secures each hunter a payoff of 3, while failure incurs a payoff of 0 for every hunter who has participated in the stag hunt.[4] Alternatively, every hunter who succeeds in bagging himself a hare will thereby ensure himself a payoff of 2 (while dooming to failure all the other hunters who are trying to hunt a stag).

What happens when the band of hunters sets out to hunt a stag? Let us assume that a certain hunter believes that every one of the other $n-1$ hunters is liable, with a slight chance of $\varepsilon > 0$, to withdraw from the stag hunt of his own volition, and that the chances of withdrawal of the various hunters are independent of one another. In the view of that hunter, the probability that all the other hunters will adhere to the common effort is only $(1-\varepsilon)^{n-1}$. The greater the number of hunters, n, the chance $(1-\varepsilon)^{n-1}$ tends to 0. If, for instance, the prospect of abandonment by each hunter is $\varepsilon = \frac{1}{10}$, then the likelihood that not one of the ten hunters will opt out is $\left(\frac{9}{10}\right)^{10} \cong 0.347$, and the prospect that 100 hunters will all, to a man, stick to the job in hand is only $\left(\frac{9}{10}\right)^{100} \cong 0.0000266$.

Therefore, the more hunters there are in the band, the more each hunter ought to fear that the mission will not succeed, and the greater the temptation he faces to withdraw from the stag hunt in order to assure himself of a hare for dinner. In this sort of scenario, the intuition presented by Rousseau comes more sharply into focus.

More generally, less extreme situations could occur in which it suffices that a part α of the hunting band will stick to the job in hand in order for the stag hunt to be crowned with success. In such a case, when at least a proportion α out of the band of hunters set out to hunt a stag, they pull it off successfully, winning a payoff of 3. By contrast, if fewer than α of the hunters band together to hunt the stag, these hunters fail and return home empty-handed (with a payoff of 0). As before, each hunter who elects to hunt a hare assures himself of a payoff of 2.

---

[4] This is a reasonable situation if a large band of hunters can hunt a large herd of deer, such that the overall kill is proportionate to the number of hunters, and the kill per hunter remains constant. In order to simplify the terminology, we will nevertheless continue to speak of "a stag" rather than a "herd of deer."

9.1.1   Whale hunting

A hunting game of this type actually takes place in a whale-hunting village on the island of Lembata in Indonesia.[5,6] In the dry season, between May and September, boats powered by oars and palm-fronds sails put out to sea every morning, to a distance of up to about 13 kilometers from the shore, to find and hunt whales. Whale hunting is a complex and dangerous task that calls for at least eight crew members – the "captain," the harpooner and his assistant, the helmsman, and others. When the boatmen spot a whale, they usually lower the sail and row powerfully in the direction of the prey. The moment the boat comes within suitable range, the harpooner, standing in the boat on a small platform especially designed for the purpose, casts his spear at the whale. The whale then plunges or drags the boat with him until it is exhausted. The danger, of course, is that the whale will drag the boat far out to sea, or that the boat will capsize.

Thus, early every morning, the "captain" of each wooden whaling boat (called a *téna*) must recruit a crew of at least eight men for the job. The villagers must decide whether to join the boat, or, alternatively, to go fishing for themselves, either alone or in pairs, seeking smaller fry near the shore (or doing other onshore jobs, such as tending to their livestock, which will include a few goats, some poultry, and some pigs). Each crew member taking part in the whale hunt will obtain, on average, a larger hunk of meat than he could get by fishing close to the shore. In addition, the crew member earns the gratitude of his extended family, since he shares the catch with them.

However, over a period of years in which it has gradually become increasingly apparent that schools of whales in the fishing zone are small and rare, the "captains" face, day by day, a tougher job in manning their boats. On the whole, crew members whose whaling boats, on a particular day, do not go to sea, don't go fishing near the shore either because to do that they need boats of a different type (coracles), nets instead of harpoons, and so forth. Thus the "strategic uncertainty" facing the whale hunters increases, and the number of boats putting out to sea every morning progressively decreases throughout the hunting season in such difficult years.

9.1.2   Laboratory experiments of the Stag Hunt game

Various laboratory experiments have been devised to examine the Stag Hunt game. In one such experiment[7] the participants repeatedly played the game with the following payoffs:

---

[5] Alvard, M. S. and D. A. Nolin (2002), "Rousseau's Whale Hunt? Coordination among Big-Game Hunters," *Current Anthropology* 43 (4), 533–559.

[6] Indonesia is not a signatory to the international convention for the prevention of whale hunting, but in any event, that convention exempts from restrictions natives who engage in whale hunting for their own subsistence.

[7] Cooper, R., D. DeJong, B. Forsythe, and T. Ross (1990), "Selection Criteria in Coordination Games: Some Experimental Results," *American Economic Review* 80, 218–233.

Player 2

		S	H
	S	100,100	0,80
Player 1	H	80,0	80,80

where the figures represent the percentage prospect of obtaining $1 from the experimenters. In this game, each player can assure himself of an 80 percent prospect of winning the dollar if he chooses strategy A. In order to close the small remaining gap to 100 percent, the two players must successfully coordinate between themselves the choice of the strategy S. But the failure of such coordination will leave the player who chooses S with no prospect of winning the dollar, and therefore the risk involved in this strategy may be perceived as high in comparison with the difference in rewards. Sure enough, in the final eleven rounds of the experiment, the players, in 97 percent of cases, chose the profile (H, H).

The picture changed when the participants were permitted to send each other messages. When player 1 was permitted, prior to each round of the game, to announce the strategy he was about to play, the players were able to coordinate the most worthwhile profile (S, S) in 53 percent of cases; but a lack of coordination occurred in 31 percent of cases, giving (S, H) or (H, S), while in the remaining 16 percent of cases the participants played (H, H). Thus, in some cases in which player 1 announced his intention of playing S, he nevertheless feared lack of cooperation on the part of player 2, and therefore, ultimately, played the safe strategy H after all. Correspondingly (or consequently), player 2 did not in fact cooperate in choosing S, even when player 1 announced his intention of choosing S. This resulted in instances of non-coordination, or in the choice of the safe strategy H by both players.

The picture improved dramatically when the experimenters permitted two-way communication, meaning that they permitted player 2 to respond and likewise to declare the strategy he intended to choose. In the last eleven rounds of the game, the participants played the efficient profile (S, S) in 91 percent of cases, while the remaining cases suffered from lack of coordination.

The Stag Hunt game is the archetype of a large group of coordination games. A coordination game, it will be recalled, is a game in which there are several Nash equilibria that can be ranked according to their efficiency.

In another coordination game experiment, there was a hierarchy of seven possible levels of cooperation between the players, where the payoff to each player depended on his choice and on the minimal level of cooperation within the group of players as a whole.[8] The choice of "7" by all players ensures the highest payoff to all, but also entails the heaviest "fines" if one player deviates and chooses a lower level of cooperation. Universal choice of a lower level of cooperation yields a lower payoff to each player, but also reduces the "fines" imposed in case of deviation on the part of any of the players.

Expressly, in this game the payoffs to each player were as follows:

		The lowest number selected by the players						
		7	6	5	4	3	2	1
	7	1.3	1.1	0.9	0.7	0.5	0.3	0.1
	6	–	1.2	1.0	0.8	0.6	0.4	0.2
	5	–	–	1.1	0.9	0.7	0.5	0.3
The player's choice	4	–	–	–	1.0	0.8	0.6	0.4
	3	–	–	–	–	0.9	0.7	0.5
	2	–	–	–	–	–	0.8	0.6
	1	–	–	–	–	–	–	0.7

In this game, there are seven equilibria – every profile of actions in which all players select the same level X of cooperation is a Nash equilibrium. How did the participants actually play?

Each participant took part in 7–10 rounds of the game. When a large number of players participated, a gradual convergence took place in the course of the game rounds, toward a players' choice of low (and "safe") levels of cooperation – to the lowest level of "1" in 77 percent of instances in the final round of the game, and to a level of "2" in another 17 percent of final-round instances.

By contrast, when there were only two players in a set, the great majority of playing pairs (twenty-one out of twenty-four pairs in the experiment) converged to coordinating on the highest level "7" of cooperation in the final round of the game. It transpires that when there are only two participants in a game and one of them is initially fearful and starts off his game rounds by selecting a low level, his fellow player is frequently prepared to "wait" for him by repeatedly selecting the level "7" until, in most instances, the first player in fact quickly overcomes his misgivings and joins the efficient "7" choice. Such a "waiting period" was not observed when the

---

[8] Van Huyck, J. B., R. C. Battalio, and R. Beil (1990), "Tacit Cooperation Games, Strategic Uncertainty, and Coordination Failure," *American Economic Review* 80, 234–248.

pair was randomly swapped in each game round. In this configuration, insistence on a "7" level of cooperation cannot serve as a signal of preparedness for effective cooperation, and the cooperation level mostly deteriorated to the lowest common denominator, namely "1."

In a similar experiment, the participants played in trios.[9] The choice of S by everybody would have secured a payoff of 90 for all, but a deviation by any one of them to H would have caused the payoff to those adhering to S to plummet to 10. Meanwhile, the universal choice of H would have only slightly reduced the reward to 80, while at the same time greatly reducing the risk inhering in deviation on the part of one of the players; a player choosing H where one of the others chooses S would get 60.

In this experiment, seven out of eight trios of participants were successful in learning to mutually coordinate on the efficient action S in the course of twenty game rounds. In practice, the participants chose S three-fourths of the time, even in the early rounds of the experiment.

The results were completely different when eight participants were (virtually) arranged in a circle, each playing the game with whoever was next to him in the circle (which is to say that as before, his payoffs depended on his choice and the choices made by his neighbors on either side; the same choice of a player pertained to his interaction with both his neighbors). Here the participants chose S from the outset only half the time, and the frequency of the selection S deteriorated progressively during the twenty game rounds. In the last round, none of the participants chose S; rather, the unanimous choice fell on H.

What is the origin of the difference in outcomes? Where each trio is isolated unto itself, mutual trust can evolve. In the circle game, by contrast, each participant is indirectly dependent also on his remote neighbors: they affect their neighbors' choices, which in turn affect those of their own neighbors, and so on and so forth; and ultimately, they also affect the participant's immediate neighbors. Thus, a reluctance to choose S is liable to spread like a plague through the whole circle, ultimately "infecting" everybody, and causing them to choose H.

Stag Hunt games, or more general games of coordination, succinctly describe many realistic situations unrelated to the world of hunting. We will now describe a few examples.

9.2   Keyboard arrangement

The generally accepted arrangement of English letter keys on the computer keyboard is called QWERTY, after the first six characters running from left to

---

[9] Berninghaus, S. K., K. M. Erhart, and C. Keser (2002), "Conventions and Local Interaction Structures," *Games and Economic behavior* 39, 177–205.

right on the top row of letters. This arrangement has nothing to do with typing convenience but originates from a period when mechanical typewriters were used for typing.

In mechanical typewriters, striking a keyboard key activated a lever, the end of which featured a relief of the corresponding letter. When activated, the lever was thrown forward to impact an inked ribbon that was stretched close across the sheet of paper held in the rollers, and the letter mould was thus imprinted on the page. A common problem in mechanical typewriters was that two levers could become entangled when two adjacent letters on the keyboard were struck one after another. The keyboard was therefore arranged in such a way that letters frequently succeeding one another in English words would be kept apart.

But preventing the typewriter levers from getting crossed was not the only criterion for the efficiency of the alpha-numerical arrangement of the keyboard. Typing speed was another important issue, and the lever problem is in any event no longer relevant in the age of personal computers. In the 1930s, August Dvorak and William Dealy therefore invented a different arrangement of keyboard characters, which could significantly improve typing speeds. The arrangement is designated DVORAK.[10]

The preferable keyboard layout, however, was not popular and the QWERTY arrangement remains dominant in practice. Since most of the world's keyboards conform to that layout, there is little point in learning and adapting to a different design. If a majority of computer users worldwide were to switch simultaneously to using the DVORAK-style keyboard, typing would become quicker and easier, and the improvement would justify the costs and the effort involved. But the existing situation, in which almost everybody is accustomed to QWERTY typing, itself likewise constitutes a Nash equilibrium among computer users.

Comprehension check

Describe a game between computer users that corresponds to the above description, and indicate its payoffs.

[10] In Microsoft Windows operating systems, for example, you can avail yourself of the option of using DVORAK by choosing Start – > Settings – > Control Panel – > Regional and Language Options – > Text Services and Input Languages and add the DVORAK layout.

9.3   Video cassette recording technology

In the 1980s, two rival technologies, VHS and Betamax, competed in the video cassette recording (VCR) and viewing market. In terms of recording quality, Betamax was considered preferable. The Japanese firm Sony produced VCRs using this technology and drove it to market. Almost all other electronics manufacturers, however, produced VHS-compatible equipment. In order to encourage consumers to purchase its VCRs, Sony promised that it would continue producing them by means of that technology, and that it would set up Betamax movie lending libraries worldwide.

For several years, the two technologies coexisted in the market. Gradually, the VHS technology bit off a larger market share and, commencing from a certain stage, the vast majority of demand was channeled to VHS-type cassette recorders. Sony thereupon also started producing VHS, relinquishing its Betamax line.

9.4   Consumer network externalities[11]

The utility consumers derive from products often depends on the number of other consumers using the same product. The facsimile machine is a classic example of this rule. If nobody, anywhere, had a fax machine, it would not be worth anybody's while to get one, because there would be no one to send faxes to or receive from. For every potential user, the utility to be got from the device progressively increases with the number of people worldwide who likewise use a fax machine. Even so, given a certain distribution of fax machines among the population, various users will gain a different level of utility from purchasing one for themselves. For example, various business owners obtaining a fax machine for their business will be able to boost their income to different extents. Accordingly, the maximum price each will be willing to pay for the machine will vary.

The simplest way to model such a state of affairs is to assume that every potential fax consumer is characterized by her **type**, $\tau > 0$. If the number of fax users in the population is $n \geq 2$, then a type τ consumer is prepared to pay at most $n\tau$ to purchase a fax machine. But if nobody but the potential consumer herself purchases a fax machine, then a type τ consumer will not shell out any cash for the device, because she will have no use for it.

---

[11] The model described here is based on Rohlfs, J. (1974), "A Theory of Interdependent Demand for a Communications Service," *The Bell Journal of Economics and Management Science* 5, 16–37.

To simplify the problem even further, let's assume that in a particular country there are A potential fax consumers, of the types $\tau = 1,2, \ldots, A$. We will assume that fax machines are now being initially offered for sale in the market at price p. Who of the consumers will purchase fax machines at a Nash equilibrium?

First, a situation could come about in which everyone believes that nobody else is going to purchase a fax machine. Thus they will all refrain from purchasing the device. In other words, a state of affairs in which nobody buys a fax machine is a Nash equilibrium.

Is there also an equilibrium in which fax machines are in demand? To check this out, we will assume that at a Nash equilibrium, $n^* \geq 2$ devices are sold. In other words, some types in the population find good reason to purchase a fax machine at the price p. Obviously, if an individual of type τ decides to purchase a fax machine (which is to say $n^* \tau \geq p$) then everyone of a higher type $\tau' > \tau$ will also wish to purchase a fax (since then $n^* \tau' > p$). In other words, we will be able to identify the minimal type τ^* who will wish to purchase a fax at price p given that n^* consumers altogether start using the fax. To keep it simple, let's assume that for the type τ^*, the equation:

$$p = n^* \tau^*$$

is satisfied. This means that the price p is the maximal price that type τ^* is prepared to pay for the device, given that n^* consumers altogether buy and use fax machines.

These n^* consumers are of the types:

$$\tau = \tau^*, \ldots, A$$

which is to say:

$$n^* = A - \tau^* + 1$$

Hence we may infer that:

$$p = n^* \tau^* = \left(A - \tau^* + 1\right)\tau^*$$

This quadratic equation in τ^* has two solutions (see Figure 9.1):[12]

$$\tau_1^* = \frac{(A+1) - \sqrt{(A+1)^2 - 4p}}{2}$$

$$\tau_2^* = \frac{(A+1) + \sqrt{(A+1)^2 - 4p}}{2}$$

Each of these solutions defines a Nash equilibrium. In the first equilibrium, all the types $\tau \geq \tau_1^*$ purchase fax machines, i.e. the number of faxes sold altogether is:

---

[12] As long as $p < \frac{(A+1)^2}{4}$.

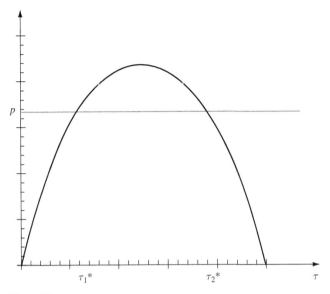

Figure 9.1

$$n_1^* = (A+1) - \tau_1^* = \frac{(A+1) + \sqrt{(A+1)^2 - 4p}}{2}$$

In the second equilibrium, only the types $\tau \geq \tau_2^*$ purchase faxes, and the overall number of devices sold is:

$$n_2^* = (A+1) - \tau_2^* = \frac{(A+1) - \sqrt{(A+1)^2 - 4p}}{2}$$

We therefore obtain that there are altogether three Nash equilibria in this game. The equilibrium τ_1^* is the most desirable of all – the one with the largest number of consumers who use the fax machines and benefit from them.

Comprehension check

The world's personal computers are currently divided into two principal types – the PCs with Microsoft Windows operating systems, and Macintosh computers. PCs are most widely used, but some consumers consider their performance to be inferior to that of the Mac, especially for graphic design applications. The greater popularity of the PC results in a situation in which a wider diversity of software programs is on offer for that type of computer.

Give a verbal and formal description of a coordination game between personal computer users, one of the equilibria of which corresponds to the state of affairs prevailing in reality in which a majority of consumers choose the PC and a minority the Macintosh.

Guidance: assume that there are two types of computer users. The first type prefers to work with Macintosh in any event. Users of the second type, constituting the majority of computer users in the population, prefer to work with that type of computer for which most software programs are written. Assume that the type of computer for which more software programs are written is the one used by the larger part of the population.

9.5   Job search and unemployment

Coordination games also have important application in describing macro-economic phenomena. We will now describe such an application, which is based on ideas from the model presented in an influential article by Diamond (1982).[13] For these and related ideas Diamond received the Nobel prize in Economics in 2010.

The inhabitants of a certain tropical island go out picking coconuts every morning. To pick a coconut, one must first climb the coconut tree. A coconut picker finding a tree that bears a coconut must decide whether to climb up and pluck it or whether to look for another tree where the coconut hangs lower, so that it will be easier to pluck. Islanders face a taboo against eating coconuts they have picked themselves. So in the afternoons, islanders who picked coconuts in the morning look for partners with whom to swap coconuts. Once the swap has taken place, each partner can eat the coconut he now has in his possession. Traditionally, coconuts, once picked, may not be kept for the next day. Therefore, an inhabitant who has picked a coconut but has not found a partner with whom to transact the swap must throw it away and does not get to eat a coconut that day.

This is, of course, "in a nutshell," a metaphor for the economic organization of modern society. The vast majority of people do not subsist solely on the products they produce themselves; they exchange most of their produce with others in consideration of different goods (by selling their produce or their labor in exchange for money, and using that money to purchase other goods and services). This is due to the sophistication and the expertise involved in manufacturing processes – most consumer goods are produced in multiple stages by very many people, using a large number of intermediate by-products of other manufacturing processes. (The tropical

---

[13] Diamond, P. (1982), "Aggregate Demand Management in Search Equilibrium," *Journal of Political Economy* 90 (5), 881–894.

island of the fable has no form of professional specialization that necessitates barter trade, and therefore barter trade is anchored in a different assumption – that of the taboo.)

Most consumer goods become obsolete and spoil over the course of time. This assumption is represented in the fable by the (simplifying) assumption that coconuts won't keep from one day to the next. This is an extreme assumption, which is designed to facilitate the computations in the model we will present. (Alternatively, the value of a coconut might have been assumed to decrease gradually over time,[14] but this complication would not yield any new insights from the model for our purposes here.)

Job seeking or searching for a business opportunity is likened, in this story, to the search for a coconut that the individual will wish to pluck. While searching, the individual is "unemployed." Having picked his coconut, he is "employed." His pay packet or profit finds expression in his chance of finding a partner with whom to swap coconuts, and if that chance comes to fruition, he will be able to eat a coconut that day. The better chance he stands of finding a partner, the higher will be his profit from picking the coconut in the morning.

The more coconut pickers there are on the island on any given morning who are looking for an opportunity to exchange their fruits in the afternoon, the better the chance of finding a partner for the swap. If the prospect of finding a partner is high, each individual will be more motivated to make the effort to pick the higher-hung coconuts, too. Yet if there is only a slight chance of finding a partner for the swap and satisfying one's appetite for a coconut, each individual will prefer to preserve his strength and look for low-hanging coconuts.

Thus numerous Nash equilibria are possible in this model. If none of the islanders picks coconuts, it is worth nobody's while to do so on his own account, because he will never be able to exchange them and get to eat coconuts.

A different situation is possible in which people attempt to pick only low-hanging fruit. Only a small number of coconuts is picked in this sort of situation, and therefore the chance of finding a partner for the swap is low. Hence, the incentive for making an effort and picking coconuts is low to begin with, justifying the islanders' tendency not to exert themselves to pick high-hung coconuts.

In a more successful equilibrium, people climb to pick the higher coconuts, too, on the expectation that the great effort involved will justify itself by providing a higher chance of finding a partner for the swap. In this equilibrium, this is indeed a self-fulfilling expectation, because a large number of coconuts, both high and low hanging, are picked on the island and many coconut pickers roam around the island in the afternoon seeking a partner with whom to exchange the fruits of their labors.

---

[14] As, in fact, Diamond (1982 – see note 13) assumes.

The moral of this story is clear. A nation may fall into a "poverty trap" in which unemployment surges and few entrepreneurs establish new businesses. Potential entrepreneurs fear there will be no demand for new produce, because the low-income population cannot afford to buy it. So these potential entrepreneurs do not open new businesses, and no employment opportunities are created for the unemployed. The population as a whole remains mired in poverty and this state of affairs justifies the entrepreneurs' fears.

At an equilibrium of prosperity, entrepreneurs expect that employees will earn high salaries and will want to spend their money on purchasing numerous goods. The entrepreneurs therefore proceed to new business initiatives, offering employment to most inhabitants, and the latter do indeed step up their consumption accordingly.

The model of Diamond (1982 – see note 13) is formulated in continuous time. We will now present a simpler model of a game that describes some of the ideas in the article.

Every afternoon, $0 \leq e \leq 1$ is the ratio of islanders who are "employed," which is to say, they roam around carrying a coconut they picked that morning and try to find a partner in a similar situation with whom to swap coconuts. Their chance of finding a swap partner is given by $b(e)$, where:

$$b : [0, 1] \rightarrow [0, 1]$$

is an increasing function: the higher the number of employed persons, the better, too, the chances of finding a partner that day. Of course, $b(0) = 0$ is satisfied; if nobody seeks a partner, no partner can possibly be found. For simplicity's sake, we will assume in this discussion that the function b is given by:

$$b(e) = e$$

In the morning hours, all the islanders are out looking for fruit-bearing coconut palms. All palms are the same height, which is also the measurement unit used by the islanders. In other words, the height of every palm tree is "1." Every day, one coconut ripens on each tree. The height of the ripe coconuts h on the trees is uniformly distributed up the tree. A person climbing to a height h in order to pick a ripe coconut invests effort $c(h)$ for that purpose, while the function:

$$c : [0, 1] \rightarrow R_+$$

is an increasing and convex[15] function that assumes positive values. The effort $c(h)$ is expressed in terms of the prospect $b(e)$ of finding a partner with whom to swap coconuts. The effort is worthwhile if:

[15] That is to say, the second derivative c'' is not negative. The convexity of the function expresses the assumption that the coconut picker gets tired as he climbs, each additional yard he has to climb being at least as hard for him to climb as the previous one he has already climbed.

$$c(h) \leq b(e)$$

but is not worthwhile, from the point of view of the islander, if:

$$c(h) > b(e)$$

We will look for a symmetric Nash equilibrium, in which on all days the proportion e^* of persons "employed" on the island of an afternoon remains constant, and all the morning's "job seekers" on the island adopt the following threshold strategy: they will climb the coconut palm they have found only if the (ripe) coconut on it hangs at a height of not more than h^*. In other words, h^* satisfies:

$$c(h^*) = b(e^*)$$

such that for every coconut at a lower height, $h \leq h^*$ the inequality $c(h) \leq b(e^*)$ is satisfied, and the islander considers his climbing effort to have paid off. Since we have assumed that $b(e) = e$,

$$c(h^*) = e^*$$

will be satisfied at equilibrium.

   We will assume that every "job seeker" finds, in the course of his searches on a given morning, just one coconut palm. Since the height of the ripe nuts on the island's trees is uniformly distributed, the chance of finding a coconut at a height that does not exceed h^* is h^*, and therefore this will also be the ratio of "employed persons" e^* proffering coconuts in the afternoon:

$$e^* = h^*$$

If we add this to the previous equation, we will obtain that every equilibrium of the type we seek is bound to satisfy the equation:

$$c(h^*) = h^*$$

Thus, the number of equilibria and the nature thereof in this model depend on the properties of the effort function $c(h)$. For example, if:

$$c(h) = h$$

then the game has a continuum of different equilibria: for every $h^* \in [0,1]$ it may be that the convention on the island is that in the morning, one climbs to a height of h^* in order to pick coconuts. This convention justifies itself because it brings about a situation in which the chance of finding a partner for swapping coconuts in the afternoon is likewise h^*, and given that chance, every islander deems it not worth his while to make an effort to pick coconuts that are higher than h^*.

Of all these equilibria, the worst is the one in which $h^* = 0$. In this equilibrium, none of the islanders picks any coconuts, because every one of them (rightly) believes that he will not find a partner with whom to swap coconuts in the afternoon. The most efficient equilibrium is the one in which $h^* = 1$. In this equilibrium, every islander picks a coconut in the morning, at whatever height he finds it on the tree, because he is convinced that he will certainly be able to exchange his coconut in the afternoon. This belief is indeed justified, since all the islanders pick coconuts in the morning hours.

Assume now, alternatively, that the effort function is given by:

$$c(h) = 2h^2$$

We have seen that:

$$c(h^*) = h^*$$

must be satisfied at equilibrium, which is to say:

$$2(h^*)^2 = h^*$$

This equation has two solutions:

$$h_1^* = 0, \quad h_2^* = \frac{1}{2}$$

The equilibrium $h_2^* = \frac{1}{2}$ at which half the coconuts are picked every morning is, of course, more efficient than the equilibrium $h_1^* = 0$ at which no coconuts are picked at all.

Finally, we will assume that the distribution of ripe coconuts on the palm trees is non-uniform, but is given by the cumulative distribution function P, which may be any increasing function:

$$P : [0, 1] \rightarrow [0, 1]$$

which satisfies $P(0) = 0$ and $P(1) = 1$.

At an equilibrium in which coconuts are plucked every morning up to a height of h^*, in the afternoon a proportion $e^* = P(h^*)$ of the inhabitants are looking for swap partners, and this is also the prospect of their finding a swap partner at that time (since we have assumed that $b(e^*) = e^*$). Therefore, the equilibria h^* of the game are the solutions to the equation:

$$P(h^*) = c(h^*)$$

If the cumulative distribution function inflects several times as it increases in the range of [0,1], it can also intersect several times with the convex function $c(h^*)$ in this range, and each of these intersection points will be a Nash equilibrium. The highest intersection point will also be the most efficient equilibrium.

For example, the cumulative distribution function:

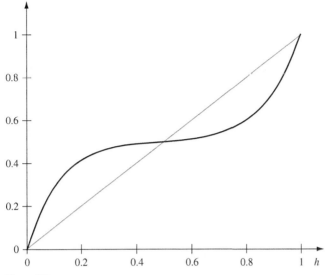

Figure 9.2

$$P(h) = \frac{1}{2} + 4\left(h - \frac{1}{2}\right)^3$$

intersects the effort function:

$c(h) = h$

at three points (see Figure 9.2):

$$h1^* = 0, \quad h_2^* = \frac{1}{2}, \quad h_3^* = 1$$

Each of these three points is a Nash equilibrium of the game.

PART IV

Uncertainty and mixed strategies

INTRODUCTION

In Chapter 10 we start addressing the issue of uncertainty. When a player is unsure what strategies his rivals will choose, we will assume that the player attaches a probability to each of the possible choice combinations. Each choice of a strategy of his own then defines the probability with which each profile of all the players' choices would be realized. Overall, each of the player's strategies defines a **lottery** over the strategy profiles in the game.

In order to decide which strategy to choose, the player then has to figure which of the lotteries induced by his strategies he prefers. We will assume that the player's preference over these lotteries is expressed by the **expected utility** accrued by this lottery – the weighted average of his utilities from his choice and the others' choices, weighted by the probabilities that he ascribes to the other players' choices. This assumption means that the utility levels now have a **cardinal** (rather than just **ordinal**) interpretation. Preferences over lotteries which can be represented by an expected utility over outcomes are named after von Neumann and Morgenstern, who isolated four axioms on the preference relation which obtain if and only if an expected-utility representation of the preferences is feasible.

These axioms do not always obtain. We bring in the example of the Allais Paradox for preferences that seem "reasonable" but which nevertheless cannot be represented by an expected utility.

We then apply the notion of expected utility to define **risk dominance** in 2×2 games. The risk-dominant strategy of a player in such a game is the one which yields him a higher expected payoff assuming that his rival chooses each of her two possible strategies with the same probability ½. A risk-dominant equilibrium in a 2×2 game is one in which both players choose their risk-dominant strategy. We observe that in the Stag Hunt game, it is the inefficient equilibrium which is risk dominant.

In Chapter 11 we launch the study of **mixed strategies**. A mixed strategy is a choice of the player among his strategies made using a lottery with specific probabilities. Extending the game by allowing the players to choose mixed strategies is called the **mixed extension of the game**. Within this extension, the original strategies (chosen with certainty) are called the **pure strategies**.

Matching Pennies is an example of a game which has no Nash equilibrium in pure strategies, but which has a Nash equilibrium in mixed strategies. In fact, by a theorem of Nash, every (mixed extension of a) matrix game has an equilibrium in pure or mixed strategies. In the appendix to the chapter we provide the outline of the proof, which relies on a fixed-point theorem.

If a player employs a mixed strategy at equilibrium, then she must be indifferent among all the pure strategies that she mixes (otherwise she would be better off choosing the one among them yielding her the highest expected payoff). This idea is somewhat counter-intuitive, and for some games this may be the source of failing to reproduce the mixed-strategy equilibrium behavior at the lab.

Mixed-strategy Nash equilibria have several potential interpretations. First, the mixed strategy of a player at equilibrium could be interpreted not as a mindful randomization but rather as the probabilistic prediction made by the player's rivals. Another interpretation would be to understand mixed strategies as simple, history-independent rules of thumb for behavior in repeated games. These could be relevant in games in which surprising the opponent is of value, such as service aces in tennis or penalty kicks in soccer. Indeed, both examples were empirically investigated to check for the use of mixed strategies by professional players, and partial positive evidence was discovered. Yet another interpretation is that for the strategic encounter each player is drawn at random from a large population, and knows only the characteristics of the average behavior of the population she is facing rather than that of the individual representative with whom she was matched. In this interpretation of a **population game**, each player chooses a determinate pure strategy, but different individuals in the population choose different pure strategies, and the mixed strategy represents the frequencies with which the different pure strategies are chosen. We offer an example in which this interpretation is particularly plausible.

In Chapter 12 we study **strictly competitive** two-player games, in which the interests of the players are diametrically opposed – whenever a player prefers a strategy profile over another, her opponent has the reverse preference. A particular instance of strictly competitive games are **zero sum** games, in which for each strategy profile the payoff of each player is just minus the payoff of her rival.

A **security** or **maxmin strategy** is one which maximizes the player's payoff under the assumption that for each strategy she may choose, her opponent will choose the strategy which will minimize her payoff. This notion is particularly relevant in strictly competitive games – in such games the opponent will indeed wish to minimize the player's payoff not due to mere cruelty but rather simply with the view of maximizing *his* own payoff.

In general, the payoff guaranteed to the player by her security strategy might be lower than her payoff at a Nash equilibrium. However, in the particular case of strictly competitive games, mixed-strategy equilibrium strategies are also security strategies, and Nash equilibrium payoffs are the same as the maxmin payoffs. Moreover, the **minimax theorem** asserts that in the mixed extension of a zero sum game, each player has a mixed security strategy, which guarantees her the same payoff she could get if she were to best reply to each particular mixed strategy of her opponent, while given this optimal behavior the opponent were to choose his strategy most spitefully to her.

Chapter 13 brings further elaborate examples of mixed strategies in general games. The first example is the Volunteer's Dilemma, in which out of a pool of potential volunteers each individual has to choose whether to volunteer for a costly mission (for which he would opt if he were the only potential volunteer) or wait and hope that somebody else will volunteer instead. Somewhat like a public good game, in the symmetric mixed-strategy equilibrium of this game each potential volunteer volunteers with a probability smaller than 1, which tends to zero as the number of potential volunteers increases; moreover, as the pool of volunteers gets larger, the overall probability that at least one person would volunteer decreases. However, laboratory experiments of this game show more optimistic outcomes than this theoretical prediction.

A further example, in which each player has more than two strategies, is the Rock-Paper-Scissors game, whose only equilibrium is in mixed strategies. Finally, the appendix to Chapter 13 elaborates an additional patent-race model, in which the competitors may choose one out of a finite number of R&D intensity levels using a mixed strategy. The mixed-strategy equilibrium is studied, and its properties compared with the findings of laboratory experiments.

Choice under uncertainty and risk dominance

In the preceding chapter we dealt, *inter alia*, with choice under strategic uncertainty, i.e. with situations in which a player is not sure what strategies the other players will adopt. The player may adopt various strategies, the choice of any one of which may lead to different possible outcomes, depending on the strategy profiles of the other players.

How will the player compare her various strategies when she is uncertain regarding the choices of her opponents? The way player i compares the strategies available to her depends on her belief about the likelihoods with which the other players will choose a particular strategy from among those available to them.

Assume that this belief can be represented by the probability $p(x_{-i})$ that player i assigns to each strategy profile $x_{-i} \in X_{-i}$ of the other players (the sum of these probabilities, of course, being 1: $\sum_{x_{-i}\in X_{-i}} p(x_{-i}) = 1$). We will denote this probabilistic belief by:

$$p_{-i} = (p(x_{-i}))_{x_{-i}\in X_{-i}}$$

Given this belief, any strategy $\tilde{x}_i$ of the player determines a lottery among the strategy profiles $(\tilde{x}_i, x_{-i})_{x_{-i}\in X_{-i}}$. In this lottery, the probability of the strategy profile $(\tilde{x}_i, x_{-i})_{x_{-i}\in X_{-i}}$ is $p(x_{-i})$.

The player cannot influence the probability $p(x_{-i})$ at which, so she believes, the other players will choose the strategy profile x_{-i}. But the strategy $\tilde{x}_i$ is subject to player i's control, and it is this strategy that determines what strategy profile $(\tilde{x}_i, x_{-i})_{x_{-i}\in X_{-i}}$ will be the one that will be realized with a probability of $p(x_{-i})$ (according to player i's belief).

If the player chooses the strategy $\tilde{x}_i'$ rather than the strategy $\tilde{x}_i$, this will give rise to a different lottery, in which – according to player i's belief - the strategy profile $(\tilde{x}_i, x_{-i})_{x_{-i}\in X_{-i}}$ has the chance $p(x_{-i})$ of being realized. In order to decide which strategy to choose, the player must decide which of these lotteries she prefers.

For example, in the Stag Hunt game with two players (section 9.1), we will assume that player 1 believes player 2 will choose to hunt a stag with the probability $p(S)$, and that with the complementary probability, $p(H) = 1 - p(S)$, he will choose to bag a hare. The belief of player 1 is thus denoted:

$$p_{-1} = (p(S), p(H))$$

If player 1 chooses to hunt a stag, he actually chooses a lottery in which the stag gets captured by the players' joint efforts with the probability $p(S)$, and with the probability $p(H)$ he returns home with no plunder (while his fellow hunter bags a hare). If player 1 chooses to bag a hare, he is actually choosing a lottery in which he returns home with a hare with certainty, whereas his fellow player returns home empty-handed with a probability of $p(S)$ and with a hare with a probability of $p(H)$. Player 1 must therefore make a choice as to which of these two lotteries he prefers, in order to decide which strategy to choose.

We will henceforth assume that the player's preferences over lotteries can be represented by her expected payoff. If player i chooses the strategy $\tilde{x}_i'$, her **expected utility**[1] under the belief p_{-i} is:

$$U_i(\tilde{x}_i; p_{-i}) = \sum_{x_{-i} \in X_{-i}} u_i(\tilde{x}_i, x_{-i}) p(x_{-i})$$

This is the weighted average of the player's levels of utility for the possible strategy profiles x_{-i} of the other players, where the weights in the weighting are the player's beliefs $p(x_{-i})$ about these strategy profiles. We will assume that player i will prefer her strategy $\tilde{x}_i$ over the strategy $\tilde{x}_i'$ (under the belief p_{-i}) if and only if the choice of $\tilde{x}_i$ yields her a higher expected utility:

$$U_i(\tilde{x}_i; p_{-i}) > U_i(\tilde{x}_i'; p_{-i})$$

In general, we will assume that the player will prefer a lottery in which the strategy profiles[2] $x \in X$ are realized with the probabilities:

$$p = (p(x))_{x \in X}$$

over the lottery in which these probabilities are:

$$\hat{p} = (\hat{p}(x))_{x \in X}$$

if and only if her expected utility from the first lottery exceeds her expected utility from the second lottery, that is, if:

$$U_i(p) = \sum_{x \in X} u_i(x) p(x) > \sum_{x \in X} u_i(x) \hat{p}(x) = U_i(\hat{p})$$

In a case such as this we say that the expectation U_i of the utility function u_i represents the preferences of player i over the lotteries on strategy profiles.

A discussion of general lotteries of this type amounts to a situation in which player i no longer necessarily chooses her strategy on her own. A state of affairs such as this could come about if the player has empowered an agent or a broker to choose her

[1] Recall that we use the terms "payoff" and "utility" interchangeably.
[2] I.e. the possible combinations of her own strategy along with strategies of the other players.

strategy on her behalf. If the other players, too, have confided the activation of their strategies to that same broker, then $p(x)$ is the probability that the player ascribes to the broker choosing to activate the strategy profile x. Different beliefs, p or $\hat{p}$, define different lotteries, which are differentiated from each other only in the probability ascribed to each strategy profile x; the utility $u_i(x)$ to player i from any given strategy profile x is identical across all these lotteries.

The assumption that the expectation U_i of the utility function u_i represents the preferences of player i over these lotteries restricts the set of payoff functions u_i that we can ascribe to the player for representing her preferences over strategy profiles. In order to see this, let's assume, for example, that player i prefers a particular strategy profile x over the strategy profile x', and prefers x' over the strategy profile x''. So far, we have been able to represent the player's preferences by every triple of numbers:

$$u_i(x) > u_i(x') > u_i(x'')$$

For example, we could have represented the preferences by the three numbers:

$$u_i(x) = 5, \quad u_i(x') = 4, \quad u_i(x'') = 1$$

And also by another triple, such as:

$$\bar{u}_i(x) = 5, \quad \bar{u}_i(x') = 2, \quad \bar{u}_i(x'') = 1$$

But the new assumption that we have introduced above gives rise to a further requirement: the **expectation** of the three numbers ought to represent the player's preferences also over the **lotteries** in which a probability is assigned to every strategy profile (these probabilities summing to 1). Consider, for example, a lottery in which each of the strategy profiles x, x'' is realized with the probability $\frac{1}{2}$. Does the player prefer this lottery over the certain outcome x' (i.e. over the lottery in which x' is realized with probability 1)? If the answer to this is affirmative, then it is possible that the expectation $\bar{U}_i$ of the three payoffs:

$$\bar{u}_i(x) = 5, \quad \bar{u}_i(x') = 2, \quad \bar{u}_i(x'') = 1$$

may represent the player's preferences over the lotteries, since indeed:

$$\frac{1}{2} \times \bar{u}_i(x) + \frac{1}{2} \times \bar{u}_i(x'') = \frac{1}{2} \times 1 + \frac{1}{2} \times 5 = 3 > 2 = \bar{u}_i(x')$$

But the expectation U_i of the three payoffs:

$$u_i(x) = 5, \quad u_i(x') = 4, \quad u_i(x'') = 1$$

does not represent the player's preferences, since:

$$\frac{1}{2} \times u_i(x) + \frac{1}{2} \times u_i(x'') = \frac{1}{2} \times 1 + \frac{1}{2} \times 5 = 3 < 4 = u_i(x')$$

Moreover, if the three numbers:

$$\bar{u}_i(x) = 5, \quad \bar{u}_i(x') = 2, \quad \bar{u}_i(x'') = 1$$

represent the player's preferences, she will prefer a lottery between x and x'' over the safe outcome x' if and only if the probability $p(x)$ of x is greater than $\frac{1}{4}$ (and the probability $p(x'')$ of x'' is smaller than $\frac{3}{4}$, since in such a case:

$$\bar{U}_i((p(x), 0, p(x''))) = p(x) \times \bar{u}_i(x) + 0 \times \bar{u}_i(x') + p_i(x'') \times \bar{u}_i(x'')$$
$$> \frac{1}{4} \times 5 + 0 \times 2 + \frac{3}{4} \times 1 = 2 = \overline{u_i}(x') = \bar{U}_i((0, 1, 0))$$

(The expression $\bar{U}_i((p(x), 0, p(x'')))$ is, of course, the expected utility of $\overline{u_i}$ when the strategy profiles (x, x', x'') are realized with the probabilities $(p(x), 0, p(x''))$, respectively. And similarly, the expression $\bar{U}_i((0, 1, 0))$ is the expected utility of $\bar{u}_i$ when the strategy profiles (x, x', x'') are realized with the probabilities $(0, 1, 0)$, i.e. the strategy profile x' is realized with certainty.)

Thus, if u_i is a utility function whose expectation represents the player's preferences over these lotteries, then it carries with it not only ordinal information but also cardinal information. A utility function of this kind is called a **Bernoulli utility function**.[3]

Comprehension check

Demonstrate that, in the above example, if the player's preferences over the lotteries are represented by the expectation of the utility function:

$$\bar{u}_i(x) = 5, \quad \bar{u}_i(x') = 2, \quad \bar{u}_i(x'') = 1 \tag{10.1}$$

then likewise the expectation of the utility function:

$$\bar{\bar{u}}_i(x) = 400, \quad \bar{\bar{u}}(x') = 100, \quad \bar{\bar{u}}(x'') = 0 \tag{10.2}$$

represents the same preferences over lotteries.

Hint: among other things, you must demonstrate that with the utility function $\bar{\bar{u}}_i$, the player prefers the certain outcome x' over a lottery between x and x'' if and only if in this lottery the chance of x is smaller than $\frac{1}{4}$.

---

[3] After Daniel Bernoulli, (1700–1789), one of the founders of probability theory.

More generally, the expectation of two utility functions:

$$\bar{u}_i : X \to R$$
$$\bar{\bar{u}}_i : X \to R$$

represents the same preferences of a player over lotteries between strategy profiles $x \in X$ if there exist numbers $a > 0$ and b such that for every strategy profile $x \in X$ it is the case that:

$$\bar{\bar{u}}_i(x) = a\bar{u}_i(x) + b$$

Indeed, a player with a utility function $\bar{u}_i$ prefers the lottery $p = (p(x))_{x \in X}$ over the lottery $\hat{p} = (\hat{p}(x))_{x \in X}$ if and only if:

$$\bar{U}_i(p) = \sum_{x \in X}\bar{u}_i(x)p(x) > \sum_{x \in X}\bar{u}_i(x)\hat{p}(x) = \bar{U}_i(\hat{p})$$

This inequality is satisfied if and only if:

$$\begin{aligned}\bar{\bar{U}}_i(p) &= \sum_{x \in X}\bar{\bar{u}}_i(x)p(x) = \sum_{x \in X}(a\bar{u}_i(x) + b)p(x) \\ &= a\left(\sum_{x \in X}\bar{u}_i(x)p(x)\right) + b > a\left(\sum_{x \in X}\bar{u}_i(x)\hat{p}(x)\right) + b \\ &= \sum_{x \in X}(a\bar{u}_i(x) + b)\hat{p}(x) = \sum_{x \in X}\bar{\bar{u}}_i(x)\hat{p}(x) = \bar{\bar{U}}_i(\hat{p})\end{aligned}$$

(In the equalities in the formula we have used the fact that $\sum_{x \in X}p(x) = 1$, and therefore $\sum_{x \in X}bp(x) = b$. The inequality in the formula depends on a being positive, because if a were negative the inequality sign would be inverted.)

Comprehension check

Examine the definitions of the utility functions (10.1), (10.2) above. What are the numbers a, b for which $\bar{\bar{u}}_i = a\bar{u}_i + b$ is satisfied?

10.1 — **Monetary payoffs and risk neutrality**

It is important to emphasize that the Bernoulli utility function does not represent monetary payoffs to the player. For example, when the utility function $\bar{u}_i$ is given by (10.1) above, player i may get, for instance, $1,000 when the action profile x is realized, $100 when the action profile x' takes place, and no monetary payoff under the action profile x''. With the utility function $\bar{u}_i$ the player prefers to be certain of getting \$100 (in the action profile x') rather than a lottery which will secure her an expectation of less than \$250 (a lottery in which x' occurs with a chance smaller than $\frac{1}{4}$ and x'' with a chance greater than $\frac{3}{4}$).[4]

We will, of course, encounter games in which the various action profiles entail monetary payoffs to the players. In such games, every action profile $x \in X$ will define a monetary payoff $\pi_i(x)$ to the player i, $i \in I$. In the above example:

$$\pi_i(x) = 1000$$
$$\pi_i(x') = 100$$
$$\pi_i(x'') = 0$$

If every player is interested only in the monetary payoff that she herself receives (i.e. given a certain monetary payoff to herself, she is indifferent among alternative monetary payoff profiles to the other players), we can describe her utility function in the game indirectly, by first defining her utility function v_i over monetary payoffs, and only then defining her utility function u_i over the action profiles $x \in X$ in the game, by:

$$u_i(x) = v_i(\pi_i(x))$$

Thus, in the above example, we can define:

$$\bar{v}_i(0) = 1, \quad \bar{v}_i(100) = 2, \quad \bar{v}_i(1000) = 5$$

In such a case, the player's utility functions from the action profiles in the game will indeed be:

$$\bar{u}_i(x) = \bar{v}_i(\pi_i(x)) = \bar{v}_i(1000) = 5$$
$$\bar{u}_i(x') = \bar{v}_i(\pi_i(x')) = \bar{v}_i(100) = 2$$
$$\bar{u}_i(x'') = \bar{v}_i(\pi_i(x'')) = \bar{v}_i(0) = 1$$

In the particular instance in which for every monetary payoff m to player i it is the case that:

$$v_i(m) = m$$

we say that player i is **risk neutral**. In such a case, the monetary payoff function π to the player is identical with her utility function u_i over the action profiles in the game.

---

[4] In particular, such a player is called **risk averse** since she prefers to obtain with certainty a sum of money (\$100) over a lottery whose average payoff equals that sum of money (\$1,000 with a chance of $\frac{1}{10}$ and \$0 with a chance of $\frac{9}{10}$).

Von Neumann–Morgenstern preferences and the Allais Paradox

Which of a player's preferences over lotteries can be represented by the expectation of a Bernoulli utility function? This question was investigated by von Neumann and Morgenstern, who isolated four properties of preferences that guarantee the possibility of such a representation, and which are satisfied whenever such a representation is possible.[5] The discussion of these properties is beyond the scope of this book, and thus we will not lay them out explicitly here. Preferences satisfying these properties are designated **von Neumann–Morgenstern (vNM) preferences**.

These characterizing properties are not self-evident, and are not always or necessarily satisfied. To demonstrate this, Maurice Allais[6] suggested the following example, which came to be known as the **Allais Paradox**.

Consider the following pair of lotteries:

Lottery A: The player receives $2 million with certainty.
Lottery B: The player receives $10 million with a chance of 10 percent, $2 million with a chance of 89 percent, and gets nothing with a chance of 1 percent.

Which of these two lotteries would you prefer? In a series of experiments it was found that most participants preferred the first lottery over the second.[7] The first lottery promises most people a tremendous improvement in living standards. Even though the second lottery also offers something of a chance for an even greater improvement, there is nonetheless a small chance that no improvement will take place at all. Most people, it would seem, prefer to avoid the risk inhering in the second lottery.

Now consider another pair of lotteries:

Lottery C: The player gets $2 million with a chance of 11 percent, and gets nothing with a chance of 89 percent.
Lottery D: The player gets $10 million with a chance of 10 percent, and nothing with a chance of 90 percent.

What choice would you make between Lottery C and Lottery D? Most participants in the experiments preferred Lottery D over Lottery C. In both these lotteries, the chance of winning a prize is fairly small. The chance is slightly greater in Lottery C but the prize is much bigger in Lottery D.

---

[5] Von Neumann, J. and O. Morgenstern (1947), *Theory of Games and Economic Behavior*, 2nd edn., Princeton University Press.

[6] Allais, M. (1953), "Le comportement de l'homme rationnel devant le risque: critique des postulats et axioms de l'ecole Americaine," *Econometrica* 21, 503–546.

[7] Camerer, C. (1995), "Individual Decision Making," in J. H. Kagel and A. E. Roth (eds.), *The Handbook of Experimental Economics*, Princeton University Press, pp. 537–703.

We will now demonstrate that if a player prefers Lottery A over Lottery B, and Lottery D over Lottery C, then her preferences cannot be represented by an expected utility function. Sure enough, if such a utility function v existed, then:

$$v(2) > 0.1v(10) + 0.89v(2) + 0.01v(0)$$

would be satisfied, since the player prefers Lottery A over Lottery B. Therefore, if we were to add $0.89(v(0) - v(2))$ to each member of the inequality, we would obtain:

$$0.11v(2) + 0.89v(0) > 0.1v(10) + 0.9v(0)$$

and hence, contrary to our assumption, the player would prefer Lottery C over Lottery D.

The Allais Paradox led to the development of alternative and more general theories concerning individuals' preferences over lotteries, and these generalizations are gradually also finding their way into game theory. Nevertheless, at the time of writing this book, game theory is for the most part still based on the assumption that the players' preferences over lotteries are of the vNM type, i.e. that they can be represented by an expected utility function. Accordingly, this is also the assumption to which we will adhere throughout this book.

10.3   Risk dominance

In Chapter 9 we dealt with coordination games in which one of the strategies of each player can assure him with certainty of a particular payoff. What will happen if the payoff from this strategy nevertheless proves to be contingent on the actions of the other players? How can we then compare the degree of risk of the various strategies, and the equilibria in the game? Consider, for example, the following two-player game, which is a slightly different version of the Stag Hunt game:

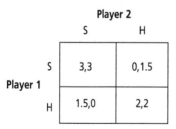

This game differs from the Stag Hunt game in that the payoff to the player who "betrays" his colleague (and bags a hare on his own) is 1.5 and not 2 as we previously assumed. The decrease in payoff may derive, for example, from the fact that the "traitor" suffers social censure for having left his partner unable to hunt the stag, causing him to return home empty-handed. However, if each of the two hunters comes home with a hare, social censure is forestalled. In this game, the strategy H – bagging a hare – is no longer a safe strategy. The payoff from this strategy depends on the other player's strategy, and it may be 1.5 or 2.

We will assume that neither player knows how the other will act, and believes there is an equal chance of $\frac{1}{2}$ that his partner will adopt one of the strategies available to him. Under this belief, strategy H – that of bagging a hare – will yield the player an expected payoff of:

$$\frac{1}{2} \times 1.5 + \frac{1}{2} \times 1 = 1.75$$

which is higher than the expected payoff he will obtain from strategy S – hunting a stag:

$$\frac{1}{2} \times 3 + \frac{1}{2} \times 0 = 1.5$$

In this sense, strategy S is riskier for the player than strategy H. At the equilibrium (H, H) each player chooses the less risky strategy. Therefore, this equilibrium is called **risk dominant**.

Definition

In a symmetric game of two players in which each player has two strategies, an equilibrium is called **risk dominant** if in this equilibrium each player chooses the strategy that maximizes her expected payoff on the assumption that the other player will choose either of the two strategies available to her with equal probability.[8]

Hence, risk dominance is one possible criterion for choosing among the equilibria in games of this type. If each player has very little information on their fellow player, they will probably choose a strategy that will maximize their payoff under the assumption that each of the other player's strategies is equally probable. This is so even if the other equilibrium is more efficient (i.e. gives each player a higher payoff), as in the above example.

Moreover, if a player believes that her fellow does not know how she herself is about to act, the player will also probably believe that her fellow will choose a strategy that will procure her the maximum expected payoff under such a balanced belief. If the game is a coordination game, the player will choose the corresponding strategy for her part, and the equilibrium that will be obtained is the risk-dominant equilibrium.

---

[8] The definition of risk dominance can be extended also to general games, but we will not pursue that extension here. See Harsanyi, J. C. and R. Selten (1988), *A General Theory of Equilibrium Selection in Games*, Cambridge, MA: The MIT Press.

Comprehension check

Give an example of a symmetric coordination game between two players with two strategies per player, in which the risk-dominant equilibrium is also the efficient equilibrium.

Comprehension check

Give an example of a symmetric game between two players with two strategies per player, in which each player has a weakly dominant strategy, but in which there is also an equilibrium at which the players play weakly dominated strategies. Prove that in every game with such properties, the equilibrium at which each of the players chooses the weakly dominant strategy is a risk-dominant equilibrium.

11 Mixed strategies

In the preceding chapters, we discussed the Nash equilibrium concept, and various criteria were proposed for focusing on a subset of the equilibria in the game. But does every game in fact have at least one Nash equilibrium? We will now show that the answer to this is negative.

11.1 The Matching Pennies game

Assume that two players each receive a single coin and are asked to place it with either heads or tails face up on the table. The players must put down their coins simultaneously. If both turn the same side of the coin face up, then player 2 must give her coin to player 1. If each coin is turned with a different face up, player 1 must give her coin to player 2.

Here is the payoffs matrix of the game; the numbers correspond to the profit or loss of each player:

		Player 2	
		Heads	Tails
Player 1	Heads	1,−1	−1,1
	Tails	−1,1	1,−1

Does this game have a Nash equilibrium? We will try to find a Nash equilibrium with the method we described in Chapter 6, by underlining the payoffs of each player when each of them chooses a best reply to the opponent's strategy:

		Player 2	
		Heads	Tails
Player 1	Heads	1,−1,	−1,1
	Tails	−1,1	1,−1

We found that the game does not have a strategy profile in which we underlined both payoffs together. In other words, there is no strategy profile in which each strategy is a best reply to the other. For example, if player 2 chooses heads, player 1 likewise will prefer to choose heads; but in this case, player 2 will prefer to choose tails, and thereupon player 1 likewise will want to choose tails; but player 2 will then counter-react by wishing to choose heads; and so forth. Therefore, this game has no Nash equilibrium.

This is an awkward state of affairs. If the basic solution concept in game theory – the Nash equilibrium – cannot provide a prediction as to the players' behavior in a simple game such as this, how can we know whether we will be able to find a Nash equilibrium when we wish to model a complex social phenomenon?

The solution to this problem comes from an unexpected direction, by means of expanding the strategy set we allow each player to use. In the present case, for example, we will assume that each player is also permitted to toss her coin and let it drop on the table. Assume that the coin has equal chances of falling on either side. Also assume that each player is risk neutral and wishes to maximize her expected payoff given her opponent's strategy.[1]

Now assume that player 2 decides to toss her coin. What will be the expected payoff of player 1 if she chooses heads? The coin tossed by player 2 will land heads up with a probability of $\frac{1}{2}$, in which case player 1 will earn a dollar; and it will land tails up with a probability of $\frac{1}{2}$, whereupon player 1 will lose a dollar. Player 1's expected payoff, therefore, will be:

$$U_1(\text{"heads", "coin toss"}) = \frac{1}{2} \times 1 + \frac{1}{2} \times (-1) = 0$$

What will player 2's expected payoff be in this strategy profile? With a chance of $\frac{1}{2}$, player 2's coin will land heads up and player 2 will lose a dollar, and with a chance of $\frac{1}{2}$ the coin will land tails up and player 2 will gain a dollar. Player 2's expected payoff will therefore be:

$$U_2(\text{"heads", "coin toss"}) = \frac{1}{2} \times (-1) + \frac{1}{2} \times 1 = 0$$

What will player 1's expected payoff be if she chooses tails when player 2 tosses her coin? With a chance of $\frac{1}{2}$, player 2's coin will land heads up and player 1 will lose a dollar, and with a chance of $\frac{1}{2}$, her coin will land tails up and player 1 will gain a dollar. Player 1's expected payoff will now be:

$$U_1(\text{"tails", "coin toss"}) = \frac{1}{2} \times (-1) + \frac{1}{2} \times 1 = 0$$

[1] Recall the definition of "risk neutral player" in Chapter 10.

And similarly, player 2's expected payoff will be:

$$U_2(\text{"tails"}, \text{"coin toss"}) = \frac{1}{2} \times 1 + \frac{1}{2} \times (-1) = 0$$

We have found that if player 2 decides to toss her coin, player 1 will be indifferent among her strategies of heads or tails, since choosing either one of them will lead to the same expected payoff. Hence, player 1 will also be indifferent among any one of these options and the option of tossing her own coin. If she chooses to toss the coin, player 1's expected payoff will likewise be:

$$U_1(\text{"coin toss"}, \text{"coin toss"})$$
$$= \frac{1}{2} U_1(\text{"heads"}, \text{"coin toss"}) + \frac{1}{2} U_1(\text{"tails"}, \text{"coin toss"})$$
$$= \frac{1}{2} \times 0 + \frac{1}{2} \times 0 = 0$$

And also player 2's expected payoff will be:

$$U_2(\text{"coin toss"}, \text{"coin toss"})$$
$$= \frac{1}{2} U_2(\text{"heads"}, \text{"coin toss"}) + \frac{1}{2} U_2(\text{"tails"}, \text{"coin toss"})$$
$$= \frac{1}{2} \times 0 + \frac{1}{2} \times 0 = 0$$

Similarly, if player 1 chooses to toss her coin, the expected payoff of each of the players will be 0 whether player 2 chooses heads, tails, or to toss her coin. Thus, in the expanded game in which we have given each player the additional coin-toss strategy, the (expected) payoffs matrix will be:

| | | Player 2 | | |
		Heads	Coin toss	Tails
Player 1	Heads	1,−1	0,0	−1,1
	Coin toss	0,0	0,0	0,0
	Tails	−1,1	0,0	1,−1

We will now look for a Nash equilibrium in the expanded game by underlining the payoffs of each player when she chooses a best reply against her opponent's strategy:

Player 2

	Heads	Coin toss	Tails
Heads	1,–1	0,0	–1,1
Player 1 Coin toss	0,0	0,0	0,0
Tails	–1,1	0,0	1,–1

Thus, in the expanded game, there exists a single Nash equilibrium, at which each player tosses her coin. Each player is indifferent among her strategies given the fact that her opponent tosses her coin, and particularly her own toss of the coin is equally favorable for her as any other strategy of hers. Therefore, if the two players reach prior agreement to toss their coins, this will be a stable agreement – one that neither will have any incentive to deviate from.

The new strategy – "the coin toss" – is called a **mixed strategy** because, by means of a lottery, it mixes the strategies of the original game with each other. In the expanded game, the strategies of the original game are called **pure strategies**.

More generally, we can expand the game even further by allowing each player to institute additional lotteries among her original strategies. For example, if we equip each player with a dice, she can use it to choose heads with a probability of $\frac{1}{3}$ or tails with a probability of $\frac{2}{3}$. The player can realize a mixed strategy of this kind by throwing the dice (without letting her opponent see what comes up!) and playing heads if the dice comes up 1 or 2, and tails if the dice comes up 3, 4, 5, or 6.

Now assume that every player $i = 1,2$ can choose heads and tails out of any lottery among her two original strategies. A mixed strategy of this kind will be represented by the probability $p_i \in [0,1]$ with which player i chooses heads. (In this mixed strategy, of course, player i chooses tails with the complementary probability of $1 - p_i$.) The game obtained by the addition of all possible mixed strategies is called **the mixed extension of the game**. In this extension, the original strategies of the game – the pure strategies of the expanded game – are represented by the lotteries in which $p_i = 1$ (a certain choice of heads) and $p_i = 0$ (a certain choice of tails). If in the mixed extension of the game there is a Nash equilibrium, we also say that this is a **Nash equilibrium with mixed strategies** of the original game.

Does the mixed extension of the game indeed have a Nash equilibrium? We have already seen that if player 2 tosses her coin, i.e. chooses the mixed strategy $p_2 = \frac{1}{2}$, then the two pure strategies heads and tails yield player 1 an expected utility of 0. Therefore any mixture p_1 by player 1 among her pure strategies will likewise yield the expected utility 0. Thus, if player 2 chooses the mixed strategy $p_2 = \frac{1}{2}$, player 1 is indifferent among all her mixed strategies. In particular, if she undertakes ahead of time to choose her mixed strategy $p_1 = \frac{1}{2}$ (i.e. to toss her coin), then she will have no incentive for deviating from that undertaking as long as she believes that player 2 will adhere to the mixed strategy $p_2 = \frac{1}{2}$. A similar consideration is valid also for player 2, and therefore the strategy profile:

$$(p_1, p_2) = \left(\frac{1}{2}, \frac{1}{2} \right)$$

is a Nash equilibrium in mixed strategies.

Are there additional equilibria in the mixed extension of the game? In order to find out, we must first discover the players' best-reply functions. In particular, for every strategy $p_2 \in [0,1]$ of player 2, we must find the best reply of player 1. If player 2 chooses the mixed strategy p_2 and player 1 chooses the strategy $p_1 = 1$ (i.e. the pure strategy 'heads'), then with a probability of p_2 the action profile (heads, heads) will be realized and player 1 will gain a dollar, and with the complementary probability $1 - p_2$ the action profile (heads, tails)[2] will be realized and player 1 will lose a dollar. Therefore, player 1's expected payoff will be:

$$U_1(1, p_2) = p_2 \times 1 + (1 - p_2) \times (-1) = 2p_2 - 1$$

If, in contrast, player 1 chooses the strategy $p_1 = 0$ (i.e. chooses tails with certainty), then the action profile (heads, tails) will be realized with a probability of p_2 and player 1 will lose a dollar, and with the complementary probability $1 - p_2$, the action profile (tails, tails) will be realized and player 1 will gain a dollar. Player 1's expected payoff will then be:

$$U_1(0, p_2) = p_2 \times (-1) + (1 - p_2) \times 1 = 1 - 2p_2$$

Thus, the pure strategy "heads" is strictly preferable in the eyes of player 1 over the pure strategy "tails" if and only if:

$$2p_2 - 1 = U_1(1, p_2) > U_1(0, p_2) = 1 - 2p_2$$

which is to say, if and only if $p_2 > \frac{1}{2}$. Intuitively, since player 1 wishes to maximize the chance that the side of the coin she chooses will correspond to the side of the coin that her opponent chooses, she will prefer to choose heads if the chance p_2 at which her opponent chooses heads is greater than $\frac{1}{2}$.

Moreover, when $p_2 > \frac{1}{2}$, player 1 will prefer the pure strategy "heads" not only over the pure strategy "tails" but also over any mixed strategy p_1 that satisfies $p_1 < 1$. This is because:

$$U_1(p_1, p_2) = p_1 U_1(1, p_2) + (1 - p_1) U_1(0, p_2)$$

[2] When we denote strategy profiles such as (heads, tails) the left-hand member (heads, in this example) relates to the strategy of player 1 and the right-hand member relates to the strategy of player 2.

and therefore, when $U_1(1, p_2) > U_1(0, p_2)$, a choice of heads with certainty, $p_1 = 1$, is the one that will maximize the expected utility $U_1(p_1, p_2)$.

Similarly, when $p_2 < \frac{1}{2}$ we will obtain that $U_1(1, p_2) < U_1(0, p_2)$, and therefore nothing but the certain choice of tails, $p_1 = 0$, will maximize the expected utility of player 1.

Finally, in the interim case in which $p_2 = \frac{1}{2}$, we will obtain $U_1(1, p_2) = U_1(0, p_2)$, i.e. a certain choice of heads or a certain choice of tails by player 1 will yield her the same expected utility. Therefore, also any mixed strategy p_1 will yield player 1 this expected utility and she will be indifferent among all the mixed and pure strategies at her disposal.

We thus infer that the best reply of player 1 is given by:

$$BR_1(p_2) = \begin{cases} 1 & p_2 > \frac{1}{2} \\ [0,1] & p_2 = \frac{1}{2} \\ 0 & p_2 < \frac{1}{2} \end{cases}$$

Note that BR_1 is not a function but rather a **correspondence**: for every value $p_2 \in [0,1]$, it associates one best reply of player 1 or a set of best replies when there is more than one best reply. For the value $p_2 = \frac{1}{2}$, all the strategies $p_1 \in [0,1]$ of player 1 are best replies – they all yield her the same expected utility.

Similarly, the best reply of player 2 is given by:

$$BR_2(p_1) = \begin{cases} 0 & p_1 > \frac{1}{2} \\ [0,1] & p_1 = \frac{1}{2} \\ 1 & p_1 < \frac{1}{2} \end{cases}$$

The graphs of the best replies of player 1 (in gray) and of player 2 (in black) are shown in Figure 11.1.

The Nash equilibrium of the game is obtained at the intersection point of the two graphs, in the mixed strategies profile:

$$(p_1, p_2) = \left(\frac{1}{2}, \frac{1}{2} \right)$$

11.2   Finding a Nash equilibrium in mixed strategies

How, in general, are we to find the equilibrium in mixed strategies in a game in which each player $i \in I$ has two pure strategies x_i^1, x_i^2?

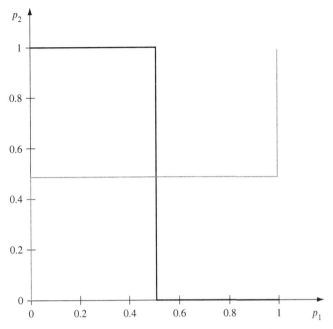

Figure 11.1

As in the preceding example, we will represent a mixed strategy of player i by means of the probability p_i that she chooses her first pure strategy x_i^1 in the original game. If player i adopts the mixed strategy p_i^* at the Nash equilibrium $p^* = \left(p_i^*, p_{-i}^*\right)$, then this strategy will be her best reply against the strategy profile p_{-i}^* of the other players. In other words, the expected payoff that the mixed strategy p_i^* yields player i is the maximum expected payoff she can guarantee herself by means of choosing one of the possible lotteries over her two strategies. This expected payoff is:

$$U_i\left(p_i^*, p_{-i}^*\right) = p_i^* U_i\left(x_i^1, p_{-i}^*\right) + \left(1 - p_i^*\right) U_i\left(x_i^2, p_{-i}^*\right)$$

In this equation, we denote by $U_i\left(x_i^1, p_{-i}^*\right)$ the expected payoff of player i when she adopts the pure strategy x_i^1 and the other players adopt the lotteries p_{-i}^*. We will make alternating use of the notation $U_i\left(x_i^1, p_{-i}^*\right)$ and of the equivalent notation $U_i\left(1, p_{-i}^*\right)$ to denote that player i chooses x_i^1 with the probability $p_i = 1$, i.e. chooses x_i^1 with certainty.

Similarly, we make alternating use of the notations $U_i\left(x_i^2, p_{-i}^*\right)$ and $U_i\left(0, p_{-i}^*\right)$. We use the notation $U_i\left(0, p_{-i}^*\right)$ to denote that player i chooses x_i^1 with the probability $p_i = 0$, and hence with the complementary probability, i.e. with probability 1, the pure strategy x_i^2.

If, at a Nash equilibrium p_i^* is a mixed strategy (in which each of the pure strategies x_i^1, x_i^2 is drawn with a positive probability), i.e. $0 < p_i^* < 1$, then it must be the case that:

$$U_i(x_i^1, p_{-i}^*) = U_i(x_i^2, p_{-i}^*)$$

since otherwise p_i^* would not be a best reply. For example, if it were the case that:

$$U_i(x_i^1, p_{-i}^*) > U_i(x_i^2, p_{-i}^*)$$

we would obtain that:

$$U_i(p_i^*, p_{-i}^*)$$
$$= p_i^* U_i(x_i^1, p_{-i}^*) + (1 - p_i^*) U_i(x_i^2, p_{-i}^*)$$
$$< p_i^* U_i(x_i^1, p_{-i}^*) + (1 - p_i^*) U_i(x_i^1, p_{-i}^*) = U_i(x_i^1, p_{-i}^*)$$

and hence the mixed strategy p_i^* would be inferior for her relative to the pure strategy x_i^1, contrary to the assumption that p_i^* is a best reply of player i to p_{-i}^*.

We hence reach an important conclusion: if at a Nash equilibrium player i adopts a mixed strategy in which she plays with positive probabilities both her two pure strategies, then we may infer that she is indifferent among the choice of any one of her pure strategies (given the equilibrium choice of the other players). Therefore, in order to discover whether there exists a Nash equilibrium in the game in which player i plays a mixed strategy, we must find a strategy profile p_{-i}^* of the other players which will ensure that player i will indeed be indifferent among her pure strategies.

In a game with two players, there is only one additional player j apart from player i. Therefore, in order to discover whether, in such a game, there is a Nash equilibrium at which player i adopts a mixed strategy, we must find a (pure or mixed) strategy p_j^* of player j that will ensure that player i will be indifferent among her two pure strategies. Thus, at such an equilibrium, the equilibrium strategy p_j^* of player j actually depends solely on the payoffs of the rival player i and not on her own payoffs. We will proceed to demonstrate this now.

11.2.1   The Battle of the Sexes

Recall the Battle of the Sexes game in section 6.1, with the payoff matrix:

		Ben	
		Cinema	Theatre
Iris	Cinema	2,1	0,0
	Theatre	0,0	1,2

In this game, it will be recalled, there are two Nash equilibria in pure strategies – the equilibrium (cinema, cinema) and the equilibrium (theatre, theatre). Does this game also have an equilibrium in mixed strategies?

As we have seen, in order for Iris to want to adopt a mixed strategy, in which she goes to the cinema with a probability of p_1 and to the theatre with the complementary probability $(1 - p_1)$, she must be indifferent between these two alternatives, i.e. both must yield her the same expected utility. We therefore need to find a mixed strategy of Ben's, in which he goes to the cinema with a probability of p_2 and to the theatre with the complementary probability $(1 - p_2)$, which will indeed cause Iris to be indifferent between her options. In other words, the probability p_2 must satisfy:

$$U_1(\text{cinema}, p_2) = U_1(\text{theatre}, p_2)$$

When Ben chooses the mixed strategy p_2, Iris's expected utility from going to the cinema is:

$$U_1(\text{cinema}, p_2) = p_2 U_1(\text{cinema}, \text{cinema}) + (1 + p_2) U_1(\text{cinema}, \text{theatre})$$
$$= p_2 \times 2 + (1 - p_2) \times 0 = 2p_2$$

while her expected utility from going to the theatre is:

$$U_1(\text{theatre}, p_2) = p_2 U_1(\text{theatre}, \text{cinema}) + (1 + p_2) U_1(\text{theatre}, \text{theatre})$$
$$= p_2 \times 0 + (1 - p_2) \times 1 = 1 - p_2$$

Therefore, in order for Iris to want to adopt any mixed strategy p_1, Ben must adopt the mixed strategy p_2 which satisfies:

$$2p_2 - 1 - p_2$$

i.e.:

$$p_2 = \frac{1}{3}$$

In other words, if a Nash equilibrium exists in the game at which Iris adopts a mixed strategy, then Ben must adopt, in this equilibrium, the mixed strategy $p_2^* = \frac{1}{3}$.

Does such a Nash equilibrium exist in fact? Does Iris have a strategy – pure or mixed – to which Ben's strategy $p_2^* = \frac{1}{3}$ is a best reply?

As we have seen, in order for any mixed strategy adopted by Ben (and in particular the mixed strategy $p_2^* = \frac{1}{3}$) to be a best reply for him, the strategy p_1 of Iris must cause Ben to be indifferent between his two pure strategies. In other words, the strategy p_1 must satisfy:

$$U_2(p_1, \text{cinema}) = U_2(p_1, \text{theatre})$$

When Iris chooses the mixed strategy p_1, it follows that if Ben goes to the cinema his expected utility will be:

$$U_2(p_2, \text{cinema}) = p_1 U_2(\text{cinema}, \text{cinema}) + (1 - p_1)U_2(\text{theatre}, \text{cinema})$$
$$= p_1 \times 1 + (1 - p_1) \times 0 = p_1$$

and if he goes to the theatre, his expected payoff will be:

$$U_2(p_1, \text{theatre}) = p_1 U_2(\text{cinema}, \text{theatre}) + (1 - p_1)U_2(\text{theatre}, \text{theatre})$$
$$= p_1 \times 0 + (1 - p_1) \times 2 = 2 - 2p_1$$

Thus, if there exists a Nash equilibrium at which Ben adopts some mixed strategy, then at this equilibrium Iris must adopt the mixed strategy p_1 which satisfies:

$$p_1 = 2 - 2p_1$$

i.e.:

$$p_1 = \frac{2}{3}$$

We therefore conclude that in this game the strategy profile:

$$\left(p_1^*, p_2^*\right) = \left(\frac{2}{3}, \frac{1}{3}\right)$$

is a Nash equilibrium with mixed strategies.

In this equilibrium, the players are indifferent between each of their own pure strategies and therefore also consent to draw lots from among them. Each of the players chooses with the probability $\frac{2}{3}$ to head for his or her favorite form of entertainment and with the complementary probability of $\frac{1}{3}$ to head for his or her less preferred form of entertainment.

As calculated above, Iris's expected utility in this equilibrium is:

$$2p_2^* = 1 - p_2^*$$

i.e. $\frac{2}{3}$. Ben's expected utility in the equilibrium is:

$$p_1^* = 2 - 2p_1^*$$

i.e. likewise, $\frac{2}{3}$.

Note that in each of the pure strategy equilibria – (theatre, theatre), (cinema, cinema) – the payoff of each player is at least 1. In the equilibrium in mixed strategies that we have just found, the expected utility of each player is lower, amounting only to $\frac{2}{3}$. This is because, in this equilibrium, there exists a positive probability that each member of the couple will pass the evening alone, an option which both view as inferior to spending time together in any form of entertainment.

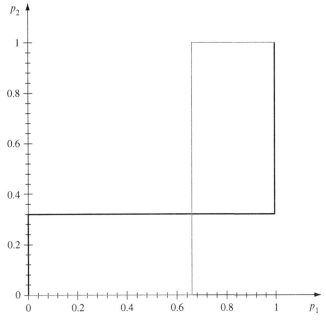

Figure 11.2

(Make your own calculation as to the probability of their spending the evening alone.) The sole virtue of the equilibrium in mixed strategies is that it is symmetric; it yields each member of the couple the same expected utility, whereas in each of the two equilibria in pure strategies, one of the two gets more enjoyment than the other from the time they spend together.

Comprehension check

Find the best-reply correspondences of Iris and of Ben in the Battle of the Sexes game.

Hint: Figure 11.2 describes the best-reply correspondences of the two players. To which of the players does the black graph correspond and to which the gray?

11.3   Mixed strategies in laboratory experiments

When people are involved in a one-off, non-iterative strategic situation, do they in fact play using mixed strategies that correspond to a Nash equilibrium? In a non-recurring strategic situation, we cannot determine whether a player has drawn lots or has made a deterministic choice of one of the strategies that were available to her, but we can check whether or not the distribution of strategies chosen by different players in that strategic situation is close to the distribution of choices over the pure strategies that a mixed equilibrium strategy prescribes. In case of proximity between the two distributions, we can say that the behavior of the population of players as a whole is consistent with the adoption of the mixed equilibrium strategy by each one of them (even though it is very likely that each player separately has actually chosen one of the strategies with certainty and has not instituted any lottery).

Goeree and Holt (2001)[3] examined this question in laboratory experiments of several different versions of the Matching Pennies game. In the first version, each participant in the experiment played, on one single occasion, in a game in which the payoffs were:

		Player 2	
		L	*R*
Player 1	*T*	$0.80, $0.40	$0.40, $0.80
	B	$0.40, $0.80	$0.80, $0.40

This game is completely symmetric, like the original Matching Pennies game. And indeed, close to half the participants who took the role of player 1 chose *T*, while the rest chose *B*; similarly, the distribution of choices of the participants in the role of player 2 was very close to the uniform distribution, 50–50 percent, between the two options. Thus, the results of the experiment are consistent with the prediction of the equilibrium in mixed strategies for this game, according to which each player will choose, with a probability of $\frac{1}{2}$ each of the pure strategies at her disposal.

The picture changed when the experimenters altered one payoff in the game matrix, thus:

		Player 2	
		L	*R*
Player 1	*T*	**$3.20**, $0.40	$0.40, $0.80
	B	$0.40, $0.80	$0.80, $0.40

[3] Goeree, J. K. and C. A. Holt (2001), "Ten Little Treasures of Game Theory and Ten Intuitive Contradictions," *American Economic Review* 91, 1402–1422.

In the new game, too, there exists no equilibrium in pure strategies. At the Nash equilibria in mixed strategies in the new game, player 1 still has to play her strategies with equal probability $(p_1^* = \frac{1}{2})$, even though one of her payoffs has changed significantly. That is because the equilibrium p_1^* strategy of player 1 must cause player 2 to be indifferent between her pure strategies. Since the payoffs of player 2 have not changed from one game to the other, the equilibrium strategy p_1^* must likewise remain intact.

It is, contrariwise, the equilibrium strategy p_2^* of player 2 that must be modified in the new game, in order to ensure that player 1 gets the same expected payoff from each of her strategies. Therefore, the strategy p_2^* in the new game must satisfy:

$$3.20p_2^* + 0.40(1 - p_2^*) = 0.40p_2^* + 0.80(1 - p_2^*)$$

i.e.:

$$p_2^* = \frac{1}{8}$$

The participants' behavior in the experiment, however, was completely different, and the distribution of their choices was not consistent with these equilibrium strategies. A great majority of 96 percent of the participants in the experiment in the role of player 1 chose strategy T, and not half of them as the Nash equilibrium prescribes. It would seem that these participants, consciously or implicitly, assumed that the possible high payoff of 3.20 compatible with the strategy T would lead, on average, to a higher payoff. And sure enough, 84 percent of the participants in the role of player 2 did in fact anticipate that player 1 would make such a choice and chose to reply with the strategy R, which assured them an average payoff of close on 0.80, the maximum possible payoff for them in the game. This percentage does indeed approximate the prediction in the Nash equilibrium, which is $1 - p_2^* = 87.5$ percent. Nevertheless, that remaining 16 percent of participants in the role of player 2 who chose L (and obtained, on average, a lower payoff of close to 0.40) justified, on average, the choice of strategy T by most of the participants taking the role of player 1: the average payoff in the experiment for this strategy was higher than the average payoff for strategy B.

To sum up, the results of the experiment are not consistent with the forecast, since in games with a unique Nash equilibrium in which the strategies are mixed, the players' behavior does not depend on their payoffs but merely on the payoffs of their opponents. An analogous result was also obtained when the experimenters modified the payoff of player 1 in the opposite direction:

Player 2

	L	R
T	$0.44, $0.40	$0.40, $0.80
B	$0.40, $0.80	$0.80, $0.40

Player 1 (rows: T, B)

In this game, a small minority of only 8 percent of the participants in the role of player 1 chose strategy T, while the great majority (92 percent) chose B. Correspondingly, 80 percent of the participants in the role of player 2 chose L, while 20 percent chose R.

11.4   Three possible interpretations of a Nash equilibrium in mixed strategies

In the original Matching Pennies game (section 11.1), the mixed strategy $p_i = \frac{1}{2}$ constitutes a natural action in the game – tossing a coin. In the Battle of the Sexes game (section 11.2.1), however, the mixed strategies do not constitute natural actions on the part of the players. How, then, are we to understand mixed strategies in this game?

Sure enough, each member of the couple in the Battle of the Sexes game can resort to the toss of a dice in order to implement the equilibrium strategies. For example, Iris may decide, ahead of time, on the following plan: she will toss the dice; if one of the numbers 1, 2, 3, or 4 comes up, she will make her way to the cinema; and if the result of the toss is 5 or 6, she will head for the theatre. But tossing the dice is not a natural action in the context of this game. In addition, it is hard to imagine a scenario in which Iris in fact feels obliged to adhere to this plan after tossing the dice: if she believes that Ben will, in fact, adhere to the mixed strategy $p_2^* = \frac{1}{3}$, she will be indifferent between the two alternatives that are available to her and has no special reason to adopt the mixed strategy $p_1^* = \frac{2}{3}$ in particular.

As we have seen, the results of experiments do not back the assumption whereby people draw lots over the alternatives available to them in one-shot strategic interactions. Does an equilibrium in mixed strategies have another, more intuitive meaning? We will now review three possible interpretations of equilibrium in mixed strategies.

11.4.1   Equilibrium in predictions

Recall that one of the interpretations we gave in Chapter 6 to the Nash equilibrium concept is not expressed in terms of the actions that the players take, but rather in terms of the predictions each of them makes concerning the expected actions of the other players. In the example above we can understand the mixed strategy $p_1^* = \frac{2}{3}$ not as an express action taken by Iris, but rather as the probability with which Ben envisages that Iris will go to the theatre. Similarly, Ben's mixed strategy $p_2^* = \frac{1}{3}$ can be understood as a probability that Ben will go to the cinema as seen by Iris. In this interpretation of the equilibrium, the players' beliefs are consistent with one another and confirm one another. This interpretation does not relate to the choices actually made by the players.

11.4.2 Simple rules of thumb in repeated games

Another possible interpretation is relevant for circumstances in which the players find themselves over and over again in the same strategic situation. It is true, in principle, that in every additional round of the game, the players can rely on all the information that is available to them and decide how to act given the actions that they and the other players have taken in all the preceding game rounds. In the last part of this book, we will analyze explicitly rational choice by players in such **repeated games**. However, it may be the case that every player is actually looking for a simple, fixed "rule of thumb" which is completely independent of the history of the game, one which will maximize her average payoff over time. A mixed strategy, in which the player uses again and again a rule of thumb by which prior to each game round she holds a lottery in order to draw the strategy she is to choose for that round, is indeed a simple rule of action of this kind. The greater the number of iterations of the game, the greater, too, will be the chance that the average payoff to the player will in fact be close to the expected payoff from the mixed strategy.[4]

Accordingly, one may think of a Nash equilibrium in mixed strategies as an equilibrium in simple decision rules, that are in no way dependent on the history of the game, when each player wishes to maximize her average payoff over the rounds of the games.

We will now examine two examples.

11.4.2.1 Tennis serves

A tennis match consists of a large number of points. Each point starts off with a serve by one of the players to her opponent. The point may be won there and then if the receiver is unable to respond to the serve,[5] or after the players exchange a number of strokes.

Each time she serves, the server can choose whether to aim the ball to the right or to the left of her opponent's point of departure. If the ball lands to the right of the receiver, she will respond to it with a forehand stroke (if she is right handed), and if it lands to her left, she will respond with a backhand stroke. The receiving player must decide whether

---

[4] This is the Law of Large Numbers from probability theory.
[5] Or, in rarer instances, if the server fluffs the two attempts available to her for launching the game.

to be more prepared for a right-directed ball or for a left-directed ball the very moment the server makes her serve, since the ball travels very fast.

As stated, every tennis match consists of a long series of points and games and therefore the players can decide on serve and preparedness directions as the match progresses as a function of the match history up to that stage. Alternatively, they can disregard the history of the match, and treat each point as a separate game that each of them wants to win. In such a case, a point can be described as a match in which each player must choose between two strategies, right or left, where the payoff of each player is her chance of winning the point. This chance depends, of course, on the strategy profile of the two players as to the court area (right or left) at which the server aims, and the direction for which the receiver prepares. Thus, the following structure of game payoffs is obtained:

		Receiver	
		Right	Left
Server	Right	$\pi_{RR}, 1 - \pi_{RR}$	$\pi_{RL}, 1 - \pi_{RL}$
	Left	$\pi_{LR}, 1 - \pi_{LR}$	$\pi_{LL}, 1 - \pi_{LL}$

The server's chances of winning are presumably higher if she serves in the direction opposite to the one for which the receiver has prepared:

$$\pi_{RR} < \pi_{LR}, \quad \pi_{LL} < \pi_{RL}$$

Likewise, the server's chances of winning are higher if the receiver has prepared to receive from the direction opposite to the serve:

$$\pi_{RR} < \pi_{RL}, \quad \pi_{LL} < \pi_{LR}$$

Question 11.1

Prove that in this game there is no Nash equilibrium in pure strategies.

Answer

Based on the above inequalities, we will underline the payoffs of each player that correspond to her best replies:

		Receiver	
		Right	Left
Server	Right	$\pi_{RR}, \underline{1 - \pi_{RR}}$	$\underline{\pi_{RL}}, 1 - \pi_{RL}$
	Left	$\underline{\pi_{LR}}, 1 - \pi_{LR}$	$\pi_{LL}, \underline{1 - \pi_{LL}}$

In this table we find that the game has no pure strategy profile in which every strategy is a best reply to the opposing strategy. In other words, the game has no Nash equilibrium in pure strategies.

Question 11.2

Assume that the payoffs in the game are:

		Receiver	
		Right	Left
Server	Right	0.1,0.9	0.7,0.3
	Left	0.8,0.2	0.4,0.6

According to this payoff matrix, the receiver has a very high chance (0.9) of winning the point if the server aims to the right and the receiver has in fact prepared to respond with a forehand stroke. The receiver's chances of winning are down to 0.6 if she has correctly prepared for a left-directed serve, to which she has perforce to respond with a backhand stroke (which is in fact more difficult for most players). But if the receiver prepares for a left-directed ball and the server surprises her by serving right, then the server has the greater chance (0.7) of winning the point; and if the server aims left while the receiver prepares for a right-directed ball, then the server's chances of winning soar to 0.8.

Find a Nash equilibrium in mixed strategies in this game. What are each player's chances of winning a point in the equilibrium you have found?

Answer

We will call the server player 1 and the receiver player 2. For each of the players $i = 1,2$, a mixed strategy of player i is represented by the chance p_i of her choosing a "right-directed" strategy.

We are looking for a Nash equilibrium in mixed strategies (p_1^*, p_2^*). In such an equilibrium, player 1 is indifferent between her two pure strategies of right or left; each of them yields her the same expected payoff. Her expected payoff from the right-hand strategy is $0.1p_2^* + 0.7(1 - p_2^*)$ and her expected payoff from the left-hand strategy is $0.8p_2^* + 0.4(1 - p_2^*)$. Therefore, an equilibrium strategy p_2^* on the part of player 2 must satisfy:

$$0.1p_2^* + 0.7(1 - p_2^*) = 0.8p_2^* + 0.4(1 - p_2^*)$$

which is to say:

$$p_2^* = 0.3$$

With this mixed strategy, the server wins the point with a chance of:

$$0.1 \times 0.3 + 0.7 \times (1 - 0.3) = 0.8 \times 0.3 + 0.4 \times (1 - 0.3) = 0.52$$

when she chooses any of her pure strategies, and therefore also when she chooses any mixed strategy whatsoever.

Similarly, at the equilibrium (p_1^*, p_2^*), player 2 is indifferent between her two pure strategies: her expected payoff from the strategy "right-directed", namely $0.9p_1^* + 0.2(1 - p_1^*)$, must be the same as her expected payoff from the strategy "left directed", $0.3p_1^* + 0.6(1 - p_1^*)$. Thus, at a Nash equilibrium, the strategy p_1^* must satisfy:

$$0.9p_1^* + 0.2(1 - p_1^*) = 0.3p_1^* + 0.6(1 - p_1^*)$$

i.e.:

$$p_1^* = 0.4$$

With this mixed strategy, the receiver wins the point with a chance of:

$$0.9 \times 0.4 + 0.2 \times (1 - 0.4) = 0.3 \times 0.4 + 0.6 \times (1 - 0.4) = 0.48$$

when she adopts any one of her pure strategies, and therefore also any mixed strategy (and in particular her equilibrium strategy, $p_2^* = 0.3$).

Thus we have found that:

$$(p_1^*, p_2^*) = (0, 4, 0.3)$$

is the equilibrium of the game in mixed strategies.

In this equilibrium, in 60 percent of points the server aims to the left, in such a way as to force the receiver to respond with a backhand stroke. Correspondingly, the receiver likewise prepares to respond with a backhand stroke with a high chance (70 percent). As a result, in a large proportion 60 percent × 70 percent = 42 percent of serves the server aims left, the receiver likewise prepares for a left-directed serve, and the server wins the point with a chance of 0.4 only (this is the payoff to the server in the lower right-hand entry of the payoff matrix).

In 40 percent of instances, the server tries to surprise her opponent and directs her opening serve to the right. A surprise tactic of this kind succeeds in 70 percent of instances, when the receiver prepares, as usual, for a left-directed serve, and altogether in 40 percent × 70 percent = 28 percent of points. When a surprise tactic of this kind succeeds, the server wins the point with a chance of 0.7.

But the receiver, for her part, will sometimes try to surprise the server and in 30 percent of points employs the diversionary tactic of preparing for a right-directed ball. If this ploy coincides with an attempted surprise on the part of the server, the rightward-aimed ball finds the receiver ready for it and the server's chance of winning the point plummets to 0.1 only. A combination of surprises of this type takes place in a small proportion 40 percent × 30 percent = 12 percent of points.

The receiver is therefore very happy when her attempt to spring a surprise coincides with a similar attempt on the part of the server. But when the receiver tries to surprise the server and prepares for a right-directed ball while the server, as usual, aims left, the receiver's chance of winning the point drops to 0.2. In the equilibrium that we found, this profile occurs in 60 percent × 30 percent = 18 percent of points.

At equilibrium, the frequency with which each player tries to surprise her opponent prevents the opponent from preferring any one of her strategies over another: the opponent has the same chance of winning whether or not the other player tries to surprise her. Therefore, a delicate balance exists at equilibrium, in which each player surprises her opponent at precisely that frequency that in fact enables the opponent likewise to try to spring a surprise every so often, at the equilibrium frequency.

11.4.2.2 Tennis serves in practice

Do professional tennis players really adopt mixed strategies?

Walker and Wooders (2001)[6] examined this question by analyzing ten lengthy tennis matches in which world-class tennis champions met at important international tournaments in the period 1974–1997. Television recordings of these matches enable the viewer to see, in each game, in which direction the server delivers his serve, though not always from which direction the receiver prepares to receive the ball. But even with these incomplete data, we can ask the following:

1. Does the server have identical chances of winning by aiming to the right (the receiver's forehand) or by aiming to the left (the receiver's backhand), as is the case at the Nash equilibrium in mixed strategies?[7]

---

[6] Walker, M. and J. Wooders (2001), "Minimax Play at Wimbledon," *American Economic Review* 91(5), 1521–1538.

[7] In the course of play, players alternate in delivering the opening service. Also, about half the serves take place from the server's right-hand (deuce) side of the court to the receiver's deuce side of the court, and the rest of the serves are delivered from the left (ad) side of the court to the left. Thus, the serves in each match can be divided into four different series, in accordance with the identity of the server and in accordance with the side of the court from which the serve is delivered. The chances of success π_{RR}, π_{RL}, π_{LR}, π_{LL} in the game may perhaps depend on these data. Therefore, Walker and Wooders (2001) each conducted a separate analysis for each of four service series.

2. Are the directions of serving in different games independent as required by a mixed strategy, or does there exist a serial correlation between serves, so that they are not independent?

Walker and Wooders (2001) found that the answer to the first question was affirmative: in the great majority of matches, the chances of success in games in which the server directed the opening serve to the right were almost identical to the chances of success in games in which it was aimed to the left.[8] But they found that the answer to the second question was negative: serve directions in the various games were not independent.[9] Nevertheless, the affirmative answer to the first question indicates that the receiving players had not managed to learn the statistical correlation between the servers' opening serves and were therefore unable to utilize them to their benefit.

11.4.2.3   Penalty kicks in soccer

The penalty kick in soccer taken from 12 yards out from the goal is another natural example in which one can examine whether professional players really adopt mixed strategies when these are called for at the Nash equilibrium of the strategic situation. In a penalty kick, the ball is placed 12 yards from the goal. The penalty taker makes a run-up to the ball and usually kicks it either to the right or the left of the goalie. It takes about one third of a second for the ball to reach the goal. An experienced goalie, therefore, will leap either to the right or to the left the moment the penalty taker touches the ball: if he moves before that, the taker will have time to spot the direction of his move and will kick in the opposite direction; if the goalie moves after the kick, he will usually be too late to reach the ball.

---

[8] Walker and Wooders (2001– see note 6) chose to analyze lengthy matches because such matches provide a rich source of data. They admit, however, that the choice of prolonged matches resulted in a certain bias in the outcomes: these matches may have lasted longer than usual precisely because the players used mixed strategies that corresponded to Nash equilibria, whereas in other professional tennis matches in the same competitions, use of non-equilibrium strategies led to a win for one of the sides within a shorter length of time. This assumption needs to be corroborated or refuted by further empirical research.

[9] In long series of independent lotteries, there exists a non-negligible chance also for short- to medium-range contiguous sequences of identical outcomes. (For example, in tossing a coin 100 times, even though the chance that the first 5 tosses will turn up heads is small, the chance that some contiguous sequence of 5 heads is to be found in the course of 100 tosses is not negligible.) In many experiments it was found that most people find it very difficult to create, by themselves, a series of outcomes that will closely imitate a series of coin-toss outcomes: people make sure that the frequency of the outcomes in a series they have created will be close to the average frequency sought throughout each series and they therefore refrain almost completely from including short to medium contiguous sequences of identical entries in the series they create. Walker and Wooders (2001) diagnosed a similar problem in a series of opening serve directions by servers in the tennis matches they analyzed.

The contest between the penalty kick taker and the goalie therefore very closely resembles that between the server and the receiver in a tennis match in the preceding example: the goalie's chance of stopping the ball is greater if he moves in the direction to which the ball is kicked, and the kicker's chance of scoring a goal is greater if he kicks in the direction opposite to that in which the goalkeeper moves. There are, however, important qualitative differences between the two events. In a tennis match, each point is one of many stages in the same game between the same players. In professional soccer, repeated encounters between any pair of players – penalty taker and goalie – are rare, usually taking place in different soccer matches, with a considerable time interval between them. A certain aspect of a repeated game does, nevertheless, exist here, too, since both professional soccer players and trainers methodically document the behavior of penalty takers and goalies facing penalty kicks and rely on that documentation when preparing for upcoming games.

11.4.2.4   Soccer penalty kicks in practice

Palacios-Huerta (2003)[10] examined the behavior of the players in a database of more than 1,400 penalty kicks in leading European leagues in the years 1995–2000. He found that the average probabilities of a goal being scored were:

		Goalie	
		Left	Right
Kick taker	Left	58.30 %	94.97 %
	Right	92.91 %	69.92 %

In this game, the unique Nash equilibrium is in mixed strategies, and in accordance with this Nash equilibrium, the kick taker must aim leftward with a chance of 41.99 percent, and the goalie must leap to the left with a chance of 38.54 percent. The actual behavior of the players in the database was very close to this prediction: 42.31 percent of kicks were aimed to the left and 39.38 percent of the goalkeepers' moves were in a leftward direction.

The database listed twenty-two penalty kick takers and twenty goalkeepers who took part in at least thirty penalty kicks each. For the great majority, it was found that each of the two strategies (left or right) did in fact yield almost the same chance of success. Moreover, no serial correlation was found between the directions of the

---

[10] Palacios-Huerta, I. (2003), "Professionals Play Minimax," *Review of Economic Studies* 70, 395–415.

kicks/leaps of the players in the sample.[11] Thus, the conclusion of the analysis is that the players' behavior was consistent with the assumption that they employ the Nash equilibrium mixed strategies.[12]

11.4.3   Population games

So far we have dealt with two interpretations of the concept of equilibrium in mixed strategies. One interpretation relates to a player's mixed strategy as a prediction by her opponent (or opponents) regarding her expected actions. According to the second interpretation, a player's mixed strategy is her simple rule of thumb for acting in a repeated game, in which the choice she makes in each round of the game is arrived at by means of a lottery, independently of the previous choices by the opponents and by herself.

A third important interpretation relates to a situation in which each of the players showing up for a game comes from a large population. In every round of the game, representatives are chosen, one from each population, to compete in the game. In other game rounds (taking place simultaneously or at different times), different representatives of the different populations compete. All individuals in a given population have the same payoff function, which will accordingly be called **the population payoff function**, while the game will be called a **population game**.

Every player in each of the populations always adopts the same pure strategy when called into play. This pure strategy is called the player's **type**. If the frequency of types in the various populations corresponds to a Nash equilibrium in mixed strategies in the game defined by the utility functions of the populations, then each type in a population has the same expected payoff.

Now assume that the player's payoff in the game expresses its ability to produce and maintain offspring of the same type, i.e. offspring who adopt the same strategy as the one it uses. A payoff of this sort is called **fitness**. At equilibrium, each type has the same expected payoff and therefore all types of the population have on average the same number of offspring. Hence, at an equilibrium in mixed strategies, the relative frequency of the various types in each population will remain constant over time.

This interpretation of a Nash equilibrium has natural applications in biological systems. In Chapter 16 we will elaborate on the subject of population games.

---

[11] As distinct from tennis, in which a serial correlation was found between the serve directions. It is important to emphasize that not even the absence of a serial correlation between the kick directions of a particular player in different penalty kicks constitutes a proof that the kicker actually conducted a lottery prior to each kick, but only that the kick directions are consistent with such a lottery being conducted.

[12] Chiappori, Levitt and Groseclose (2002) reached similar conclusions by analyzing a smaller penalty kicks database: Chiappori, P. A., Levitt, S. D., and Groseclose, T. (2002), "Testing Mixed Strategy Equilibrium when Players are Heterogeneous: The Case of Penalty Kicks in Soccer," *American Economic Review* 92 (4), 1138–1151.

Comprehension check: consumers and technicians[13]

Everyone sometimes has to resort to the services of an expert technician – a plumber, an electrician, a garage owner, etc. In some cases the technician, to the consumer's delight, determines that the malfunction in question is slight and can be cheaply corrected. In other cases, the technician states that the malfunction is complicated and calls for costly repair. Thereupon, the more naive consumer accepts the technician's ruling without question and agrees to pay for the expensive repair. The more sophisticated consumer, however, will seek a second opinion, hoping that another technician will find that the problem was not so complicated after all and will do the job at low cost. But if the second technician also determines that the problem is complicated, the consumer will often go back to the first technician, regretting both the cost of the repair and the additional time wasted.

The initial suspicion displayed by sophisticated consumers is not without cause. Some technicians, of course, are honest and will not try to sell the consumer a costly repair for an easily fixed problem. Some technicians, however, being less than honest, will always represent to the consumer that the problem is a complicated one.[14] In that way they can collect a high payment even when the repair is easy and simple. They do, however, run the risk that they might be dealing with a sophisticated consumer who may well go somewhere else and not come back unless convinced that the repair really is a complicated one.

Consider the game between the consumer population and the technician population. Suggest a payoff matrix for the game, the nature of which corresponds to the following description:

1. In an encounter with an honest technician, a naive consumer has a higher expected utility than a sophisticated consumer; in an encounter with a dishonest technician, a naive consumer has a lower expected utility than a sophisticated consumer.
2. A dishonest technician will be able to mislead a naive consumer and will obtain a higher utility than an honest technician; in an encounter with a sophisticated consumer, it is, by contrast, the honest technician who has a higher expected utility.

Answer the following questions:

---

[13] The question is based on Osborne, M. J. (2004), *An Introduction to Game Theory*, Oxford University Press, p. 123.

[14] To keep things simple, we will assume that dishonest technicians don't get rumbled: of course, sophisticated consumers who have refused a costly repair and subsequently discovered the fraud may tell their friends the story, but we will assume here that the information fails to reach a substantial proportion of the consumer population.

A. Does the game have a Nash equilibrium in pure strategies?

B. What must be the percentage of honest technicians (out of total technicians) that will ensure that both types of consumers have the same expected utility in a random encounter between a consumer and a technician?

C. What must be the percentage of naive consumers in the consumer population that will ensure that both types of technicians have the same expected utility?

D. What can be said about the combination of the two values you have found in B and C above?

Appendix: Proving the existence of a Nash equilibrium in mixed strategies

Despite the fact that mixed strategies are not always a natural concept, they appeared as far back as Nash's original article in which he presented his equilibrium concept.[15] The reason is that in any game with a finite number of strategies, there exists a Nash equilibrium in pure or mixed strategies. Thus, the mixed strategy notion provides a solution (or solutions) to every game with a finite number of strategies.

In this book, we will not adduce express proof of this existence theorem, instead contenting ourselves with furnishing an explanation of the ideas with the aid of which the theorem is proved. All proofs of the theorem rely on a family of important mathematical theorems called **fixed point theorems**.

In this present discussion, we will continue to focus on a case in which for every player $i \in I$ there are two pure strategies, such that we can present this mixed strategy of hers by the probability $p_i \in [0,1]$ in which she plays the first of the two strategies. At the same time, we note that the ideas we will present here are general and are also valid in the case in which every player has some finite number of pure strategies (as well as in even more general instances with which we will not deal expressly in this book). In Chapter 13 we will define explicitly mixed strategies for games with finitely many strategies for each player.

The set of mixed strategies $p_i \in [0,1]$ of every player i is bounded, closed,[16] and convex.[17] For every mixed strategy profile of the other players, $p_{-i} = (p_j)_{j \neq i}$, we

---

[15] Nash, J. F. (1950), "Equilibrium Points in N-person Games," *Proceedings of the National Academy of Sciences* 36, 48–49; Nash, J. F. (1951), "Non-Cooperative Games," *Annals of Mathematics* 54 (2), 286–295.

[16] I.e. contains its boundary points 0 and 1.

[17] I.e. for every pair of mixed strategies $p_i, p_i' \in [0, 1]$, their weighted average $\alpha p_i + (1 - \alpha)p_i'$ is likewise a mixed strategy, for every $\alpha \in [0,1]$.

will denote by $BR_i(p_{-i})$ player i's set of best replies against p_{-i}. As we saw in the examples of the Matching Pennies and Battle of the Sexes games, a player sometimes has more than one best reply to a strategy (or a strategy profile) of the player (or players) against whom she is competing. The set of best replies $BR_i(p_{-i})$ satisfies the following properties:

1. $BR_i(p_{-i})$ is not **empty**, i.e. player i always has at least one best reply to any strategy profile p_{-i} of the other players.[18]
2. $BR_i(p_{-i})$ is a **convex** set.[19] (For example, in the Matching Pennies game or the Battle of the Sexes game, we saw that the set of best replies was always an entire interval which is indeed a convex set, or a single point which likewise constitutes a convex set.)
3. $BR_i(p_{-i})$ is a **closed** set, i.e. it contains its boundary points.[20] (For example, in the Matching Pennies game or the Battle of the Sexes game we saw that when the best reply set was the interval $[0,1]$, it did in fact contain the boundary points 0 and 1.)
4. The correspondence that associates to any $p_{-i} \in [0,1]$ the best reply set $BR_i(p_{-i})$ has a **closed graph**. In other words, if p_{-i}^n is a series of mixed strategy profiles of the other players, which converges to the limiting strategy profile p_{-i}:

---

[18] This property derives from the following facts:
1. For any given strategy profile p_{-i} of the other players, the expected utility $U_i(p_i, p_{-i})$ of player i varies continuously as a function of p_i.
2. The strategy set $p_i \in [0,1]$ of player i is a closed and bounded set.
3. For every continuous function defined on a closed and bounded set, there is a point in the set at which the function attains its maximum value.

[19] For a given strategy profile p_{-i} of the other players, to every pair of best replies
$$p_i, p_i' \in BR_i(p_{-i})$$
the expected utility function U_i attains the same maximum value:
$$U_i(p_i, p_{-i}) = U_i(p_i', p_{-i}) = M$$
Therefore, U_i will attain the same maximal value also for the strategy $\alpha p_i + (1-\alpha)p_i'$ for $0 < \alpha < 1$:
$$U_i(\alpha p_i + (1-\alpha)p_i', p_{-i})$$
$$= \alpha U_i(p_i, p_{-i}) + (1-\alpha)U_i(p_i', p_{-i}) = \alpha M + (1-\alpha)M = M$$
Hence we conclude that also the strategy $\alpha p_i + (1-\alpha)p_i'$ is a best reply to p_{-i}, i.e.
$$\alpha p_i + (1-\alpha)p_i' \in BR_i(p_{-i})$$

[20] For a given strategy profile p_{-i} of the other players, the expected utility function $U_i(p_i, p_{-i})$ obtains the same maximum value M in the strategy set $BR_i(p_{-i})$. Therefore, the function $U_i(p_i, p_{-i})$ obtains the same maximum value M also at the boundary points of $BR_i(p_{-i})$, since U_i is a continuous function. Hence it follows that the strategies that are the boundary points of $BR_i(p_{-i})$ are likewise optimal as against p_{-i}, and therefore they themselves belong to the best reply set $BR_i(p_{-i})$.

$$\lim_{n \to \infty} p^n_{-i} = p_{-i}$$

and $p^n_i \in BR_i(p^n_{-i})$ is a sequence of best replies of player i against these strategy profiles, which converges to a mixed strategy p_i:

$$\lim_{n \to \infty} p^n_i = p_i$$

then the limit strategy p_i is a best reply to the limit strategy profile p_{-i}:[21]

$$p_i \in BR_i(p_{-i})$$

Now, for every strategy profile $(p_i)_{i \in I}$ of all the players, we will define the correspondence:

$$BR\big((p_i)_{i \in I}\big) = \Big\{ (p'_i)_{i \in I} : \quad p'_i \in BR_i(p_{-i}), \quad i \in I \Big\}$$

BR associates to every strategy profile of **all the players** $(p_i)_{i \in I}$ those strategy profiles $(p'_i)_{i \in I}$ in which for every player $i \in I$, her strategy p'_i is a best reply to the strategy profile $(p_{-i}) = (p_j)_{j \neq i}$ of the other players. The correspondence BR is defined by means of the correspondences BR_i and therefore BR also has a closed graph, and for every strategy profile $(p_i)_{i \in I}$, the set $BR\big((p_i)_{i \in I}\big)$ is convex, closed, and non-empty.

The correspondence BR is useful because the strategy profile $(p^*_i)_{i \in I}$ is a Nash equilibrium of the game (i.e. a strategy profile in which the strategy of each player is a best reply to the strategies of the other players) if and only if:

$$(p^*_i)_{i \in I} \in BR\Big((p^*_i)_{i \in I} \Big)$$

that is to say, if and only if $(p^*_i)_{i \in I}$ is a fixed point of the correspondence BR. Therefore, in order to prove that there exists a Nash equilibrium in the game, one must show that the correspondence BR does indeed have a fixed point.

To this effect we can now employ the following fixed point theorem.

Theorem 11.1: Kakutani's fixed point theorem

If Y is a closed, bounded, and convex domain, and for every $y \in Y$ the correspondence f associates to y a set $f(y) \subseteq Y$ which is convex, closed, and non-empty, and moreover the correspondence f from Y to Y has a closed graph, then f has a fixed point y^*. In other words, there exists a point $y \in Y$ which satisfies:

$$y^* \in f(y^*)$$

---

[21] Here, this property follows from the fact that the expected utility function U_i is continuous.

If we now apply the theorem to the domain Y which is the set of the mixed strategy profiles of the players:

$$y = [0, 1] \times \ldots \times [0, 1]$$

and to the correspondence:

$$f = BR$$

we can hence deduce that the correspondence BR has a fixed point $(p_i^*)_{i \in I}$. This fixed point is a Nash equilibrium of the game.

12 Security strategies, strictly competitive games and the minimax theorem

12.1 Security strategies

The development of game theory gained heightened momentum at the end of the Second World War, during the cold war between the United States and the USSR. Following the world war, the two powers embarked on an arms race, both stock-piling ever increasing quantities of nuclear weapons. The nuclear bombardment of the Japanese towns of Hiroshima and Nagasaki at the end of the Second World War exemplified the horror involved in the use of this type of weapon. "Worst-case" scenarios kept strategic advisers intensively busy.

One of the first solution concepts developed in game theory does indeed relate to the assumption that the opponent has evil intent, and that all that remains to the player is to try to moderate, insofar as possible, the damage that the opponent is liable to inflict. A strategy achieving that aim is called a **security strategy**.

Consider, for instance, the following game:[1]

12.1.1 Example

		Player 2		
		L	M	R
Player 1	T	2,0	3,3	0,2
	B	1,3	0.5,0	3,1

What is player 2's security strategy in this game?

In order to find the security strategy, player 2 must examine each of her strategies and ask herself first: "If I adopt this strategy, what is the lowest payoff I am liable to obtain?"

---

[1] In this and later examples, unless expressly indicated otherwise, we are relating to the game itself and not to its mixed extension, i.e. we are discussing pure strategies only.

- If she chooses L, she is liable to obtain a payoff as low as 0 (if player 1 chooses T).
- If she chooses M, she is liable to obtain a payoff as low as 0 (if player 1 chooses B).
- If she chooses R, she is liable to obtain a payoff as low as 1 (if player 1 chooses B).

Therefore, player 2's security strategy is R: if she chooses this strategy, her payoff will be at least 1. If she chooses any of her other strategies, her payoff might be 0.

12.1.2   Definition of a security strategy

We will now proceed to define explicitly the security strategy concept:

Definition $\hat{x}_i$ is a **security strategy** of player i if it maximizes the minimal payment she is liable to obtain as a result of the other players' choices. In other words, $\hat{x}_i$ is a security strategy if it is the case that:

$$\min_{x_{-i} \in X_{-i}} u_i(\hat{x}_i, x_{-i}) \geq \min_{x_{-i} \in X_{-i}} u_i(x_i, x_{-i})$$

for every $x_i \in X_i$.

A security strategy is often also called a maxmin strategy, since it **maximizes** the player's payoff under the assumption that no matter what strategy she chooses, her opponents will choose a strategy profile that will **minimize** her payoff.

Comprehension check

Verify that:

1. If, in a given game, one of the players i has a dominant strategy $\tilde{x}_i$, then this strategy is likewise her security strategy.
2. If, in a given game, one of the players i has a strategy x_i that is dominated by another strategy x'_i, then the strategy x_i is not her security strategy.

Question 12.1   Find player 1's security strategy in the game in the example in section 12.1.1.

Answer
- If player 1 chooses T, the lowest payoff she is liable to get is 0 (in the event that player 2 chooses R).
- If player 1 chooses B, the lowest payoff she is liable to obtain is 0.5 (in the event that player 2 chooses M).

Therefore, player 1's security strategy is B: it guarantees her a minimal payoff which is higher than the minimal payoff which T guarantees.

Question 12.2   Does the game in example 12.1.1 have a Nash equilibrium in pure strategies? If so, find it.

Answer   For every player and for every one of her opponent's pure strategies, we will underline in the game matrix the payoff corresponding to the best reply of the player to that strategy of the opponent:

Player 2

		L	M	R
Player 1	T	2,0	3,3	0,2
	B	1,3	0.5,0	3,1

The strategy profile (T,M) is the only one in which we have underlined the payoffs of the two players. Therefore, this is the only strategy profile in which the strategy of each player is a best reply to her opponent's strategy, i.e. this is the only Nash equilibrium in the game in pure strategies.

Thus, we have found that in example 12.1.1, the security strategy profile (B,R) is completely different from the Nash equilibrium strategy profile (T,M). What is the reason for this difference?

When player 2 prepares for the worst-case scenario from her point of view, she ignores the question of whether such a scenario is reasonable. For example, when player 2 considers the strategy M, she fears a scenario in which player 1 chooses B. This in spite of the fact that player **1 will certainly not want** to choose B (but, on the contrary, will opt for T) if she knows that player 2 is choosing M. Indeed, if player 2 chooses M, then player 1 must act erroneously or irrationally in order not to choose T. Nevertheless, assuming the worst-case scenario, player 2 also takes this slight risk into account and refrains, on account of it, from choosing M.

Similarly, assuming the worst-case scenario, player 1 refrains from choosing T since she fears a state of affairs in which player 2 will choose R – even though player 2, if she is rational, will not choose R (but rather M) if she knows that player 1 is choosing T.

Comprehension check

Give an example of a 2×2 game (with two players and two strategies per player) in which there is a unique equilibrium which is obtained by iterative elimination of strongly dominated strategies, but the equilibrium strategy profile is distinct from the players' security strategy profile. (Hint: design the payoffs in such a way that the strategy of player 1, which is eliminated in the first elimination round, yields player 2 her lowest payoff in the game if she adopts her equilibrium strategy.)

Question 12.3

Assume that player 1 also takes into account mixed strategies. What is her security strategy in the mixed extension of the game in example 12.1.1? What is the (expected) payoff that this security strategy guarantees player 1?

Answer

A mixed strategy of player 1 is characterized by the probability $p \in [0,1]$ with which she chooses T (and hence she chooses B with the complementary probability $1 - p$).

- If player 2 chooses L, the expected payoff of player 1 will be $2p + (1 - p)$.
- If player 2 chooses M, the expected payoff of player 1 will be $3p + 0.5(1 - p)$.
- If player 2 chooses R, the expected payoff of player 1 will be $3(1 - p)$.

These payoffs, as a function of the strategy p, are described in Figure 12.1:

- in black – if player 2 chooses L;
- in gray – if player 2 chooses M;
- in the dashed black line – if player 2 chooses R.

For every mixed strategy p, the lowest expected payoff that player 1 is liable to obtain is described by the lower contour line of these graphs:

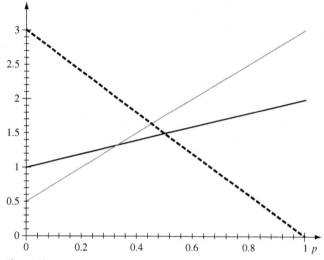

Figure 12.1

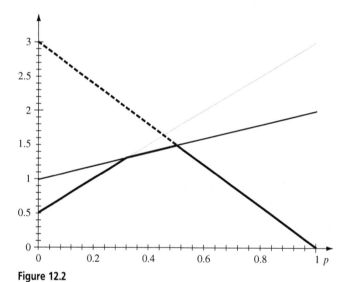

Figure 12.2

- by the gray line for the strategies $p \in \left[0, \frac{1}{3}\right]$;
- by the black line for the strategies $p \in \left[\frac{1}{3}, \frac{1}{2}\right]$;
- by the dashed line for the strategies $p \in \left[\frac{1}{2}, 1\right]$.

The lower contour line is shown in bold in Figure 12.2. It describes the minimal expected payoff that player 1 is liable to obtain. In order to choose a security strategy, she seeks the strategy $\hat{p}$ which will maximize this minimal expected payoff. In other words, $\hat{p}$ is the strategy that maximizes the lower contour line.

In the present example, $\hat{p} = \frac{1}{2}$. This security strategy gives player 1 an expected payoff of 1.5. This is higher than the payoff of 0.5 which she could guarantee herself by means of the pure strategy B (i.e. by means of the strategy $p = 0$).

Among the pure strategies, strategy B confers the highest payoff on the player assuming the worst-case scenario. But if player 1 is indifferent to the risk that she herself is assuming, and is interested solely in her expected payoff when adopting a mixed strategy, she can guarantee herself the highest expected payoff by means of the mixed strategy $\hat{p} = \frac{1}{2}$.

The strategy $\hat{p} = \frac{1}{2}$ guarantees that for any strategy of player 2, the expected payoff of player 1 will be the average of the payoffs she can obtain from her two strategies:

- The expected payoff of player 1 will be 1.5 if player 2 chooses L.
- The expected payoff of player 1 will be 1.75 if player 2 chooses M.
- The expected payoff of player 1 will be 1.5 if player 2 chooses R.

This **averaging** moderates the volatility of the payoff to player 1 which inheres in her choice of one of the pure strategies at her disposal. When player 1 chooses T, her payoffs may range between 0 and 3, and when she chooses B her payoffs may range between 0.5 and 3. When she chooses the mixed strategy $\hat{p} = \frac{1}{2}$, the fluctuation range of the (expected) payoff is much smaller – between 1.5 and 1.75. Moreover, the lowest bound of this payoffs range – 1.5 – is higher than the lowest bound with any one of the pure strategies.

Will player 1's security strategy be different if she assumes that Player 2 may also adopt a mixed strategy? The answer to this question is negative. A mixed strategy on the part of player 2 is a lottery between her pure strategies.[2] Given a mixed strategy p of player 1, one of the **pure** strategies of player 2 (the color corresponding to which is shown in bold in Figure 12.2) is most harmful to player 1, whereas the other strategies of player 2 are equally harmful or less harmful to player 1. Therefore, if player 2 adopts a mixed strategy, the expected payoff to player 1 will never be smaller than that described on the lowest, bold contour line in the figure. This bold graph accordingly describes the minimal expected payoff that player 1 is liable to obtain (as a function of her mixed strategy p) whether player 2 adopts pure or mixed strategies. In other words, this graph describes the function that player 1 wishes to maximize when she prepares for what is, from her point of view, the worst-case scenario, and the strategy $\hat{p} = \frac{1}{2}$ maximizes that function.

---

[2] Player 2 has three pure strategies. In the next chapter, we will formally define the meaning of a mixed strategy on the part of a player who has more than two pure strategies.

12.1.3   The payoff at a Nash equilibrium as compared with the payoff guaranteed by a security strategy

In the example in 12.1.1 above we saw that the strategy B guarantees player 1 the payoff 0.5, and the strategy $\hat{p} = \frac{1}{2}$ guarantees her a higher expected payoff, 1.5. This expected payoff is still smaller than the payoff of 3 that player 1 obtains at the Nash equilibrium (T, M).

This is a logical state of affairs: when player i is preparing for the worst-case scenario, she does not necessarily respond optimally to the chosen strategy profile x^*_{-i} of the other players, but rather to that hypothetical strategy profile of theirs, $\tilde{x}_{-i}$, which is liable to inflict the maximum damage upon her, given the strategy she herself chooses.

Proposition 12.1

....

The player's payoff at a Nash equilibrium is never smaller than the payoff she could guarantee herself by means of a security strategy.

Proof[3]

Assume that $\left(x^*_i, x^*_{-i}\right)$ is a Nash equilibrium. In particular, x^*_i is a best reply of player i to x^*_{-i}. That is:

$$U_i\left(x^*_i, x^*_{-1}\right) \geq U_i\left(x_i, x^*_{-i}\right)$$

for every strategy $x_i \in X_i$ of player i. For every such strategy it is, of course, the case that:

$$U_i\left(x_i, x^*_{-i}\right) \geq \min_{x_{-i} \in X_{-i}} U_i(x_i, x_{-i})$$

(the payoff $U_i\left(x_i, x^*_{-i}\right)$ of player i is not smaller than the payoff $\min_{x_{-i} \in X_{-i}} U_i(x_i, x_{-i})$ that she would have obtained had the other players colluded against her in order to inflict the greatest possible damage given the strategy x_i).

From the two inequalities jointly we deduce that:

$$U_i\left(x^*_i, x^*_{-i}\right) \geq \min_{x_{-i} \in X_{-i}} U_i(x_i, x_{-i})$$

---

[3] In setting forth this proof, we will denote by x_i the strategy of player i. The proof is valid for any game, and in particular for a game that is the mixed extension of another basic game. In this case, the strategies x_i of player i in the mixed extension game are her mixed strategies of the basic game.

for every strategy $x_i \in X_i$ of player i. In particular, the inequality persists if player i chooses her security strategy $\hat{x}_i$, i.e. the one which maximizes $\min_{x_{-i} \in X_{-i}} U_i(x_i, x_{-i})$:

$$U_i(x_i^*, x_{-i}^*) \geq \min_{x_{-i} \subset X_{-i}} U_i(\hat{x}_i, x_{-i}) = \max_{x_i \in X_i} \min_{x_{-i} \in X_{-i}} U_i(x_i, x_{-i})$$

QED

12.2   Strictly competitive games and zero sum games

Are there games in which the equilibrium payoffs are identical to the payoffs the players can guarantee themselves by means of security strategies? Are there games in which the players' security strategies are equilibrium strategies?

In the example in 12.1.1 we saw that the gap between the security strategy B of player 1 and her equilibrium strategy derives from player 1's extreme fears. In preparing for the worst-case scenario, she balks at choosing T for fear that her opponent will choose R. This in spite of the fact that the choice of T on her part will cause her opponent to opt, contrariwise, for the choice of M – a choice that will lead to a high payoff profile for both of them.

Player 1's fears are, however, understandable in games in which the interests of the two players are **strictly opposed**. If a low payoff to player 1 always entails a high payoff to player 2, then player 1 rightly fears that player 2 is constantly trying to injure her – not out of ill will for its own sake but simply out of player 2's wish to increase her own payoff. In this case, the game is said to be strictly competitive.

Definition   A **strictly competitive game** is a game between two players in which, for each pair of strategy profiles $x, x' \in X$, player 1 prefers x over x' if and only if player 2 prefers x' over x, i.e.:

$$U_1(x) > U_1(x')$$

if and only if:

$$U_2(x') > U_2(x).$$

This state of affairs is satisfied, for example, in games between two players in which, for every strategy profile (x_1, x_2), the sum of the players' payoffs amount to zero:

$$U_1(x_1, x_2) + U_2(x_1, x_2) = 0$$

i.e.

$$U_1(x_1, x_2) = -U_2(x_1, x_2)$$

Definition   A game in which for every strategy profile (x_1, x_2) the sum of the players' payoffs is zero is called a **zero sum game**.

The Matching Pennies game in section 11.1 is an example of a zero sum game. In effect, any game between two risk-neutral players, in which a loss for one of them entails a monetary payment from her to her opponent, is a zero sum game. For example, if, in a game of chess, the loser pays her opponent a certain sum of money (while in case of a draw no payments are made), then when the monetary profit of either player is identical to her (Bernoulli) utility function, the game is a zero sum game.

In a strictly competitive game, doing one's best against the opponent also means being cautious of her. Every equilibrium strategy is also a security strategy, and therefore there is no gap between the equilibrium payoffs and those payoffs that can be guaranteed by means of a security strategy. This is the import of the following theorem.

Theorem 12.1

If (p_1^*, p_2^*) is a Nash equilibrium in mixed strategies[4] in a two-player strictly competitive game, then:

- p_1^* is a security strategy of player 1 and p_2^* is a security strategy of player 2;
- the payoff that each player obtains at equilibrium is the highest payoff that she can guarantee herself in the game:

$$U_1\left(p_1^*, p_2^*\right) = \max_{p_1} \min_{p_2} U_1(p_1, p_2)$$

$$U_2\left(p_1^*, p_2^*\right) = \max_{p_2} \min_{p1} U_2(p_1, p_2)$$

Proof

p_2^* is a best reply of player 2 to p_1^*, i.e. for every mixed strategy p_2 of player 2, it is the case that:

---

[4] So far we have defined (in Chapter 11) mixed strategies for games in which each player has two pure strategies. In the next chapter we will extend the concept of a mixed strategy (which is a lottery between the player's pure strategies) also to the case in which a player has finitely many pure strategies. Theorem 12.1 and any discussion further along in this chapter hold good, *verbatim*, also for the more general case, in which each player has some finite number of pure strategies.

$$U_2\left(p_1^*,p_2^*\right) \geq U_2\left(p_1^*,p_2\right)$$

Since the game is one with strictly opposing interests, then for every mixed strategy p_2 of player 2 it is the case that:

$$U_1\left(p_1^*,p_2^*\right) \leq U_1\left(p_1^*,p_2\right)$$

In other words, given that player 1 chooses p_1^*, then at the equilibrium $\left(p_1^*,p_2^*\right)$ player 1 obtains her lowest possible payoff:

$$U_1\left(p_1^*,p_2^*\right) = \min_{p_2} U_1\left(p_1^*,p_2\right)$$

Moreover, for every mixed strategy p_1 of player 1, it is the case that:

$$U_1\left(p_1^*,p_2^*\right) \geq U_1\left(p_1,p_2^*\right) \geq \min_{p_2} U_1(p_1,p_2)$$

The first inequality derives from the fact that the equilibrium strategy p_1^* is a best reply of player 1 to p_2^*; the second inequality derives from the fact that the payoff $U_1\left(p_1,p_2^*\right)$ of player 1 is not smaller than the payoff $\min_{p_2} U_1(p_1,p_2)$ that she would obtain if player 2 were to try to inflict on her as much damage as possible, given the strategy p_1.

Thus, we conclude that for every mixed strategy p_1 of player 1, it is the case that:

$$\min_{p_2} U_1\left(p_1^*,p_2\right) = U_1\left(p_1^*,p_2^*\right) \geq \min_{p_2} U_1(p_1,p_2)$$

Hence it follows that p_1^* is a security strategy of player 1, and it is the case that:

$$U_1\left(p_1^*,p_2^*\right) = \max_{p_1} \min_{p_2} U_1(p_1,p_2)$$

thus proving the claim of the theorem for player 1.

The proof for player 2 is analogous, and is obtained by reversing the names of the players in the course of the argument.

QED

In the case of a zero sum game, in which $U_2 = -U_1$, it is the case that:

$$\min_{p_1} U_2(p_1,p_2) = -\max_{p_1} U_1(p_1,p_2)$$

(This is because if a function $F(p_1)$ attains its maximum value M at the point $\tilde{p}_1$, then the function $G(p_1) = -F(p_1)$ attains its minimal value at that same point $\tilde{p}_1$, and that minimal value is $G(\tilde{p}_1) = -F(\tilde{p}_1) = -M$. In the above equality, we have used this property for the function $F(p_1) = U_1(p_1, p_2)$, for some fixed p_2.)

Hence it follows that:

$$\max_{p_2} \min_{p_1} U_2(p_1,p_2) = \max_{p_2}\left(- \max_{p_1} U_1(p_1,p_2) \right) = - \min_{p_2} \max_{p_1} U_1(p_1,p_2)$$

(This is because, if any function $f(p_2)$ attains its minimal value m at the point $\tilde{p}_2$, then the function $g(p_2) = -f(p_2)$ attains its maximum value at that same point $\tilde{p}_2$, and that maximum value is $g(\tilde{p}_2) = -f(\tilde{p}_2) = -m$. In the second equality in the above equation, we have used this property for the function $f(p_2) = \max_{p_1} U_1(p_1,p_2)$.)

With the aid of this equality, in the next section we can infer from Theorem 12.1 the following important theorem.

12.3   The minimax theorem

Theorem 12.2: The minimax theorem

In every zero sum game it is the case that:

$$\max_{p_1} \min_{p_2} U_1(p_1,p_2) = \min_{p_2} \max_{p_1} U_1(p_1,p_2)$$

$$\max_{p_2} \min_{p_1} U_2(p_1,p_2) = \min_{p_1} \max_{p_2} U_2(p_1,p_2)$$

Likewise, if (p_1^*,p_2^*) is a Nash equilibrium in mixed strategies in a zero sum game between two players, then:

$$\max_{p_1} \min_{p_2} U_1(p_1,p_2) = \min_{p_2} \max_{p1} U_1(p_1,p_2) = U_1(p_1^*,p_2^*)$$

And similarly:

$$\max_{p_2} \min_{p_1} U_2(p_1,p_2) = \min_{p_1} \max_{p2} U_2(p_1,p_2) = U_2(p_1^*,p_2^*)$$

Proof

Assume that (p_1^*,p_2^*) is a Nash equilibrium of the game. We have shown that in a zero sum game it is the case that:

$$\max_{p_2} \min_{p_1} U_2(p_1,p_2) = - \min_{p_2} \max_{p_1} U_1(p_1,p_2)$$

From Theorem 12.1 we know that:

$$U_2(p_1^*,p_2^*) = \max_{p_2} \min_{p_1} U_2(p_1,p_2)$$

Since the game is a zero sum game, we also know that:

$$U_1\left(p_1^*,p_2^*\right) = -U_2\left(p_1^*,p_2^*\right)$$

and from Theorem 12.1 we know that:

$$U_1\left(p_1^*,p_2^*\right) = \max_{p_1}\min_{p_2} U_1(p_1,p_2)$$

From these four equalities taken together we deduce that:

$$\max_{p_1}\min_{p_2} U_1(p_1,p_2) = U_1\left(p_1^*,p_2^*\right) = -U_2\left(p_1^*,p_2^*\right)$$

$$= -\max_{p_2}\min_{p_1} U_2(p_1,p_2) = \min_{p_2}\max_{p_1} U_1(p_1,p_2)$$

as required.

In an analogous way, it can be proved that for player 2:

$$\max_{p_2}\min_{p_1} U_2(p_1,p_2) = \min_{p_2}\max_{p_1} U_2(p_1,p_2) = U_2\left(p_1^*,p_2^*\right)$$

The proof is obtained by reversing the names of the players in the above argument.

Finally, in the appendix to Chapter 11, we proved that in every game (with a finite number of strategies per player) there exists a Nash equilibrium in mixed strategies. This theorem also holds true for zero sum games, and we can infer from it that in every zero sum game there does in fact exist a Nash equilibrium $\left(p_1^*,p_2^*\right)$ in mixed strategies. Therefore, from the equalities:

$$\max_{p_1}\min_{p_2} U_1(p_1,p_2) = \min_{p_2}\max_{p_1} U_1(p_1,p_2) = U_1\left(p_1^*,p_2^*\right)$$

$$\max_{p_2}\min_{p_1} U_2(p_1,p_2) = \min_{p_1}\max_{p_2} U_2(p_1,p_2) = U_2\left(p_1^*,p_2^*\right)$$

we may deduce that:

$$\max_{p_1}\min_{p_2} U_1(p_1,p_2) = \min_{p_2}\max_{p_1} U_1(p_1,p_2)$$

$$\max_{p_2}\min_{p_1} U_2(p_1,p_2) = \min_{p_1}\max_{p_2} U_2(p_1,p_2)$$

QED

12.3.1   Comments on the minimax theorem

A. What is the meaning of the equality:

$$U_1^* = \max_{p_1}\min_{p_2} U_1(p_1,p_2) = \min_{p_2}\max_{p_1} U_1(p_1,p_2)$$

for Player 1? The equality:

$$U_1^* = \max_{p_1}\min_{p_2} U_1(p_1,p_2)$$

expresses the fact that for every mixed strategy p_2 of player 2, player 1 can find a mixed strategy p_1, which is dependent on strategy p_2 and guarantees her a payoff of not less than U_1^*. On the other hand, the equality:

$$U_1^* = \min_{p_2} \max_{p_1} U_1(p_1, p_2)$$

expresses a stronger argument: player 1 has a certain mixed strategy, p_1, which guarantees her a payoff of not less than U_1^* for every mixed strategy p_2 that player 2 may choose.

In a zero sum game, U_1^* is called the **value of the game**.

B. It is not difficult to prove that from the equalities:

$$\max_{p_1} \min_{p_2} U_1(p_1, p_2) = \min_{p_2} \max_{p_1} U_1(p_1, p_2)$$

$$\max_{p_2} \min_{p_1} U_2(p_1, p_2) = \min_{p_1} \max_{p_2} U_2(p_1, p_2)$$

it also follows that in a zero sum game, every profile of security strategies of the players constitutes a Nash equilibrium. We are unable to go into the details of this argument, for lack of space.

C. In proving the minimax theorem we relied on the existence of a Nash equilibrium in mixed strategies, which we proved in the appendix to Chapter 11, by relying on a fixed point theorem. However, the minimax theorem can also be proved without reliance on a fixed point theorem, but rather by using simpler mathematical tools, called **separation theorems**.

Game theory was first developed in the first half of the twentieth century for the particular instance of zero sum games. John von Neumann proved the minimax theorem in 1928 while applying one of the separation theorems. It was only in 1951 that John Nash proved the existence of the equilibrium which is named after him also in games which are not zero sum games, by applying a fixed point theorem.

To sum up our discussion, we note that most strategic situations are not amenable to description by means of zero sum games. Even sworn enemies, it being given that one of them is fated to win, would prefer that the conflict between them take place at low intensity and not through an all-out war which would be ruinous for both. Accordingly, in most strategic situations competitive aspects exist alongside interests that are common to both parties. For this reason, the greater part of this book is not restricted solely to the analysis of zero sum games.

13

Mixed strategies in general games

In Chapter 11, we defined mixed strategies in games in which every player has two pure strategies. In all the examples cited in Chapter 11, only two players took part in the game.

We will begin this chapter with an example of a game with many players in which there is a Nash equilibrium in mixed strategies. In the game in this example, every player has two strategies. In the second part of this chapter, we will extend the definition of mixed strategies to games in which every player has more than two pure strategies, and explore examples of such games.

13.1 The Volunteer's Dilemma

Consider a group of honest people who witness the perpetration of a crime. Each of these people may prefer that one of the other people in the group come to the aid of the victim or call the police, because volunteering to do so is bothersome and might put the volunteer at risk. What are the Nash equilibria in this sort of social situation, and what are their properties? How do they depend on the number of witnesses?

This question was analyzed by Diekmann (1985).[1] Assume that each of the witnesses, $i = 1, \ldots, n$, has zero utility if nobody volunteers. If at least one of them volunteers to act on behalf of the victim, those who did not volunteer have a positive utility V, expressing their satisfaction with the assistance rendered to the victim. Each of the volunteers has a utility $V - C$. The term C expresses the effort or the risk experienced by the volunteer. We will assume that $V - C > 0$, i.e. that a unique witness to the crime would prefer to volunteer rather than to stand aside.

For every witness in this game there exists a Nash equilibrium in which she is the unique volunteer. Such an equilibrium is a focal point equilibrium if that witness has any quality that distinguishes her as being especially suited to volunteering (such as physical strength, medical knowhow and so forth). This witness realizes that all the others expect her to volunteer and that nobody is about to volunteer in her stead. This being so, she prefers to volunteer rather than leave the victim unaided.

---

[1] Diekmann, A. (1985), "Volunteer's Dilemma," *Journal of Conflict Resolution* 29, 605–610.

But what will happen when none of the witnesses stands out as being obviously well suited for the task? Does the game also have a symmetric equilibrium, in which each of the witnesses volunteers for the task with the same probability p, $0 < p < 1$?

In a symmetric equilibrium in mixed strategies, every witness adopts one of the two strategies (to volunteer, not to volunteer) with positive probability.

If a witness does not volunteer, his utility depends on the actions of the other $n - 1$ witnesses. If none of them volunteers, the witness's utility is 0. If at least one of the $n - 1$ other witnesses volunteers, the witness's utility is V (the victim gets help without the witness having to make any effort or assume any risk).

At the equilibrium we seek, the chance that a particular witness will not volunteer is $1 - p$. Since the witnesses' choices are independent, the chance that none of the other $n - 1$ witnesses will volunteer is $(1 - p)^{n-1}$. The chance of the complementary event, that at least one of the other $n - 1$ witnesses will volunteer, is $1 - (1 - p)^{n - 1}$.

Accordingly, the expected utility of a non-volunteering witness is:

$$0 \cdot (1 - p)^{n-1} + V\left(1 - (1 - p)^{n-1}\right)$$

On the other hand, if the witness volunteers, his payoff is $V - C$, irrespective of the extent to which the other witnesses volunteer: the victim gets help and the witness bears the involved effort or risk.

In order for the witness's mixed strategy to be a best reply, the two strategies (to volunteer, not to volunteer) must yield the witness the same expected utility:

$$V - C = 0 \cdot (1 - p)^{n-1} + V\left(1 - (1 - p)^{n-1}\right)$$

Hence:

$$(1 - p)^{n-1} = \frac{C}{V}$$

or:

$$1 - p = \left(\frac{C}{V}\right)^{\frac{1}{n-1}}$$

What happens when the number of witnesses n progressively increases? How does the number of witnesses n affect the chance $(1 - p)^n$ that none of them will bestir himself in aid of the victim?

The ratio $\frac{C}{V}$ is smaller than 1. Therefore, the larger n becomes, the chance that a particular witness will not volunteer,

$$1 - p = \left(\frac{C}{V}\right)^{\frac{1}{n-1}}$$

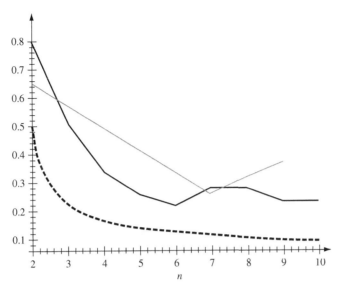

Figure 13.1

increases progressively, tending to 1! The larger the crowd of witnesses, the more likely it is that any one of them will tend to rely on the possibility that somebody else will volunteer.

What is the effect of this negative tendency on the overall chance that nobody will volunteer? The chance that nobody will volunteer,

$$(1-p)^n = (1-p)^{n-1}(1-p) = \left(\frac{C}{V}\right)\left(\frac{C}{V}\right)^{\frac{1}{n-1}}$$

increases progressively and tends to $\frac{C}{V}$. Thus, as the number of witnesses increases, the dwindling preparedness of any individual to volunteer exerts a stronger negative effect on the overall prospect of anyone volunteering than the positive effect exerted by the increase in the potential number of volunteers. As a result, as the total number of witnesses progressively increases, the chance, at a Nash equilibrium, that at least one of them will lend a helping hand perversely records a progressive decrease, converging to $1 - \frac{C}{V}$.

In experiments of the game for $\frac{C}{V} = \frac{1}{2}$, the level of volunteerism was significantly higher than predicted at this symmetric Nash equilibrium. Figure 13.1 describes, with a broken line, the chance of volunteerism expected from any single witness at a Nash equilibrium for sets of volunteers numbering between two and ten individuals, compared with the outcomes of the Diekmann (1986) experiment[2] (in black) and the outcomes of the Frazen (1995)[3] experiment (in gray).

[2] Diekmann, A. (1986). "Volunteer's Dilemma: A Social Trap without a Dominant Strategy and Some Empirical Outcomes," in A. Diekmann and P. Mitter (eds.), *Paradoxical Effects of Social Behavior: Essays in Honor of Anatol Rapoport*, Heidelberg: Physica-Verlag, pp. 187–197.
[3] Frazen, A. (1995), "Set Size and One Shot Collective Action," *Rationality and Society* 7, 183–200.

Frazen (1995) also tried the game with larger sets, of 21, 51, and 101 participants. He found that the rate of volunteerism in large sets such as these remained relatively high, in a range of 20–30 percent. As a result, the chance of nobody volunteering is negligible, in contrast to the prediction that this chance will approach 50 percent in the symmetric Nash equilibrium that we have analyzed here.

Comprehension check

Compare this example to the one in section 7.1 of investment in a public good. What are the similarities and the differences between the two examples? Your comments should relate, *inter alia*, to the effect of the number of players on the nature of the equilibrium, and the nature of the best-reply function in the two examples. Is the Volunteer's Dilemma a game of cooperation or one of conflict between the witnesses? Are the players' mixed strategies in the Volunteer's Dilemma strategic complements or strategic substitutes (i.e. if one of the witnesses i increases his chance of volunteering, p_1, will each of the other witnesses $j \neq i$ wish to increase or decrease his chance of volunteering p_1)?

13.2 Mixed strategies in games with more than two pure strategies per player

So far, we have defined the mixed extension for games in which each player has only two strategies. The definition can easily be extended to the case in which each player i has a finite number K_i of strategies:

$$X_i = \left\{x_i^1, \ldots, x_i^{Ki}\right\}$$

In order to describe a mixed strategy of player i, i.e. a lottery conducted by player i between her (pure) strategies, we must denote for every strategy $x_i^k \in X_i$ the probability p_i^k with which the player chooses x_i^k. In a mixed strategy of this kind, which will be denoted:

$$\bar{p}_i = \left(p_i^1, \ldots p_i^{K_i}\right)$$

the sum of probabilities should of course be equal to 1:

$$\sum_{k=1}^{K_i} p_i^k = 1$$

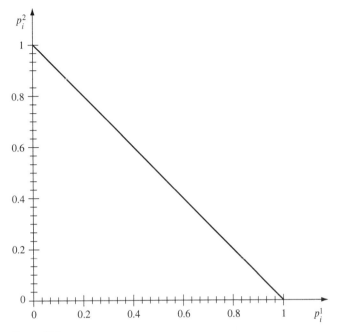

Figure 13.2

In the particular instance we have dealt with so far, with only two pure strategies per player (i.e. $K_i = 2$ for every player $i \in I$), we represented the lottery by the probability p_i^1 with which the player chose her first pure strategy, x_i^1. If a player has K strategies, $2 \leq K$, we will specify the probabilities of each of her pure strategies. For example, in the case that $K = 2$, we will specify:

$$\bar{p}_i = \left(p_i^1, p_i^2\right)$$

Of course, $p_i^2 = 1 - p_i^1$. A set of all possible lotteries is described, therefore, by the interval described in Figure 13.2, which is a set of all the profiles $\left(p_i^1, p_i^2\right)$ that satisfy $p_i^1 + p_i^2 = 1$. These profiles are the mixed strategies of player i in this case.

If player i has three pure strategies $X_i = \left\{x_i^1, x_i^2, x_i^3\right\}$, i.e. $K = 3$, her mixed strategies is the set of all the profiles $\left(p_i^1, p_i^2, p_i^3\right)$ that satisfy $p_i^1 + p_i^2 + p_i^3 = 1$; it is described by the shaded triangle in Figure 13.3.

In general, we will denote by $\Delta(X_i)$ the set of mixed strategies of player i in the mixed extension of the game. In mathematical terminology, this set is called a **simplex**.

When the players adopt the mixed strategies:

$$\bar{p}_j = \left(p_j^1, \dots p_j^{K_j}\right), \quad j \in I$$

the lottery results are independent of one another, since every player holds her own lottery simultaneously with the other players and independently of them. Hence it follows, for example, that the strategy profile:

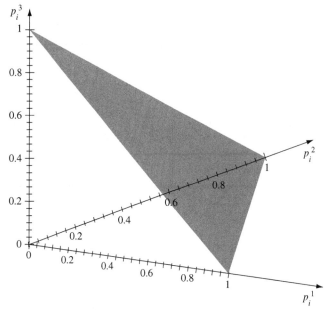

Figure 13.3

$$\left(x_j^1\right)_{j\in I} \in X = \Pi_{j\in1}X_j$$

in which each player chooses her first strategy, will be realized with probability:

$$\Pi_{j\in I}p_j^1$$

which is the product of the probabilities p_j^1 with which each of the players $j \in I$ chooses the first strategy in her own strategy set. In general, the strategy profile:

$$x = (x_J^{k_j})_{j\in I}$$

(in which player j chooses strategy number k_j in her strategy set) will be realized with the probability:

$$P(x) = \Pi_{j\in I}p_j^{k_j}$$

In order to find the expected utility $U_i\left((\bar{p}_j)_{j\in I}\right)$ of player i when the players $j \in I$ choose the mixed strategies:

$$\bar{p}_j = (p_j^1, \dots, p_j^{K_j}), \quad j \in I$$

we must make the following computation: for every strategy profile $x \in N$ of the players, we should multiply the utility $U_i(x)$ of player i of this profile by the probability $P(x)$ that this profile will in fact be realized, and sum up over all possible strategy profiles:

$$U_i\left(\left(\bar{p}_j \right)_{j \in I} \right) = \Sigma_{x \in X} P(x) U_i(x)$$

$$= \Sigma_{(x_j^{k_j})_{j \in I} \in X} \left(\Pi_{j \in I} p_j^{k_j} \right) \cdot U_i\left((x_j^{k_j})_{j \in I} \right)$$

Now, the Nash equilibrium in mixed strategies is simply a Nash equilibrium in the mixed extension of the game we have just defined, in which the strategy set of every player $i \in I$ is $\Delta(X_i)$, and her utility $U_i\left((\bar{p}_j)_{j \in I} \right)$ from the strategy profiles $(\bar{p}_j)_{j \in I}$ of the players is given above. In other words, the mixed strategy set $(\bar{p}_j^*)_{j \in I}$ is a Nash equilibrium if for every player $i \in I$ it is the case that:

$$U_i\left(\bar{p}_i^*, (\bar{p}_j^*)_{j \neq i} \right) \geq U_i\left(\bar{p}_i, (\bar{p}_j^*)_{j \neq i} \right)$$

for every mixed strategy $\bar{p}_i \in \Delta(X_i)$ of player i.

We will now turn to explore two games with mixed-strategy equilibria of this kind.

13.2.1 Rock-Paper-Scissors

Recall the following children's game. Two players simultaneously raise their right hand in one of three shapes: a rock, paper, or a pair of scissors. We will denote each of these options with the first letter of the word: R, P, and S. If both choose the same shape, the game ends in a draw. Otherwise, one of them loses and the other wins. The winner is determined by means of the following rule: rock "blunts" and beats scissors, scissors "cut" and beat paper, and paper "wraps" and thereby beats rock. Each player gets a payoff of 1 if she wins, -1 if she loses, or 0 if the game ends in a draw.

The following is the payoffs matrix of the game:

		Player 2		
		R	P	S
	R	0,0	−1,1	1,−1
Player 1	P	1,−1	0,0	−1,1
	S	−1,1	1,−1	0,0

Question 13.1

Show that this game has no equilibrium in pure strategies.

Answer

For each player, we will underline each of her payoffs in a strategy profile in which her strategy is a best reply to the other player's strategy:

Player 2

		R	P	S
	R	0,0	−1,<u>1</u>	<u>1</u>,−1
Player 1 P		<u>1</u>,−1	0,0	−1,<u>1</u>
	S	−1,<u>1</u>	<u>1</u>,−1	0,0

We have not found a strategy profile in which we have underlined both strategies, i.e. a profile in which each of the strategies is a best reply to the other. Therefore this game has no Nash equilibrium in pure strategies.

How can we determine whether a mixed strategy profile $(\bar{p}_i)_{i\in I}$ is a Nash equilibrium in the game? A mixed strategy $\bar{p}_i$ of player i is a best reply to a strategy profile $\bar{p}_{-i}$ of the other players if, with a positive probability, player i mixes only among those pure strategies x_i^*, the choice of which would maximize the player's expected utility:

$$u_i^* = U_i\left(x_i^*, \bar{p}_{-i}\right) = \max_{x_i \in X_i} U_i(x_i, \bar{p}_{-i})$$

(Such a best reply $\bar{p}_i$ will likewise yield player i an expected utility u_i^*, since $\bar{p}_i$ mixes between pure strategies x_i^*, each of which yields the player the expected utility u_i^*.)

Therefore, $\bar{p}_i$ is a best reply to $\bar{p}_{-i}$ if and only if the following two conditions are satisfied:

1. Each of the pure strategies of player i that are played with a positive probability in the mixed strategy $\bar{p}_i$ yield player i the same expected utility u_i^*: if one of these pure strategies x_i were to yield the player a higher expected utility than (at least one of) the others, then the choice of x_i would strictly increase the player's expected utility, contrary to the assumption that $\bar{p}_i$ is a best reply.
2. All the pure strategies x_i' of player i that are played with zero probability in the mixed strategy $\bar{p}_i$ (if any) yield player i an expected utility that does not exceed u_i^*: if such a pure strategy x_i' were to yield the player an expected

utility which is higher than u_i^*, the choice of x_i' would strictly increase the player's expected utility, contrary to the assumption that $\bar{p}_i$ is a best reply.

Question 13.2

Find all the equilibria in mixed strategies in the game Rock-Paper-Scissors.

Answer

In Question 13.1, we found that the game has no equilibrium in pure strategies. We will now examine whether the game has a Nash equilibrium in which one of the players mixes between two out of her three pure strategies.

Assume that at a Nash equilibrium $(\bar{p}_1, \bar{p}_2)$ player 1 mixes only between strategies R and P, and does not adopt strategy S at all. In such a case, strategy R of player 2 is strongly dominated by her strategy P. Therefore, player 2 will not adopt her strategy R at equilibrium, i.e.:

$$p_2^R = 0$$

In order for the mixed strategy $\bar{p}_1$ of player 1 to be a best reply, an equilibrium strategy $\bar{p}_2$ on the part of player 2 must cause player 1 to be indifferent between the two strategies that she mixes. In other words:

$$U_1(R, \bar{p}_2) = U_1(P, \bar{p}_2)$$

i.e.:

$$p_2^R U_1(R, R) + p_2^P U_1(R, P) + p_2^S U_1(R, S)$$
$$= p_2^R U_1(P, R) + p_2^P U_1(P, P) + p_2^S U_1(P, S)$$

Or, explicitly:

$$0 \cdot 0 + p_2^P \cdot (-1) + p_2^S \cdot 1 = 0 \cdot 1 + p_2^P \cdot 0 + p_2^S \cdot (-1)$$

Furthermore, it must also be the case, of course, that:

$$p_2^P + p_2^S = 1$$

From the solution of this pair of equations (and from the fact that $p_2^R = 0$), we obtain that:

$$\bar{p}_2 = (p_2^R, p_2^P, p_2^S) = \left(0, \frac{2}{3}, \frac{1}{3}\right)$$

Given $\bar{p}_2$, the payoff of player 1 when she adopts the strategy R is:

$$U_1(R, \bar{p}_2) = p_2^R U_1(R, R) + p_2^P U_1(R, P) + p_2^S U_1(R, S)$$
$$= 0 \cdot 0 + \frac{2}{3} \cdot (-1) + \frac{1}{3} \cdot 1 = -\frac{1}{3}$$

(Verify that this is also the expected payoff of player 1 if she chooses the strategy P.) However, if player 1, given $\bar{p}_2$, chooses strategy S, then her expected payoff will be higher:

$$U_1(S,\bar{p}_2) = p_2^R U_1(S,R) + p_2^P U_1(S,P) + p_2^S U_1(S,S)$$

$$= 0 \cdot (-1) + \frac{2}{3} \cdot 1 + \frac{1}{3} \cdot 0 = \frac{2}{3}$$

Therefore, mixing between the strategies R and P only is not a best reply of player 1 to $\bar{p}_2$. Hence we deduce that there is no Nash equilibrium at which player 1 mixes only between her first two strategies, R and P.

Based on similar considerations, there is no Nash equilibrium in the game at which player 1 mixes only two out of her pure strategies. Due to the symmetry between the players' payoffs in the game, neither is there a Nash equilibrium at which player 2 mixes two out of her three pure strategies. It remains to determine whether there exists an equilibrium at which the two players mix all their pure strategies.

Assume that there exists an equilibrium $(\bar{p}_1,\bar{p}_2)$ at which player 1 mixes all of her pure strategies. In this equilibrium, player 1 has the same expected utility from each of her strategies:

$$U_1(R,\bar{p}_2) = U_1(P,\bar{p}_2) = U_1(S,\bar{p}_2)$$

i.e.:

$$p_2^R U_1(R,R) + p_2^P U_1(R,P) + p_2^S U_1(R,S)$$
$$= p_2^R U_1(P,R) + p_2^P U_1(P,P) + p_2^S U_1(P,S)$$
$$= p_2^R U_1(S,R) + p_2^P U_1(S,P) + p_2^S U_1(S,S)$$

or, explicitly:

$$p_2^R \cdot 0 + p_2^P \cdot (-1) + p_2^S \cdot 1$$
$$= p_2^R \cdot 1 + p_2^P \cdot 0 + p_2^S \cdot (-1)$$
$$= p_2^R \cdot (-1) + p_2^P \cdot 1 + p_2^S \cdot 0$$

It must also be the case that:

$$p_2^R + p_2^P + p_2^S = 1$$

From the solution of this system of three equations we obtain:

$$\bar{p}_2 = \left(p_2^R, p_2^P, p_2^S\right) = \left(\frac{1}{3}, \frac{1}{3}, \frac{1}{3}\right)$$

(Verify this!) From a symmetric calculation we will also obtain that:

$$\bar{p}_1 = (p_1^R, p_1^P, p_1^S) = \left(\frac{1}{3}, \frac{1}{3}, \frac{1}{3}\right)$$

and therefore:

$$(\bar{p}_1, \bar{p}_2) = \left(\left(\frac{1}{3}, \frac{1}{3}, \frac{1}{3}\right), \left(\frac{1}{3}, \frac{1}{3}, \frac{1}{3}\right)\right)$$

is the unique equilibrium in the game. At this equilibrium, the expected payoff of every player is 0. (Verify this!)

Note that the equilibrium strategies that we found in the game Rock-Paper-Scissors are also the players' security strategies. For example, if player 2 adopts any mixed strategy:

$$(\tilde{p}_2^R, \tilde{p}_2^P, \tilde{p}_2^S)$$

while player 1 adopts her equilibrium strategy:

$$\bar{p}_1 = (p_1^R, p_1^P, p_1^S) = \left(\frac{1}{3}, \frac{1}{3}, \frac{1}{3}\right)$$

then the expected payoff of player 1 is 0:

$$U_1 = \left(\left(\frac{1}{3}, \frac{1}{3}, \frac{1}{3}\right)(\tilde{p}_1^R, \tilde{p}_1^P, \tilde{p}_1^S)\right)$$

$$= \frac{1}{3}\left(\tilde{p}_2^R U_1(R, R) + \tilde{p}_2^P U_1(R, P) + \tilde{p}_2^S U_1(R, S)\right)$$

$$+ \frac{1}{3}\left(\tilde{p}_2^R U_1(P, R) + \tilde{p}_2^P U_1(P, P) + \tilde{p}_2^S U_1(P, S)\right)$$

$$+ \frac{1}{3}\left(\tilde{p}_2^R U_1(S, R) + \tilde{p}_2^P U_1(S, P) + \tilde{p}_2^S U_1(S, S)\right)$$

$$= \frac{1}{3}\left(\tilde{p}_2^R \cdot 0 + \tilde{p}_2^P \cdot (-1) + \tilde{p}_2^S \cdot 1\right)$$

$$+ \frac{1}{3}\left(\tilde{p}_2^R \cdot 1 + \tilde{p}_2^P \cdot 0 + \tilde{p}_2^S \cdot (-1)\right)$$

$$+ \frac{1}{3}\left(\tilde{p}_2^R \cdot (-1) + \tilde{p}_2^P \cdot 1 + \tilde{p}_2^S \cdot 0\right)$$

$$= \frac{1}{3}\left(\tilde{p}_2^R \cdot (0 + 1 + (-1)) + \tilde{p}_2^P \cdot ((-1) + 0 + 1) + \tilde{p}_2^S \cdot (1 + (-1) + 0)\right)$$

$$= \frac{1}{3}\left(\tilde{p}_2^R \cdot 0 + \tilde{p}_2^P \cdot 0 + \tilde{p}_2^S \cdot 0\right) = 0$$

However, there is no other strategy that can guarantee player 1 an expected payoff greater than zero. For example, if player 1 plays R with a probability greater than $\frac{1}{3}$, then player 2 can cause the expected payoff of player 1 to be negative, by choosing her strategy P with a probability greater than $\frac{1}{3}$, and thus her "paper" will beat player 1's "rock" in more than a third of the cases.[4]

This is a particular case of Theorem 12.1 of the preceding chapter. The game Rock-Paper-Scissors is a zero sum game, and in particular it is a strictly competitive game. According to Theorem 12.1, equilibrium strategies in such a game are also security strategies.

Appendix: Patent race – an additional model

In the example in section 7.3, we presented a model of competition between firms investing in research in order to develop a new technology. The firms are required to decide how much effort and money to invest in development, while the firm making the greater investment also has a higher chance of being the first to complete and to patent the invention.

What will happen, however, if a higher investment in development leads with certainty to winning the patent? This question was addressed by Rapoport and Amaldoss (2000)[5] and Amaldoss and Jain (2002).[6]

Assume that two firms are competing over the patent. The firm that invests more in research will be the first to develop the technology and will register a patent on it, while the second firm's investment will come to nothing. Assume also that if both firms invest equally in research, they will develop the technology simultaneously, and in such a case the competition between them over selling the product and the legal battle over the patent rights will offset all their profits from the sales, such that neither firm will gain anything from its investment. What should each firm do in such a state of affairs? What level of investment in research is it worth their while to choose?

---

[4] For example, you can verify that if player 1 adopts a mixed strategy:

$$\left(\hat{p}_1^R, \hat{p}_1^P, \hat{p}_1^S\right) \neq \left(\frac{1}{3}, \frac{1}{3}, \frac{1}{3}\right)$$

then player 2 can cause player 1's expected payoff to be negative by choosing the mixed strategy:

$$\left(\breve{p}_2^R, \breve{p}_2^P, \breve{p}_2^S\right) = \left(\hat{p}_1^S, \hat{p}_1^R, \hat{p}_1^P\right)$$

[5] Rapoport, A. and W. Amaldoss (2000), "Mixed Strategies and Iterative Elimination of Strongly Dominated Strategies: An Experimental Investigation of States of Knowledge," *Journal of Economic Behavior and Organization* 42, 483–521.

[6] Amaldoss, W. and S. Jain (2002), "David vs. Goliath: An Analysis of Asymmetric Mixed-Strategy Games and Experimental Evidence," *Management Science* 48 (8), 972–991.

Technical appendices posted at: http://mansci.pubs.informs.org/e_companion_pages/AJ.PDF

If one of the firms invests in research at the maximum possible level, there is no way the other firm can uniquely win the patent and profit from the investment, and therefore it is worthwhile for the second firm to bow out of the contest and invest nothing. In this case, however, the first firm will find it worthwhile to make only a minimal investment in research, which, absent any competition, will suffice to guarantee that it wins the patent. But at that point it will be worthwhile for the second firm to invest a little more, to bypass the development rate of the first firm, and to win the patent ...

This, then, is an example of a strategic situation with no Nash equilibrium in pure strategies: there is no combination of investment levels by the firms each one of which is a best reply to the other firm's level of investment. Does the game have an equilibrium in mixed strategies? If so, what is its nature?

Question 13.3

Assume that each of the firms $i = 1,2$ has to choose one of three possible levels of investment:

$$c_i = 0, 1, 2$$

The expected revenue of a firm which wins the patent alone is:

$$r_i = 4$$

If firm i invests more than the competing firm j, i.e. in the event that $c_i > c_j$, then the net profit of firm i will be:

$$U_i(c_i, c_j) = r_i - c_i$$

whereas firm j will lose its entire investment:

$$U_j(c_i, c_j) = -c_j$$

Yet if both firms choose the same investment level, i.e. in the event that $c_i = c_j$, then both firms will lose their entire investment:

$$U_i(c_i, c_j) = U_j(c_i, c_j) = -c_i = -c_j$$

Answer the following questions:

1. Does the game have an equilibrium in pure strategies? If so, what is it?
2. Assume that both firms are risk neutral. Show that the game has an equilibrium in mixed strategies, at which the probabilities of each of the firms $i = 1,2$ investing at the different investment levels $c_i = 0,1,2$ are given by:

$$\bar{p}_i = (p_i^0, p_i^1, p_i^2) = \left(\frac{1}{4}, \frac{1}{4}, \frac{1}{2}\right)$$

What is the expected payoff of each firm at this equilibrium?

3. Prove that at any Nash equilibrium of the game, at least one of the firms invests 0 with a positive probability.
4. Prove that the equilibrium in Question 13.2 is the unique equilibrium in the game.

Answer   1. Let's write the payoff matrix of the game explicitly:

Firm 2

		0	1	2
	0	0,0	0,3	0,2
Firm 1	1	3,0	−1,1	−1,2
	2	2,0	2,−1	−2,−2

We will underline the payoffs corresponding to best replies:

Firm 2

		0	1	2
	0	0,0	0,$\underline{3}$	0,2
Firm 1	1	$\underline{3}$,0	−1,1	−1,$\underline{2}$
	2	2,$\underline{0}$	$\underline{2}$,−1	−2,−2

We have found that this game does not have a pair of pure strategies each of which is a best reply against the other. Therefore, this game has no Nash equilibrium in pure strategies.

2. In order to prove that:

$$\bar{p}_i = \left(p_i^0, p_i^1, p_i^2\right) = \left(\frac{1}{4}, \frac{1}{4}, \frac{1}{2}\right), \quad i = 1, 2$$

is a Nash equilibrium, we must demonstrate that if one of the firms i adopts the mixed strategy $\bar{p}_i$, then the other firm j is indifferent among all its pure strategies (and, accordingly, in particular, will be willing to mix among them with the probabilities $\left(\frac{1}{4}, \frac{1}{4}, \frac{1}{2}\right)$).

Indeed, if firm i adopts the mixed strategy $\bar{p}_i$, then the expected profits of firm j from its pure strategies are:

$$U_j(0,\bar{p}_i) = \frac{1}{4} \times 0 + \frac{1}{4} \times 0 + \frac{1}{2} \times 0 = 0$$

$$U_j(1,\bar{p}_i) = \frac{1}{4} \times 3 + \frac{1}{4} \times (-1) + \frac{1}{2} \times (-1) = 0$$

$$U_j(2,\bar{p}_i) = \frac{1}{4} \times 2 + \frac{1}{4} \times 2 + \frac{1}{2} \times (-2) = 0$$

Therefore, even when firm j mixes among its pure strategies, its expected payoff is 0. This, then, is the expected payoff of each of the firms at this Nash equilibrium.

3. We will denote by c_i the minimal level of investment that firm i invests with a positive probability at a given Nash equilibrium. Assume that $c_j \geq c_i$, i.e. the minimal investment of firm j in this equilibrium is greater than or equal to the minimal investment of firm i. We will assume, for the moment, that no firm ever invests 0, i.e. $c_j \geq c_i > 0$, and we arrive at a contradiction. Indeed, in this case, firm i will always lose its entire investment when it invests $c_i > 0$, since in such a case firm j invests at least as much as i and therefore i does not win the patent. Firm i can therefore improve its expected payoff if instead of investing c_i it invests 0 (with the same probability), and hence it follows that i's strategy in which $c_i > 0$ is not a best reply and cannot be a Nash equilibrium.

4. In 3 above we found that at least one of the firms, i, invests 0 at equilibrium. The payoff of firm i in such a case will be 0 (it will invest nothing and will never win the patent). In 1 above we found that the game has no equilibrium in pure strategies. Therefore, at a Nash equilibrium, firm i mixes between the strategy 0 and another pure strategy or other pure strategies at its disposal. Hence at this equilibrium, firm i is indifferent between the strategy 0 and this (or these) other strategy (or strategies) that yields it an expected payoff of 0. In the event that i chooses strategy $c_i = 1$ with a positive probability, the equilibrium strategy $\bar{p}_j = \left(p_j^0, p_j^1, p_j^2\right)$ must satisfy:

$$U_i\left(1,\bar{p}_j\right) = p_j^0 \times 3 + p_j^1 \times (-1) + p_j^2 \times (-1) = 0$$

$$U_i\left(2,\bar{p}_j\right) = p_j^0 \times 2 + p_j^1 \times 2 + p_j^2 \times (-2) \leq 0 \qquad (13.1)$$

$$p_j^0 + p_j^1 + p_j^2 = 1$$

and in the event that i plays the strategy $c_i = 2$ with a positive probability, the equilibrium strategy $\bar{p}_j = \left(p_j^0, p_j^1, p_j^2\right)$ must satisfy:

$$U_i\left(1,\bar{p}_j\right) = p_j^0 \times 3 + p_j^1 \times (-1) + p_j^2 \times (-1) \le 0$$
$$U_i\left(2,\bar{p}_j\right) = p_j^0 \times 2 + p_j^1 \times 2 + p_j^2 \times (-2) = 0 \tag{13.2}$$
$$p_j^0 + p_j^1 + p_j^2 = 1$$

In the first case, from the solution of the system (13.1) we will obtain $p_j^0 = \frac{1}{4}$, $p_j^1 + p_j^2 = \frac{3}{4}$ and $p_j^2 \ge \frac{1}{2}$. Since, in this case, j chooses the strategy $c_j = 0$ with a positive probability, and this strategy yields it an expected payoff of 0, the strategy $c_j = 2$ that it adopts with a positive probability should also yield it, at equilibrium, an expected payoff of 0, and the strategy $c_j = 1$ should yield it an expected payoff that is not positive. In other words, the equilibrium strategy $\bar{p}_i = (p_i^0, p_i^1, p_i^2)$ must satisfy:

$$U_j(1,\bar{p}_i) = p_i^0 \times 3 + p_i^1 \times (-1) + p_i^2 \times (-1) \le 0$$
$$U_j(2,\bar{p}_i) = p_i^0 \times 2 + p_i^1 \times 2 + p_i^2 \times (-2) = 0 \tag{13.3}$$
$$p_i^0 + p_i^1 + p_i^2 = 1$$

From the solution to this system we obtain in particular that $p_i^2 = \frac{1}{2}$. But if at equilibrium firm i does in fact choose the investment level $c_i = 2$ with a positive probability, then in the system (13.1) equality must obtain in the second row, i.e. the choice of $c_i = 2$ must also yield firm i an expected payoff of 0. The solution of the system (13.1) with equality, i.e. the solution of the system:

$$U_i\left(1,\bar{p}_j\right) = p_j^0 \times 3 + p_j^1 \times (-1) + p_j^2 \times (-1) = 0$$
$$U_i\left(2,\bar{p}_j\right) = p_j^0 \times 2 + p_j^1 \times 2 + p_j^2 \times (-2) = 0 \tag{13.4}$$
$$p_j^0 + p_j^1 + p_j^2 = 1$$

is:

$$\bar{p}_j = (p_j^0, p_j^1, p_j^2) = \left(\frac{1}{4}, \frac{1}{4}, \frac{1}{2}\right)$$

In particular, at a Nash equilibrium, firm j mixes among all its pure strategies, and therefore its expected payoff from the choice of any one of them is equal to 0, which is its (expected) payoff when it invests $c_j = 0$. In order for firm j to be, indeed, indifferent among its pure strategies, the equilibrium strategy $\bar{p}_i = (p_i^0, p_i^1, p_i^2)$ of firm i must therefore satisfy:

$$U_j(1,\bar{p}_i) = p_i^0 \times 3 + p_i^1 \times (-1) + p_i^2 \times (-1) = 0$$
$$U_j(2,\bar{p}_i) = p_i^0 \times 2 + p_i^1 \times 2 + p_i^2 \times (-2) = 0 \qquad (13.5)$$
$$p_i^0 + p_i^1 + p_i^2 = 1$$

The unique solution of this system of equations is:

$$\bar{p}_i = (p_i^0, p_i^1, p_i^2) = \left(\frac{1}{4}, \frac{1}{4}, \frac{1}{2}\right)$$

What happens in the second instance, in which the system (13.2) obtains? The solution of this system is $p_j^2 = \frac{1}{2}$, $p_j^0 + p_j^1 = \frac{1}{2}$, $p_j^1 \geq \frac{1}{4}$. Since, in this case, firm j chooses strategy $c_j = 1$ with a positive probability, and this strategy yields it an expected payoff of 0, then the strategy $c_j = 1$, which it adopts with a positive probability, must also yield it at equilibrium an expected payoff of 0. In other words, the equilibrium strategy $\bar{p}_i = (p_i^0, p_i^1, p_i^2)$ must satisfy:

$$U_j(1,\bar{p}_i) = p_i^0 \times 3 + p_i^1 \times (-1) + p_i^2 \times (-1) = 0$$
$$U_j(2,\bar{p}_i) = p_i^0 \times 2 + p_i^1 \times 2 + p_i^2 \times (-2) = 0 \qquad (13.6)$$
$$p_i^0 + p_i^1 + p_i^2 = 1$$

The solution of this system of equations is $\bar{p}_i = (p_i^0, p_i^1, p_i^2) = \left(\frac{1}{4}, \frac{1}{4}, \frac{1}{2}\right)$. Since firm i chooses all its strategies with a positive probability, at equilibrium all its strategies must yield it the same expected payoff of 0. Therefore, the equilibrium strategy $\bar{p}_j = (p_j^0, p_j^1, p_j^2)$ of firm j must satisfy the system of equations (13.5), the solution of which is:

$$\bar{p}_j = (p_j^0, p_j^1, p_j^2) = \left(\frac{1}{4}, \frac{1}{4}, \frac{1}{2}\right)$$

Thus, we have found that in both cases, the unique possible equilibrium is the one specified in 2.

Question 13.4

We will now generalize Question 13.3 in two different ways.

First, we will no longer assume that it is necessarily the case that $r_1 = r_2$. When $r_1 \neq r_2$, the revenue r_1 of firm 1 when it wins the patent is not identical to the revenue r_2 that firm 2 pockets if it wins the research and development race.

Second, we will allow for $k + 1$ different levels of investment – each of the firms $i = 1, 2$ must choose an investment level:

$$c_i = 0, 1, \ldots, k$$

where $k \geq 2$.

Consistently with the preceding question, we will continue to assume that $r_1 > k$, $r_2 > k$, such that upon winning the patent, the winning firm pockets a positive profit.

1. Prove that the game has no Nash equilibrium in pure strategies.
2. Show that the following mixed strategy profile is a Nash equilibrium of the game:

$$\bar{p}_1 = (p_1^0, p_1^1, p_1^2 \ldots, p_1^k) = \left(\frac{1}{r_1}, \frac{1}{r_1}, \frac{1}{r_1}, \cdots, 1 - \frac{k}{r_2} \right)$$

$$\bar{p}_2 = (p_2^0, p_2^1, p_2^2 \ldots, p_2^k) = \left(\frac{1}{r_2}, \frac{1}{r_2}, \frac{1}{r_2}, \cdots, 1 - \frac{k}{r_2} \right)$$

Answer

1. We will rule out the existence of a Nash equilibrium in pure strategies by reviewing the various instances of pure strategy profiles (c_i, c_j). We will divide them into five possible cases and show that no profile in any of these cases is a Nash equilibrium, since at least one of the firms can improve its position if it chooses a different level of investment than the one prescribed for it in the profile.

   Case 1: $c_i = c_j = 0$. In such a case, neither firm either gains or loses. Since $c_j = 0$, firm i can improve its position by making a positive investment $c_i > 0$, winning the patent and guaranteeing itself a positive profit.

   Case 2: $c_i = c_j > 0$. In such a case, both firms lose their investment. Given that $c_j > 0$, firm i can improve its position by not investing at all, and avoiding any loss.

   Case 3: $c_i < c_j < k$. In such a case, firm i does not win the patent and has no positive profit. Given that $c_j < k$, firm i can guarantee itself a positive profit by investing k and winning the patent.

   Case 4: $0 < c_i < c_j = k$. In this case, firm i does not win the patent and loses its investment. Given that $c_j = k$, firm i can avoid its loss by investing 0.

   Case 5: $0 = c_i < c_j = k$. In such a case, firm j wins the patent, but with the maximum possible investment. Since $c_i = 0$, firm j can increase its profits if it makes a positive investment smaller than k, that will still guarantee its winning the patent.

2. If firm 1 adopts the strategy:

$$\bar{p}_1 = (p_1^0, p_1^1, p_1^2 \ldots, p_1^k) = \left(\frac{1}{r_2}, \frac{1}{r_2}, \frac{1}{r_2}, \cdots, 1 - \frac{k}{r_2} \right)$$

it mixes among all its pure strategies and in particular it chooses, with the positive probability $\frac{1}{r_2}$, not to make any investment at all and to guarantee itself a payoff of 0. Therefore, in order to show that the mixed strategy $\bar{p}_1$ is a best reply of firm 1 to the strategy:

$$\bar{p}_2 = (p_2^0, p_2^1, p_2^2 \ldots, p_2^k) = \left(\frac{1}{r_1}, \frac{1}{r_1}, \frac{1}{r_1}, \ldots, 1 - \frac{k}{r_1}\right)$$

of firm 2, we must ascertain that, given $\bar{p}_2$, firm 1 is indifferent among its pure strategies and that they all therefore – like the strategy of refraining from investment – guarantee it an expected payoff of 0.

This is indeed the case: if firm 1 chooses to invest $c_1 > 0$, it wins the patent and makes a profit of $r_1 - c_1$ as long as firm 2 invests a smaller amount. But firm 1 loses its investment if firm 2 invests an identical or a larger amount. Given $\bar{p}_2$, the expected payoff of firm 1 is:

$$U_1(c_1, \bar{p}_2) = (r_1 - c_1) \sum_{n=0}^{c_1-1} p_2^n + (-c_1) \sum_{n=c_1}^{k} p_2^n$$

$$= (r_1 - c_1) \sum_{n=0}^{c_1-1} \frac{1}{r_1} + (-c_1) \sum_{n=c_1}^{k-1} \frac{1}{r_1} + (-c_1)\left(1 - \frac{k}{r_1}\right)$$

$$= (r_1 - c_1)c_1 \frac{1}{r_1} + (-c_1)(k - c_1)\frac{1}{r_1} + (-c_1)\left(1 - \frac{k}{r_1}\right)$$

$$= c_1 \frac{1}{r_1}[(r_1 - c_1) - (k - c_1) + k] - c_1 = c_1 - c_1 = 0$$

as we sought to demonstrate. We have therefore shown that $\bar{p}_1$ is a best reply to $\bar{p}_2$. The same argument, with a reversal of roles between firms 1 and 2, proves that $\bar{p}_2$ is a best reply to $\bar{p}_1$, and therefore the strategy profile $(\bar{p}_1, \bar{p}_2)$ is a Nash equilibrium.

Note: Actually, $(\bar{p}_1, \bar{p}_2)$ can be shown to be the unique Nash equilibrium in this game. The proof generalizes the method we used in Question 13.3, parts 3, 4, in order to prove the uniqueness of the equilibrium in the particular case we discussed there.

In the equilibrium we saw in the last question, the firm that profits less from winning the patent is the very one that makes the maximum investment k with a higher probability. For example, if $r_1 < r_2$, i.e. if firm 1 has a lower payoff than firm 2 when it wins the patent, then at the equilibrium $(\bar{p}_1, \bar{p}_2)$ the probability with which firm 1 makes the maximum investment k is:

$$p_1^k = 1 - \frac{k}{r_2},$$

This probability is higher than firm 2's probability of investing k:

$$p_2^k = 1 - \frac{k}{r_1},$$

Moreover, the average investment of firm 1, which is equal to:

$$\frac{1}{r_2}[0 + 1 + \ldots + (k-1)] + \left(1 - \frac{k}{r_2}\right)k = \frac{1}{r_2}\frac{k(k-1)}{2} + \left(1 - \frac{k}{r_2}\right)k$$

$$= k\left\{\frac{1}{2r_2}[(k-1) - 2k] + 1\right\} = k\left(1 - \frac{k(k+1)}{2r_2}\right)$$

is higher than the average investment of firm 2, which is equal to:

$$\frac{1}{r_1}[0 + 1 + \ldots + (k-1)] + \left(1 - \frac{k}{r_1}\right)k = k\left(1 - \frac{k(k+1)}{2r_1}\right)$$

and firm 1's chance of winning the patent is higher than that of firm 2. Indeed, firm 1 wins the patent if one of the two following conditions is satisfied:

1. Firm 1 invests k (the chance of this happening at equilibrium is $1 - \frac{k}{r_2}$), while firm 2 invests less than k (the probability of this happening at equilibrium is $\frac{k}{r_1}$, which is equal to the sum of the probabilities that it invests $0, \ldots, k-1$). The probability of this combination of circumstances at equilibrium is therefore $\left(1 - \frac{k}{r_2}\right)\frac{k}{r_1}$. Or:

2. Firm 1 invests amount $0 < c_1 < k$ (with a chance of $\frac{1}{r_2}$) and firm 2 invests a smaller amount (with probability $\frac{c}{r_1}$, which is equal to the sum of the probabilities that it invests $0, \ldots, c-1$). Hence the probability of this combination of circumstances at equilibrium is $\frac{1}{r_2}\frac{c_1}{r_1}$.

Accordingly, the overall probability with which firm 1 wins the patent is:

$$\left(1 - \frac{k}{r_2}\right)\frac{k}{r_1} + \sum_{c_1=1}^{k-1}\frac{1}{r_2}\frac{c_1}{r_1} = \left(1 - \frac{k}{r_2}\right)\frac{k}{r_1} + \frac{1}{r_2 r_1}\frac{k(k-1)}{2}$$

$$= \frac{k}{2r_2 r_1}[2(r_2 - k) + k - 1] = \frac{k(2r_2 - k - 1)}{2r_2 r_1}$$

This probability is **higher** than firm 2's probability, similarly calculated, of winning the patent:

$$\left(1 - \frac{k}{r_1}\right)\frac{k}{r_2} + \sum_{c_2=1}^{k-1}\frac{1}{r_1}\frac{c_2}{r_2} = \frac{k(2r_1 - k - 1)}{2r_2 r_1}$$

What causes firm 2, which, if it wins the patent will gain higher revenues, to behave complacently and to invest, on average, less than its rival? How can this strategy be optimal for it at equilibrium?

The nature of the equilibrium is non-intuitive in the present case, since an outcome such as this would not, in fact, be obtained in a non-strategic situation. In order to understand the difference between **strategic analysis** and the analysis of the decision problem faced by a single decision maker, we will examine what would have happened if firm 1 had adopted some fixed strategy:

$$\overline{p}_1 = (p_1^0, p_1^1, p_1^2 \cdots, p_1^k)$$

which is completely independent of the behavior of firm 2. In this case, if firm 2 had invested c_2, the following two outcomes could have been realized:

1. It would have won the patent and earned $r_2 - c_2$ if firm 1 had invested less than c_2. The chance of that would then have been $p_1^0 + p_1^1 + \cdots + p_1^{c_2-1}$.
2. Firm 2 would have lost its investment if firm 1 had invested at least c_2. The chance of that would then have been $p_1^{c_2} + \cdots + p_1^k$.

Thus, an increase in the investment c_2 would have boosted the chance of winning $p_1^0 + p_1^1 + \cdots + p_1^{c_2-1}$, reduced the profit $r_2 - c_2$ given a win, and increased the size of the investment that would come to nothing in case of a loss. Alternatively, reducing the investment c_2 would reduce the chance of winning, increase the profit – given a win – and reduce the loss in the event that the firm does not win the patent. To sum up, firm 2 would try to strike a balance between these considerations and would choose that level of investment that would maximize its expected payoff:

$$U_2(c_2, \overline{p}_1) = (p_1^0 + p_1^1 + \ldots + p_1^{c_2-1})(r_2 - c_2) + (p_1^{c_2} + \ldots + p_1^k)(-c_2)$$
$$= (p_1^0 + p_1^1 + \ldots + p_1^{c_2-1})r_2 - c_2$$

Denote by c_2^* the optimal level of investment (or, if there are a number of investment levels that are all optimal, we will denote the highest of them by c_2^*). If $c_2^* < k$, i.e. if c_2^* is not the maximum possible investment level, then raising the level of investment by a single unit, from c_2^* to $c_2^* + 1$, would not be worthwhile for firm 2 (since by definition $c_2^* + 1$ is suboptimal for firm 2); such an increase would add $p_1^{c_2^*}r_2 < 1$ to the first term in the expected utility and subtract 1 from the second term. From the fact that the increase from c_2^* to $c_2^* + 1$ is suboptimal we deduce that $p_1^{c_2^*}r_2 < 1$. But if r_2 were much larger, this inequality would be reversed, and the optimal (maximum) investment of firm 2 would increase.

This is therefore the basis for our intuition that a higher revenue from the patent should lead the firm to increase its investment in research and development. As stated, however, this intuition is confirmed only under the assumption that the other firm behaves naively, in total disregard of its rival when choosing its investment strategy, and does not try to influence it by means of its strategy choice.

What happens when both firms behave in a strategic fashion? We have already seen that this game has no equilibrium in pure strategies; at equilibrium, each firm must invest 0 with a positive probability, and therefore 0 must also be the expected utility of each firm from any investment strategy that it adopts with a positive probability. When a firm makes a positive investment c, it wins the patent with a positive probability (since its rival sometimes invests 0). But when firm 1 is the one that wins the patent, it earns only $r_1 - c$, less than the profit $r_2 - c$ of firm 2 when firm 2 wins the patent with an investment of c. Therefore, in order for the expected utility of both firms to be 0 at equilibrium, firm 1's average probability of winning must be higher at equilibrium, in order to counterbalance the lower profit given a win.

13.3.1   The patent race in laboratory experiments

How is the game actually played in laboratory experiments? Amaldoss and Jain (2002) conducted an experiment in which they examined the game with the parameters $k = 2$, $r_1 = 4$, and $r_2 = 7$. In this game the Nash equilibrium is:

$$\bar{p}_1 = (p_1^0, p_1^1, p_1^2) = \left(\frac{1}{7}, \frac{1}{7}, \frac{5}{7}\right)$$

$$\bar{p}_2 = (p_2^0, p_2^1, p_2^2) = \left(\frac{1}{4}, \frac{1}{4}, \frac{1}{2}\right)$$

At that equilibrium, firm 1 invests on average 1.57 and wins the patent with a chance of 39.29 percent, while firm 2 invests 1.25 on average and wins the patent with a chance of 17.86 percent. Each participant in the experiment represents one of the firms and in each round of the game he is facing (by means of a lottery conducted anonymously, through a computer network) one of the participants representing the other firm. Thirty-six students altogether participated in the experiment, in 160 game rounds.

Amaldoss and Jain (2002) found that, on average of the total participants taking the role of firm 1, those participants played in a manner not very different from what would be expected at a Nash equilibrium. They adopted the investment strategies $c_1 = 0,1,2$ with the frequencies (23 percent, 7 percent, 70 percent), invested 1.47 on average, and won 37 percent of the game rounds. However, the behavior of the participants in the role of firm 2 did not correspond to the equilibrium prediction. On average over all participants in the role of firm 2, those participants invested $c_2 = 0,1,2$ with the frequencies (12 percent, 40 percent, 48 percent)[7] and 1.36 on average.

---

[7] However, the deviation from equilibrium behavior lessened in the later rounds of the game.

They also won in 23.5 percent of the game rounds, more than the predicted rate of winning at the Nash equilibrium.

In another experiment, Amaldoss and Jain (2002) increased the revenue of firm 1 from winning the patent to $r_1 = 6$. Theoretically, such a change should not influence the equilibrium strategy of firm 1, but rather that of firm 2, which is now:

$$\vec{p}'_2 = (p_2'^0, p_2'^1, p_2'^2) = \left(\frac{1}{6}, \frac{1}{6}, \frac{4}{6}\right)$$

The results of the experiment qualitatively support the theoretically predicted change. In this experiment, the distribution of the investments made by the representatives of firm 2 was indeed diverted in the direction of an increase of the investment, becoming (5 percent, 30 percent, 65 percent), with a higher average of 1.597. The distribution of the investments of the representatives of firm 1 in this experiment was (25 percent, 12 percent, 63 percent) – a distribution similar to the one that was found in the first experiment.

Rapoport and Amaldoss (2000) examined in an experiment the symmetric case in which $r_1 = r_2 \equiv r$, for $k = 5$. In such a case, when $r = 8$, the equilibrium strategy of the two firms is:

$$(p^0, p^1, p^2, p^3, p^4, p^5) = \left(\frac{1}{8}, \frac{1}{8}, \frac{1}{8}, \frac{1}{8}, \frac{1}{8}, \frac{3}{8}\right)$$

The distribution of the choices of the participants in the experiment was, to a large extent, close to this prediction:

(16.9 percent, 11.6 percent, 8.8 percent, 11.8 percent, 9 percent, 41.8 percent)

For $r = 20$, the equilibrium strategy is:

$$(p^0, p^1, p^2, p^3, p^4, p^5) = \left(\frac{1}{20}, \frac{1}{20}, \frac{1}{20}, \frac{1}{20}, \frac{1}{20}, \frac{15}{20}\right)$$

and the distribution of the participants' choices in the experiment was:

(14.1 percent, 5.5 percent, 5.3 percent, 5.3 percent, 6.9 percent, 62.8 percent)

In none of these experiments was any support found for the assumption that individual players independently conduct a lottery over their choices across the different game rounds. A significant serial correlation was found in the participants' choices over time, and a large difference was also found in the distributions of the actions of the various players. Thus, these experiments lend a certain amount of support to the theory on the aggregate level, when calculating the average observed behavior of a large number of players, but not at the individual level of behavior of any particular player.

PART V

Advanced topics in strategic form games

INTRODUCTION

Part V collects several advanced topics in strategic form games. Chapter 14 discusses the solution concept called **rationalizability**, based on the notion of a **never-best-reply strategy**, one which is not a best reply for any belief the player may have about her rivals' choice profiles. A strongly dominated strategy is never-best-reply, but we show that there are games in which never-best-reply strategies need not be strongly dominated by some other (pure) strategy; however, every never-best-reply strategy always turns out to be dominated by some *mixed* strategy in the mixed extension of the game.

Since a rational player will never choose a strategy which is never-best-reply, it makes sense to define an iterative elimination process in which, at each round, strategies that are never-best-reply (in the game remaining at that stage) are eliminated. The strategies surviving this elimination process are called **rationalizable**. Only rationalizable strategies will be played by players who are rational and believe that there is common certainty among the players that they are all rational.

Chapter 15 addresses the topic of equilibrium stability under an updating process, such as the **best-reply dynamics** in which the players respond optimally to their peers' behavior in the previous round of the game. The chapter provides the basic definition of a discrete dynamical system, the notion of a fixed point in it, and various notions of stability of fixed points. In an updating dynamics such as the best-reply dynamics, the Nash equilibria of the game are fixed points of the dynamics, but there are games in which some Nash equilibria are unstable fixed points. Such Nash equilibria are hence a weaker prediction for the outcome of the game. We study this phenomenon for two of the coordination games which were defined in Chapter 9.

Chapter 16 studies the basics of **evolutionarily game theory**, in which the game takes place within a large population of individuals. Each individual is of some particular **type** "programmed" to play one of the strategies (of a symmetric game) in a random match with another member of the population, and the individual's payoff represents his **fitness** to have offspring. The frequency of types in the population at a given point in time corresponds, therefore, to a mixed strategy which is the distribution of choices in the population.

Under the **replicator dynamics**, the composition of types in the population evolves from one generation to the next according to the assumption that each individual "breeds true" (its offspring are of the same type as its own), and the number of its offspring – its fitness – is simply its payoff in its random encounter to play the game with another individual from the population. The replicator dynamics thus defines a dynamical system of the strategy choice distribution within the population.

We explore the replicator dynamics in several games, including the Hawk-Dove game and the Rock-Paper-Scissors game. The strategies of the latter correspond to the mating strategies of males of a particular species of lizard, and the replicator dynamics indeed reflects the empirical findings of zoologists regarding the evolution of strategy distribution among males along the breeding seasons.

Each stable fixed point of the replicator dynamics is a symmetric Nash equilibrium of the game (though the replicator dynamics might additionally have some *unstable* fixed points which are not Nash equilibria). Conversely, the symmetric Nash equilibria of the game are fixed points of the replicator dynamics; however, we show in several examples that some of these Nash equilibria might be unstable and are hence a weaker prediction for the possible long-run composition of the population.

Another notion of stability for population games is that of an evolutionarily stable strategy (ESS). A mixed strategy is an ESS if it repels from the population any mutant who plays an alternative mixed strategy and whose penetration level to the population is small enough. It should be emphasized that despite the above phrasing, the notion of ESS is static, and it involves no explicit dynamics; this is apparent in the following equivalent definition for an ESS – a mixed strategy is an ESS if it is a symmetric Nash equilibrium, such that if the ESS is just as good as another ("mutant") mixed strategy when tipped against the ESS, the ESS yields a higher payoff when tipped against the mutant than the payoff yielded by the mutant when tipped against the mutant.

In the replicator dynamics, each individual in the population employs a pure strategy (and it is the frequency of the individuals' choices which corresponds to a mixed strategy). With an ESS, in contrast, each individual in the population employs the same mixed strategy. Another difference between the two notions is that an ESS considers explicitly the potential appearance of mutants. In the replicator dynamics, in contrast, any (pure) strategy which is not initially played by some (possibly small but strictly positive) fraction of the individuals in the population cannot appear in the population at a later generation.

Weakly dominated strategies are not evolutionarily stable. Since some symmetric games do have symmetric Nash equilibria in which a dominated strategy is played, also the notion of ESS defines a refinement for the set of Nash equilbria. In general, this refinement may be different than the refinement defined by stable fixed points of the replicator dynamics.[1]

---

[1] In the continuous-time version of the replicator dynamics, every ESS is also asymptotically stable in the replicator dynamics.

Another selection criterion among equilibria, this time for multi-player coordination games, is introduced in Chapter 17. This selection criterion is obtained by approximating the original coordination game by a *global game*, in which each player gets a noisy signal about the main parameter of the game – the minimal fraction of players which needs to choose the "risky" strategy in order for them to get a payoff which is higher than that assured by the "safe" action.

A prime example of such a game is that of currency attacks: enough investors have to short sell the currency of a particular country in order for it to be eventually devalued in the foreign exchange markets, and each investor gets only a somewhat noisy signal about the overall size of the attack which is needed for it to succeed.

The game as such has two Nash equilibria – all potential investors attack or all decline to attack (and save themselves the transaction cost of the investment). However, in the associated global game, as the noisy signal of the investors gets smaller and tends to zero, only one equilibrium survives, depending on the parameters of the game: the higher the yield of a successful "attack" relative to the transaction cost, the smaller the extent of coordination needed for a success in order to mobilize essentially all of the investors to take part in the attack; but when too many investors (in comparison with the ratio of potential gains to transaction cost) need to "jump into the water" together in order for cooperation to succeed, the investors refrain from attacking.

14

Rationalizable strategies

14.1   A never-best-reply strategy

In Chapter 4, we introduced the concept of a strongly dominated strategy. The strategy x_i of player i is strongly dominated if the player has another strategy x_i' which strongly dominates x_i, i.e. guarantees the player a higher payoff than the strategy x_i for every strategy x_j of her rival j:[1]

$$U_i(x_i', x_j) > U_i(x_i, x_j)$$

In a case such as this, the inequality persists also for any mixed strategy $\bar{p}_j$ of the rival. That is to say, for any belief $\bar{p}_j \in \Delta(X_j)$ of player i concerning the probability with which her rival chooses among the pure strategies available to her, it is the case that:

$$U_i\left(x_i', \bar{p}_j\right) > U_i\left(x_i, \bar{p}_j\right)$$

In particular, the strategy x_i of player i will never be a best reply for her. Given any belief $\bar{p}_j$ which player i holds concerning the frequency distribution of her rival's actions, she can improve her expected payoff if she adopts the strategy x_i' instead of the strategy x_i.

Definition   We say that a pure strategy x_i of player i is **never-best-reply** if for every belief $\bar{p}_j$ of hers on the likelihoods with which her rival j will use his available strategies, player i has another pure strategy $x_i^{\bar{p}_j}$ that yields her a higher expected payoff:

$$U_i\left(x_i^{\bar{p}_j}, \bar{p}_j\right) > U_i\left(x_i, \bar{p}_j\right).$$

In the specific case in which x_i is dominated by x_i', the strategy x_i is never-best-reply: for every belief $\bar{p}_j$ of player i on the distribution of her rival's strategies, the strategy $x_i^{\bar{p}_j} = x_i'$ yields player i a higher expected payoff than the strategy x_i.

---

[1] Or a strategy profile of her rivals. For the sake of simplicity in presentation, we will focus here on the case of a game between two players.

Can a player have a strategy x_i that is a never-best-reply, and yet x_i will not be dominated by any other pure strategy x_i'? She certainly can, as the following example demonstrates.

14.1.1   Example: a never-best-reply strategy which is nevertheless not a dominated strategy

Player 2

	L	R
T	4,2	0,1
M	0,2	4,1
B	1,0	1,3

Player 1: T, M, B

In this game, the strategy B of player 1 is not a (strongly or weakly) dominated strategy. It is not dominated by the strategy T, since B is preferable to T if player 2 plays R. The strategy B is likewise not dominated by the strategy M, since B is preferable to M if player 2 plays L.

Nevertheless, B is a never-best-reply strategy. If Player 2 plays L, strategy T is preferable for player 1 over B; and if player 2 plays R, strategy M is preferable for player 1 over B. Moreover, also for every belief of player 1 concerning the probabilities $(p, 1-p)$ with which player 2 will adopt her strategies (L, R), the strategy B of player 1 will never be inferior to either one of her other two strategies: if $p > \frac{1}{4}$, then the strategy T will yield player 1 a higher expected utility than B:

$$U_1(T,p) = 4p > 1 = U_1(B,p)$$

and if $p < \frac{3}{4}$ then the strategy M will yield player 1 a higher expected utility than B:

$$U_1(T,p) = 4(1-p) > 1 = U_1(B,p)$$

Thus, for every belief of player 1 concerning the distribution of her rival's strategies, one of the strategies, either T or M (and sometimes even both of them – when $\frac{1}{4} < p < \frac{3}{4}$), will yield her a higher expected payoff. Figure 14.1 describes, as a function of the belief p, the expected payoff of player 1 if she chooses T (in black), M (in gray) or B (in black dashed line). The domains in which T or M are preferable to B are in bold.

A rational player will not choose a never-best-reply strategy even if it is not dominated by any other of his strategies. In the example we have just seen, player 1 will not choose B. If player 2 believes that player 1 is rational, player 2 believes that

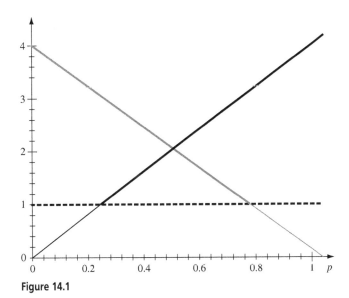

Figure 14.1

player 1 will only choose either T or M. As a result, she believes it is worth her while to play L (since R would be preferable for her over L only if player 1 were to play B). If player 1 realizes this, she will choose T. Thus, we can deduce that under common knowledge of rationality, the players will play the profile (T, L) – in spite of the fact that in this game, iterative elimination of strongly dominated strategies does not yield a unique prediction: neither player has a strongly dominated strategy in the game. Thus, common knowledge of rationality can provide us with a stronger prediction concerning the outcome of the game than the prediction we obtain from the process of iterative elimination of strongly dominated strategies.

Both concepts do nevertheless coincide in the mixed extension of the game. If player i has a strategy x_i that is a never-best-reply, we can always find a mixed strategy of hers $\bar{p}'_i$ that strongly dominates the strategy x_i. This is the import of the following proposition.

Proposition 14.1
· ·
(Pearce 1984, Bernheim 1984)[2]

In a game in which player i has a finite number of pure strategies, a pure strategy x_i of the player is never-best-reply for her if and only if it is strongly dominated by some mixed strategy $\bar{p}'_i$ of hers in the mixed extension of the game:

---

[2] Pearce, D. G. (1984), "Rationalizable Strategic Behavior and the Problem of Perfection," *Econometrica* 52, 1029–1050. Bernheim, B. D. (1984), "Rationalizable Strategic Behavior," *Econometrica* 52, 1007–1028.

$$U_i(x_i, \bar{p}_{-i}) < U\left(\bar{p}'_i, \bar{p}_{-i}\right)$$

for every strategy profile $\bar{p}_{-i}$ of the other players.

The proof of this proposition is presented in the appendix to this chapter. The proof relies on the minimax theorem presented in Chapter 12.

Question 14.1

Proposition 14.1 guarantees that in the game in section 14.1.1 there exists a mixed strategy $\bar{p}'_1$ of player 1 that strongly dominates the strategy B in the mixed extension of the game. Explain why the above proposition does indeed provide that guarantee, and find such a strategy $\bar{p}'_1$.

Answer

In the game in section 14.1.1, the strategy B is never-best-reply for player 1. The above proposition guarantees that in such a case there exists a mixed strategy $\bar{p}'_1$ of player 1 that strongly dominates B. For example, the strategy $\bar{p}'_1 = \left(\frac{1}{2}, \frac{1}{2}, 0\right)$ gives player 1 the expected utility:

$$U_1\left(\bar{p}'_1, \bar{p}_2\right) = \frac{1}{2}U_1(T, \bar{p}_2) + \frac{1}{2}U_1(M, \bar{p}_2)$$

$$= \frac{1}{2}\left(p_2^L U_1(T, L) + p_2^R U_1(T, R)\right) + \frac{1}{2}\left(p_2^L U_1(M, L) + p_2^R U_1(M, R)\right)$$

$$= \frac{1}{2}\left(p_2^L \times 4 + p_2^R \times 0\right) + \frac{1}{2}\left(p_2^L \times 0 + p_2^R \times 4\right) = 2\left(p_2^L + p_2^R\right) = 2$$

which is higher than the expected utility of 1 that player 1 can obtain by choosing the strategy B.

14.2   Rationalizable strategies

We have thus shown that in the mixed extension of a game with a finite number of strategies per player, the set of pure strategies of a player that is not strongly dominated is identical to the set of strategies which is a best reply, each, to some belief of the player concerning her rival's behavior. This is the set of strategies out of which a rational player will choose.

Therefore, the set of pure strategies surviving iterative elimination of strongly dominated strategies (by pure or mixed strategies) is identical to the set of pure strategies that the players will adopt under common knowledge of rationality. Profiles of such strategies constitute the largest set $X'_i \times X'_j$ of strategy profiles that satisfies the following pair of properties:

1. Every strategy $x_i' \in X_i'$ is a best reply of player i to some belief $\bar{p}_j' \in \Delta(X_j')$ of player i concerning the probabilities with which player j will choose among his strategies in X_j'.

2. Every strategy $x_j' \in X_j'$ is a best reply of player j to some belief $\bar{p}_i' \in \Delta(X_i')$ of player j concerning the probabilities with which player i will choose among her strategies in X_i'.

The strategies of each player in this set are called the player's **rationalizable strategies**. In particular, the set of rationalizable strategy profiles $X_i' \times X_j'$ includes all the pure-strategy Nash equilibria of the game (since at a Nash equilibrium $\left(x_i^* \times x_j^*\right)$, the strategy of each player *is* optimal for her, given that she is certain that the other player will adhere to her equilibrium strategy). Also in the mixed strategy equilibria of the game, the equilibrium strategies mix only among the strategies in $X_i' \times X_j'$. This is because, at an equilibrium in mixed strategies, any strategy adopted by a player with a positive probability is a best reply to the distribution of the pure strategies of her rival at that equilibrium.

However, in any game in which there are several equilibria (and in which each player adopts different pure strategies at different equilibria), such as in the Battle of the Sexes game, not every rationalizable strategy profile in $X_i' \times X_j'$ is a Nash equilibrium. In such games, iterative elimination of never-best-reply strategies will not yield a sharp prediction about the outcome of the game.

Appendix: Proof of Proposition 14.1

If x_i is strongly dominated by $\bar{p}_i'$, then for any belief $\bar{p}_j'$ of player i about the likelihood of her rival's strategies, the expected utility of player i, if she adopts $\bar{p}_i'$, will always be higher than the utility she would obtain by adopting x_i:

$$U_i\left(\bar{p}_i', \bar{p}_j\right) > U_i\left(x_i, \bar{p}_j\right)$$

Thus, $\bar{p}_i^{\bar{p}_j} = \bar{p}_i'$ is preferable for player i over x_i under the belief $\bar{p}_j$, and hence x_i will never be optimal for player i in the mixed extension of the game.

It remains to prove the reverse direction of the proposition: if x_i is never-best-reply, then there exists a mixed strategy $\bar{p}_i'$ that strongly dominates x_i in the mixed extension of the game. In order to prove this, we will use the minimax theorem. We will define a new game with the same strategies for both players. The payoff function:

$$V_i\left(\tilde{x}_i, \tilde{x}_j\right) = U_i\left(\tilde{x}_i, \tilde{x}_j\right) - U_i\left(x_i, \tilde{x}_j\right)$$

for player i in the new game will be the difference between her payoff $U_i(\tilde{x}_i, \tilde{x}_j)$ in the original game and the payoff she would have obtained had she chosen x_i. The payoff function of player j in the new game will now be $V_j(\tilde{x}_i, \tilde{x}_j) = -V_i(\tilde{x}_i, \tilde{x}_j)$, so that the new game will be a zero sum game.

Since x_i is a never-best-reply strategy in the original game, we know that, given player i's belief $\bar{p}_j$ concerning her rival's strategies (i.e. given that player i believes that the rival is adopting the mixed strategy $\bar{p}_j$), player i has a mixed strategy $\bar{p}_i^{\bar{p}_j}$ which yields her a higher expected utility than she would have gotten had she chosen x_i:

$$U_i\left(\bar{p}_i^{\bar{p}_j}, \bar{p}_j\right) > U_i\left(x_i, \bar{p}_j\right)$$

In other words, for every mixed strategy $\bar{p}_j \in \Delta(X_j)$ of player j, it is the case that:

$$\max_{\bar{p}_i \in \Delta(X_i)} U_i\left(\bar{p}_i, \bar{p}_j\right) > U_i\left(x_i, \bar{p}_j\right)$$

or:

$$\max_{\bar{p}_i \in \Delta(X_i)} V_i\left(\bar{p}_i, \bar{p}_j\right) = \max_{\bar{p}_i \in \Delta(X_i)}\left[U_i\left(\bar{p}_i, \bar{p}_j\right) - U_i\left(x_i, \bar{p}_j\right)\right] > 0$$

In particular, this inequality is satisfied for that mixed strategy $\hat{p}_j \in \Delta(X_j)$ for which $\max_{\bar{p}_i \in \Delta(X_i)} V_i\left(\bar{p}_i, \bar{p}_j\right)$ is minimal:

$$\max_{\bar{p}_i \in \Delta(X_i)} V_i\left(\bar{p}_i, \hat{p}_j\right) = \min_{\bar{p}_j \in \Delta(X_j)} \max_{\bar{p}_i \in \Delta(X_i)} V\left(\bar{p}_i, \bar{p}_j\right) > 0$$

From the minimax theorem[3] (section 12.3) we deduce that:

$$\min_{\bar{p}_j \in \Delta(X_j)} \max_{\bar{p}_i \in \Delta(X_i)} V_i\left(\bar{p}_i, \bar{p}_j\right) = \max_{\bar{p}_i \in \Delta(X_i)} \min_{\bar{p}_j \in \Delta(X_j)} V_i\left(\bar{p}_i, \bar{p}_j\right) > 0$$

This means that even if for any mixed strategy $\bar{p}_i$ of player i, player j chooses that mixed strategy $\bar{p}_j^{\bar{p}_i}$ that will minimize the payoff $V_i\left(\bar{p}_i, \bar{p}_j\right)$ of player i, player i can still find a security strategy $\bar{p}_i'$ that will secure her a positive payoff:

$$V_i\left(\bar{p}_i', \bar{p}_j^{\bar{p}_i'}\right) = \max_{\bar{p}_i \in \Delta(X_i)} \min_{\bar{p}_j \in \Delta(X_j)} V_i\left(\bar{p}_i, \bar{p}_j\right) > 0$$

[3] In Chapter 12 we proved the minimax theorem for games in which each player has only two pure strategies. However, as we noted there, the theorem holds true also for games in which each player has any finite number of pure strategies. The proof that was given there is also valid for the more general case in which each player has finitely many pure strategies.

In other words, for every mixed strategy $\bar{p}_j$ of player j, it is the case that:

$$V_i\left(\bar{p}'_i, \bar{p}_j\right) > 0$$

or:

$$U_i\left(\bar{p}'_i, \bar{p}_j\right) - U_i\left(x_i, \bar{p}_j\right) > 0$$

Therefore, in the original game, x_i is a strategy that is strongly dominated (by $\bar{p}'_i$), as we sought to demonstrate.

QED

15 Stability of equilibria

At a Nash equilibrium a balance is struck between the players' strategies: each player chooses a strategy that is optimal for her, given the strategies chosen by the other players. The equilibrium concept does not deal with the question of how such a balance is created, or what will happen if it is upset. In other words, the equilibrium is a static concept and does not address the question of what dynamics (if any) could possibly cause the players to choose, or to gradually approach, the equilibrium strategies.

A large number of dynamic processes are conceivable in which, over time, each player repeatedly updates her choice, and in so doing studies the moves of the other players and the payoffs she is getting. Of course, different processes will correspond to different assumptions concerning the players' degree of sophistication, the information available to them, the memory resources and computational capability at their disposal, and so on. Accordingly, an important branch of modern game theory is called Learning in Games and this topic is one of the frontiers of game-theoretic research.[1]

We will now proceed to describe two key types of updating processes.

15.1 Updating processes

15.1.1 Eductive processes

In eductive processes, the game is played one single time. Before it starts, each player mulls over various possible strategy profiles that both she and the other players may adopt, and in an iterative process progressively narrows down the possibilities that appear to her as reasonable.

In preceding chapters, we have already encountered two such types of eductive processes:

- iterative elimination of strongly dominated strategies;
- iterative elimination of weakly dominated strategies.

---

[1] See, for example, Fudenberg, D. and D. K. Levine (1998), *The Theory of Learning in Games*, Cambridge, MA: The MIT Press.

We have also seen that in certain games (such as Divvying up the Jackpot) the eductive process of iterative elimination of weakly dominated strategies can lead the players to exclude certain Nash equilibria.

15.1.2   Actual updating processes

In these processes, the players play the same game over and over again, and can change their choice of strategies from one game round to the next. The possible rules in accordance to which the players may update their choices are numerous. We will describe several of them:

- **Best-reply dynamics**: in the first round, the players adopt some given strategy profile, which is the starting point for the updating process. In each additional game round, each player chooses a best reply to the strategy profile played by the other players in the preceding round.
- **Fictitious play**: before each game round, each player checks in what proportion of the preceding game rounds each strategy profile of the other players was played. The player believes that this proportion defines the probability with which that same action profile will be played in the next round. Given this belief, the player chooses a strategy that will maximize her expected payoff in the next round. Prior to the first round, the belief of each player is determined in the same way by a distribution over the opponents' strategy profiles in an imaginary history of game rounds. These distributions constitute the starting point for the updating process.
- **Regret matching dynamics**: following each game round, every player i asks herself: *"If, in the past, whenever I played the strategy x_i that I have just chosen, I had instead chosen a particular different strategy x'_i, by how much could I have improved my average payoff?"* In the next round, the player tends to choose strategies x'_i that would have enabled such improvement, and the probability with which she will choose between the strategies that would enable improvement monotonically increases in the extent of the improvement; nevertheless, with a certain (predetermined) probability, the player will persistently adhere to the strategy she applied in the preceding round. The starting point for the updating process is a particular strategy profile that the players adopt in the first round.
- **Reinforcement learning**: each player updates the score she assigns to her strategies after each game round. The player increases the score she assigns to the strategy she just played if the payoff she obtained is higher than her average payoff in the game rounds so far, and reduces the score she assigns to that strategy in the opposite case. In the next round, the higher the score assigned to a particular strategy, the greater the player's chance of choosing that strategy. Prior to the first round, each player has a certain given score for her strategies, and that score is the point of departure for the updating process.

- **Aspiration-based updating**: each player aspires to her average payoff not falling below a certain threshold. She adheres to that strategy as long as the average payoff she has obtained so far is not below the threshold. If, after several game rounds, the average payoff declines to below the threshold, she randomly chooses another strategy. (In another version of the process, the threshold is repeatedly updated in the course of the game, rising and falling as a function of the actual average payoff.) The starting point of the process is defined by the strategy adopted by each player in the first round.

- **Bayesian learning**: at the beginning of the process, each player has a probabilistic belief about all the possible histories of action profiles (of the other players) that may show up in the course of all the game rounds. These beliefs define the starting point of the process. After each game round, each player updates her beliefs concerning the future game rounds by applying Bayes' rule, which involves excluding from the reckoning all histories that have not actually materialized. In particular, after such an update, each player entertains a belief concerning the probabilities of the other players' possible action profiles in the next game round. It is in light of this updated belief that each player chooses a strategy that will maximize her expected payoff in the next game round.

These updating processes differ substantially from one another. First, they are distinguished by the degree of information upon which they rely. In the "best-reply dynamics" every player relies solely on the actions actually chosen by the players in the preceding round, whereas in fictitious play, regret matching and Bayesian learning, each player relies on the entire history of the game up to that stage. By contrast, in reinforcement learning and aspiration-based updating, the players do not know or do not recall how their rivals played in the preceding rounds, and each player is familiar with her own payoffs only. Second, the players are distinguishable from one another in terms of their degree of sophistication. In Bayesian learning, the players choose their actions in terms of their beliefs regarding the future behavior of their rivals,[2] based on how they played in the past. In all the other dynamics, however, the players are myopic and use various rules of thumb based solely on the development of the game in the preceding rounds.

Despite all these differences, one aspect is common to all these updating processes: if at the start of the process all players play a particular Nash equilibrium of the game,[3] they will continue to play that equilibrium over and over again. In other words, any Nash equilibrium of the game is a **fixed point** or a **rest point** of each of the processes.

---

[2] Even though every player ignores the fact that her rivals, too, are adopting the same learning process and does not try to influence their beliefs (and thereby their actions) by the very choices she makes.

[3] Or, in accordance with the opening attributes of each process, they imagine that that equilibrium has always been played, or believe that it will be played henceforward.

This naturally gives rise to the following questions. Assume that in the first round of the process, the players' strategies, although not exactly Nash equilibrium strategies, are very close to being Nash equilibria. (A deviation of this kind may be caused, for example, by a minor error on the part of one of the players after the players had agreed beforehand to play that same Nash equilibrium repeatedly.) Will the updating process lead the players to converge back to that Nash equilibrium? Will the players be using, throughout the entire updating process, only strategy profiles that are close to that equilibrium, or are they also liable to greatly distance themselves from it in some of the rounds? We will now proceed to formulate these questions in a precise fashion.

15.2 Dynamical systems

In each of the updating processes we have described, and after each game round t, the state of affairs can be described by means of a state variable $y \in Y$ which provides a sufficient description from which it is possible to deduce (by applying the updating or learning rule) how the other players will play in the next game round. For example, in best-reply dynamics, y is simply the strategy profile that the players played in round t; in reinforcement learning, the variable y describes the score that each player ascribes to each of her strategies; and so on.[4]

The updating process may be described by a function:

$$f : Y \to Y$$

defining the state variable $f(y)$ of the process in the next round assuming that in the previous round the state variable was y.

More generally, the space of state variables $Y \subseteq \mathbb{R}^k$ and the transition function:

$$f : Y \to Y$$

define a dynamical system in discrete time.[5]

Given the initial state of the system $y_0 \in Y$, the development of the state of the system over time is given by the sequence of state variables:

$$y_0, \quad y_1 = f(y_0), \quad y_2 = f(y_1), \ldots \quad y_{n+1} = f(y_n), \ldots$$

The state $y^* \in Y$ is called a **fixed point** of the system if it is the case that:

$$y^* = f(y^*)$$

---

[4] Thus, the state variable y is simply a vector of numbers. If k numbers are required in order to describe the situation, then the space of state variables Y is a subset of the space $\mathbb{R}^k$ — the Euclidean space of k-dimensional vectors.

[5] More precisely, this is an autonomous dynamical system, i.e. a dynamical system in which the updating rule f itself does not change over time.

Thus, if from the outset the system is in the state $y_0 = y^*$, then it will remain there:

$$y_0 = y^*$$
$$y_1 = f(y^*) = y^*$$
$$y_2 = f(f(y^*)) = f^2(y^*) = y^*$$
$$\vdots$$
$$y_n = f^n(y^*) = y^*$$
$$\vdots$$

(f^n is the function f when activated n times, one after the other.)

When do we say that a fixed point y^* of a dynamical system is **stable**?

Definition

A fixed point y^* is called **stable**[6] if a slight deviation from y^* will never lead the system to a large deviation from y^*.[7]

A fixed point of the system is called **asymptotically stable** if it is **stable**, and when the system deviates slightly from y^*, it converges back to it.[8]

The set of all the states $y_0 \in Y$ from which the system converges to y^* is called **the basin of attraction** of y^*.

After these general definitions for dynamical systems, we will address the particular case in which the dynamical system is that of the best-reply dynamics. In this case, the state variable y of the system is simply the strategy profile x that the players played in the preceding game round. In other words, the set of state variables Y is therefore the players' set of strategy profiles X.

---

[6] Stability of this kind is also called **Liapunov stability**.

[7] In precise terms, the fixed point y^* is stable if for every $r > 0$ we can find $\varepsilon > 0$, such that for every initial state y_0 the distance of which from y^* is smaller than ε,

$$d(y_0 - y^*) < \varepsilon$$

the system will never reach a distance of more than r from y^*:

$$d(f^n(y_0) - y^*) < r, \quad n = 1, 2, \ldots$$

[8] In precise terms, a fixed point y^* of the system is asymptotically stable if it is stable, and in addition there exists $q > 0$ such that from any initial state y_0 the distance of which from y^* is less than q,

$$d(y_0 - y^*) < q$$

it is the case that:

$$y_n = f^n(y_0) \xrightarrow[n \to \infty]{} y^*$$

What is the transition function f that corresponds to this updating process? Every player $i \in I$ chooses a strategy that is a best reply for her against the action profile that the players played in the preceding round.[9] That is, the transition function:

$$f : X \rightarrow X$$

is defined by:

$$f(x) = (BR_i(x_{-i}))_{i \in I}$$

(Recall that, given the strategy profile x, x_{-i} is the strategy profile of all the players other than i, and $BR_i(x_{-i})$ is the best reply of player i to that strategy profile.)

Question 15.1

Show that the strategy profile x^* is a Nash equilibrium in the game if and only if x^* is a fixed point of the best-reply dynamics.

Answer

The strategy profile x^* is a Nash equilibrium if and only if for every player $i \in I$:

$$x_i^* = BR_i(x_{-i}^*)$$

i.e.:

$$x^* = (\ldots x_i^*, \ldots) = (\ldots BR_i(x_{-i}^*), \ldots) = f(x^*)$$

Or, in other words, x^* is a fixed point of the best-reply dynamics f.

Is every Nash equilibrium in the game also asymptotically stable? In other words, is every Nash equilibrium also an asymptotically stable fixed point of best-reply dynamics? We will now show that the answer to this question is negative. There exist games in which some of the equilibria are not stable (and therefore they are also not asymptotically stable). Hence, such equilibria constitute weaker predictions regarding the players' behavior: if at such an equilibrium the balance in the players' behavior is upset even slightly, the best-reply dynamics will lead the players far away from that equilibrium.

On the other hand, an asymptotically stable equilibrium is a robust prediction of the players' behavior. In an asymptotically stable equilibrium, a slight deviation by the players from the equilibrium will lead them to converge back to it under the best-reply dynamics. Moreover, throughout the convergence process, the players' behavior will remain close to their behavior at equilibrium.

---

[9] We will focus here on games in which every player always has a unique best reply.

15.2.1　Examples of games in which only some of the equilibria are stable

In Chapter 9, section 9.4, we discussed the coordination problem among consumers in the presence of network externalities, and we illustrated it by an example of demand for fax machines. We found that there are three equilibria in this game. At one equilibrium, nobody purchases a fax machine. At the other two equilibria, the number of consumers purchasing fax machines is given by:

$$n_1^* = \frac{(A+1) + \sqrt{(A+1)^2 - 4p}}{2}$$

$$n_2^* = \frac{(A+1) - \sqrt{(A+1)^2 - 4p}}{2}$$

In order to check which of these equilibria is stable in the best-reply dynamics, we will first examine who will be the purchasers of the fax machines, and how many purchasers there will be if in the previous game round n customers acquired the device.[10]

Recall that the A potential consumers taking part in the game are of the types

$$\tau = 1, \ldots A$$

When n consumers purchase faxes, a consumer of type τ is willing to pay at most $n\tau$ for the device. Therefore, if n consumers purchased fax machines in the preceding game round, the lowest type that is prepared to purchase a device in the current round is:

$$\tau = \frac{p}{n}$$

when the market price of a fax machine is p.[11] It follows that the number of consumers who will wish to purchase the device in the current round is:

$$A + 1 - \tau = A + 1 - \frac{p}{n}$$

in case this is not a negative number. If the number of consumers n who purchased faxes in the preceding round is so small that $A + 1 - \frac{p}{n} < 0$, then none of the consumers will wish to purchase a fax in the current round.

---

[10]　Here we are assuming that in every game round, every consumer must pay for the fax machine if she wishes to use it, even if she has already purchased a fax machine in one of the preceding game rounds. This payment may be chargeable for maintenance, warranty, and service. For the sake of simplicity, we assume that in every game round, this payment is identical to that paid by the consumer when she first purchased the fax machine.

[11]　More precisely, since the types are integers, this is the type $\lfloor \frac{p}{n} \rfloor$ (the largest integer that does not exceed $\frac{p}{n}$). Accordingly, in the following calculations, too, the number of consumers must always be rounded to whole numbers.

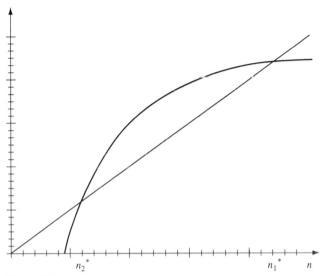

Figure 15.1

Figure 15.1 describes the expression $A + 1 - \frac{p}{n}$ as a function of n, together with the diagonal at 45°. The two equilibria, n_1^* and n_2^*, correspond to the two points of intersection: if in the preceding round n_1^* consumers purchased fax machines, then in the current round, too, n_1^* consumers will wish to become fax owners; the same holds true for n_2^*. The third equilibrium is located at the origin: if nobody purchased a fax in the preceding round ($n = 0$), then the expression $A + 1 - \frac{p}{n}$ is negative, i.e. nobody will wish to purchase a fax in the current round either.

We can now use this graph to examine the stability of these equilibria.

The equilibrium n_1^*: assume that in the preceding round, the number of fax purchasers n was slightly higher than n_1^*:

$$n > n_1^*$$

We see that in this domain it is the case that:

$$A + 1 - \frac{p}{n} < n$$

i.e. the number of consumers in the current round will be less than n, but still greater than n_1^* (since, when $n > n_1^*$, it is the case that $A + 1 - \frac{p}{n} > A + 1 - \frac{p}{n_1^*} = n_1^*$). Thus, in the following stages, the number of consumers will gradually decrease and converge to n_1^* (see Figure 15.2).

Now assume that in the preceding round, the number of fax purchasers n was smaller than n_1^* but greater than n_2^*:

$$n_2^* < n < n_1^*$$

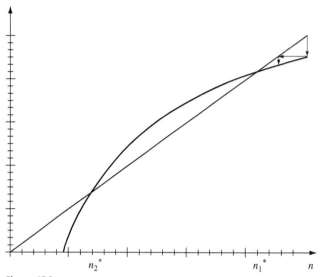

Figure 15.2

In this domain it is the case that:

$$A + 1 - \frac{p}{n} > n$$

Therefore, in the current round, the number of fax purchasers will be greater than n, and in the forthcoming rounds it will continue to rise and will converge towards n_1^* (see Figure 15.3).

(In Figures 15.2 and 15.3, every vertical arrow describes the change in the number of fax purchasers; each horizontal arrow connects the number of fax purchasers n from the preceding round to the 45° diagonal, and reaches the point from which it will be possible, with the aid of a vertical arrow, to find the number of fax purchasers $A + 1 - \frac{p}{n}$ in the current round; and so forth.)

Hence two conclusions follow:

- The equilibrium n_1^* is asymptotically stable in best-reply dynamics: a small deviation from it leads to re-convergence to it, and not to diverging away from it.
- The equilibrium n_2^* is unstable (and hence it is not asymptotically stable either) in best-reply dynamics: even the very slightest upward deviation from this equilibrium leads to divergence away from it (towards n_1^*).

It now remains to examine the domain:

$$0 < n < n_2^*$$

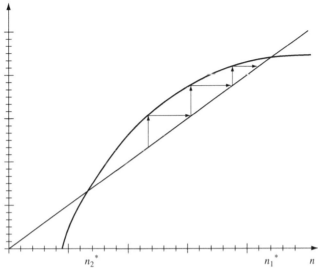

Figure 15.3

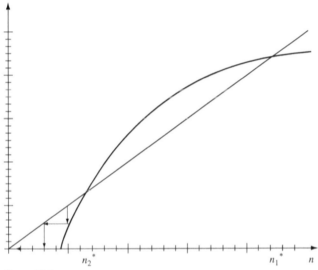

Figure 15.4

In this domain it is the case that:

$$A + 1 - \frac{p}{n} < n$$

and therefore the number of fax purchasers in the current round will be less than n. In the following rounds, this number will decrease even further, becoming vanishingly close to 0 (see Figure 15.4). In this domain, in fact, the number of purchasers will revert to 0 after a finite number of rounds: the moment when the number of fax purchasers n' in a particular round satisfies:

$$A + 1 - \frac{p}{n'} \leq 0$$

the number of purchasers in the succeeding round will be 0.

Hence, the equilibrium at which nobody purchases fax machines is asymptotically stable in best-reply dynamics: a slight deviation from it leads to re-convergence to it, and not to divergence away from it.

What can we deduce from this about the commodity markets in which there exist externalities which are contingent on the size of the consumer network? The equilibrium n_2^* constitutes the **critical mass** which the marketers of such products will aspire to reach. The equilibrium n_2^* is not stable in itself, but the moment the number of consumers surpasses it, there may be a snowball effect in which more and more consumers decide to purchase the product, toward the efficient equilibrium n_1^*. When market penetration of the product falls below the critical mass n_2^*, the demand for the product progressively deteriorates, and it gradually vanishes from the market.

Question 15.2	Examine the three equilibria in the job search and unemployment model in Chapter 9, section 9.5 (pp. 149ff.), when the effort function is given by: $$c(h) = h$$ and the cumulative distribution function of the height of the coconuts on the trees is given by: $$p(h) = \frac{1}{2} + 4\left(h - \frac{1}{2}\right)^3$$ See Figure 15.5. Which of the three equilibria are asymptotically stable in best-reply dynamics? Which of them are not stable?
Answer	Assume that on a particular day, e of the islanders were "employed" and spent the afternoon looking for partners with whom to exchange the coconuts they had picked that morning. The next morning, in the best-reply dynamics, the islanders are to decide which coconuts to pick, assuming that the chance of finding a swap partner in the afternoon will be $b(e) = e$. Therefore, they will only pick nuts at a height of not more than e (since the effort $c(h)$ that is required in order to pick a nut at height h is h, and the effort of climbing is perceived as justifying itself only if that effort is not greater than the chance of finding a swap partner). As a result, that afternoon, $P(e)$ of the islanders will have nuts to swap. Next morning, the islanders will pick coconuts

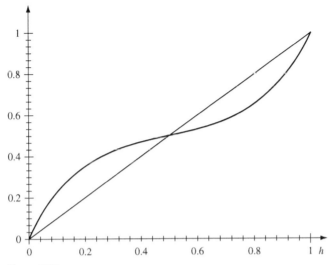

Figure 15.5

at a height of not more than $P(e)$, and in the afternoon, $P(P(e)) = P^2(e)$ of the islanders will seek partners for the swap; etc.

P is an increasing function and satisfies $P(\frac{1}{2}) = \frac{1}{2}$. For $0 < e < \frac{1}{2}$ it is the case that:

$$e < P(e) < P\left(\frac{1}{2}\right) = \frac{1}{2}$$

and for $\frac{1}{2} < e < 1$ it is the case that:

$$e < P(e) < P\left(\frac{1}{2}\right) = \frac{1}{2}$$

Accordingly, for $0 < e < \frac{1}{2}$ it is the case that:

$$e < P(e) < P^2(e) < P^3(e) < \dots < \frac{1}{2}$$

and the sequence $P^n(e)$ converges to $\frac{1}{2}$;
and for $\frac{1}{2} < e < 1$ it is the case that:

$$e > P(e) > P^2(e) > P^3(e) > \dots > \frac{1}{2}$$

and the sequence $P^n(e)$ converges to $\frac{1}{2}$ (see Figure 15.6).

Hence the equilibrium $h^* = \frac{1}{2}$ is asymptotically stable, and the two other equilibria, $h^* = 0$ and $h^* = 1$, are unstable.

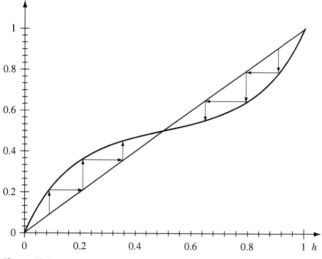

Figure 15.6

Comprehension check

Repeat Question 15.2 for the cumulative distribution function:

$$P(h) = \begin{cases} 4h^3 & 0 \le h \le \frac{1}{2} \\ 1 + 4(h-1)^3 & \frac{1}{2} \le h \le 1 \end{cases}$$

the graphic description of which is given in Figure 15.7.

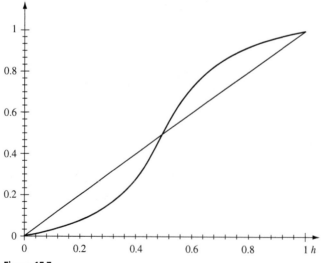

Figure 15.7

16 Games and evolution

The solution concepts we have dealt with so far were based on the assumption that the players taking part in the game are rational. Is game theory useful only under the assumption of rationality?

It may perhaps be surprising to discover that the answer to this question is negative. In this chapter, we will replace the assumption of rationality by which the players try to maximize their payoff with an assumption that is the very antithesis of rationality. We will assume that every player is devoid of the capacity to choose, being pre-programmed to play a unique particular strategy.

How can a theory of strategic choice be relevant for players who make no choice? Despite the apparent contradiction, we will see how the tools of game theory can serve for analyzing the evolution of characteristic properties or *types* of individuals in large populations. The fascinating connection between game theory and biology was explicitly proposed by Maynard Smith and Price (1973)[1] and was later developed in the classic book of Maynard Smith (1982).[2]

In population games, a player's strategy is its **type**. In an animal population, the player is an individual in the population and its type is a genetic property that it bears – its genotype. This is a property that it inherits from its parents and bequeaths to its offspring. This idea can also be extended to a discussion of social and cultural norms in human societies: an individual's type may be a social norm that the individual has assimilated and internalized in the course of the socialization process and which she will also bequeath to her children.

In the games we dealt with in the preceding chapters, the participants in the strategic encounter always constituted a constant (and usually small) set of players, and the encounter between them was a one-shot non-recurring interaction. In population games, by contrast, the encounters take place over and over again between pairs of individuals chosen in each encounter by random pairwise matching.[3]

---

[1] Maynard Smith, J. and G. R. Price (1973), "The Logic of Animal Conflict," *Nature* 246, 15–18.
[2] Maynard Smith, J. (1982), *Evolution and the Theory of Games*, Cambridge University Press.
[3] More generally speaking, the set of players in each encounter may also include more than two players, and in particular the entire population ("playing the field"). In this book, we will not address these generalizations, but will focus on a model of random encounters between pairs of individuals.

In any random encounter in the course of a population game, the individuals do not perform any process of choice; the payoff of each individual is determined by the profile of the types of individuals in the encounter. What, then, does this payoff express? If the individual makes no choice, what significance is there to the fact that the individual would have obtained a higher payoff had it been of a different type?

In population games, the individual's payoff reflects fitness to reproduce: individuals with a higher payoff have a larger number of offspring.

We will focus on a case in which the game in every encounter is symmetric, i.e. a game in which an individual's payoff depends solely on its type and that of its rival, and not on the question of whether, in the random encounter, the individual was selected for the role of player 1 or player 2.

Definition   **A symmetric game between two players** is a game in which both players have the same set of strategies:

$$S \equiv X_1 = X_2 = \left\{ s^1, \dots, s^K \right\}$$

and for each pair of strategies $s, s' \in S$, it is the case that:

$$U_1(s, s') = U_2(s', s).$$

In a symmetric game we denote $U(s, s') \equiv U_1(s, s')$.

Definition   **A symmetric equilibrium** (in pure or mixed strategies) **in a symmetric game between two players** is a Nash equilibrium in which both players adopt the same strategy.

In this chapter, we will focus on a case in which all payoffs in the game are positive: $U(s, s') > 0$.

16.1) The replicator dynamics

How does the composition of types in a population change from one generation to the next? We will assume the following:

1. All the offspring of a particular individual have exactly the same type as that of the parent. Thus, reproduction is asexual and with no mutations.
2. The individual's payoff in the game – its fitness – is simply the number of offspring it produces.

In every generation, a population is characterized by its aggregate size and by the distribution of the various types within it. The first state variable – the size of the population – is the number N. The second state variable – the distribution of types in the population – can be thought of as a mixed strategy:

$$\bar{p} = (p^1, \ldots, p^K) \in \Delta(S)$$

Thus, there exist in a population $p^k N$ individuals of the type s^k and each individual in the population has a probability p^k of randomly encountering a rival of the type s^k.[4]

| **Definition** | The above pair of rules 1 and 2 defines a **dynamical system**[5] of the evolution over time of the distribution of types in the population, called **the replicator dynamics**. |

Assume that the size of the population in generation t is N_t and the *distribution* of types in the population is:

$$\bar{p}_t = (p_t^1, \ldots, p_t^K)$$

An individual of the type s^ℓ encounters an individual of the type s^k with the probability p_t^k and in such a case has $U(s^\ell, s^k)$ offspring. Therefore, the average number of offspring of an individual of type s^ℓ is:

$$U(s^\ell, \bar{p}_t) = \sum_{k=1}^{K} p_t^k U(s^\ell, s^k)$$

and the average number of offspring across all the individuals in the population is:

$$U(\bar{p}_t, \bar{p}_t) = \sum_{l=1}^{K} p_t^\ell U(s^\ell, \bar{p}_t)$$

Since in generation t the population has $p_t^\ell N_t$ individuals of type s^ℓ, in generation $t + 1$ the population will have $(p_t^\ell N_t) U(s^\ell, \bar{p}_t)$ individuals of type s^ℓ, and altogether the number of individuals in the population in generation $t + 1$ will be:[6]

---

[4] We assume here, implicitly, that from the outset the population is very large. If the population is of the size N, it has $p^k N$ individuals of the type s^k. Therefore, the probability that an individual of the type s^ℓ will randomly encounter a rival of a different type s^k out of the other $N-1$ individuals in the population is $\frac{p^k N}{N-1} \approx p^k$. The quality of the approximation progressively improves as the size of the population N increases. Similarly, the probability that an individual of the type s^ℓ will randomly encounter a rival of the same type is $\frac{p^\ell N-1}{N-1} \approx p^\ell$ and the quality of the approximation improves progressively as the size of the population N increases.

[5] As defined in Chapter 15.

[6] Here we assume that all the parents who produced offspring in generation t are no longer alive in generation $t + 1$.

$$N_{t+1} = \sum_{\ell=1}^{K} \left(p_t^\ell N_t\right) U\left(s^\ell, \bar{p}_t\right) = N_t \sum_{\ell=1}^{K} p_t^\ell U\left(s^\ell, \bar{p}_t\right) = N_t U\left(\bar{p}_t, \bar{p}_t\right)$$

Therefore, the proportion of individuals of type s^ℓ in the population in generation $t+1$ is:

$$p_{t+1}^\ell = \frac{p_t^\ell N_t U\left(s^\ell, \bar{p}_t\right)}{N_{t+1}} = \frac{p_t^\ell U\left(s^\ell, \bar{p}_t\right)}{U\left(\bar{p}_t, \bar{p}_t\right)} \tag{16.1}$$

Thus, we have found that the distribution of types in the population in generation $t+1$ does not depend on the absolute size N_t of the population in generation t, but only on the distribution of the types in generation t (and, of course, on the payoff function U, which remains the same and does not vary over time).

Thus, if for every possible distribution of types: $\bar{p} = \left(p^1, \ldots p^\ell, \ldots p^K\right) \in \Delta(S)$ we define:

$$f(\bar{p}) = \left(\frac{p^1 U\left(s^1, \bar{p}\right)}{U\left(\bar{p}, \bar{p}\right)}, \ldots \frac{p^\ell U\left(s^\ell, \bar{p}\right)}{U\left(\bar{p}, \bar{p}\right)}, \ldots \frac{p^K U\left(s^K, \bar{p}\right)}{U\left(\bar{p}, \bar{p}\right)}\right)$$

then $f: \Delta(s) \to \Delta(s)$ is the transition function defining the replicator dynamics: from equation (16.1) we find that $f(\bar{p}_t) = \bar{p}_{t+1}$.[7]

Question 16.1

Show that in the replicator dynamics, if types s^ℓ who are present in the population (i.e. those for whom $p_t^\ell > 0$) and whose average fitness $U\left(s^\ell, \bar{p}_t\right)$ exceeds the average fitness $U\left(\bar{p}_t, \bar{p}_t\right)$ of the entire population, i.e. if it is the case that:

$$U\left(s^\ell, \bar{p}_t\right) > U\left(\bar{p}_t, \bar{p}_t\right)$$

then their proportion in the population increases at the expense of those types s^k whose average fitness $U\left(s^k, \bar{p}_t\right)$ is lower than the average population fitness $U\left(\bar{p}_t, \bar{p}_t\right)$. Likewise, show that the proportion of the various types in the population remains fixed from one generation to the next if and only if all the types present in the population have the same average fitness.

Answer

This is an immediate conclusion from equation (16.1), from which we see that if $p_t^\ell > 0$,[8] then it is the case that:

---

[7] The replicator dynamics was first presented by Taylor, P. and L. Jonker (1978), "Evolutionary Stable Strategies and Game Dynamics," *Mathematical Biosciences* 40, 145–156 in a more realistic fashion: each generation is divided into a large number n of equal time intervals, and in each such time interval only $1/n$ of the individuals interact in random pairs and produce offspring in accordance with rules 1 and 2. In the limit when $n \to \infty$, the continuous-time replicator dynamics is obtained; this was the dynamics defined by Taylor and Jonker (1978). In order to distinguish between the two definitions, the dynamic system that we have defined here is explicitly called the discrete-time replicator dynamics.
[8] If $p_t^\ell = 0$ then the two members of (16.1) cannot be divided by p_t^ℓ.

$$\frac{p_{t+1}^\ell}{p_t^\ell} = \frac{U\left(s^\ell,\bar{p}_t\right)}{U\left(\bar{p}_t,\bar{p}_t\right)}$$

Thus, the incidence of the type s^ℓ increases in the population, $p_{t+1}^\ell > p_t^\ell$, i.e.:

$$\frac{p_{t+1}^\ell}{p_t^\ell} > 1$$

if and only if:

$$\frac{U\left(s^\ell,\bar{p}_t\right)}{U\left(\bar{p}_t,\bar{p}_t\right)} > 1$$

That is, if and only if the average fitness of the type s^ℓ exceeds the average fitness of the population as a whole:

$$U\left(s^\ell,\bar{p}_t\right) > U\left(\bar{p}_t,\bar{p}_t\right)$$

The proportion of a type s^ℓ which is present in the population remains constant:

$$p_{t+1}^\ell = p_t^\ell > 0$$

if and only if:

$$U\left(s^\ell,\bar{p}_t\right) = U\left(\bar{p}_t,\bar{p}_t\right)$$

Therefore, the proportion of all types in the population remains unchanged from one generation to the next if and only if all the types which are present in the population have the same average fitness, which is equal, in this case, to the average fitness of the entire population, $U\left(\bar{p}_t,\bar{p}_t\right)$.

(This conclusion is not valid for a type which is not present in the population, i.e. a type s^ℓ for whom $p_t^\ell = 0$, if such a type exists. For such a type we deduce from (16.1) that $p_{t+1}^\ell = 0$, whether $U\left(s^\ell,\bar{p}_t\right) = U\left(\bar{p}_t,\bar{p}_t\right)$ or not.)

We will now turn to demonstrate these ideas in the following example.

16.1.1   The Hawk-Dove game

The individuals in a particular population compete with one another over the use of a scarce resource such as territory. Without use of the resource, the fitness of an individual is $F > 0$. An individual obtaining the resource without a fight has fitness $F + V$. The term $V > 0$ is the fitness increment for the individual resulting from the use of the resource. However, if the individual obtains the resource only after contending with another individual, its fitness drops to $F + V - C$. The term C is the decrease in fitness resulting from the fight.

The population consists of two types of individuals: "hawks" and "doves." When two hawks meet, they fight one another. Each of them wins the resource with equal probability, and therefore the expected fitness of each one of them is $F + \frac{V}{2} - C$. When two doves meet, they do not fight and each of them wins the resource with equal probability. As a result, the expected fitness of each of them is $F + \frac{V}{2}$. When a hawk meets a dove, the dove concedes the resource and the hawk obtains it without a fight. In such a case, the fitness of the hawk is $F + V$, and the fitness of the dove is F. Thus, in this symmetric game, the payoff function U (of player 1) describes the levels of fitness:

<table>
<tr><td></td><td></td><td colspan="2" align="center">Individual 2</td></tr>
<tr><td></td><td></td><td align="center">Hawk</td><td align="center">Dove</td></tr>
<tr><td></td><td align="right">Hawk</td><td align="center">$F + \frac{V}{2} - C$</td><td align="center">$F + V$</td></tr>
<tr><td align="left">Individual 1</td><td></td><td></td><td></td></tr>
<tr><td></td><td align="right">Dove</td><td align="center">F</td><td align="center">$F + \frac{V}{2}$</td></tr>
</table>

We will denote the hawk strategy by h and the dove strategy by d. We will assume that the population is heterogeneous, i.e. we will assume that both types are present in the population.

If in generation t, the distribution of types in the population is $\bar{p}_t = (p_t^h, p_t^d)$ (which satisfies, of course, $p_t^h + p_t^d = 1$), then the expected fitness of an individual of type h is:

$$U(h, \bar{p}_t) = p_t^h U(h, h) + p_t^d U(h, d)$$
$$= p_t^h \left(F + \frac{V}{2} - C \right) + p_t^d (F + V) = F + \frac{V}{2} + p_t^d \frac{V}{2} - p_t^h C$$

and the expected fitness of an individual of type d is:

$$U(d, \bar{p}_t) = p_t^h U(d, h) + p_t^d U(d, d) = p_t^h F + p_t^d \left(F + \frac{V}{2} \right)$$
$$= F + p_t^d \frac{V}{2}$$

Therefore, the average fitness of an individual in the population is:

$$U(\bar{p}_t, \bar{p}_t) = p_t^h U(h, \bar{p}_t) + p_t^d U(d, \bar{p}_t)$$
$$= p_t^h \left(F + \frac{V}{2} + p_t^d \frac{V}{2} - p_t^h C \right) + p_t^d \left(F + p_t^d \frac{V}{2} \right)$$
$$= F + p_t^d \frac{V}{2} + p_t^h \left(\frac{V}{2} - p_t^h C \right)$$

From Question 16.1 we know that the dove population will increase in the next generation $(p_{t+1}^d > p_t^d)$ if and only if:

$$U(d, \bar{p}_t) - U(\bar{p}_t, \bar{p}_t) = -p_t^h \left(\frac{V}{2} - p_t^d C \right) > 0$$

i.e. if and only if:

$$p_t^h > \frac{V}{2C}$$

Two cases are possible here:

A. If $\frac{V}{2C} > 1$ then the inequality $p_t^h > \frac{V}{2C}$ will never materialize. In such a case, the dove population will progressively decrease from one generation to the next, and the hawk population will progressively increase. Appendix A to this chapter details the proof of the fact that the proportion of the doves tends to zero over the course of time. This result is not surprising, since when $\frac{V}{2} > C$, "hawk" is a dominant strategy.

B. If $\frac{V}{2C} < 1$, then neither of the strategies is dominant. In this case, the population of doves in generation $t + 1$ will be larger than the population of doves in generation t $(p_{t+1}^d > p_t^d$ and accordingly $p_{t+1}^h < p_t^h)$ if the hawk population is relatively large, $p_t^h > \frac{V}{2C}$; in the opposite case, in which the hawk population is relatively small, $p_t^h < \frac{V}{2C}$, the hawk population will increase and the dove population will decrease $(p_{t+1}^h > p_t^h$ and hence $p_{t+1}^d < p_t^d)$.

Only in the case in which $p_t^h = \frac{V}{2C}$ will the distribution of types remain constant from generation to generation. Thus, the distribution of types $(p^h, p^d) = \left(\frac{V}{2C}, 1 - \frac{V}{2C} \right)$ is a **fixed point of the replicator dynamics**. This is also the unique Nash equilibrium in the one-shot game between two players, the payoffs matrix of which is the one described above and replicated here with both players' payoffs specified explicitly:

		Individual 2	
		Hawk	Dove
Individual 1	Hawk	$F + \frac{V}{2} - C, F + \frac{V}{2} - C$	$F + V, F$
	Dove	$F, F + V$	$F + \frac{V}{2}, F + \frac{V}{2}$

(Verify this is indeed the unique Nash equilibrium!)

Let's assume, for example, that $F = 3$, $V = 8$, $C = 6$. Figure 16.1 describes by a thick line, for these values, the graph of the function $f(p^h) = p^h \frac{U(h, \bar{p})}{U(\bar{p}, \bar{p})}$ which determines (in accordance with the rule in (16.1)) the proportion of the hawks in

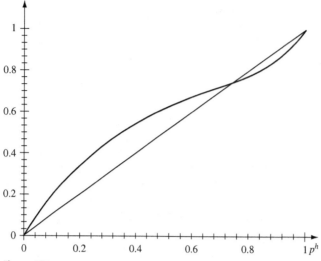

Figure 16.1

the population in the next generation as a function of their proportion in the population in the current generation.

We see that the proportion of hawks will be on the rise and will tend to:

$$\frac{V}{2C} = \frac{2}{3}$$

when their proportion is smaller than this bound, in the interval $p^h \in \left(0, \frac{2}{3}\right)$ (because $\frac{2}{3} > f(p^h) > p^h$), while the proportion of hawks will decrease and will tend to this bound in the domain $p^h \in \left(\frac{2}{3}, 1\right)$ (since in this domain $\frac{2}{3} < f(p^h) < p^h$). Finally, it is of course the case that $f\left(\frac{2}{3}\right) = \frac{2}{3}$.

16.2   The fixed points of the replicator dynamics and Nash equilibrium

The replicator dynamics describe the change of relative proportion of the different types in a population. This is, as stated, a completely mechanical dynamic: the individuals do not take any decisions but breed – to a greater or a lesser extent – in accordance with their fitness, which depends on their type and the type of the other individual whom they have randomly encountered.

Nevertheless, the fitness function U also defines a symmetric game between two players who make decisions, a game of the kind we discussed in the preceding chapters. Is there any nexus between rational behavior on the part of decision-making players in this game and the mechanical replicator dynamics of individuals in the large population? In particular, does any nexus exist between the Nash equilibria of the game and the fixed points of the replicator dynamics, in which the distribution of types in the population remains constant from one generation to the next?

We will now see that such a nexus does indeed exist. If we identify the distribution of types in the population $\bar{p} \in \Delta(S)$ with the mixed strategy profile in which each of the two players adopts the mixed strategy $\bar{p}$, we will see the following:

1. Every symmetric Nash equilibrium in the game is also a fixed point of the replicator dynamics.
2. Not every fixed point is a symmetric Nash equilibrium.
   However:
3. Every stable fixed point is a symmetric Nash equilibrium.
   Moreover:
4. There exist games with symmetric Nash equilibria that are not stable. In this sense, the replicator dynamics "single out" some of the equilibria and "discard" the rest. In other words, the property of stability defines a **refinement** of the concept of Nash equilibrium: stability is an additional property that we may require an equilibrium to fulfill.

We will now proceed to provide the proof of these connections.

Question 16.2

Show that if $(\bar{p}, \bar{p})$ is a Nash equilibrium in mixed strategies of the symmetric game with the payoff function U, then $\bar{p} = (p^1, \ldots, p^K)$ is a fixed point of the replicator dynamics.

Answer

If $(\bar{p}, \bar{p})$ is a Nash equilibrium in mixed strategies of the game, then all the strategies s^ℓ that are played with a positive probability $p^\ell > 0$ at this Nash equilibrium yield the same expected utility. In Question 16.1, we saw that in such a case, in the replicator dynamics the proportions of the different types in the population remain unchanged from generation to generation, i.e. $\bar{p}$ is a fixed point of the replicator dynamics.

Question 16.3

Is the opposite claim also true, i.e. is it the case that for every fixed point $\bar{p}$ of the replicator dynamics, $(\bar{p}, \bar{p})$ is a Nash equilibrium of the symmetric game with the payoff function U?

Answer

Not necessarily. In order for $(\bar{p}, \bar{p})$ to be a Nash equilibrium, it is not enough that all the strategies that are played with a positive probability should yield that same expected utility; it must also be the case that other strategies, that are not played at all, yield a lower (or at least an equal) expected utility. But the replicator dynamics may have fixed points that do not satisfy this property.

For example, if $\bar{p}$ is a pure strategy, i.e. in the distribution of types in the population only one particular type is present, then $\bar{p}$ is a fixed point of the replicator dynamics: the replicator dynamics do not allow for "mutations" to evolve out of different types, and hence types that are not present in the population from the outset cannot breed, even if, were they to be present, their payoff would be higher than average.

If that same unique type existing in the population corresponds to a dominated strategy, then the profile $(\bar{p}, \bar{p})$ is not a Nash equilibrium. For example, in the social dilemma game (in the example in section 3.2.1)

Player 2

		C	D
	C	2,2	0,3
Player 1	D	3,0	1,1

the "social" strategy C is dominated by the "selfish" strategy D, and therefore the strategy profile in which both players choose C does not constitute a Nash equilibrium. Yet, under the replicator dynamics, a population that initially consists of only "social" individuals will remain so along the generations.

It is clear, however, that fixed points of the replicator dynamics at which the only type which is present is a dominated type s^k are unstable.[9] A slight shift from a fixed point of this sort to a population in which there appear a very small number of individuals of the type s^ℓ which dominates s^k will lead, under the replicator dynamics, to divergence from the fixed point.

What about fixed points that *are* stable?

Proposition 16.1

For every stable fixed point $\bar{p}$ of the replicator dynamics, $(\bar{p}, \bar{p})$ is a Nash equilibrium.

This proposition is not hard to prove – the proof is given in Appendix B to this chapter.

---

[9] Stability and asymptotic stability of fixed points are defined in Chapter 15.

16.2.1   **Social dilemma**

If in a social dilemma game (the Prisoner's Dilemma game mentioned in section 3.2.1.1), when the population consists exclusively of "social" types C, we replace a small number of individuals by "selfish" types D, then a D-type individual will always have better fitness than a social type, whether the other party to the encounter is a type C or a type D:

$$U(D,C) > U(C,C)$$
$$U(D,D) > U(C,D)$$

This is because D is a dominant strategy in this game. Therefore, even in a population that has, from the outset, only a handful of D-type individuals, the proportion of type D in the population will increase progressively. In the limit, the type D will become completely predominant in the population in the sense that its share in the population will tend to 1. At any finite time, type C will still have positive representation in the population, but that relative representation will diminish gradually over the generations, tending to 0.

Note that the average fitness of the population *as a whole* will gradually decrease! This is because $U(C, C) > U(D, D)$. When the vast majority of the population consists of individuals of the type C, the replicator dynamics confer an advantage on the type D whose fitness is higher than the fitness of the other type in the given population. But the replicator dynamics do not guarantee that, with the passage of time, the (average) fitness of the entirety of individuals in the population will continue to increase. Thus, in a contest between the types C and D of the same species, type D will seize control of the population. The takeover by the type D of the population of the species will lead to a moderation in the rate of growth of the population.

This insight has implications for the contest between different species occupying the same habitat. Assume that in the habitat of the species under discussion (which includes two types, C and D) there exists also another species, X, whose rate of growth g is independent of the composition of the population of the first species (i.e. the rate of increase of the species X does not depend on the percentage of individuals of the first species which are of type C). We will also assume that the growth rate g of the species X is greater than the growth rate $U(D, D)$ of the population of individuals of the first species when it consists solely of individuals of the type D, but smaller than the growth rate $U(C,C)$ of a population that has only individuals of the type C:

$$U(D,D) < g < U(C,C)$$

We will assume that the populations of the two species are competing for the limited supply of food in that habitat, and that there can therefore exist in the habitat, at any point in time, precisely one million individuals of the two species altogether. We will further assume that at a certain point in time, half the individuals in the habitat are of the first species, the vast majority of them being of type C, and the other half belong to the other species, X. At first, the relative share of the first species in the habitat will steadily increase (i.e. more than half a million individuals will be of the first species), since $g < U(C, C)$. However, since the ratio of individuals of type D in the population of the first species will increase, the growth rate of the population of the first species will correspondingly decline. When a majority of the population of the first species will be of the type D, the growth rate of the population of the first species will be smaller than that of the species X since $U(D, D) < g$. Therefore, there will come a point in time at which the population of the first species will number less than half a million individuals; it will go on decreasing and will ultimately tend toward total extinction.

Hence the Darwinian laws of natural selection cannot be applied to the entire species: evolutionary pressures will not necessarily lead to a takeover by that genotype that will maximize the growth rate of the species. The argument that the logic of natural selection can be applied not only to the level of the type but also to the level of species has been advanced in biological literature and dubbed **group selection**. But we have now seen how game-theoretic tools plainly demonstrate that this argument is not valid in general.

16.2.2   The Stag Hunt game

Question 16.4

The payoffs in the Stag Hunt game that we presented in Chapter 9 are:

		Hunter 2	
		Stag	Hare
Hunter 1	Stag	3,3	0,2
	Hare	2,0	2,2

A. Find all the Nash equilibria in the game (in pure and/or mixed strategies).
B. Find all the fixed points of the replicator dynamics.
C. Which of these fixed points are stable?

Answer

A. In Chapter 9, we have already found that (stag, stag) and (hare, hare) are Nash equilibria in pure strategies. Likewise, the game has an equilibrium in mixed strategies, at which every hunter chooses the "stag" strategy with a probability of $p^S = \frac{2}{3}$. (When one of the hunters adopts this mixed strategy, the expected utility of the other hunter from any one of his strategies is 2. Therefore he is indifferent among them; and in particular, he, too, is prepared to adopt the mixed strategy in which $p^S = \frac{2}{3}$.) Note that each of these equilibria is a symmetric equilibrium: in each of them the two players adopt the same strategy.

B. We know – from Question 16.2 – that in each of the three symmetric equilibria that we found in A the equilibrium strategy is a fixed point of the replicator dynamics.[10]

Do there exist additional fixed points of the replicator dynamics to which no symmetric equilibrium strategy corresponds? From Question 16.3 we know that in order for there to be a fixed point that is not a symmetric equilibrium strategy, there should exist a strategy $\bar{p}$ that mixes between the strategies in some subset of strategies S', and also a strategy s which is not present in S' but yields against $\bar{p}$ a higher expected payoff than do the strategies in S'.

In the present game, there are only two such possible combinations of a subset S', a strategy $\bar{p}$ and a strategy $s \notin S'$:

Combination 1: $S' = \{Stag\}$, $\bar{p}$ assigns probability 1 to the strategy "Stag" and $s =$ Hare. In this combination, the strategy s is inferior against $\bar{p}$ relative to the strategy "Stag" that is present in S' (since only "Stag" is a best reply to "Stag").

Combination 2: $S' = \{Hare\}$, $\bar{p}$ assigns probability 1 to the strategy "Hare" and $s =$ Stag. In this case, too, as against $\bar{p}$ the strategy s is inferior to the strategy in S' (since only "Hare" is a best reply to "Hare").

Therefore, no additional fixed points of replicator dynamics exist in this game.

C. We will now examine the stability of the three fixed points we have found:

1. The fixed point "Stag." We will assume that the vast majority $p^S > \frac{2}{3}$ of the population of hunters are stag hunters, and only a small proportion of the population

$$p^H = 1 - p^S < \frac{1}{3}$$

are "Hare" hunters. Randomly paired off, the hunters set out on the hunt together.

[10] Question 16.2 deals with a symmetric equilibrium in mixed strategies and is accordingly also valid for the particular case in which the symmetric equilibrium strategy $\bar{p}$ is actually a pure strategy, in which one of the pure strategies is played with a probability of 1.

The average fitness of a hunter always hunting a stag is:

$$U\left(S, \left(p^S, p^H\right)\right) = p^S U(S, S) + p^H U(S, H) = 3p^S > 3 \cdot \frac{2}{3} = 2$$

while the fitness of a hunter always bagging a hare is only:

$$U\left(H, \left(p^S, p^H\right)\right) = p^S U(H, S) + p^H U(H, H) = 2p^S + 2\left(1 - p^H\right) = 2$$

Therefore, the proportion of stag hunters in the population will gradually increase over time, while the proportion of hare hunters in the population will steadily decrease and tend to zero. Therefore, the fixed point at which the entire population consists of stag hunters is stable (and also asymptotically stable: a slight deviation from it leads to re-convergence towards the fixed point).

2. The fixed point "Hare." We will assume that at least one-third of the population are "hare hunters" and the rest are "stag hunters." The hunters are randomly paired off and set out on the hunt together.

    The average fitness of a hare hunter is:

$$U\left(H, \left(p^S, p^H\right)\right) = p^S U(H, S) + p^H U(H, H) = 2p^S + 2\left(1 - p^H\right) = 2$$

while the average fitness of a stag hunter is only:

$$U\left(S, \left(p^S, p^H\right)\right) = p^S U(S, S) + p^H U(S, H) = 3p^S < 3 \cdot \frac{2}{3} = 2$$

Therefore, the proportion of hare hunters in the population will steadily increase, while the proportion of stag hunters in the population will decrease, tending to zero. Therefore, the fixed point at which the entire population consists of hare hunters is asymptotically stable.

3. The fixed point:

$$\left(p^S, p^H\right) = \left(\frac{2}{3}, \frac{1}{3}\right)$$

is not stable. A slight deviation from it to a population in which $p^S > \frac{2}{3}$ will gradually lead towards a population composed entirely of stag hunters, as we saw in A above. Similarly, a slight perturbation toward a population in which $p^S < \frac{2}{3}$ will lead the dynamic system to converge towards a population consisting exclusively of hare hunters, as we saw in B.

Thus, the criterion of stability in the replicator dynamics defines the sifting out of some of the equilibria in certain symmetric games. In effect, there are symmetric games with a unique Nash equilibrium, which is unstable in the replicator dynamics. We will now examine such an example.

16.2.3 Rock-Paper-Scissors

In the example in section 13.2.1 we analyzed the following Rock-Paper-Scissors game:

Player 2

	R	P	S
R	0,0	−1,1	1,−1
P	1,−1	0,0	−1,1
S	−1,1	1,−1	0,0

Player 1: P rows labeled R, P, S

and we found that the game has a unique Nash equilibrium at which each player chooses each of her strategies with a probability of $\frac{1}{3}$.

If we increase each of the payoffs in the game by 2, we will obtain a new game:

Player 2

	R	P	S
R	2,2	1,3	3,1
P	3,1	2,2	1,3
S	1,3	3,1	2,2

in which both players have the same von Neumann–Morgenstern preferences among the lotteries.[11] Therefore, also in the new game $(\frac{1}{3},\frac{1}{3},\frac{1}{3})$ is the unique Nash equilibrium. In the new game, all payoffs are positive, and therefore, in the replicator dynamics, the payoffs can represent the fitness levels of the individuals in the population.[12]

We know from Question 16.3 that the equilibrium $(\frac{1}{3},\frac{1}{3},\frac{1}{3})$ is a fixed point of replicator dynamics. Is this fixed point stable? What will happen if the initial composition of types in the population is very close, but not identical, to $(\frac{1}{3},\frac{1}{3},\frac{1}{3})$?

Let's assume that in the initial composition of the population, the type Rock has the highest proportion. As a result, the share of the type Scissors in the population will gradually decrease, becoming from a certain point onwards smaller than the share of Paper. At this stage, the type Paper will have the highest average fitness. Therefore, its share in the population will constantly increase until it becomes the most common type in the population.

[11] See Chapter 10.
[12] Instead of increasing the payoffs by 2 we could have increased the payoffs also by any other constant greater than 1 – an increase that would have resulted in all payoffs in the payoffs matrix being positive.

As a result, the proportion of the type Rock will gradually decrease, becoming, sooner or later, even lower than that of the type Scissors. At this stage, Scissors will have the highest fitness and will ultimately become the most common type in the population. The share of Paper will now steadily decline, and its incidence will ultimately be less than that of the type Rock. Rock will now be the type with the highest average fitness, and will gradually retake its position as the most common type in the population, and so on.

From this description we understand that the distribution of proportions will spiral around the fixed point $\left(\frac{1}{3},\frac{1}{3},\frac{1}{3}\right)$. Will this spiral gradually converge back in the direction of the fixed point, or, alternatively, become ever more distant from it? Or will it circle around $\left(\frac{1}{3},\frac{1}{3},\frac{1}{3}\right)$ in a fixed radius, without either approaching or moving away from the fixed point?

The sequence of points in Figure 16.2 describes the development of the proportions of types, beginning from an initial distribution that is close to the fixed point $\left(\frac{1}{3},\frac{1}{3},\frac{1}{3}\right)$ (which is marked by the square).

We see that the spiral of proportions steadily diverges away from the fixed point $\left(\frac{1}{3},\frac{1}{3},\frac{1}{3}\right)$ and therefore this fixed point is not stable.[13] Since $\left(\frac{1}{3},\frac{1}{3},\frac{1}{3}\right)$ is the unique equilibrium in the game, this game has no Nash equilibrium that is also a stable fixed point of replicator dynamics.

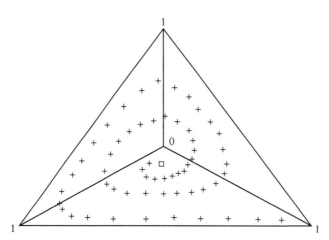

Figure 16.2

[13] The distribution of the types' proportions in the continuous version of replicator dynamics that we mentioned in footnote 7 will circle in a fixed radius around $\left(\frac{1}{3},\frac{1}{3},\frac{1}{3}\right)$; but if we even slightly increase the payoff of each strategy as against itself to $2 + \varepsilon$, for an arbitrarily small $\varepsilon > 0$, the spiral will circle outward, and will steadily diverge from the fixed point, similarly to the dynamic in Figure 16.2. For $\varepsilon < 0$, the spiral will steadily approach in the direction of the fixed point, and in this case the fixed point will be stable (and also asymptotically stable).

16.2.3.1   **Lizards play Rock-Paper-Scissors**

The replicator dynamics in a game of the type Rock-Paper-Scissors actually take place in a species of lizards called the common side-blotched lizard (*Uta stansburiana*) that lives in the coastal region of California. This species of lizard has males of three types:

- Orange-throated males are aggressive, and defend large domains where they keep harems of up to seven females each.
- Blue-throated males are less aggressive, defend smaller domains, and keep small harems, usually of three females.
- Yellow-throated males are very submissive, and mimic females. Thus they can steal into the domains of other males and mate with the females living there.

Sinervo and Lively (1996)[14] researched the lizard population in the years 1990–1995. They found that in 1990–1991, the blue-throated males were the most common type in the population; by the year 1993, their share in the population had fallen significantly, while the share of the orange-throated had peaked; by 1994, the most common throat color was yellow; and in 1995, the distribution of types resembled that of 1990.

What is the reason for this dynamic?

- The orange-throated males are more violent than the blue-throated. Therefore, the orange-throated are able to overrun the domains of the blue-throated and mate with the females there. Hence, in a year in which the population has a relatively large number of blue-throated males, the orange-throated are able to mate with a large number of females, and their share in the population increases in the following year.
- The orange-throated have domains that are too large for them to defend properly from the encroachments of the yellow-throated males. Thus, in a year in which there are many orange-throated males, the yellow-throated will, perversely enough, be the ones who succeed in mating with a relatively large number of females, boosting their share in the population in the next generation.
- The blue-throated have small domains which they can therefore defend properly, and they are able, in most cases, to prevent the yellow-throated from making incursions and mating with the females in the domain. As a result, in a year in which the number of yellow-throated males is the largest, the blue-throated produce a relatively large number of offspring, boosting their share in the population in the following year.

Thus, the "game" between the types of lizards is of a similar nature to the Rock-Paper-Scissors game: the orange-throated males beat the blue-throated, the blue-throated overcome the yellow-throated, but the yellow-throated defeat the orange-throated. As we have seen, in a case of this kind the replicator dynamics lead to a spiral

---

[14] Sinervo, B. and C. M. Lively (1996), "The Rock-Paper-Scissors Game and the Evolution of Alternative Male Strategies," *Nature* 380, 240–243.

development of the distribution of types in the population, in which, over the generations, the three different types gain ascendancy in the population in iterative cyclical order.

16.3   Evolutionarily stable strategies

When Maynard Smith and Price (1973) first "mated" game theory with biology, they did not present an explicit dynamic model like that of the replicator dynamics; rather, they proposed a static model, whose motivation has a dynamic narrative. We will now present the Maynard Smith and Price concept of evolutionarily stable strategies (ESS) and will then proceed to examine the nexus between it and the explicit dynamic model of the replicator dynamics.

Imagine a population of individuals subjected to random pairwise matching which plays a symmetric game with a payoff function U. Here, too, we will go on designating U by the name "fitness function," even though here we are not describing an explicit dynamic process of the production of offspring by the individuals in the population.

Every individual in the population is characterized by its type, which is the strategy $\bar{p}$ that it chooses in the encounter. This strategy may be a pure or a mixed strategy.

We will initially assume that the population is homogeneous, and all the players therein are of the type $\bar{p}$. In this case, the average fitness of all the individuals in the population is $U(\bar{p},\bar{p})$.

What will happen if a mutant of a type $\tilde{p}$ invades the population? In other words, what will happen if a small proportion of individuals in the population is now of the type that adopts the strategy $\tilde{p}$ when it encounters another individual?

If the mutant's share in the population is $\varepsilon > 0$, then the average fitness of individuals of the type $\bar{p}$ will be:

$$(1 - \varepsilon)U(\bar{p},\bar{p}) + \varepsilon U(\bar{p},\tilde{p})$$

since every such individual will encounter a partner of the type $\bar{p}$ with a probability of $1 - \varepsilon$ (and will obtain an expected fitness of $U(\bar{p},\bar{p})$), and with the complementary probability ε it will encounter an individual of the type $\tilde{p}$ (and will gain an expected fitness of $U(\bar{p},\tilde{p})$). Similarly, the average fitness of the individuals of the type $\tilde{p}$ will be:

$$(1 - \varepsilon)U(\tilde{p},\bar{p}) + \varepsilon U(\tilde{p},\tilde{p})$$

Will the mutant $\tilde{p}$ be repelled by the incumbent type $\bar{p}$, or will $\tilde{p}$ succeed in taking root in the population? If:

$$(1 - \varepsilon)U(\bar{p},\bar{p}) + \varepsilon U(\bar{p},\tilde{p}) > (1 - \varepsilon)U(\tilde{p},\bar{p}) + \varepsilon U(\tilde{p},\tilde{p}) \qquad (16.2)$$

then the fitness of the incumbent type $\bar{p}$ will be higher than that of the mutant $\tilde{p}$. In such a case, we say that the mutant will be repelled.

Definition

The mixed strategy $\bar{p}$ is **evolutionarily stable** if a population of individuals of the type $\bar{p}$ repels any mutant with a small rate of penetration into the population, i.e. if the inequality (16.2) is satisfied for a small enough $\varepsilon > 0$. In other words, the strategy $\bar{p}$ is evolutionarily stable if for every mutant $\tilde{p} \neq \bar{p}$ there exists $\varepsilon_{\tilde{p}} > 0$ such that the inequality (16.2) is satisfied for every $\varepsilon < \varepsilon_{\tilde{p}}$.

Proposition 16.2 (an equivalent definition of an evolutionarily stable strategy)

The strategy $\bar{p}$ is evolutionarily stable if and only if for every strategy $\tilde{p} \neq \bar{p}$ either:

$$U(\bar{p},\bar{p}) > U(\tilde{p},\bar{p}) \qquad (16.3)$$

or:

$$U(\bar{p},\bar{p}) = U(\tilde{p},\bar{p}) \qquad \text{and} \qquad U(\bar{p},\tilde{p}) > U(\tilde{p},\tilde{p}) \qquad (16.4)$$

Proof

It is obvious that the property (16.4) entails the inequality (16.2). Likewise, if (16.3) is satisfied, then the inequality (16.2) is certainly satisfied for a small enough $\varepsilon > 0$.[15] Therefore, if for every $\tilde{p} \neq \bar{p}$ either the property (16.3) or the property (16.4) is satisfied, then the strategy $\bar{p}$ is evolutionarily stable.

The converse is also true: if $\bar{p}$ is evolutionarily stable, then for every $\tilde{p} \neq \bar{p}$ the property (16.3) or the property (16.4) is satisfied. Indeed, if there exists a mutant $\tilde{p} \neq \bar{p}$ for which (16.3) or (16.4) do not obtain, then there are only two possibilities:

1. One possibility is that $U(\bar{p},\bar{p}) < U(\tilde{p},\bar{p})$.
   In this case:

   $$(1 - \varepsilon)U(\bar{p},\bar{p}) + \varepsilon U(\bar{p},\tilde{p}) < (1 - \varepsilon)U(\tilde{p},\bar{p}) + \varepsilon U(\tilde{p},\tilde{p})$$

   for a small enough $\varepsilon > 0$, in contrast to (16.2), and therefore $\bar{p}$ is not evolutionarily stable.

[15] Explicitly, for $\varepsilon < \varepsilon_{\tilde{p}} = \frac{D}{M+D}$, where M is the maximal value that the fitness function U can attain, and D is the difference $D = U(\bar{p},\bar{p}) - U(\tilde{p},\bar{p}) > 0$.

2. The second possibility is that:

$$U(\bar{p},\bar{p}) = U(\tilde{p},\bar{p})$$

and:

$$U(\bar{p},\tilde{p}) \leq U(\tilde{p},\tilde{p})$$

In such case, for every $\varepsilon > 0$ we have:

$$(1-\varepsilon)U(\bar{p},\bar{p}) + \varepsilon U(\bar{p},\tilde{p}) \leq (1-\varepsilon)U(\tilde{p},\bar{p}) + \varepsilon U(\tilde{p},\tilde{p})$$

in contrast to (16.2). Therefore, also in this case $\bar{p}$ is not evolutionarily stable.

QED

The equivalent definition that is formulated in the proposition is frequently more amenable to verification, since it does not require finding the "penetration barrier" $\varepsilon_{\tilde{p}} > 0$ for every mutant $\tilde{p}$. In the equivalent definition, the properties (16.3) and (16.4) are formulated directly in terms of the fitness function U.

Question 16.5

Show that if $\bar{p}$ is evolutionarily stable, then $\bar{p}$ is also a symmetric Nash equilibrium of the game.

Answer

According to the assumption, $\bar{p}$ is evolutionarily stable. From Proposition 16.2 it follows that for every $\tilde{p} \neq \bar{p}$ the properties (16.3) or (16.4) are satisfied. In particular, for every $\tilde{p} \neq \bar{p}$ it is the case that $U(\bar{p},\bar{p}) > U(\tilde{p},\bar{p})$ or $U(\bar{p},\bar{p}) = U(\tilde{p},\bar{p})$. Therefore $\bar{p}$ is a symmetric Nash equilibrium of the game.

Is every strategy $\bar{p}$ in a symmetric Nash equilibrium also evolutionarily stable? The answer is negative. If there exists a strategy $\tilde{p} \neq \bar{p}$ for which $U(\bar{p},\bar{p}) = U(\tilde{p},\bar{p})$, then it is not necessarily also the case that $U(\bar{p},\tilde{p}) > U(\tilde{p},\tilde{p})$ as is required in property (16.4). We will now demonstrate this possibility.

16.3.1   Example of an equilibrium strategy that is not evolutionarily stable

Consider the game:

Player 2

		A	B
	A	0,0	0,0
Player 1			
	B	0,0	1,1

The profile (A,A) is a symmetric Nash equilibrium. This is so despite the fact the strategy A is weakly dominated by the strategy B. In this game it is the case that:

$$U(A,A)= U(B,A)$$

However:

$$U(A,B)\neq U(B,B)$$

Therefore property (16.4) is not satisfied, and strategy A is not evolutionarily stable.

16.3.2 A weakly dominated strategy is not evolutionarily stable

In general, if the strategy $\bar{p}$ in a symmetric Nash equilibrium is weakly dominated by some other strategy $\tilde{p} \neq \bar{p}$, then the strategy $\bar{p}$ is not evolutionarily stable. In such case $U(\tilde{p},\bar{p}) \geq U(\bar{p},\bar{p})$, but on the other hand, it is also the case that $U(\bar{p},\bar{p}) \geq U(\tilde{p},\bar{p})$, since $\bar{p}$ is an equilibrium strategy. But since $\bar{p}$ is weakly dominated by $\tilde{p}$, it is the case that $U(\tilde{p},\tilde{p}) \geq U(\bar{p},\tilde{p})$. Hence property (16.4) is not satisfied and $\bar{p}$ is not evolutionarily stable.

Thus, the criterion of evolutionary stability defines a refinement of the Nash equilibrium concept.

16.4 Evolutionary stability versus stability in the replicator dynamics

We have examined two possible approaches to defining the concept of **stability** in a population in which individuals are paired at random to play a game that determines their fitness. We first defined the notion of a stable fixed point under the replicator dynamics, and then went on to define an ESS. Let's now recapitulate the similarities and differences between the two concepts.

- The concept of a stable fixed point in the replicator dynamics relies on an explicit dynamic process: the composition of the population changes from one generation to the next in accordance with the fitness of the types, and remains constant only at the fixed point. By contrast, the concept of an evolutionarily stable strategy relies on a criterion of **immunity** against the penetration of a mutant into the population. The immunity criterion also examines whether the fitness of the mutant is lower than that of the most common type, but does not rely on a dynamic process that examines the evolution of the population composition over time.
- At a stable fixed point of the replicator dynamics, the composition of the population may certainly be **heterogeneous** – many and various types can co-exist in the population with different proportions. Yet in defining the concept of an ESS,

the reference point is a **homogeneous** population, in which all individuals adopt the same strategy. This reference point is repeatedly examined in the face of a small rate of penetration by a unique mutant type. Thus, at every stage of the analysis, there is no reference to more than two types in the population (the incumbent type and the mutant).

- In the replicator dynamics, each type is characterized by means of a pure strategy that it plays. Nevertheless, an evolutionarily stable strategy can certainly be a mixed strategy: each individual in the population is equipped with a mechanism that enables him to hold lotteries among its pure strategies. The assumption that a type of a species is able to conduct such lotteries is problematic, of course. However, as in the replicator dynamics, each individual is "programmed" to execute the strategy of its type. In neither approach are the individuals rational, nor do they conduct any process of conscious choice.

- The concept of an ESS explicitly relates to the possibility of the advent of mutations. In contrast, the replicator dynamics do not permit the advent of mutants in the population: the set of types making up the population at the beginning of the process is the one that will be present in the population throughout the generations (although the incidence of some of its types may tend to zero with the passage of time). In the replicator dynamics, it is possible to model the advent of mutations only indirectly, by adding to the population a handful of individuals of the mutant type, and checking to what extent and how this change affects the development path of the population's composition over time.

- The two concepts constitute a refinement of the concept of a symmetric Nash equilibrium.

Is there a connection between equilibrium strategies that are also evolutionarily stable and equilibrium strategies that are also stable fixed points of the replicator dynamics? It turns out that no such link necessarily exists: there are games with Nash equilibria that are stable in both senses, but there are also games with a Nash equilibrium that is stable in one of the senses but not in the other.[16]

Hence, there is no complete correlation between the two approaches to defining stability. The replicator dynamics are closer in spirit to a dynamic description of evolutionary processes, biological or social, but also more complex for purposes of explicit analysis. The concept of an evolutionarily stable strategy frequently serves as a short-cut in the analysis, and in many – although not all – games it leads to the same conclusions regarding the nature of stable population states.

---

[16] However, in the continuous version of replicator dynamics (see footnote 7), every ESS is an asymptotically stable fixed point of the replicator dynamics.

Appendix A: The Hawk-Dove game

Further to section 16.1.1, case A, we will prove that starting from any initial heterogeneous distribution (p_0^h, p_0^d), if $\frac{V}{2} > C$ then the replicator dynamics will converge to a homogeneous population consisting exclusively of hawks, and the share of doves will converge to zero. Indeed, for every generation t it is the case that:

$$\frac{p_{t+1}^d}{p_t^d} = \frac{U(d, \bar{p}_t)}{U(\bar{p}_t, \bar{p}_t)} = \frac{F + p_t^d \frac{V}{2}}{F + p_t^d \frac{V}{2} + p_t^h \left(\frac{V}{2} - p_t^h C\right)}$$

$$= \frac{1}{1 + \frac{p_t^h \left(\frac{V}{2} - p_t^h C\right)}{F + p_t^d \frac{V}{2}}} \leq \frac{1}{1 + \frac{p_0^h \left(\frac{V}{2} - C\right)}{F + \frac{V}{2}}} < 1$$

Hence:

$$p_{t+1}^d = \frac{p_{t+1}^d}{p_t^d} \frac{p_t^d}{p_{t-1}^d} \cdots \frac{p_1^d}{p_0^d} p_0^d \leq \left[\frac{1}{1 + \frac{p_0^h \left(\frac{V}{2} - C\right)}{F + \frac{V}{2}}} \right]^{t+1} p_0^d \xrightarrow[t \to \infty]{} 0$$

QED

Appendix B: Proof of Proposition 16.1

We have to show that if $\bar{p} = (p^1, \ldots, p^K)$ is a fixed point of the replicator dynamics but $(\bar{p}, \bar{p})$ is not a Nash equilibrium, then $\bar{p}$ is not stable. In other words, we must show that there exists a distance $r > 0$, such that even the very slightest deviation from $\bar{p}$ is liable to lead the replicator dynamic to stray from $\bar{p}$ to a distance greater than r. Let's demonstrate this.

We have already seen, in Question 16.1, that if $\bar{p}$ is a fixed point, then all types s^ℓ present in the population (i.e. those for whom $p^\ell > 0$) have the same average fitness, which is equal to the average fitness of the population as a whole:

$$U(s^\ell, \bar{p}) = U(\bar{p}, \bar{p})$$

Therefore, if $(\bar{p}, \bar{p})$ is not a Nash equilibrium of the game, there exists a pure strategy s^k that is never chosen in the mixed strategy $\bar{p}$ (i.e. $p^k = 0$), while that strategy yields, as against $\bar{p}$, a higher expected payoff than the strategy s^ℓ for every s^ℓ that is played with a positive probability in the strategy $\bar{p}$:

$$U(s^k, \bar{p}) - U(s^\ell, \bar{p}) = d > 0$$

Likewise, we will note that the expected payoff U of player 1 is a continuous function of the strategy adopted by player 2: if player 2 changes the probabilities she adopts in her mixed strategy from $\bar{p}$ to $\tilde{p}$, and the change is small enough, then $U\left(s^k, \bar{p}\right)$ will not diminish by more than $\frac{d}{4}$ and $U\left(s^\ell, \bar{p}\right)$ will not increase by more than $\frac{d}{4}$.

In other words, there exists a positive number $r > 0$ such that if the distance between $\bar{p}$ and $\tilde{p}$ is smaller than r:

$$|\tilde{p} - \bar{p}| < r$$

then it will be the case that:

$$U\left(s^k, \tilde{p}\right) - U\left(s^\ell, \tilde{p}\right) > \frac{d}{2} > 0$$

i.e.:

$$\frac{U\left(s^\ell, \tilde{p}\right)}{U\left(s^k, \tilde{p}\right)} < 1 - \frac{d}{2U\left(s^k, \tilde{p}\right)} \leq 1 - \frac{d}{2M}$$

where M is the highest payoff that the player can obtain in the game.

We will choose r also to be smaller than $\frac{p^\ell}{2}$, such that in any distribution of types $\tilde{p} = \left(\tilde{p}^1, \ldots, \tilde{p}^K\right)$ that satisfies $|\tilde{p} - \bar{p}| < r$, the incidence $\tilde{p}^\ell$ of the type s^ℓ in the population satisfies $\tilde{p}^\ell > \frac{p^\ell}{2}$.

We will now assume that we are changing the distribution of the original population $\bar{p}$ by substituting individuals of the type s^k for a tiny proportion of individuals in the population – as small as we like and smaller than r. In the new distribution of types, $\tilde{p}_0 = \left(\tilde{p}_0^1, \ldots, \tilde{p}_0^K\right)$, the type s^k is present. How would the replicator dynamics develop starting from $\tilde{p}_0$? We will now see that a generation will ultimately come in which the distribution of types in the population will diverge from the fixed point $\bar{p}$ to a distance exceeding r, giving rise to the conclusion that $\bar{p}$ is not a stable fixed point.

To this end we will momentarily assume that, on the contrary, the distribution of types in the population will never stray from the fixed point $\bar{p}$ to a distance that is greater than r, and we will arrive at a contradiction.

From the equation (16.1) we obtain that the distribution of types $\tilde{p}_1 = \left(\tilde{p}_1^1, \ldots, \tilde{p}_1^K\right)$ after one generation satisfies, in particular:

$$\tilde{p}_1^k = \frac{\tilde{p}_0^k U\left(s^k, \tilde{p}_0\right)}{U\left(\tilde{p}_0, \tilde{p}_0\right)}, \quad \tilde{p}_1^\ell = \frac{\tilde{p}_0^\ell U\left(s^\ell, \tilde{p}_0\right)}{U\left(\tilde{p}_0, \tilde{p}_0\right)}$$

and therefore:

$$\tilde{p}_1^\ell \leq \frac{\tilde{p}_1^\ell}{\tilde{p}_1^k} = \frac{\tilde{p}_0^\ell U\left(s^\ell, \tilde{p}_0\right)}{\tilde{p}_0^k U\left(s^k, \tilde{p}_0\right)} < \frac{\tilde{p}_0^\ell}{\tilde{p}_0^k}\left(1 - \frac{d}{2M}\right)$$

Similarly, in the distribution of the types $\tilde{p}_2 = (\tilde{p}_2^1, \ldots, \tilde{p}_2^K)$ after two generations, it will be the case that:

$$\frac{\tilde{p}_2^\ell}{\tilde{p}_2^k} = \frac{\tilde{p}_1^\ell U(s^\ell \tilde{p}_1)}{\tilde{p}_1^k U(s^k \tilde{p}_1)}$$

According to our assumption, $\tilde{p}_2$ will still not diverge from $\bar{p}$ to a distance of more than r, and therefore it will be the case that:

$$\tilde{p}_2^\ell \leq \frac{\tilde{p}_2^\ell}{\tilde{p}_2^k} = \frac{\tilde{p}_1^\ell U(s^\ell, \tilde{p}_1)}{\tilde{p}_1^k U(s^k, \tilde{p}_1)}$$

$$< \left[\frac{\tilde{p}_0^\ell}{\tilde{p}_0^k}\left(1 - \frac{d}{2M}\right)\right]\left(1 - \frac{d}{2M}\right) = \frac{\tilde{p}_0^\ell}{\tilde{p}_0^k}\left(1 - \frac{d}{2M}\right)^2$$

Similarly, it follows by induction that after t generations, the distribution of the types $\tilde{p}_t = (\tilde{p}_t^1, \ldots, \tilde{p}_t^K)$ will satisfy:

$$\tilde{p}_t^\ell \leq \frac{\tilde{p}_t^\ell}{\tilde{p}_t^k} < \frac{\tilde{p}_0^\ell}{\tilde{p}_0^k}\left(1 - \frac{d}{2M}\right)^t \underset{t \to \infty}{\longrightarrow} 0$$

Therefore, were our assumption $|\tilde{p}_t - \bar{p}| < r$ to be true for every $t = 0,1,2 \ldots$, i.e. if $\tilde{p}_t$ would never diverge from $\bar{p}$ to a distance greater than r, then the incidence $\tilde{p}_t^\ell$ of the type s^ℓ in the population would tend to zero over the course of generations. In particular, there would arrive a generation T in which it would be the case that $\tilde{p}_T^\ell < \frac{\varrho^\ell}{2}$. But this state of affairs is not feasible, since we chose r to be small enough so that for every distribution of types $\tilde{p}$ whose distance from $\bar{p}$ does not exceed r, it is the case that $\tilde{p}^\ell < \frac{\varrho^\ell}{2}$.

From the contradiction we have encountered, we conclude that $\tilde{p}_t$ will sooner or later diverge from the fixed point $\bar{p}$ to a distance greater than r. Therefore, the fixed point $\bar{p}$ is not stable.

QED

17 Global games

17.1 Equilibrium selection criteria

As we have seen, many games have more than one Nash equilibrium. In such games, additional criteria are needed in order to reach a more accurate prediction as to how the players will choose to play. Every such criterion is a **selection criterion** for choosing among the equilibria in the game.

In preceding chapters, we have already dealt with a number of such criteria. First, we saw examples of games in which, at some of the equilibria, some or all of the players choose weakly dominated strategies. In the Divvying up the Jackpot game, for example, we argued that it is natural to focus on equilibria at which the players do not choose such strategies. This is one possible criterion for excluding some of the equilibria in certain games.

We later discussed equilibria that are focal point equilibria – either because the payoff profile in such equilibria is more symmetric than in other equilibria, or because they are conspicuous by reason of external or historic causes that find expression not in the payoffs themselves but rather in the verbal description of the game.

In Chapter 9, we discussed two additional selection criteria. We defined when one equilibrium is more *efficient* than another. According to this criterion, if one of the equilibria in the game is more efficient than all the rest, the players will focus on that equilibrium. Moreover, if there is an equilibrium that is less efficient than another equilibrium, the players will not focus on the less efficient equilibrium.

The efficiency criterion does not always dovetail with another criterion we have examined – that of *risk dominance*. It is in games with multiple equilibria that the players are actually liable to be unsure as to how their rivals will play, and they may therefore choose strategies that appear to them as more secure on average. In a symmetric game of two players, they will hence play a risk-dominant equilibrium, which is not always the most efficient equilibrium.

In this chapter, we will present another approach for choosing among equilibria, one that is especially well suited to choosing between equilibria in coordination games.

17.2   Global games

In Chapter 9, we discussed a family of multi-player games of the Stag Hunt type which are characterized by the following payoffs: when at least fraction α out of the players choose "to invest," the investment is crowned with success and the players who "invested" get a payoff A. However, if fewer than α of the players "invest," the investment fails and the players who "invested" get a payoff 0. Any player can guarantee himself a payoff c by choosing to "refrain from investing." The game has two equilibria – one at which all the players invest and the other at which all refrain from investing.

We will now extend the definition of the game to cases in which α is not a proportion of the set of players, cases in which $\alpha \leq 0$ or $\alpha > 1$:

- If $\alpha \leq 0$ then even an investment by a single player will guarantee him the payoff A. In such a case, the game has a unique equilibrium at which all the players invest.
- If $\alpha > 1$ then even if all the players invest, the investment will fail and all the investors will get 0. In such a case, the game has a unique equilibrium, at which all the players refrain from investing.

17.2.1   Attacks on currency exchange rates

A game of this sort is suitable, for example, for describing financial crises resulting from coordinated attacks by investors on currency exchange rates. The exchange rate of any national currency is determined by means of the supply and demand for that currency by international investors who are willing and able to trade in it as against the currencies of other countries.[1]

Typically, every country wishes to avoid a sharp and sudden devaluation of its currency on international currency markets. Such devaluation will hinder the import of vital goods that are not produced domestically, since importers will have to exchange more local currency units for each unit of the foreign currency needed to purchase goods in another country.

However, in an age of international trade in which goods and people move ever more freely from one country to another, currency exchange rates reflect the relative purchasing power of currencies in the various countries. As long as a certain class of commodities is produced in two different countries that permit mutual trade, commodity prices in Country A cannot possibly be much higher for any lengthy period of time than the prices of the same commodity in Country B (as calculated following exchange rate conversions between the two countries' currencies). If the price

---

[1] Of course, any country can outlaw such trading, but foreign investors would then have difficulty in investing in its economy.

difference becomes large enough, importers in Country A will start importing those commodities from Country B. Therefore, if the production of such goods in Country A is not suspended, the currency exchange rates of Country A will depreciate relative to the currency of Country B, making import economically unviable.

Let's assume that a particular country fears an imminent deterioration in its economic situation (for example, due to expectations of an increase in its defense spending). Such deterioration would adversely affect the efficiency of the production of consumer goods in that country, and is liable, ultimately, to result in a devaluation of its currency relative to other currencies.

Speculative investors can try to coordinate among themselves a certain move that will bring about an immediate and sharp depreciation of that country's domestic currency exchange rate. Such a move is called a **currency attack**. These investors can dump, all at once, whatever amounts they hold in the domestic currency, using it to purchase foreign currency. Moreover, they can execute future **short sale** transactions of large amounts of the domestic currency in exchange for foreign currency. A future sale of a sum of money in a particular currency is an obligation to pay that amount in that currency after a certain interval of time; and the sale is **short** when the vendor is not, at that moment, in possession of the amount he has undertaken to sell.

Every investor is, of course, restricted as to the volume of short selling in which he can engage. This is because he must put up other financial assets that he holds as collateral so as to guarantee his undertaking to sell the currency that is not yet in his possession. Short selling, therefore, involves transaction costs for the investor, which we will denote by c. For example, c might be the interest that the investor would obtain if his financial assets were not deposited as collateral but were invested in some other channel.

A sharp increase in the supply of the local currency will cause it to be devalued on international foreign exchange markets, unless there is a simultaneous increase in the demand for that currency. In the absence of any depreciation, the investor, in order to make good on his undertaking to sell short, will ultimately have to purchase domestic currency as against the amount X of foreign currency that he obtained when he carried out the future transaction, and he will lose the transaction cost c. Yet if a sharp depreciation takes place immediately after he sells short, the investor, on the expiry date of the future obligation, will be able to purchase the domestic currency (which he undertook to sell) for an amount Y of foreign currency which is significantly lower than the amount X of foreign currency that he obtained when he made the short sale prior to the devaluation. The difference:

$$A = X - Y$$

will then be the investor's profit from the transaction.

The central bank of the country under attack can try to stave off the attack and preserve the exchange rates of the domestic currency by purchasing, on its own account, the entire quantity of domestic currency that is up for sale. In order to implement such a purchase, it must spend the foreign currency reserves it holds. These reserves are, of course, limited, and the country needs them in order to import goods it does not produce itself. The central bank can also raise the interest rate on domestic currency savings in order to boost the perceived profit that foreign investors will be able to obtain if they purchase rather than sell the domestic currency. But raising the interest rate on savings means also raising the interest rate on loans, making it difficult for entrepreneurs to borrow the money they need for investing in projects that will promote the country's growth.

Therefore, when the currency exchange rate comes under attack, the country's central bank must decide whether to try to stave off the attack while stabilizing the currency exchange rate, or, alternatively, to refrain from intervening and enable the devaluation to take place. Of course, The decision depends on the volume of foreign currency reserves available to the central bank for buying up the flood of domestic currency supply, and on its estimate of the domestic economic state of affairs. The central bank will refrain from intervening if it estimates that the country's economic position will in any event deteriorate to such an extent that the imminent devaluation of the currency is inevitable, or if the foreign currency reserves at its disposal are sparse. The central bank may decide to intervene and prevent the devaluation if it estimates that the country's economic position does not warrant devaluation, and if it holds adequate foreign currency reserves.

These economic data are represented in the above model by the parameter α. When $\alpha \leq 0$, the devaluation will in any event take place in a short time. When $\alpha > 1$, the country's economic situation is sound, and the central bank will in any event prevent a currency devaluation. When $0 < \alpha \leq 1$, the decision of the central bank depends on the scope of the attack. If at least α of the potential participants in the attack do actually take part in it, the central bank will yield and enable the devaluation to take place. However, faced with an attack of smaller scope, the central bank will rally to the cause to preserve the value of the domestic currency, and will purchase the amounts of the domestic currency that are being offered for sale in the attack, while utilizing, to that end, part of its foreign currency reserves. The greater α is, the better shape the domestic economy is in, and the larger the number of investors who must make common cause in order for the attack on the currency exchange rates to lead to devaluation.

Thus, the payoff to the investor will be A if at least a proportion α out of the potential investors decide to invest and a devaluation takes place, but the payoff will be 0 if the scope of the attack is smaller and the devaluation is avoided. As stated, the investor can guarantee himself a profit c if he refrains from participating in the attack and invests his assets in other channels.

The final decade of the twentieth century was characterized by several financial crises and attacks on currency exchange rates worldwide – in South America, in East Europe and in the Far East. One of the most outstanding crises broke out in Thailand in 1997.

Prior to the crisis, the exchange rate of the Thai baht was linked to a basket of international currencies. Following news of a deterioration in the balance of payments in Thailand, and the dangerous exposure of the financial sector to real estate investments, on May 7, 1997 foreign investors began exerting massive pressure on the exchange rates of the Thai currency, giving rise to similar pressure on the currency exchange rates of other South East Asian countries – Indonesia, Malaysia, and the Philippines. To counterbalance that pressure, the central banks of those countries coordinated a short-term interest rate increase. Moreover, the central bank of Thailand also attempted to cope with the foreign investors in a more focused manner by raising the interest rate for investors outside of Thailand by as much as an annualized 1300 percent (!), as well as intervening directly in foreign currency trading by posting a demand for the baht on futures markets in face of the supply put up by speculators. As a result, by the end of June 1997, those investors sustained losses of $1–1.5 billion.

Even so, the bulwarks set up by the Bank of Thailand gradually began to be breached. First, the interest rate in Thailand itself started to rise because the tremendous difference between the interest rate to Thai residents and the interest rate to foreign residents set in motion mounting attempts to bridge this gap by means of various circular transactions. In addition, Thailand's capacity to put up the supply for the baht in future transactions was stretched almost to breaking point, given the foreign currency reserves at its disposal.

Therefore, on July 2, 1997, the Bank of Thailand announced that it was cancelling the linkage of the baht to the currency basket, and the exchange rate of the baht *vis-à-vis* the US dollar thereupon plunged. Altogether, the exchange rates of the baht tumbled in July 1997 by some 50 percent, while at the same time pressure mounted against the currencies of neighboring states. On July 11, Indonesia expanded the band within which it permitted its currency to fluctuate, and in the space of ten days its exchange rates plunged to the new lowest limit. Thus, as a result of these devaluations, the investors who had bet against the exchange rates of Thailand and Indonesia in July 1997 pocketed enormous profits.

In order to model events of this type, we will assume that the economic position of any country – as reflected in the value of the parameter α – is able, from the outset, to float within a broad range. At any given moment, the value of the parameter may be fairly accurately known to all potential investors, but usually, none of them knows the precise value. We will now see how this assumption can affect the analysis of the game.

We will assume, for example, that $A = 5$ and $c = 3$. Likewise, we will assume that α can, with equal probabilities, obtain any one of the values:

$$\alpha = -\frac{2}{10}, \ -\frac{1}{10}, \ 0, \ \frac{1}{10}, \ \ldots, \ \frac{9}{10}, \ 1, \ 1\frac{1}{10}, \ 1\frac{2}{10}$$

No player knows exactly the true value of α, but rather learns its value with a slight degree of inaccuracy: a player relies on a signal s which, with equal probabilities, gets any one of the values:

$$\alpha - \varepsilon, \alpha, \alpha + \varepsilon$$

Given the value of α, the signals that the various players rely on are independent of one another. We will first focus on the case in which $\varepsilon = \frac{1}{10}$.

We will now try to understand how a player will play at equilibrium while relying on the signal s that he has received. When $\varepsilon = 0$ and hence $\alpha \in (0,1)$ is known with complete precision to all the players, we saw in Chapter 9 that two different Nash equilibria exist (all the players "invest" or all "refrain from investing"). But when α is not precisely known to the players, we will see that for certain values of α only one of the two equilibria persists when $\varepsilon = \frac{1}{10}$. For low values of α, the unique equilibrium that survives is the one at which (almost) everybody invests, and for high values of α the unique equilibrium that survives is the equilibrium at which (almost) everybody refrains from investing. Thus, the players' behavior is sensitive to the degree of coordination required for the investment to succeed, and the investment takes place only if its success does not depend on cooperation by too large a fraction of the players. This contrasts with the symmetric situation under precise knowledge of α, in which the game has two very different Nash equilibria.

What gives rise to the categorical difference between the equilibria under complete information and the equilibrium with "almost full" information (i.e. with a very small ε)? What is the source of the non-continuity in the solution of the model when ε is positive but close to zero?

When $\varepsilon = 0$, not only does every player know the precise value of α, he also knows that all the other players know exactly what α is; and he also knows that all the others know that everybody knows the exact value of α; and so on. In other words, when $\varepsilon = 0$, the value of α is common knowledge among the players.

What happens when ε is small but positive? A player who received a signal s knows that the true value of α lies in the small neighborhood $\{s - \varepsilon, s, s + \varepsilon\}$, and in his view, each of these possibilities is equally probable.[2] (Work out for yourself why this probability is uniform![3])

In particular, the player understands that other players may receive signals s that are different from the signal s that he himself received. Another player who obtained a signal s' believes that α is distributed uniformly in the set $\{s' - \varepsilon, s', s' + \varepsilon\}$. Therefore, not only can the beliefs of distinct players differ from one another, but, moreover, no player knows for sure what the beliefs of the other players are. Therefore, the players' beliefs are not common knowledge among the players even when α is very small. Carlsson and van Damme (1993) coined the term "global game" in order to describe such a state of affairs.[4]

Let's examine how the players who received different signals will behave.

- How will a player who gets a signal $s \in \{-\frac{3}{10}, -\frac{2}{10}, -\frac{1}{10}\}$ choose to behave? Such a player knows that the true value of α is smaller than or equal to zero. Therefore, he realizes that it is worth his while "to invest" regardless of the actions of the other players (since an investment will guarantee him the maximal payoff of $A = 5$ even if all the other players choose not to invest).
- How will a player who gets the signal $s = 0$ choose to behave?

   Such a player believes that with a probability of $\frac{1}{3}$ the true value of α is $-\frac{1}{10}$. If this is the case, his investment will be successful and will yield him a payoff of $A = 5$ irrespective of the actions of the other players.

   The player believes that with a probability of $\frac{1}{3}$ the true value of α is 0. In this case, too, an investment will yield him success and a payoff of $A = 5$ regardless of the actions of the other players.

   Therefore, a player who receives the signal $s = 0$ believes that an investment will yield him a payoff of $A = 5$ with a probability of at least $\frac{2}{3}$ and hence an expected payoff of at least:

$$\frac{2}{3} \times A = \frac{2}{3} \times 5 = 3\frac{1}{3}$$

This is higher than the payoff $c = 3$ that he can guarantee himself if he refrains from investing. Therefore, a player who receives the signal $s = 0$ will choose to invest.

---

[2] Except for players who received very low or very high signals s. For example, a player who received a signal $s = -\frac{3}{10}$ knows with certainty that the value of α is the lowest possible: $\alpha = -\frac{2}{10}$.

[3] In order to do so, use the conditional probability formula ("Bayes' rule").

[4] Carlsson H. and E. van Damme (1993), "Global Payoff Uncertainty and Risk Dominance," *Econometrica* 61 (5), 989–1018.

   See also Morris, S. and H. S. Shin (2002), "Global Games: Theory and Applications," in M. Dewatripont, L. Hansen, and S. Turnovsky (eds.), *Advances in Economics and Econometrics, the Eighth World Congress*, Cambridge University Press, pp. 56–114.

- How will a player who received the signal $s = \frac{1}{10}$ choose to behave?

    Such a player believes that with a probability of $\frac{1}{3}$ the real value of a is 0. In such a case, an investment will be successful and yield him a payoff of $A = 5$ regardless of the actions of the other players.

    The player believes that with a probability of $\frac{1}{3}$ the real value of a is $\frac{1}{10}$. In such a case, $\frac{1}{3}$ of the players will receive the signal $s' = 0$. As we have seen, players who receive the signal $s' = 0$ choose to invest. An investment by $\frac{1}{3}$ of the players does indeed guarantee the success of the investment when $\alpha = \frac{1}{10}$. Therefore, the player concludes that if $\alpha = \frac{1}{10}$, an investment will yield him a payoff at the level of $A = 5$.

Therefore, a player who receives the signal $s = \frac{1}{10}$ believes that with a probability of $\frac{2}{3}$ (if $\alpha = 0$ or if $\alpha = \frac{1}{10}$), an investment will yield him a payoff of $A = 5$. The player infers from this that if he invests, the expected payoff he will obtain will be at least:

$$\frac{2}{3} \times A = \frac{2}{3} \times 5 = 3\frac{1}{3}$$

This is a higher payoff than the payoff $c = 3$ that he can guarantee himself if he refrains from investing. Therefore, a player who receives the signal $s = \frac{1}{10}$ will choose to invest.

Comprehension check

A. Show similarly that a player who receives the signal $s = \frac{2}{10}$ will choose to invest.

B. Show that a player who receives the signal $s = \frac{3}{10}$ will choose to invest.

Thus we have shown that all the players who receive a signal $s \leq \frac{3}{10}$ will choose to invest. We notice that as long as $\alpha \leq \frac{2}{10}$ all the players will in fact receive a signal s that does not exceed $\frac{3}{10}$.

Hence, as long as $\alpha \leq \frac{2}{10}$, all the players will invest.

> ## Comprehension check
>
> Next, think of a player who receives the signal $s = \frac{4}{10}$. Explain why the above method of proof will not succeed in proving that such a player will choose to invest.
>
> Hint: such a player believes, of course, that with a probability of $\frac{2}{3}$ (in the event that $\alpha = \frac{3}{10}$ or $\alpha = \frac{4}{10}$) at least $\frac{1}{3}$ of the players will invest (who are these players?), but the player also knows that in one of these cases (when $\alpha = \frac{4}{10}$), an investment by $\frac{1}{3}$ of the players will not suffice for the success of the investment ... Complete the argument!

We will now examine how players receiving high signals will act.
Players receiving the signals:

$$s = 1\frac{1}{10}, 1\frac{2}{10}, 1\frac{3}{10}$$

believe that with a probability of at least $\frac{2}{3}$ $\alpha > 1$ and that the investment will not succeed even if all the players take part in it. Therefore, such players will choose not to invest, since investing will yield them an expected payoff not exceeding:

$$\frac{1}{3} \times A + \frac{2}{3} \times 0 = \frac{1}{3} \times 5 + \frac{2}{3} \times 0 = 1\frac{2}{3}$$

This expected payoff is less than the payoff $c = 3$ that a player can guarantee himself if he refrains from investing.

Question 17.1

Prove, similarly, that players receiving the signal:

$$s = 1$$

will decide not to invest.

Answer

A player who receives the signal $s = 1$:

- believes that with a probability of $\frac{1}{3}$ the true value of α is $1\frac{1}{10}$. In such a case, the investment will fail regardless of the actions of the other players;
- believes that with a probability of $\frac{1}{3}$ the true value of α is 1. In such a case, $\frac{1}{3}$ of the players will get the signal $s = 1\frac{1}{10}$ and will refrain from investing. In other words, at most $\frac{2}{3}$ of the players will invest. Since $\alpha = 1$ and an investment by all the players is required in order for the investment to succeed, the player concludes that if $\alpha = 1$ then the investment will fail.

Therefore, a player who gets the signal $s = 1$ believes that the investment will fail with a probability of at least $\frac{2}{3}$ (in the event that $\alpha = 1\frac{1}{10}$ or $\alpha = 1$), and therefore the investment will yield him an expected payoff not exceeding:

$$\frac{1}{3} \times A + \frac{2}{3} \times 0 - \frac{1}{3} \times 5 + \frac{2}{3} \times 0 = 1\frac{2}{3}$$

This expected payoff is less than the payoff $c = 3$ that the player can guarantee himself if he refrains from investing. Therefore, a player receiving the signal $s = 1$ will choose not to invest.

Comprehension check

Prove, similarly, that players receiving the signals:

$$s = \frac{9}{10}, \frac{8}{10}, \frac{7}{10}$$

will decide not to invest. (You can prove this sequentially for each separate event or by induction.)

Comprehension check

Show that the argument in the preceding exercise is not valid for $s = \frac{6}{10}$. Hint: a player who receives the signal $s = \frac{6}{10}$ assigns a probability of $\frac{1}{3}$ to $\alpha = \frac{6}{10}$, and in such a case he knows that $\frac{1}{3}$ of the players (all those who received the signal $s' = \frac{7}{10}$) will not invest. But if all the other players (those who receive the signals $\frac{6}{10}$ or $\frac{5}{10}$) choose to invest, then the overall fraction of investors will be $\frac{2}{3}$, i.e. greater than $\alpha = \frac{6}{10}$, and the investment will succeed. Complete the argument!

Thus we have shown that players who receive a signal satisfying $s \geq \frac{7}{10}$ will choose not to invest. Likewise, we note that as long as $\alpha \geq \frac{8}{10}$, all the players will in fact receive signals that satisfy $s \geq \frac{7}{10}$ and will not invest. In other words, for $\alpha \geq \frac{8}{10}$ the unique equilibrium is the one at which all the players refrain from investing.

Can we obtain a tighter prediction also for interim values of α if we reduce the degree of uncertainty ε? The answer is affirmative. In order to simplify the calculations, we will now assume that α is distributed uniformly in the interval $[-0.2, 1.2]$ (i.e. α can receive any value in this interval and not only multiples of $\frac{1}{10}$). We will likewise assume that given the value of α, the signals received by the players are distributed uniformly in the interval $[\alpha - \varepsilon, \alpha + \varepsilon]$ (i.e. all the values in this interval can be obtained, and not only the three values $[\alpha - \varepsilon, \alpha, \alpha + \varepsilon]$ as we previously assumed).

We will now focus on the case in which $\varepsilon = 0.05$, i.e. ε is smaller than in the example we analyzed above.

Assume for the moment that we have already succeeded in proving that all the players who receive signals that satisfy $s < 0.3$ will decide to invest. We note that as long as $\alpha \leq 0.315$, at least 35 percent of the players will get signals that satisfy $s < 0.3$ and will therefore decide to invest.[5] In such a case, the investment will in fact succeed, since the actual percentage of investors (35 percent) exceeds the minimal percentage of investors that is required if the investment is to succeed (which is 31.5 percent or less).

Likewise, we note that every player will decide to invest if he believes that the chances of success of the investment are greater than 0.6.[6] In particular, if a player receives a signal that satisfies $s < 0.305$, he believes that there is a probability greater than 0.6 that $\alpha \leq 0.315$ and he will therefore choose to invest.[7]

Thus, from the assumption that all the players who receive signals $s < 0.3$ will decide to invest, we have succeeded in proving that another set of players, too, will decide to invest, namely all those who receive signals that satisfy $s \in [0.3, 0.305]$.

How far will this type of argument stretch? In response to what signal s^* will a player receiving it be indifferent between investing and refraining from investment (assuming that all players receiving lower signals invest and all players receiving higher signals refrain from investing)?

A player receiving a signal s^* believes that α is distributed uniformly in the interval $[s^* - 0.05, s^* + 0.05]$. If he is indifferent between investing and refraining

[5] When $\alpha = 0.315$, the players' signals are distributed uniformly over the interval $[0.265, 0.365]$, and therefore exactly 35 percent of the players – those who get signals in the interval $[0.265, 0.3)$ – will decide to invest. If $\alpha \leq 0.315$, the percentage of players receiving signals $s < 0.3$ will be more than 35 percent.

[6] Because then the expected payoff that is obtained will be greater than $0.6 \times A = 0.6 \times 5 = 3$, i.e. the expected payoff from the investment will exceed the guaranteed payoff $c = 3$ that can be obtained by refraining from investment.

[7] If a player receives the signal $s = 0.305$ he believes that α is uniformly distributed over the interval $[0.255, 0.355]$, and therefore he believes that $\alpha < 0.315$ (i.e. that $\alpha \in [0.255, 0.315]$) with a probability of 0.6. If a player receives a signal that satisfies $s < 0.305$, he believes with a probability greater than 0.6 that $\alpha < 0.315$ and that the investment will hence succeed.

from investment, this indicates that he believes that the investment has a chance of 0.6 of succeeding. That is to say, he believes that for any $\alpha \in [s^* - 0.05, s^* + 0.01]$ the investment will succeed and that for any $\alpha \in [s^* - 0.05, s^* + 0.01]$ the investment will fail. In other words, for any:

$$\alpha \leq s^* + 0.01$$

at least α of the players decide to invest and the investment succeeds, i.e. the proportion that gets a signal $s \in (\alpha - 0.05, s^*)$ and invests is at least α. Formally:

$$\frac{s^* - (\alpha - 0.05)}{0.1} \geq \alpha$$

The maximal s^* for which these two inequalities obtain simultaneously is the one for which an equality obtains in both expressions:

$$\alpha = s^* + 0.01$$

and:

$$\frac{s^* - (\alpha - 0.05)}{0.1} = \alpha$$

If we substitute the first equality into the second, we obtain:

$$\frac{s^* - ((s^* + 0.01) - 0.05)}{0.1} = s^* + 0.01$$

and hence:

$$s^* = 0.39$$

We will now repeat the analysis from the opposite direction. Let's assume that we have already succeeded in proving that all the players who obtain a signal $s > 0.7$ will refrain from investing. As long as $\alpha \geq 0.69$, at least 40 percent of the players will get signals that satisfy $s > 0.7$ and will therefore refrain from investing.[8] In such a case, the investment will fail because the percentage of investors – at most 60 percent – is below the minimal percentage (at least 69 percent) of investors required for the investment to succeed.

Likewise, we note that any player will refrain from investing if he believes that the probability that the investment will fail is greater than 0.4.[9] In particular, if a player

---

[8] When $\alpha = 0.69$, the players' signals are uniformly distributed in the interval [0.64, 0.74] and therefore precisely 40 percent of the players – those who get signals in the interval [0.7, 0.74] – will certainly refrain from investing. If $\alpha > 0.69$, then the percentage of players getting signals $s > 0.7$ will be greater than 40 percent.

[9] Because then the chances of success of the investment are less than 0.6, and the expected payoff he will obtain will be smaller than $0.6 \times A = 0.6 \times 5 = 3$. Thus, the expected payoff from the investment will be lower than the guaranteed payoff $c = 3$ that he can obtain if he refrains from investing.

gets a signal that satisfies $s > 0.68$, he believes there is a probability greater than 0.4 that $\alpha \geq 0.69$ and will therefore choose not to invest.[10]

Thus, from the assumption that all the players getting signals that satisfy $s > 0.7$ will refrain from investing, we have succeeded in proving that an additional set of players will also refrain from investing – namely all those who get signals that satisfy $s \in (0.68, 07]$.

How far can we stretch this type of argument toward ever lower signals s? In response to what signal will a player receiving it be indifferent between investing and refraining from investment (assuming that all players receiving lower signals invest and all players receiving higher signals refrain from investing)? In fact, in the above analysis we have already found that this signal is $s^* = 0.39$! All the players who receive a signal that satisfies $s > 0.39$ will refrain from investing, while all the players who receive a signal that satisfies $s < 0.39$ will invest.[11] Accordingly:

- If $\alpha \leq 0.4$, at least 40 percent of the players will get signals that satisfy $s < 0.39$ and will invest, thus guaranteeing the success of the investment. Two cases are possible:
  - When $\alpha \in (0.34, 0.4]$, some of the players will receive signals that satisfy $s > 0.39$ and will refrain from investing but, in retrospect, will regret having done so when the success of the investment becomes apparent.
  - When, $\alpha \leq 0.34$ all the players will get signals that satisfy $s < 0.39$ and will invest.
- If $a > 0.4$, fewer than 40 percent of the players will get signals that satisfy $s < 0.39$ and will invest, and therefore the investment will fail. Here, too, there are two sub-cases:
  - When $\alpha \in [0.4, 0.44)$, some of the players will get signals that satisfy $s < 0.39$ and invest, but will later regret having done so, since the investment will fail.
  - When $\alpha > 0.44$, all the players will get signals that satisfy $s > 0.39$ and will refrain from investing.

Thus we have seen that $\alpha^* = 0.4$ is the boundary value such that for any $\alpha \leq \alpha^*$ a successful investment takes place, while for every $\alpha > \alpha^*$ the investment fails or simply does not take place.

---

[10] If a player gets the signal $s = 0.68$, he believes that α is distributed uniformly over the interval $[0.63, 0.73]$ and therefore he believes that $\alpha \geq 0.69$ (i.e. that $\alpha \in [0.69, 0.73]$) with a probability of 0.4. If a player gets a signal $s > 0.68$, he believes with a probability greater than 0.4 that $\alpha \geq 0.69$ and that the investment will hence fail.

[11] A player who received exactly the signal $s = 0.39$ will be indifferent between investing and refraining from investment and can therefore choose to go either way.

We note that:

$$\alpha^* = 1 - \frac{c}{A}$$

(It will be recalled that $A = 5$ is the payoff that investors get when the investment succeeds, while $c = 3$ is the payoff that any player can guarantee himself by refraining from investment.)

We will now see that the equation $a^* = 1 - \frac{c}{A}$ for the threshold value α^* will be satisfied for any combination of values $A > c > 0$. To that end, we will first calculate in response to what signal s^* a player receiving it will be indifferent between investing and refraining from investment (assuming that all players receiving lower signals invest and all players receiving higher signals refrain from investment).

A player who receives a signal s^* believes that α is distributed uniformly in the interval $[s^* - \varepsilon, s^* + \varepsilon]$. If he is indifferent between investing and refraining from investment, this indicates his belief that the investment has $\frac{c}{A}$ chances of succeeding. (Make sure you understand why!) That is to say, he believes that for every $\alpha \in [s^* - \varepsilon, \alpha^*]$ the investment will succeed and for every $\alpha \in (\alpha^*, s^* + \varepsilon)$ the investment will fail when α^* is the value that satisfies:

$$\frac{\alpha^* - (s^* - \varepsilon)}{2\varepsilon} = \frac{c}{A}$$

(The left member $\frac{\alpha^* - (s^* - \varepsilon)}{2\varepsilon}$ is indeed the probability, in the eyes of the player, that $\alpha \in [s^* - \varepsilon, \alpha^*]$, since he believes that α is uniformly distributed over an interval that is 2ε in length: the interval $[s^* - \varepsilon, s^* + \varepsilon]$.)

In other words, when:

$$\alpha \leq \alpha^*$$

at least α of the players decide to invest and the investment succeeds, i.e. the fraction of players who receive a signal $s \in [\alpha - \varepsilon, s^*)$ and hence invest is at least α. Formally, for every $\alpha \leq \alpha^*$ it is the case that:

$$\frac{s^* - (\alpha - \varepsilon)}{2\varepsilon} \geq \alpha$$

(For a given value of α and for $s^* \geq (\alpha - \varepsilon)$ the left member is indeed the proportion of players who get a signal that satisfies $s < s^*$ since the signals that the players receive are distributed uniformly over an interval of length 2ε, namely the interval $[\alpha - \varepsilon, \alpha + \varepsilon]$.) For $\alpha = \alpha^*$ an equality will obtain, i.e.:

$$\frac{s^* - (\alpha^* - \varepsilon)}{2\varepsilon} = \alpha^*$$

Or:

$$s^* = (1 + 2\varepsilon)\alpha^* - \varepsilon$$

If we substitute this in the preceding equation:

$$\frac{\alpha^* - (s^* - \varepsilon)}{2\varepsilon} = \frac{c}{A}$$

we will obtain:

$$\frac{\alpha^* - ([(1 + 2\varepsilon)\alpha^* - \varepsilon] - \varepsilon)}{2\varepsilon} = \frac{c}{A}$$

or:

$$\alpha^* = 1 - \frac{c}{A}$$

as we sought to show.

The ratio $\frac{c}{A}$ expresses the nature of the safe alternative of refraining from invest-ment (with the payoff c) compared with the attractiveness of a successful investment (yielding the payoff A). No matter how great this ratio, we have shown that the investment in the global game will succeed only if an investment is required on the part of a proportion of the players that is smaller than α^*, as described in Figure 17.1.

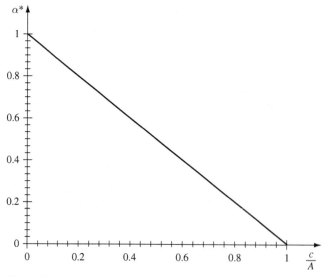

Figure 17.1

This is an intuitive result. On the one hand, if the alternative of refraining from investment is very good (c is high relative to A), then the players will wish to take part in the investment only if its success is guaranteed even when a small proportion of the players takes part in it (a low α^*). On the other hand, if the success of the investment yields a payoff that is higher relative to the safe alternative (A is high relative to c), the players will tend to invest even if a substantial proportion of the players (a high α^*) must coordinate among themselves in order for the investment to succeed.

Comprehension check

We will assume, as before, that at least α of the investors must participate in order for the investment to succeed; we will assume that the success of the investment will yield the investors a payoff of $A = 1$. Now, however, the payoff that the safe alternative ensures differs slightly from one investor to another – this payoff is now c_i for investor i. The payoffs c_i are distributed uniformly over a small interval $[\theta - \varepsilon, \theta + \varepsilon]$. Player i knows her payoff c_i (and the value ε) but does not know what the other players' payoffs are and therefore does not know what θ is. The parameter θ itself is uniformly distributed in the interval $[-\delta, 1 + \delta]$, where $\delta > \varepsilon$.

Show, employing the method we used above, that for every:

$$\alpha \leq \alpha^* = 1 - \theta$$

there is a unique equilibrium in which a successful investment takes place (i.e. at least α of the players invest) and for every:

$$\alpha > \alpha^* = 1 - \theta$$

there is a unique equilibrium in which nobody invests, or too small a set of players (less than α of the players) chooses to invest and the investment fails.

17.3   Global games in laboratory experiments

In our discussion so far we have defined a number of criteria for selecting among equilibria that are relevant to coordination games of the type we have dealt with in

Chapter 9: efficiency, risk dominance, and global games. These criteria offer various predictions as to how the players will behave. How do people behave in reality?

This question was examined in an experiment in which the participants were asked to choose between the two possible strategies for different values of A, c and α.[12] In some runs of the experiment, the players benefited from full information on those values, while in other runs some of them were given information with some small inaccuracy (independently distributed across the players), similar to the model we examined above.

The results of the experiment support the conclusion that the global games model is an important point of reference for predicting the participants' behavior. Of the participants in the experiment, 92 percent used threshold strategies, i.e. they invested only for profiles in which, according to the data available to them, the ratio between A and c was large enough and the critical mass α necessary for success was small enough. Such threshold behavior also took place when the players had full knowledge of those parameters. In general, no great difference was found between the average thresholds of the participants under full information of the parameters and under partial information.[13] Even when the participants had full information, their behavior responded to the parameters in a manner similar to that predicted by the global games model: an increase of the payoff A from a successful investment and a decrease in the critical mass α necessary for the success of the investment led the participants to invest with a higher probability.

---

[12] Heinemann, F., R. Nagel, and P. Ockenfels (2004), "The Theory of Global Games on Test: Experimental Analysis of Coordination Games with Public and Private Information," *Econometrica* 72, 1583–1599.

[13] Although under partial information, the variance in the players' behavior was larger.

PART VI

Dynamic games

- INTRODUCTION -

In Chapter 18, we introduce extensive form games, which describe the potential evolution of a dynamic game using a game tree. In each node of the tree some player (or players) should choose their action(s), and each branch emanating from such a node stands for an action (or action profile) that the player(s) active at that node can choose. Each leaf of the tree – a node from which no further branches extend – stands for a possible termination point of the dynamic interaction, and specifies the payoffs of the players upon this termination. Each leaf corresponds uniquely to a path of consecutive branches from the root to that leaf.[1]

A strategy of a player in an extensive form game is a complete plan of action, which specifies what the player would do at each of the nodes where she may be called upon to play, if and when that node is ever reached. Each profile of the players' strategies defines a path from the root to a leaf[2] specifying the payoffs of the players. Thus, associating each strategy profile of the players with these payoffs defines the strategic form of the extensive form game. The Nash equilibria of this strategic form are the Nash equilibria of the extensive form game.

The strategic form abstracts from the dynamic aspect of the game. As a result, some extensive form games have implausible Nash equilibria, based on a non-credible threat – an action that the player wouldn't actually like to take upon reaching his time to decide, but that at the Nash equilibrium the player doesn't need to take anyway, because due to the fear from this incredible threat a player acting prior to him preempts altogether by deviating the game to another path; this alternative path may be beneficial for the player who posed the non-credible threat but detrimental to the preempting player who acted before him.

In order to discard non-credible threats, Chapter 19 discusses an alternative, finer solution concept for extensive form games called subgame perfect equilibrium. A profile of strategies of the players is a subgame perfect equilibrium if it is a Nash equilibrium in every subgame of the game.

---

[1] Some games may have an unbounded horizon, and contain infinite paths that start from the root. In such games, each infinite path itself is associated with a payoff for each player (since the path has no terminal leaf to which these payoffs could be associated).

[2] Or an infinite path starting from the root.

In games with no infinite paths in which a single player has to choose his action at every node and can do so in an optimal manner, the subgame perfect equilibria of the game can be found by means of the backward induction procedure: in every node leading only to leaves, one specifies an action of the active player in that node leading to her highest possible final payoff, and the node is replaced by the leaf (with the corresponding payoffs) to which that action led. The procedure is then repeated "backwards" until the root itself is replaced by a leaf (with payoffs to the players). The actions specified along the procedure compose the players' strategies in a subgame-perfect equilibrium. Moreover, in case the game has more than one subgame perfect equilibrium (because some player at some node has more than one optimal action), all the subgame perfect equilibria of the game can be found with this procedure.

We demonstrate two applications of subgame perfect equilibria and backward induction. The first is the Stackelberg model of a quantity competition between two firms, as in the Cournot model (introduced in Chapter 8), when this time one of the firms chooses its quantity before its rival. We show that this game has infinitely many Nash equilibria but only one subgame perfect equilibrium. In the subgame perfect equilibrium, the leading firm will choose a higher quantity than in the simultaneous move Cournot equilibrium, thus capturing a higher share of the market and leading its rival to a modest reaction. The leader's chosen quantity is not a best reply to the quantity eventually chosen by its rival; the gains of the leading firm from committing itself to an early aggressive move, by virtue of its strategic effect of inducing a feeble reaction by the rival, more than compensate the leader for its loss due to the fact that the quantity to which it committed is somewhat suboptimal *vis-à-vis* the rival's quantity.

The second example is the "publisher's dilemma" of how to price the hardcover and paperback editions of the same book. The paperback price is the maximal amount that the relaxed readers – those who are not keen to be among the first to read the book upon its publication – are willing to pay once the paperback edition is eventually released. The book lovers, meanwhile, would be willing to pay even more if they waited for the paperback edition, and this extra willingness to pay is their informational rent: the publisher must discount it from the maximal price they are willing to pay for the first hardcover edition if it wants them to buy the hardcover immediately rather than inducing them to forgo a too pricy hardcover in favor of waiting for the paperback. If, however, the decline along time in the maximal willingness to pay of enough book aficionados is mild, and it remains far above the maximal willingness to pay of the relaxed readers even when the paperback edition is due, the informational rent might be so high that the publisher may wish to pool the readers rather than separate them. In such a case only one version of the book will be published and sold at the maximal price the relaxed readers are willing to pay upon publication.

The notion of commitment takes center stage in Chapter 20. In the Stackelberg model the leader commits to a higher, tougher action. In other games, however, e.g. in the public good game, the leading player will choose to commit to a softer action – a lower investment level that will induce its follower to increase its investment. We show that the question whether the leader will wish to commit to a higher or to a lower action (compared with its choice of the simultaneous move game) depends on the nature of the game as we classified it in Chapter 7. In games of conflict with strategic substitutes (such as quantity competition) and in games of cooperation with strategic complements (like the partnership game) the leader will pre-commit to a higher strategy. In contrast, in games of cooperation with strategic substitutes (like the public good investment game) and in games of conflict with strategic complements the leader will pre-commit itself to a milder strategy relative to its choice in the simultaneous move game.

There are situations in which the leader does not commit itself to a specific action but rather to a reaction rule. For example, a firm can invest in branding its product as being of a superior category relative to its competitor's product, thus increasing the price that customers are willing to pay for the branded product; alternatively, the leader can invest in renovating its production line, thus reducing its production cost; or, if the firms are in different countries, the government in the leader's country may choose to subsidize each unit that its firm produces. Each of these tactics implies that the entire reaction curve of the leader shifts outwards, making its optimal quantity higher for whichever quantity that the competitor may choose to produce. In some cases, this may deter the follower from producing any positive quantity at all, thus driving it out of the industry or deterring it from entering in the first place.

However, if both firms can commit themselves in advance to a more aggressive reaction curve by advertising their products, the strategic interaction becomes a two-stage game in which the firms first decide how much to advertise, and given the investment levels in advertising and the corresponding reaction curves, they play the Cournot Nash equilibrium of the ensuing game. At the subgame perfect equilibrium, both firms invest in advertising and end up competing more toughly with one another; if only they could "tie their own hands" and avoid the advertising investment, they would both be better off.

A similar situation arises when governments subsidize their home firms so as to make them more aggressive in the international markets. The World Trade Organization (WTO) agreements are aimed at avoiding (or diminishing) these subsidies simultaneously, so that firms in all countries would benefit. The temptation to deviate unilaterally from such agreements is large, which explains why the WTO agreements proceed in small steps following multiple rounds of negotiation.

Chapter 21 deals with shortcomings and conceptual limitations of the backward induction procedure. The first example to this effect is the ultimatum game, in which a proposer has to suggest how to divide a sum of money between himself and the responder, who can then either accept the proposed split – in which case the division is implemented, or reject it – in which case neither party gets anything. At a subgame perfect equilibrium of this game the proposer should offer the responder either nothing or a minimal share and the responder should accept. However, in a wide range of experiments of this game all around the world, the offers were observed to range typically between 20 and 50 percent of the entire pie, and smaller proposals were typically rejected. The appendix to Chapter 21 discusses a more elaborate model, based on the notion of stochastic stability, which may shed light on this discrepancy.

The second example is the centipede game, in which two players can choose, alternately, whether to end the game or to continue it. Exiting guarantees the player a payoff which is slightly larger than she would get if were she were to continue and her rival would quit immediately afterwards; however, continuation by the other player would already make continuation for the first player better than exiting. Unfortunately, though, there is eventually a last stage to the game, in which the player prefers to exit rather than to continue and the game ends either way. Applying the backward induction logic implies that the first player should exit at the very beginning of the game, bypassing large gains to both players if they were to continue at least several steps into the game – which is what subjects typically do in laboratory experiments of the game.

Indeed, if the second player's turn to play ever arrives, he knows that the first player has already deviated from her backward induction strategy. It is hence not obvious why the second player should be certain that the first player would resume her backward induction strategy (and exit) if he, the second player, would continue one step further. But if the first player is indeed unsure that the second player entertains such certainty, and may hence just as well continue rather than quit, this boosts the first player's incentive to continue in the first place.

The logic of this example is applied to the "chain-store paradox," in which a chain store "swears" to fight (in a mutually detrimental way) any new competitor near any of its branches. By backward induction the chain store should accommodate a competitor in the last location to which a local competitor hasn't yet entered; and by backward induction it should then accommodate rather than fight all local competitors. Still, chain stores with many branches do often fight local new entrants.

In Chapter 22, the model of extensive form games is extended to allow for nodes with moves of nature (called also "chance nodes"), in which the branches emanating from the node are followed according to a fixed given probability distribution. This extended model is then used to study two examples.

The first example encompasses the concept of brinkmanship – a strategic move that increases the chances of undesired escalation, which the opponent fears more than the party which initiated the move. This notion is then applied to the analysis of the Cuban missile crisis, in which Kennedy's decision to impose a naval blockade on Cuba is interpreted as such a brinkmanship move. The strategic situation is then analyzed using an extensive form game including a chance move.

The second example deals with nuisance suits – low-chance claims which are filed to court with the aim of inducing the defendant to compromise on an out-of-court settlement. The court decision is modeled here as a chance move (since the chances of each possible ruling depend on factors outside the control and knowledge of the parties). Nuisance suits are effective because filing the claim serves as a commitment device to pursue the claim unless an out-of-court-settlement is reached, and this idea is made explicit via the analysis of the appropriate extensive form game. One possible solution to this intriguing phenomenon is also proposed, namely to allow the defendant to require the court to forbid an out-of-court settlement (which the court should then approve). We analyze the amended game incorporating this proposal and show how the proposed measure provides the defendant with a counter-commitment device, which may deter nuisance suits in the first place.

18 Extensive form games

So far, we have dealt with strategic form games. In strategic form games, all the players are presented as choosing their strategies simultaneously. Therefore, strategic form games hinder an explicit representation of strategic situations in which some of the players act after other players have already chosen their actions, or strategic situations in which some or all of the players act more than once over the course of time.

Games in which the strategic situation is represented as evolving over time are called **extensive form games**. In the remaining part of the book, we will discuss several types of extensive form games.

First we will deal with games with a finite number of stages, at each of which one of the players chooses between several actions that are available to him. We will then proceed to discuss a more general case – games with a finite number of stages, in which a number of players may simultaneously choose their actions in at least some of the stages of the game. In the sequel, we will address the even more general case of games that may continue over an unbounded number of stages and in which, at any stage of the game, a number of players may choose their actions simultaneously. Finally, we will go on to deal with the particular case of **repeated games**, in which at every stage of the game all the players repeatedly play one particular strategic form game. We will draw a comparison between the case in which the number of repetitions is finite and the case in which the number of repetitions is unbounded.

All the extensive form games we will discuss in this book are **perfect information games**: at any stage at which a player or players are called upon to choose their actions, they know what actions all the other players have taken at all precedent stages of the game. The discussion of the more general cases, involving **imperfect information**, in which certain players possess, at some stages of the game, only partial information on players' actions in precedent stages, is beyond the scope of this book.[1]

---

[1] A note concerning terminology: the classic definition of extensive form games with perfect information does not include games in which a number of players act simultaneously at some or all stages of the game. According to the classic definition of extensive form games, action at any stage of the game is taken by a unique player. In order to describe a stage in a game in which a number of players choose their actions simultaneously, the players must be arranged in some arbitrary order, and the stage must be divided into substages – one substage per player: after the first player has chosen her action, the second player is called upon to act, without knowing what the first player has chosen; after which the third player (if there is one) is called upon to act without knowing what the first two players have chosen; and so on. Formally, this amounts to an extensive form game with imperfect information.

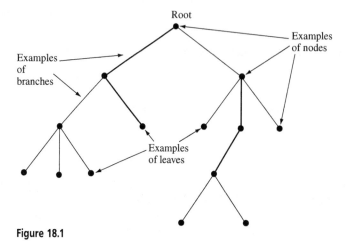

Figure 18.1

The game tree

How can an extensive form game be described? The simplest way to outline the development of possible actions in such a game is with the aid of the **game tree**.

What is a tree? A tree is made up of a set of **nodes**, some of which ramify into **branches**. Each branch emerges from a unique node and leads to another unique node. The tree has a unique node to which no branch leads – the **root** of the tree. Every other node in the tree has only one unique branch leading to it. Nodes from which no branches ramify are called **leaves**. A **path** on the tree is a sequence of nodes, such that for every node in the sequence – other than the first node – there is a branch that leads to it from the node preceding it in the sequence. Every node in the tree has a unique path that begins at the root and ends at that node.

In order to sketch a tree, we will mark the nodes by means of points and the branches by means of lines. An example of a tree is shown in Figure 18.1. The figure portrays a tree. Two paths in the tree are emphasized with a thick line. We see that a path need not necessarily begin at the root or end at a leaf.

The arbitrary arrangement of the players in such a representation is artificial, and certain solution concepts are sensitive to the arbitrary arrangement. Therefore, some of the texts in game theory (Osborne and Rubinstein 1994, Osborne 2004) refrain from such artificial representation and allow for simultaneous moves in the definition of extensive form games. We adopt this approach here.

Osborne, M. and A. Rubinstein (1994), *A Course in Game Theory*, Cambridge, MA: MIT Press; Osborne, M. (2004), *An Introduction to Game Theory*, Oxford University Press.

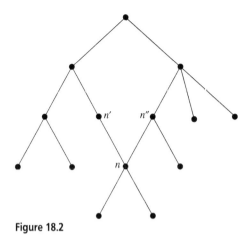

Figure 18.2

Question 18.1

Does Figure 18.2 describe a tree?

Answer

The graph in Figure 18.2 is not a tree, since two different nodes, n' and n'', lead to the node n.

We say that a tree describes an extensive form game when:

- To every node in the tree that is not a leaf we attribute:
  - a player or a set of players. These are the players active at that node;
  - a set of available **actions** for each player acting in the node.
- Corresponding to every action profile of the active players in the given node there is a branch forking out from the node and leading to a new node.

  Formally, we denote the set of nodes in the tree by N, the set of players playing at the node n by I_n, and by A_i^n the set of actions player $i \in I_n$ can take at the node n. Every action profile of the players in I_n:

$$x_i = \left(a_i^n\right)_{i \in I_n} \in A^n = \Pi_{i \in I_n} A_i^n$$

  describes a branch forking out from the node n and leading to a new node.

- Every leaf of the tree describes a possible termination of the game. Therefore, with every leaf ℓ we will associate a payoff profile $\pi^\ell = \left(\pi^\ell_i\right)_{i \in I} \in \mathbb{R}^I$ – one payoff per player $i \in I$.

This concludes the formal description of an extensive form game with a finite number of stages.

What happens in extensive form games in which the strategic interaction can continue forever, without bound? A case in which the strategic interaction continues indefinitely is described by an infinite path in the game tree. Therefore:

> If the tree has infinite paths that start at the root, we will associate a payoff profile to each such path – one payoff per player.

This concludes the description of an extensive form game (with perfect information) that can last a finite or an infinite number of stages.

Figure 18.3 describes an extensive form game between two players. Player 1 is the first to play at node 1 (i.e. $I_1 = \{1\}$). She must choose between two actions available to her – a or b (i.e. $A^1 = A^1_1 = \{a, b\}$). If she chooses b, the game ends – the payoff to player 1 is 1 and the payoff to player 2 is 0. If, however, player 1 chooses a, it will be player 2's turn to play at node number 2 (i.e. $I_2 = \{2\}$). In this case, player 2 can choose between two actions, c or d (i.e. $A^2 = A^2_2 = \{c, d\}$). The choice of d will lead to the termination of the game, with a payoff of 0 to player 1 and a payoff of 3 to player 2. The choice of c by player 2 will lead to node number 3, at which player 1 has to play once more. (With the formal notation, $I_3 = \{1\}$ and $A^3 = A^3_1 = \{e, f\}$.) Each of the actions available to player 1 at this node – e and f – leads to the termination of the game. The choice of e will cause the payoff to each player to be 4; the choice of f will lead to the payoff profile (5,2).

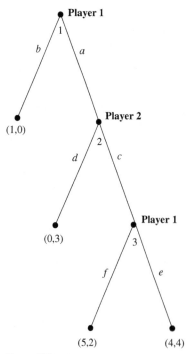

Figure 18.3

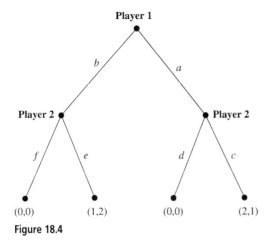

Player 1

b   a

Player 2   **Player 2**

f   e   d   c

(0,0)   (1,2)   (0,0)   (2,1)

Figure 18.4

Figure 18.4 describes another game between two players. Player 1 is the first to play and she has to choose between the actions a and b. If she chooses a, player 2 must choose between the actions c and d, which lead to the payoff profiles (2,1) or (0,0), respectively. If, however, player 1 chooses action b, then player 2 must choose between the actions e and f, which lead to the payoff profile (1,2) or (0,0), respectively.

18.2 Strategies in extensive form games

. . . .

A player's strategy in an extensive form game is an operation plan. It defines what the player does at any node at which she may be called upon to play. Here is a formal definition.

Definition   If N_i is the set of nodes at which player i acts, and for each node $n \in N_i$ we denote by A_i^n the set of actions available to player i at the node n, then **a strategy of player i** is an operation plan:

$$x_i = (a_i^n)_{n \in N_i} \in A_i = \Pi_{n \in N_i} A_i^n$$

that describes the action a_i^n that the player will adopt if and when she reaches the node $n \in N_i$.

In the game in Figure 18.3, player 1's strategy is described by a pair of actions: the action that she takes at the beginning of the game, and the action that she will take if and when her turn to play arrives again. Thus, in this game, player 1 has four possible strategies:

$$(a, e), (a, f), (b, e), (b, f)$$

Player 2 has two possible strategies, c and d, which describe the action that player 2 will take if and when her turn to play arrives.

In the game in Figure 18.4, player 1 has two possible strategies: a and b. Player 2 has four possible strategies:

$$(c, e), (c, f), (d, e), (d, f)$$

Each such strategy describes what player 2 will do at each of the nodes in the game at which she may be called upon to play.

In the game in Figure 18.3, player 1's choice of action b brings the game to an immediate end, ruling out any possible situation in which player 1 herself will be called upon to play for a second time. What, then, is the meaning of player 1's strategy (b, f)? Why should player 1's operation plan denote the action that she would have taken had she reached a node which is actually avoided due to steps previously taken by her in that very same operation plan? There are two alternative rationales for this:

1. The operation plan denotes what the player intends to do at each node. In practice, however, there is a slight chance that the player will not succeed in choosing the action that she intended to take, but will randomly take one of the other actions available to her. If this is indeed the case, then at every node there is a positive probability for any action profile of the players, and not only for the action profile dictated by their operation plans. Therefore, every path in the tree has a positive probability, and in particular there is a positive probability of arriving at every node in the tree. Hence the necessity for each player to specify in her operation plan what she will do also at nodes that are excluded by her own.
2. The player's operation plan is relevant not only for the player herself. The other players, too, mentally analyze the player's possible operation plans. For example, player 2 may consider what she is best advised to do given various possible operation plans of player 1. Various operation plans of player 1 may lead to nodes other than those that will be reached by the operation that player 1 intends to adopt in practice. Therefore, player 1's plans following every possible evolution of the game are relevant to the considerations taken into account by the other players as they plan their moves.

For example, in the game in Figure 18.3, if and when player 2 is called to play, she asks herself what will be the implications of her choice of c, and needless to say those implications depend on how player 1 will act in such case. Therefore, if player 1's strategy does not include a full description of her operation plan at every node of the game at which she can possibly be called to play, player 2 cannot know what action it is worth her while to choose.[2]

18.2.1   The strategic form of an extensive form game

As we usually do, we will denote by X_i the set of strategies (which, in an extensive form game, are the possible operation plans) of player $i \in I$ and by $X = \prod_{i \in I} X_i$ the players' set of strategy profiles.

Each strategy profile of the player defines a path in the game, from the root onwards to one of the leaves. Why? The strategies (i.e. the operation plans) of the player or players playing at the beginning of the game – at the root – define, *inter alia*, how the player or players act there. The combination of their actions at the root defines a branch proceeding from the root and leading to another node. The strategies of the player or players playing at this succeeding node define their actions there. This action profile defines a branch forking out from that node and leads to yet another node, and so on.

For example, in the game in Figure 18.4, the strategy profile $(b, (d, e))$ defines the bold path in Figure 18.5. In this figure, we have denoted with arrows the actions chosen by each player in the strategy profile $(b, (d, e))$. For example, the action d by player 2 is marked with an arrow since it is part of his operation plan in the strategy (d, e). This is in spite of the fact that when player 1 chooses b, the action d of player 2 is not on the path determined by the players' strategy profile $(b, (d, e))$.

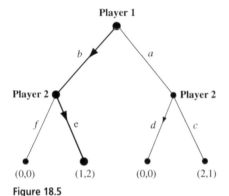

Figure 18.5

<hr>

[2] It should be emphasized that in certain places in the literature, a distinction is drawn between the term **plan of action** of player i, denoting the player's choice only at nodes that the plan of action itself does not exclude, and the term **strategy** (or operation plan), denoting the action profile of player i at all her nodes N_i as we have defined here.

The path of play in the game ultimately leads to a leaf ℓ, at which the payoffs of all the players $\pi^\ell = \left(\pi_i^\ell\right)_{i\in I} \in \mathbb{R}^I$ are specified. For example, the bold path in Figure 18.5, which is determined by the strategy profile $(b, (d, e))$, leads to the payoff profile $(1, 2)$.

In general, the players' strategy profile $x = (x_i)_{i\in I} \in X$ defines a path that ends at leaf ℓ^x, with the payoffs $\pi^{\ell^x} = \left(\pi_i^{\ell^x}\right)_{i\in I} \in \mathbb{R}^I$ to the players. The payoff function of player $i \in I$:

$$u_i : X \to \mathbb{R}$$

thus associates the payoff:

$$u_i(x) = \pi_i^{\ell^x}$$

of player i to any strategy profile $x \in X$ of the players.

Even if the strategy profile x leads to an infinite path of play, by definition this path is associated with a payoff profile which we will denote by $\pi^x = \left(\pi_i^x\right)_{i\in I} \in \mathbb{R}^I$. The payoff functions u_i in the game will then be defined by:

$$u_i(x) = \pi_i^x$$

The payoff functions u_i define a strategic form game that is called the strategic form of the extensive form game.

Question 18.2

What is the strategic form of the game described in Figure 18.3?

Answer

In this game, player 1 has four strategies and player 2 has two strategies. The payoffs appear in the following table:

Player 2

		c	d
	(a, e)	4, 4	0, 3
	(a, f)	5, 2	0, 3
Player 1	(b, e)	1, 0	1, 0
	(b, f)	1, 0	1, 0

Question 18.3

What is the strategic form of the game described in Figure 18.4? Find the Nash equilibria in the game.

Answer

In this game, player 1 has two strategies and player 2 has four strategies. Each strategy profile defines a path in the game tree, which leads to a leaf at which the players' payoffs are specified. These appear in the following table:

Player 2

		(c, e)	(c, f)	(d, e)	(d, f)
	a	2,1	2,1	0,0	0,0
Player 1					
	b	1,2	0,0	1,2	0,0

In this table, we have underlined the payoffs of each player which correspond to her best replies. The strategy profiles in which both payoffs are underlined are Nash equilibria. Thus, we have found that this game has three Nash equilibria.

At the two equilibria $(a,(c,e))$ and $(a,(c,f))$ in Question 18.3, player 1 chooses a and player 2 actually chooses c. At the third equilibrium, player 1 chooses b and player 2 ends up choosing e. This is a Nash equilibrium, because given the strategy (d, e) of player 2, the strategy b of player 1 is a best reply: player 1's choice of a rather than b would have led to a payoff of 0 for both players rather than to the payoff profile $(1, 2)$. The strategy (d, e) of player 2 carries a threat on the part of player 2 "to burn down the clubhouse," i.e. to choose the action d, which is bad for both players, if player 2 adopts the action a rather than the action b that leads to the highest possible payoff for player 2.

Yet something odd takes place at the third equilibrium. Player 2, after all, moves following player 1 and not at the same time as her. If player 1 deviates from her equilibrium strategy and chooses a, will player 2 still want to adhere to the strategy (d, e) and play d? Of course not! The choice of d will yield player 2 a payoff of 0, whereas the choice of c will yield player 2 a higher payoff.

Thus, the equilibrium $(b,(d,e))$ ignores the temporal dimension of the game. This equilibrium has some internal logic only if player 2 has some way of committing to the strategy (d, e) even if player 1 chooses a.

If player 2 has some way of irreversibly committing himself to the plan of action (*d, e*) before knowing what action player 1 has chosen, then the game is actually one in which the players choose their strategies simultaneously (or else player 2 chooses his strategy even before player 1). In such a case, the tree in Figure 18.4 does not describe the order of choice in the game. But if the tree in Figure 18.4 faithfully describes the possible order of moves in the game, then the threat posed by player 2 to respond with action *d* to a choice of *a* by player 1 is not a credible threat; if player 1 chooses *a*, player 2 will prefer to respond with *c*.

Therefore, in extensive form games, we will want to focus solely on a subset of Nash equilibria – equilibria that do not include empty threats of this kind. We will address this issue in the next chapter.

19 Non-credible threats, subgame perfect equilibrium and backward induction

19.1

19.1 Subgames of an extensive form game

In the preceding chapter, we saw that in extensive form games there may be Nash equilibria that are based on non-credible threats. How can we screen out such equilibria? What additional condition do we need to define? This chapter addresses this issue.

Every node $n \in N$ in a tree defines a **subgame**. This subgame is an extensive form game in its own right, and it contains only those branches and nodes that are found on paths proceeding from n onwards. A description of a subgame will accordingly be obtained by eliminating all nodes and branches that are not on paths proceeding from n. For example, the game tree in Figure 19.1 is a subgame of the game in Figure 18.3.

Question 19.1

What are the subgames in the game in Figure 18.4?

Answer

In this figure, there are three subgames. One of them is the entire game as described in Figure 18.4. The two others are genuine subgames. In each of them, the unique player is player 2. The games are described in Figure 19.2.

Question 19.2

How many subgames are there in an extensive form game?

Answer

Every node in the tree that is not a leaf is a root of the subtree proceeding from it. Therefore, the number of subgames in a given game tree is equal to the overall number of nodes in the tree, minus the number of leaves.

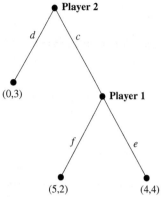

Figure 19.1

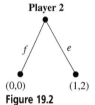

Figure 19.2

A player's strategy in an extensive form game naturally defines the player's strategy also in every subgame: this is simply the player's operation plan in the subgame.

Formally, assume that the set of nodes in the game is N and the set of nodes in the subgame is $N' \subset N$. Accordingly, assume that in the entire game, player i plays at the set of nodes $N_i \subseteq N$, and therefore, in the subgame N', player i plays at the set of nodes $N_i' = N' \cap N_i$. The player's strategy in the game as a whole, $x_i = \left(a_i^n \right)_{n \in N_i}$, defines the induced strategy $x_i' = \left(a_i^n \right)_{n \in N_i'}$ in the subgame (in which the player's operation plan is defined only in the set of nodes N_i').

19.2   Subgame perfect equilibrium

In order for a Nash equilibrium in an extensive form game not to be based on non-credible threats, we must require that at equilibrium, each player's strategy will be a best reply to her rivals' strategies not only in the game as a whole but also in every subgame.[1] A Nash equilibrium meeting this condition is called a **subgame perfect equilibrium**.

Definition   The strategy profile $x^* = \left(x_j^*\right)_{j\in I} \in X$ of the players is a **subgame perfect equilibrium** if it induces a Nash equilibrium in every subgame.

Question 19.3   Find a subgame perfect equilibrium in the game in Figure 18.4.

Answer   A subgame perfect equilibrium should also induce an equilibrium in every subgame and in particular in the subgames in Figure 19.2. In these subgames, player 2 is the unique player, and therefore her equilibrium strategy in every subgame is simply her optimal strategy. In the game at the top of Figure 19.2 the optimal strategy is c, and in the game at the bottom of that figure the optimal strategy is e. Therefore, at a subgame perfect equilibrium, the equilibrium strategy of player 2 is (c,e). The best reply of player 1 to this strategy is a. Therefore, in this game, there is a unique subgame perfect equilibrium – the strategy profile $(a,(c, e))$.

Thus, the two additional Nash equilibria that we found in Question 18.3 are not subgame perfect equilibria. In particular, the Nash equilibrium $(b,(d, e))$ that is based on a non-credible threat posed by player 2 is not a subgame perfect equilibrium.

A subgame perfect equilibrium is never based on non-credible threats: at every stage of the game, every player does her best irrespective of any developments prior to that stage. Therefore, at a subgame perfect equilibrium, "revenge" taken by a player against the behavior of her rivals at earlier stages is meaningless, and her behavior is dictated solely by her interests from that stage onwards.

[1] In a subgame in which there is a unique player, a "Nash equilibrium" is simply an optimal strategy for that player.

19.3 Backward induction

We will now focus our discussion on extensive form games with the following two properties:

- At each of the nodes in the game tree there is only one player.
- The tree has a finite number of nodes.

In many games of this type there exists a simple procedure by means of which a subgame perfect equilibrium can be found. This procedure is called **backward induction**. In the backward induction process, we "fold" the game tree backwards, stage by stage. At every stage:

- we identify on the tree a node n all of the branches extending from which lead to leaves. By assumption, a unique player i is playing at the node n;
- we identify the payoffs of player i at the various leaves that she can reach from the node n;
- we choose a leaf ℓ at which the payoff to player i is the highest among the payoffs to the player at those leaves. In the operation plan of player i, at the node n she will choose ℓ. (If there are several leaves at which the payoff to player i is maximal, the leaf ℓ will be one of those leaves. In such a case, the backward induction procedure does not uniquely define the selected leaf ℓ, and any choice of such leaf ℓ is permissible in the backward induction process. Different choices may lead to different results in the backward induction procedure);
- we will delete from the tree the branches proceeding from n and the leaves to which they lead, such that n becomes a leaf. To the leaf n on the pruned tree we will associate the payoff profile of ℓ.

After having repeatedly folded the game tree backwards in this way, we will ultimately remain with a unique node – the root of the tree, which has become a leaf. The operation plans we have constructed throughout the process define a strategy profile that is a subgame perfect equilibrium, and the payoff profile that we ultimately associated to the root is the payoff profile of the players at this equilibrium.

Question 19.4

Carry out the backward induction procedure for the game in Figure 18.3.

Answer

In this game, there is a unique node leading to leaves – the second node at which player 1 may be called to play. At this node, the optimal action for player 1 is f, which leads to the payoff profile (5, 2). If we replace this node by a leaf in which the payoff profile (5, 2) is specified, we will obtain the game tree described in Figure 19.3.

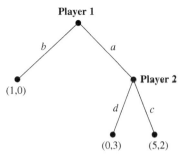

Figure 19.3

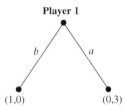

Figure 19.4

In the "folded" game that has been obtained there is once again a unique node leading to leaves – the node at which player 2 plays. The optimal action for her is d, which leads to the payoff profile $(0, 3)$. If we substitute the node of player 2 with this payoff profile, the game tree that will be obtained appears in Figure 19.4.

In the game obtained following this further folding, player 1 is the only one playing. The optimal action for her is b, which leads to the payoff profile $(1, 0)$.

The operation plans that we constructed in the course of the backward induction procedure are $((b, f), d)$. This is the unique subgame perfect equilibrium in the game.

Question 19.5

Using backward induction, find a subgame perfect equilibrium in the game appearing in Figure 19.5.

Answer

In this game, the node of player 2 is the only one leading to leaves of the tree. At both these leaves, player 2 gets the same payoff, namely 10. In such a case, the backward induction process permits us to choose any one of these actions.

If action c is chosen, we will obtain the folded game tree appearing in Figure 19.6 in which the optimal action for player 2 is b. Hence we will obtain the subgame perfect equilibrium (b, c).

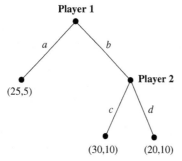

Figure 19.5

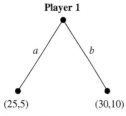

Figure 19.6

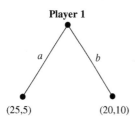

Figure 19.7

If the action *d* is chosen, we will obtain the folded game tree appearing in Figure 19.7, in which the optimal action for player 1 is *a*. Hence, we will obtain a subgame perfect equilibrium (*a, d*).

In Question 19.5, we saw how a game may have several subgame perfect equilibria. At the same time, the example also illustrates the fact that in a certain sense, such games are "rare": in order for there to be, in the backward induction procedure, a player who is indifferent between two actions that are available to her, the payoffs that each such action will yield must be identical. Therefore, if the payoffs of each player in the various leaves of the tree are even slightly different from one another, in the backward induction procedure we will be able to choose only a unique optimal action per player at every stage of the folding of the tree.

Can the backward induction procedure also be used in cases in which the game tree has an infinite number of nodes? Here we distinguish between two cases:

1. **The tree has an infinite path.** The backward induction process will not enable us to crop nodes along such a path.
2. **The tree does not have an infinite path, but it does have nodes from which there proceed an infinite number of branches.** In such a case, the backward induction process may be used, and this process will either lead to the finding of a subgame perfect equilibrium, or will show that there is no such equilibrium.

Indeed, at a tree-folding stage in which the branches lead from a particular node n to an infinite number of leaves, the player who is playing at n might not have an optimal strategy, and therefore we might be unable to continue folding the tree. (We will see an example of this phenomenon at the end of section 19.3.1 below.)

- If this is the situation in every possible folding of the tree along the backward induction procedure, we will conclude that the game has no subgame perfect equilibrium.
- However, if we find a way of folding the tree by backward induction until we reach the root, then the operation plans of the players constructed in this process will constitute a subgame perfect equilibrium.

We will now see an example of a game between two players in which each player has an infinite number of possible actions.

19.3.1   Quantity competition with a leading firm – the Stackelberg model

In Chapter 8 we presented the Cournot model of quantity competition between two firms. The firms operate in a market in which the demand for a product is given by $Q = A - P$, while $Q = q_1 + q_2$ is the sum of the quantities that the two firms produce. Firm i invests the amount c_i in order to produce a unit of the product. In Chapter 8, we found the Nash equilibrium between the two firms, at which both firms simultaneously choose what quantity to produce. In the particular case in which production costs are negligible, $c_1 = c_2 = 0$, we obtained that at a Nash equilibrium each firm produces the quantity:

$$q_1^* = q_2^* = \frac{A}{3}$$

What will happen, however, if firm 1 is able to determine the quantity it produces before firm 2 determines its quantity? In such a case, we will obtain an extensive form game between the two firms. This game is known in the literature as the

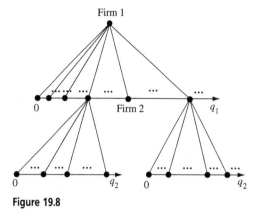

Figure 19.8

Stackelberg model. In this game firm 1 has an infinite number of possible actions – it must choose a non-negative quantity q_1 of units for production. Given this choice, firm 2 has to choose the quantity q_2 that it will produce. See Figure 19.8.

We will now find a subgame perfect equilibrium between the two firms, using backward induction.

Firm 2 is the one whose action will lead to the termination of the game and to the determination of the payoffs to the two players. If firm 1 has already produced q_1 units and firm 2 chooses to produce q_2 units, then the market price for a unit of the product will be $P = A - q_1 - q_2$, and the profit of firm 2 will be:

$$\Pi_2(q_2; q_1) = Pq_2 = (A - q_1 - q_2)q_2$$

This profit will be maximized when the derivative of the profit function vanishes:

$$\frac{d\Pi_2}{dq_2} = A - q_1 - 2q_2 = 0$$

i.e. the profit will be maximized at the quantity:

$$q_2^*(q_1) = \frac{A - q_1}{2} \tag{19.1}$$

This, then, is the strategy of firm 2 at a subgame perfect equilibrium: if firm 1 has produced q_1 units, firm 2 will produce $\frac{A-q_1}{2}$ units.[2] We are already familiar with this expression from the discussion of the Cournot model – this is simply the best-reply function of firm 2.

What about firm 1? Firm 1 understands that if it produces q_1 units, firm 2 will produce $\frac{A-q_1}{2}$ units, and therefore the overall quantity of units in the market will be:

---

[2] And if $\frac{A-q_1}{2} < 0$, firm 2 will produce nothing.

$$Q = q_1 + \frac{A - q_1}{2} = \frac{A + q_1}{2}$$

In such a case the price will be:

$$P = A - Q = A - \frac{A + q_1}{2} = \frac{A - q_1}{2}$$

and firm 1's profit will be:

$$\Pi_1(q_1) = Pq_1 = \frac{A - q_1}{2} q_1$$

This profit will be maximized when the derivative of the profit function vanishes:

$$\frac{d\Pi_1}{dq_1} = \frac{A}{2} - q_1 = 0$$

i.e. at the quantity:

$$q_1^* = \frac{A}{2}$$

Given that quantity, the number of units that firm 2 will produce is:

$$q_2^*(q_1^*) = \frac{A - q_1^*}{2} = \frac{A - \frac{A}{2}}{2} = \frac{A}{4}$$

Recall that in the Cournot model, when the two firms determined their production quantities simultaneously, each firm produced $\frac{A}{3}$ units. We see, therefore, that when firm 1 is the first to decide what quantity to produce, it enjoys an advantage and increases its production quantity to $\frac{A}{2}$ units. As a result its profit increases from:

$$\Pi_1^{Cournot} = \left(A - \frac{A}{3} - \frac{A}{3}\right)\frac{A}{3} = \frac{A^2}{9}$$

to:

$$\Pi_1^{Stackelberg} = \left(A - \frac{A}{2} - \frac{A}{4}\right)\frac{A}{2} = \frac{A^2}{8}$$

At the same time, firm 2 reduces the quantity it produces from $\frac{A}{3}$ to $\frac{A}{4}$ and its profit declines from:

$$\Pi_2^{Cournot} = \left(A - \frac{A}{3} - \frac{A}{3}\right)\frac{A}{3} = \frac{A^2}{9}$$

to:

$$\Pi_2^{\text{Stackelberg}} = \left(A - \frac{A}{2} - \frac{A}{4} \right) \frac{A}{4} = \frac{A^2}{16}$$

Thus, firms 1's leading position secures an advantage. Why? Choosing the quantity first is advantageous because it enables firm 1 to commit to a quantity q_1^* that it produces, and thereby to actually dictate to firm 2 the quantity it is to produce, i.e. firm 1 knows that in any event firm 2 will choose a quantity q_2 such that the combination of the quantities (q_1, q_2) of the two firms will be on the reaction curve (19.1) of firm 2. But when firm 1 is in the lead, in the Stackelberg model it asks itself: "What combination of quantities (q_1, q_2) on the reaction curve (19.1) of firm 2 will secure me a maximum profit?" and chooses to produce the quantity q_1^* in that combination. On the other hand, in the Cournot model, when firm 1 chose what quantity to produce simultaneously with firm 2, firm 1 asked itself: "For what combination of quantities (q_1, q_2) on the reaction curve (19.1) of firm 2 is the quantity q_1 a best reply from my point of view to the quantity q_2?" As we have seen here, the answers to these two questions need not be identical.

Thus, at a subgame perfect equilibrium in the Stackelberg model, the strategy of firm 1 is not on its own reaction curve (the reaction curve of firm 1 appears in gray in Figure 19.9). If, after firm 2 has chosen to produce $\frac{A}{4}$, firm 1 were able to "change its mind" and produce a quantity smaller than $q_1^* = \frac{A}{2}$, then firm 1 would indeed have modified the quantity being produced: the best reply of firm 1 to the quantity $\frac{A}{4}$ that firm 2 is producing would then be to produce $\frac{3}{8}A$ and not $\frac{A}{2}$. In other words, at a

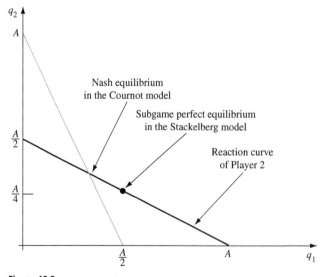

Figure 19.9

Stackelberg equilibrium, firm 1 commits itself to a strategy which it knows, from the outset, is not a best reply to the strategy that firm 2 will subsequently choose. Firm 1 does this because its profit from causing its rival to produce a small quantity ($\frac{A}{4}$) is greater than its loss due to the fact that its reply to that quantity is not optimal. The next chapter will be dedicated to a discussion of commitment in strategic situations.

We have thus found that in the Stackelberg model, which is an extensive form game, the strategy profile $q_1^* = \frac{A}{2}$, $q_2^*(q_1) = \frac{A-q_1}{2}$ is a subgame perfect equilibrium. The strategy of firm 2 is to produce $\frac{A-q_1}{2}$ if and when firm 1 produces q_1. The strategy $q_2^*(q_1) = \frac{A-q_1}{2}$ is indeed a best reply of firm 2 to a situation in which firm 1 produces the quantity q_1. As against this strategy, the strategy $q_1^* = \frac{A}{2}$ is optimal for firm 1. But the strategy $q_1^* = \frac{A}{2}$ would not be optimal for firm 1 if firm 2 were to choose to produce the quantity $\frac{A}{4}$ irrespective of the quantity that firm 1 produced before it. This is the case even though the quantity $\frac{A}{4}$ is ultimately exactly the quantity $q_2^*(q_1^*)$ that firm 2 indeed produces at the subgame perfect equilibrium of the game, at which firm 1's strategy is $q_1^* = \frac{A}{2}$ and firm 2's strategy is to produce the quantity $q_2^*(q_1) = \frac{A-q_1}{2}$, which is conditioned on the quantity q_1 that firm 1 produced prior thereto.

Transiting from a Nash equilibrium in a simultaneous move game to a subgame perfect equilibrium in the same game in which one of the players chooses its strategy first – such a transition can never hurt the leading player: the leading player can always revert to choosing the strategy that it adopted at the Nash equilibrium in the simultaneous move game ($q_1 = \frac{A}{3}$ in the present example) and in such a case the other player, who is next in turn to play, will also play the same best reply that it chose at the Nash equilibrium of the simultaneous move game ($q_2 = \frac{A}{3}$ in the example). But as we saw in the example of the Stackelberg game, the leading player often has another strategy ($q_1^* = \frac{A}{2}$ in the example) that causes the second player to respond (at a subgame perfect equilibrium) in such a way that the payoff of the leading player will ultimately be higher.

Thus, using backward induction, we have found the unique equilibrium which is a subgame perfect equilibrium in the Stackelberg model. Note that in this game there are also numerous additional Nash equilibria. For example, the game has a Nash equilibrium at which firm 2 perversely expects firm 1 to produce, $q_1 = \frac{A}{4}$, while for its own part it produces $q_2 = \frac{A}{2}$, and threatens to dump the market and to produce $q_2 = A - q_1$ if firm 1 produces any other quantity $q_1 \neq \frac{A}{4}$. Under this threat, if firm 1 does indeed produce $q_1 = \frac{A}{4}$ it will pocket a positive profit, but if it produces more and firm 2 makes good on its threat, the market price will be $P = 0$ and the profit of firm 1 will be 0.

The problem with this Nash equilibrium is, of course, that the threat posed by firm 2 is non-credible. Even if firm 1 produces a quantity $q_1 \neq \frac{A}{4}$, when the time comes and firm 2 actually has to decide how much to produce, it will not want to carry out its threat and flood the market since doing so would cause its profit, too, to fall to 0. When the time to decide arrives, firm 2 will want to produce the quantity $q_2^*(q_1)$ that we calculated in (19.1), since this is the best reply from its own point of view. At a subgame perfect equilibrium, in contrast, this is indeed the choice of firm 2 and firm 1 takes this into account when choosing how much to produce.

In this example we have also seen that the backward induction procedure was successful in pinning down a subgame perfect equilibrium despite the fact that the set of actions of every player in the game is infinite. But if, for example, we were to limit the set of actions of firm 1 to be $q_1 \in [0, \frac{A}{2})$, i.e. if firm 1 could produce only any quantity strictly smaller than $\frac{A}{2}$, then firm 1 would have at its disposal no best reply to maximize its profits; for every quantity $q_1 < \frac{A}{2}$ it were to choose to produce, it could always find a greater quantity q_1':

$$q_1 < q_1' < \frac{A}{2}$$

that would yield it an even larger profit.

This is an example of the fact that when a player's set of actions is infinite, it could be the case that none of those actions is optimal for the player. But as we have seen, such a case is obtained under an artificial assumption – that firm 1 can produce any quantity which is strictly smaller than $\frac{A}{2}$ but cannot produce the quantity $\frac{A}{2}$ itself. In practical examples, in which there are no such artificial assumptions, we will not usually encounter a situation in which a player has no optimal action, and in particular we will usually be able to find a subgame perfect equilibrium even in games in which the players have an infinite number of actions.

In the following example, several players act simultaneously at some of the stages. In general, in such a game a subgame perfect equilibrium cannot be found by means of backward induction. Nevertheless, thanks to the structure of the payoffs in the following example, a subgame perfect equilibrium can be found in the game by using backward induction considerations.

19.3.2   The publisher's dilemma – pricing over time

A publishing house is about to launch one more book in a popular series by a well-known writer. On the day the book is launched, long lines of enthusiastic readers will form outside the bookstores. Having squatted on the sidewalk the previous evening, they will spend the night in sleeping bags, chatting excitedly until the wee hours. For the privilege of being the first to get their hands on the book, these readers will, of course, be prepared to pay a high price. Other potential readers, at the same time, will spend a tranquil night in their own beds. They will be happy to read the book a few months after it first appears and are not willing to pay for it more than they would for other books.

Unfortunately for the publishing house, the bookstore vendors have no way of distinguishing between the two types of purchasers: not all readers of the first type sport round spectacles and an impish expression. Moreover, an attempt to sell the book at different prices to variously bespectacled customers will not pass muster in court. If the publishing house wants to sell the book at different prices to different types of customers, it must find some other means of distinguishing between them.

One of the ways to do this is to publish the book in two different bindings – hardcover and paperback. A hardcover book is more durable and therefore the publishers are justified in charging a higher price for it in spite of the fact that the production costs of both hardcover and paperback books, using state-of-the-art technologies, are virtually identical. These costs are in any event negligible relative to the price at which the book is sold in the store.

But what of the book-lovers stampeding the stores on the day the book is launched? Will they prefer the more expensive hardcover edition over the cheaper paperback edition? Not necessarily. These book-lovers are interested, first and foremost, in the content of the book rather than its form. They are prepared to pay a higher price for a copy of the book in order to be among its first readers, but once inside the bookstore, the great majority of them will prefer to purchase the cheapest copy they can find there.

Accordingly, in order to cause these customers to pay a high price for the book, the publishers must issue the first edition in hardcover only. The hard cover will provide the justification for charging the higher price, whereas, in practice, the price actually collected by the publishing house will be the highest price that purchasers of the first type – the book-lovers – will be willing to pay at the immediate launch.

After several months in which all the book-lovers buy expensive hardcover copies, the book is critiqued in the press, and blogs and other forms of correspondence flood the Internet, it will be time to offer the book to the second type of readers of the more relaxed sort, who are not driven to pay more for this book than for any similar one. In order to justify the cut in price, the publishing house will now issue the book in a second, paperback edition, at a more affordable price.

Bookstores thus become a game arena between the publishing house and the reading public. The publishing house has to decide on the per-copy price of the book in the first edition, and, given that price, each reader has to decide whether to purchase the book at once or to await the paperback edition. On issuing the cheaper edition, the publishing house has to decide on the price at which a paperback copy of the book will retail. Given that price, every reader not yet having purchased the book has to decide whether or not to make the purchase.

We will assume that the number of purchasers n of the first type – the book-lovers – is twice as small as the number of purchasers $2n$ of the second type – the relaxed readers. Similarly, we will assume, for simplicity's sake, that the production and distribution costs of the book are negligible, and the publishing house therefore prints $3n$ copies of the book starting straight from the hardback, and anyone wanting to buy the book can do so immediately.

A purchaser of the first type is prepared to pay at most $170 for a hardback copy. But if, for any reason, he fails to acquire a hardback copy, he will be prepared to pay at most $50 for a paperback copy of the book – once it has been critiqued and the rumors concerning its content have been circulated. A purchaser of the second type is prepared to pay at most $60 for a hardback copy of the book and not more than $30 for a paperback copy (if he did not purchase a hardback copy). When a purchaser is prepared to pay at most $x for a copy of the book, and he purchases it at price p, the purchaser's net utility is the difference $x - p$.

Question 19.6

Calculate the sale of the second edition

Assume that none of the relaxed readers has purchased a hardback copy of the book. What price is it worthwhile for the publisher to fix for a paperback copy? What will the utility of each purchaser be at that price?

Answer

The publishing house can specify a price that will cause all types of readers to purchase the book. The highest price that will bring this to pass is $30 per copy.[3] At this price, the profit of the publishing house will be at least $2n \times 30 = 60n$.

Alternatively, the publishing house can aim the paperback edition solely at the book-lover population – if any of its members have not yet purchased the book. The highest price these purchasers will be prepared to pay for the book is $50 per copy. At that price, the publishing house's profit will be at most $n \times 50 = 50n$.

Thus, the first strategy – that of setting a price of $30 – will maximize the publisher's profit from the sale of the paperback (i.e. under the assumption that none of the relaxed readers purchased a copy of the first edition). The utility of each relaxed reader will be 0 – he is purchasing the book at the highest price he is willing to pay. On the other hand, book-lovers purchasing a paperback copy have a utility of $50-30 = 20$. This is the difference between the maximum price ($50) that the book-lover would have been willing to pay and the price he actually paid

[3] At a higher price the relaxed readers will not purchase the book; if the price per copy is one cent lower, at $29.99, the relaxed readers will strictly prefer to purchase it and will not be indifferent between purchasing and refraining from purchasing. In order to simplify the calculations, we will assume here, and in similar cases later, that even at a price of $30 per copy all the relaxed readers will purchase the book.

($30). This difference is called the **informational rent** of the book-lover: the fact that he is a book-lover is known to him, but not to the publishing house, and the publisher therefore cannot charge him a different price from that which it collects from any other purchaser.

Question 19.7

Universal sale of the first edition

Assume that the publishing house wishes to sell the hardback edition to all potential customers. At what price must it retail a copy of the hardback edition? What will its profit then be?

Answer

In order to sell copies of the hardback edition also to relaxed readers, the price of a hardback copy cannot exceed $60. This is the maximum price at which all readers will purchase copies of the hardback. At this price, the profit of the publishing house will be $3n \times 60 = 180n$.

Question 19.8

Selling the first edition to book-lovers

Assume that the publishing house plans to sell the paperback edition at a price of $30 per copy, as calculated in Question 19.8. What is the maximum price at which it will be able to sell a copy of the hard-cover edition to book-lovers? What utility will each book-lover obtain by purchasing the book? What will be the total profit derived by the publisher from the sale of the two editions?

Answer

In Question 19.8 we saw that if a book-lover waits for the paperback in order to purchase the book, his utility (which is his informational rent) will be 20. Therefore, for him to want to purchase a hardback copy, the price of the hardback must guarantee the book-lover a utility of at least 20. Such a utility will be obtained only if the price of a hardback copy does not exceed $150. (In such a case, the utility to the book-lover will be exactly $170 - 150 = 20$. At a price of $149.99 per copy, the book-lover will strictly prefer to purchase a the hardback edition. To simplify our calculations, we will assume that the book-lover will purchase a hard-cover book even at a price of $150 per copy.) At such a price, the publishing house's profit from the sale of the hardbacks will be $150n$.

In Question 19.8, we saw that the profit of the publishing house from the sale of the paperback edition will be $60n$. Therefore, total profit from the sale of both editions will amount to $150n + 60n = 210n$. This exceeds the profit of $180n$ that the publishing house would have obtained had it sold the hard-cover edition to all readers at a price of $60 per copy.

Comprehension check

With the aid of the calculations in Questions 19.6–19.8, give an exact description of the strategies of each of the players (the publishing house, each of the book-lovers, each of the relaxed readers) at the subgame perfect equilibrium described in those exercises. Remember to outline, for each player, a full operation plan, describing his actions also in the event that one or more players taking their turn before him deviated from their equilibrium strategies.

Comprehension check

Repeat the calculations for the case in which the relaxed readers are prepared to pay $80 for a hardback copy. What will be the optimal strategy of the publishing house in this case?

20 Commitment

20.1 Commitment to action

In section 19.3.1, we described the Stackelberg model, in which one firm is the first to decide what quantity to produce, while the other firm decides what quantity it will produce only after having observed how much the first firm has produced. We saw that at the unique subgame perfect equilibrium of the game, the leading firm effectively chooses the combination of quantities that will maximize its profits from among all the combinations of quantities on its rival's reaction curve. But in this combination of quantities, the quantity that the first firm produces does not constitute a best reply to the quantity that the second firm ultimately produces: if, after the second firm has chosen its strategy at a Stackelberg equilibrium, the first firm were to get a chance to change its mind and produce a smaller quantity than it had already produced, then it would certainly prefer to do so. Thus, the leading firm's advantage is reflected in the fact that by its action, it can commit and bind itself to an action that at the end of the day is not necessarily optimal for it. The leading firm's loss redounds to its advantage, since its commitment to an "over-aggressive" strategy leads its rival to behave "submissively."

In the decision problem of a unique decision maker, the decision maker can derive no advantage from deciding to adopt an action which will prove, in retrospect, to have been suboptimal for her.[1] One of the most important insights of game theory is that in strategic situations, a player's ability to commit to her strategy – a strategy that is not necessarily optimal, given the reactions of her rivals – can secure her an important advantage.

In the Stackelberg model, the leading firm chooses to commit itself to an aggressive strategy (as compared with the Nash equilibrium strategy in the Cournot model,

---

[1] A person may decide to refrain from purchasing a large package of ice-cream for fear of being unable to withstand the temptation of devouring it all at once rather than enjoying a single portion each day. In this example, however, the person is actually playing "against the embodiment of himself": he fears that his preferences of the next day, with the block of ice-cream in residence in his refrigerator, will be different from his current preferences. In this sense, the person faces a strategic situation rather than a decision problem of a single decision maker. Confronting temptation, and, more generally, preferences that are "dynamically inconsistent," is one of the topics currently addressed by game-theoretic research.

in which both firms simultaneously choose how much to produce). Is it the case that in every game, the leading player will find it worthwhile to choose a strategy that is more aggressive than its equilibrium strategy at the simultaneous move game? We will now see an example demonstrating the opposite case.

20.1.1   Investment in a public good with a leading player

In the example in section 7.1, we analyzed the game of investment in a public good. Every player i has to decide what portion g_i of her resources e she wishes to invest in the public good. In the case of two players, the payoff functions were:

$$u_1(g_1, g_2) = (e - g_1)(1 + g_1 + g_2)$$
$$u_2(g_1, g_2) = (e - g_2)(1 + g_1 + g_2)$$

and the best-reply functions were:

$$BR_1(g_2) = \frac{e - 1 - g_2}{2}$$
$$BR_2(g_1) = \frac{e - 1 - g_1}{2}$$

A Nash equilibrium consisted of the investment profile:

$$g_1^* = g_2^* = \frac{e - 1}{3}$$

What will happen if player 1 can choose her investment before player 2? In this case, player 1 knows that an investment on her part of g_1 will entail an investment of $BR_2(g_1)$ on the part of player 2. Therefore, she will opt for the investment g_1 which will maximize her utility:

$$u_1(g_1, BR_2(g_1)) = (e - g_1)(1 + g_1 + BR_2(g_1))$$
$$= (e - g_1)\left(1 + g_1 + \frac{e - 1 - g_1}{2}\right)$$

This is a decreasing function of g_1 in the entire domain $g_1 \geq 0$ (verify this!) and therefore the utility of player 1 will be maximized at the investment level:

$$g_1^{**} = 0$$

This investment level is lower than the investment level $g_1^* = \frac{e-1}{3}$ at a Nash equilibrium (that we found in the example in section 7.1), where the two players choose their level of investment simultaneously.

What will happen to the utility level of player 1 at this equilibrium, compared with her utility at the Nash equilibrium of the simultaneous move game in section 7.1? In a game in which player 1 is the first to choose her investment level, her level of utility must be equal to or higher than her level of utility in the simultaneous move game.

The reason for this is that in both games, the equilibrium strategy profile is on the best-reply curve of player 2. In a game in which player 1 chooses first, she actually chooses the strategy profile that is optimal from her point of view on the reaction curve of player 2. If the equilibrium in the simultaneous move game was indeed optimal for player 1 from among all the strategy profiles on the reaction curve of player, 2, then player 1 would adhere to that strategy even when given the opportunity to choose her level of investment first. The fact of her choosing to change her investment level from $g_1^* = \frac{e-1}{3}$ to $g_1^{**} = 0$ therefore proves that her utility is higher in the game in which she moves first.

> ## Comprehension check
>
> Calculate explicitly the utility level of player 1 at the simultaneous move Nash equilibrium and at the equilibrium in which player 1 moves first, and show that her utility at the equilibrium of the game in which she moves first is indeed higher. Calculate also the utility level of player 2 at both equilibria. In which of the two games is her utility at equilibrium higher?

What is the difference between the Stackelberg model and the public good game? Why, in the Stackelberg model, does the leading player choose to commit to a more aggressive strategy than at the Nash equilibrium of the simultaneous move game, while in the case of investment in a public good, the leading player chooses, contrariwise, a strategy at which her investment in the public good is more moderate?

In the Stackelberg model, the game is one of conflict, while in the public good game, the game is one of cooperation.[2] Is this the source of the difference? We will now see that it is only one of the factors affecting the degree of aggressiveness of the strategy that is optimal for the leading player, compared with her behavior at a Nash equilibrium of the simultaneous move game.

20.1.2   Partnership with a leading player

Consider again the game described in section 6.4.1. In this game, two business partners must each choose her level of investment at work. As a function of the investment levels x_1, x_2 by the partners, their utility will be, respectively:

---

[2] The definition of games of conflict and cooperation appears at the beginning of Chapter 7.

$$u_1(x_1, x_2) = 2x_1 + 2x_2 + \frac{1}{2}x_1x_2 - x_1^2$$

$$u_2(x_1, x_2) = 2x_1 + 2x_2 + \frac{1}{2}x_1x_2 - x_2^2$$

The best-reply functions are:

$$BR_1(x_2) = 1 + \frac{x_2}{4}$$

$$BR_2(x_1) = 1 + \frac{x_1}{4}$$

At a Nash equilibrium, both partners choose the same level of effort:

$$x_1^* = x_2^* = \frac{4}{3}$$

In contrast, if partner 1 is the first to choose her level of effort, she will choose it so as to maximize her utility:

$$u_1(x_1, BR_2(x_1)) = u_1\left(x_1, 1 + \frac{x_1}{4}\right)$$

$$= 2x_1 + 2\left(1 + \frac{x_1}{4}\right) + \frac{1}{2}x_1\left(1 + \frac{x_1}{4}\right) - x_1^2$$

This maximal level of utility will be obtained at the level of effort $x_1^{**} = \frac{12}{7} > x_1^*$. See Figure 20.1.

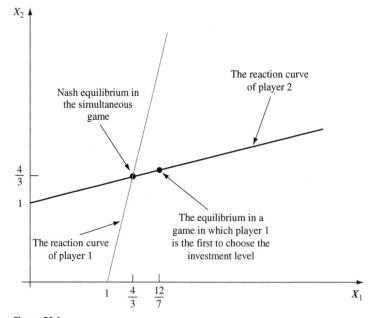

Figure 20.1

Thus we have seen that in one game of cooperation (investment in a public good), the leading player will adopt a more moderate strategy than at the Nash equilibrium of the simultaneous move game, while in another game of cooperation (the partnership game), the leading player will adopt a more aggressive strategy than at the Nash equilibrium of the simultaneous move game. What is the source of the difference?

The public good game is a game of cooperation with strategic substitutes (a game in which the players' reaction curves have a negative slope).[3] In games of cooperation with strategic substitutes, a small enough shift along the reaction curve of player 2 away from the intersection point of the reaction curves will increase the utility of player 1 if the shift takes place in the direction in which player 1 becomes more moderate (and player 2 adopts a more aggressive strategy).

Since player 1 knows that player 2 will choose a reply that is optimal from her point of view, and the strategy profile will therefore be on the reaction curve of player 2, in a game of cooperation with strategic substitutes player 1 will adopt a more moderate strategy than at a Nash equilibrium of the simultaneous move game.

This state of affairs is reversed in games of cooperation with strategic complements (in which reaction curves have a positive slope), as in the case of the partnership game. In such games, a small enough shift of the strategy profile along the reaction curve of player 2, away from the point of intersection of the two reaction curves, will increase the utility of player 1 if the shift takes place in the direction in which player 1 becomes more aggressive (and player 2 also adopts a more aggressive strategy).

Since player 1 knows that player 2 will choose a response that is optimal from her point of view, and the strategy profile will therefore be on the reaction curve of player 2, in a game of cooperation with strategic complements, player 1 will adopt a more aggressive strategy than at the Nash equilibrium of the simultaneous move game.

The picture changes once more when we move from games of cooperation to games of conflict. For example, the Stackelberg model is a game with strategic substitutes: the reaction curves have a negative slope. But since the game is a game of conflict, a slight shift along the reaction curve of player 2 (from the point of intersection of the two reaction curves) will benefit player 1 if made in the direction in which player 1 becomes more aggressive and player 2 more moderate. That's why the leading firm in the Stackelberg model chooses a more aggressive strategy than at the Nash equilibrium of the Cournot model.

Figures 20.2–20.5 describe the four possible profiles of cooperation/conflict and strategic substitutes/complements.

In light of this analysis, it is not surprising that borderline cases may also occur in which the leading player chooses neither to moderate nor to exacerbate her action,

---

[3] The definition of games with strategic substitutes appears at the beginning of Chapter 7.

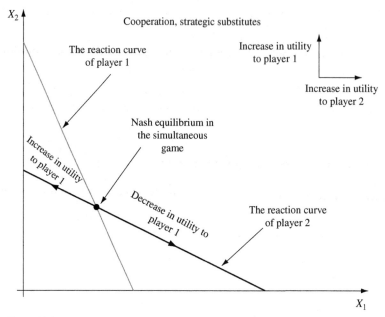

Figure 20.2

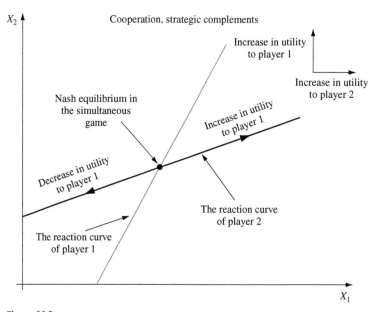

Figure 20.3

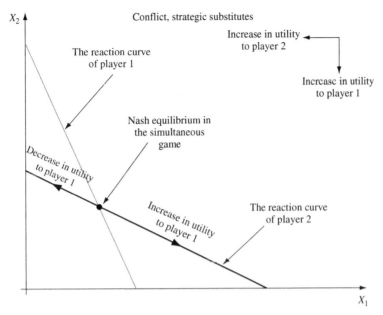

Figure 20.4

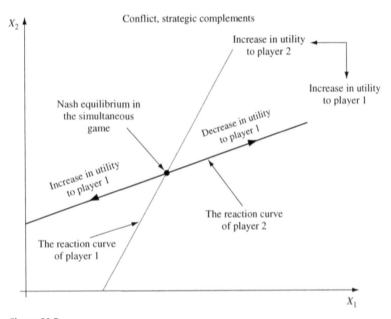

Figure 20.5

but rather to adhere to the strategy that she would have adopted in the simultaneous move game. We will explore such a case in the following example.

20.1.3   Patent race with a leading firm

In the example in section 7.3 we analyzed a game between two firms competing over the development of a patent. Given their levels of investment in the development, $x_1 > 0$, $x_2 > 0$, the competitors' utility functions are:

$$u_1(x_1, x_2) = \frac{9x_1}{x_1 + x_2} - x_1$$

$$u_2(x_1, x_2) = \frac{9x_2}{x_1 + x_2} - x_2$$

Accordingly, their reaction functions are:

$$BR_1(x_2) = 3\sqrt{x_2} - x_2$$
$$BR_2(x_1) = 3\sqrt{x_1} - x_1$$

and at a Nash equilibrium it is the case that:

$$x_1^* = x_2^* = \frac{9}{4}$$

If firm 1 is the first to choose its investment in development, its choice will be made so as to maximize its payoff assuming that its rival reacts optimally:

$$u_1(x_1, BR_2(x_1)) = \frac{9x_1}{x_1 + BR_2(x_1)} - x_1$$

$$= \frac{9x_1}{x_1 + \left(3\sqrt{x_1} - x_1\right)} - x_1 = 3\sqrt{x_1} - x_1$$

This payoff will be maximal at the level of investment:

$$x_1^{**} = \frac{9}{4}$$

which is identical to the level of investment of firm 1 in the simultaneous move game.

This is a game of conflict in which a Nash equilibrium of the simultaneous move game is located precisely at the point at which the game changes from a game of strategic complements (increasing reaction curves) to a game of strategic substitutes (decreasing reaction curves). See Figure 20.6. Therefore, given the above analysis, it is not surprising that even when firm 1 can be the first to choose its level of investment, it does not deviate from its level of investment at the Nash equilibrium of the simultaneous move game.

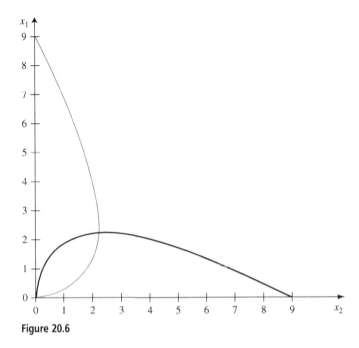

Figure 20.6

20.2   Commitment to reaction

Thus far in this chapter we have analyzed games in which one of the players chooses her strategy before her rival. There are also more complex situations, in which both players act simultaneously at the second stage, while at the first stage, one of them has an opportunity to move her own reaction curve in the simultaneous move subgame that will take place at the second stage.

Such a move of the reaction curve of the first player changes its point of intersection with the reaction curve of the second player, and accordingly it brings about a diversion of the equilibrium strategy profile of the players at the second stage along the reaction curve of the second player. Therefore, in a two-stage game of this kind, the first player chooses – albeit indirectly – to divert the strategy profile in a direction that is beneficial to her along the reaction curve of the second player. As we have seen, in a large variety of games, such diversion (in one of the directions) will indeed increase the payoff of the first player.

We will now explore several examples of such commitment to reaction.

20.2.1   Branding

Many manufacturers operate in the mineral water market. The differences in the quality of the water marketed by the various manufacturers are sometimes very small. Nevertheless, some manufacturers brand their bottled water as a product of exceptional quality, collecting a higher price than their competitors. With the aid of suitable advertising, they position their product in consumer awareness as a prestigious brand. A similar phenomenon takes place in many other sectors.

In order to model this phenomenon we will now turn to an example of a quantity competition between two firms. We will assume that firm 1 cannot produce before firm 2, and that production will take place simultaneously, as in the Cournot model. Firm 1, however, resorts to the services of an advertising agency, which advertises firm 1's product as a superior brand. As a result of the publicity, firm 1 succeeds in selling its product at a price that is higher than the price at which firm 2 sells each product unit: when the quantities they produce are q_1, q_2 respectively, the price per product unit of firm 2 is $A - q_1 - q_2$ while the price per product unit of firm 1 is $A - q_1 - q_2 + m$. In other words, the products of the two firms have different demand curves. The difference $m \in \left[0, \frac{A}{2}\right]$ between the prices depends on the scope of advertisement.

The advertising agency requires prepayment by firm 1, even before the commencement of the advertising campaign, of the amount of $M = mq_1^{**}$ where q_1^{**} is the quantity that firm 1 plans to produce at equilibrium. In other words, what the advertising agency requires of firm 1 is that the entire incremental proceeds that will ostensibly derive, at the end of the day, from the product being made into a brand will be paid to the advertising agency.

Firm 1, on the face of it, cannot, with this state of affairs, profit from the advertising campaign. Careful consideration, though, reveals that this is not the case: marketing firm 1's product as a superior brand will alter the equilibrium in the quantity competition between firm 1 and firm 2. The relative share of firm 1 in the market may increase as a result of the publicity, at the expense of the share of firm 2. This fact in and of itself may boost firm 1's profit, even when stated net of the payment to the advertising agency.

Following the advertising campaign, the profit of firm 1 (as a function of the quantities q_1, q_2) will be:

$$\Pi_1(q_1, q_2) = (A - q_1 - q_2 + m)q_1 - M$$

(Note that firm 1 paid the amount M to the advertising agency even before the competition began. The amount M was determined on the basis of the quantity that firm 1 expected to produce at equilibrium. But at the time of the competition with firm 2, firm 1 can no longer influence the amount M, and therefore that amount does not depend on q_1 at the competition stage.)

The profits of firm 2 will be:

$$\Pi_2(q_1, q_2) = (A - q_1 - q_2)q_2$$

The best-reply functions in this game are:

$$BR_1(q_2) = \frac{A - q_2 + m}{2}$$

$$BR_2(q_1) = \frac{A - q_1}{2}$$

At a Nash equilibrium, the quantities that the firms produce will be:

$$q_1^{**} = \frac{A + 2m}{3}$$

$$q_2^{**} = \frac{A - m}{3}$$

(Verify this!) At a Cournot equilibrium, it will be recalled, each firm produced the quantity $\frac{A}{3}$. Thus, as a result of branding, the market share of firm 1 increased and the market share of firm 2 decreased. Moreover, the total sales volume of the two firms together recorded an increase.

At equilibrium, the profit of firm 1 will be:

$$\Pi_1(q_1^{**}, q_2^{**}) = (A - q_1^{**} - q_2^{**} + m)q_1^{**} - M = (A - q_1^{**} - q_2^{**} + m)q_1^{**} - mq_1^{**}$$

$$= (A - q_1^{**} - q_2^{**})q_1^{**} = \left(A - \frac{A + 2m}{3} - \frac{A - m}{3}\right)\frac{A + 2m}{3}$$

By backward induction, firm 1 can now decide on the optimal volume of advertisement of the brand, such that the price excess m will maximize its total profits. The profit $\Pi_1(q_1^{**}, q_2^{**})$ is maximized when $m = \frac{A}{4}$ and, as a result:

$$q_1^{**} = \frac{A + 2 \times \frac{A}{4}}{3} = \frac{A}{2}$$

$$q_2^{**} = \frac{A - \frac{A}{4}}{3} = \frac{A}{4}$$

These are precisely the quantities that we found at equilibrium in the Stackelberg model. Why is this the case?

In the Stackelberg model, firm 1 committed to the quantity it would produce before firm 2, while in the present model, firm 1 does not commit directly to its production quantity before firm 2, but it does commit itself, in a preliminary move, in a different way: the advertising campaign, which fosters greater preparedness

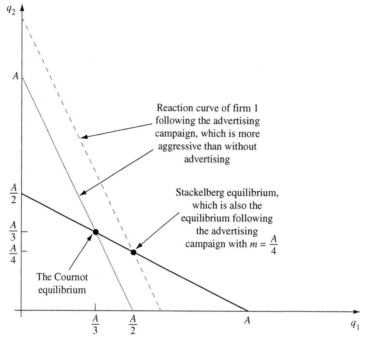

Figure 20.7

among consumers to pay for the product, causes firm 1 to react more aggressively to any strategy of firm 2, as described in Figure 20.7.

The fact that the payment M to the advertising firm was made in advance, before the competition began, resulted in a situation in which firm 1 did in fact become more aggressive during the competition, securing it a result that it could have achieved by being the first to commit directly to the quantity it proposed to produce, as in the Stackelberg model.

Comprehension check

Compute firm 1's profit $\Pi_1 \left(q_1^{**}, q_2^{**} \right)$ when $m = \frac{4}{4}$ and verify that it is indeed higher than its profit at the Cournot equilibrium (in which there is no branding and each firm produces $\frac{4}{3}$).

Could you have also concluded without an explicit computation that firm 1's profit with some level of branding is higher than its profit at the Cournot equilibrium (despite the advertising expenses $M = mq_1^{**}$)?

Hint: What would have happened if firm 1 were to choose $m = 0$?

This model has served in the literature for describing a diverse range of economic phenomena. We will now describe two such examples.

20.2.2   Entry deterrence

In the above analysis we assumed, for the sake of simplicity, that the firms' production costs are negligible. A similar analysis would have been valid if the firms $i = 1, 2$ had, respectively, production costs of $c_i > 0$ per product unit. In such a case, we would have replaced the constant A in the profit function $\prod_i$ of firm i, ($i = 1, 2$) with the constant A, where:

$$A_i = A - c_i$$

We explicitly made such an analysis in section 8.1 (pp. 119ff.).

We will now assume that in this state of affairs, firm 1 can reduce its per-unit production costs from c_1 to $c_1 - m$ by investing the amount T in improving its production technology prior to the commencement of production and the competition with firm 2. In such a case, the firms' profit functions will be:

$$\Pi_1(q_1, q_2) = (A_1 - q_1 - q_2 - m)q_1 - T$$
$$\Pi_2(q_1, q_2) = (A_2 - q_1 - q_2)q_2$$

At a Cournot equilibrium, the market share of firm 1 will increase while the market share of firm 2 will decrease as m gets larger (see the analysis of the Cournot model in section 8.1).

Comprehension check

A. Outline the details of the game pertaining to this example, draw the reaction functions, and compute the Cournot equilibrium quantities and profits.

B. Show that if $m \geq A + c_1 - 2c_2$, at the Cournot equilibrium firm 2 will choose not to produce anything at all.

Thus, a situation could come about in which the investment of firm 1 in the improvement of its production technology will actually deter firm 2 from entering into the production sector in which firm 1 engages. As a result, firm 1 will operate as a monopoly in that sector, and its profits will be greater than in a state of competition with firm 2. If this incremental profit exceeds the amount T that firm 1 has to invest in order to improve its technology from the outset, this investment is indeed worthwhile for firm 1. By means of this investment, firm 1 commits itself to react aggressively in a competition with firm 2 if and when the latter decides to compete with it: the reaction curve of firm 1 will shift "outwards," as in Figure 20.7.

In this state of affairs, it is entirely possible that the investment T would not have been worthwhile for firm 1 if it could have been sure from the outset that firm 2 was not going to compete with it. Therefore, if firm 2 ultimately refrains from entering into the sector, firm 1's investment in improving its technology may appear, in retrospect, to have been a mistake. However, an analysis of this kind disregards the **credible deterrence effect** that the investment in technology procured for firm 1. The credibility was achieved thanks to the fact that firm 1 invested in improving its technology before the time at which firm 2 was in a position to commence production. In a case such as this, it was the investment in improving the technology that gave firm 1 the standing of a monopoly. Therefore, the investment is justified from its point of view even if the reduction in production costs and the increase in quantity that firm 1 decides to produce as a result brings about an incremental profit that would not have justified the initial investment T that firm 1 would have made if it could have been sure, from the outset, that it would have no competitors.

In other words, firm 2 strategy's is to reach an optimal decision as to how much to produce (if anything), given the size of firm 1's preliminary investment. As against this strategy, firm 1's strategy of investment in the improvement of its technology may be optimal at a subgame perfect equilibrium. Such a strategy would not have necessarily been optimal for firm 1 if firm 2 had decided not to produce anything at all regardless of whether firm 1 had improved its technology.

20.2.3   Government subsidies for production

Two firms, in two different countries, export their output to a third country, in which the demand function for the product is $Q = A - P$ (i.e. if the per-unit price of the product is P, then the total quantity Q purchased by consumers is $Q = A - P$). Therefore, if firms 1 and 2 export to that country the quantities q_1 and q_2, respectively, the overall quantity that will be offered for sale there will be $Q = q_1 - q_2$, and the per-unit product price will be $P = A - Q = A - q_1 - q_2$.

We will now assume that only one country supports its exporter, and pays it a subsidy at the level of m for every product unit that it exports. The profit function of firm 1 will now be:

$$\Pi_1(q_1, q_2) = (A - q_1 - q_2)q_1 + mq_1 = (A - q_1 - q_2 + m)q_1$$

whereas the profit function of firm 2 remains:

$$\Pi_2(q_1, q_2) = (A - q_1 - q_2)q_2$$

These profit functions are analogous to those in the advertisement example in section 20.2.1. As we saw there, when firm 1 chooses m optimally, the quantities produced at a subgame perfect equilibrium will be $q_1^{**} = \frac{4}{2}, q_2^{**} = \frac{4}{4}$, with larger profits to firm 1 and smaller profits to firm 2 compared with the profits at a Cournot equilibrium that would be obtained without any subsidy.

Assume that the government of the subsidizing country is interested only in the total profits that will enter the country, and also assume for the sake of simplicity that these are the profits of firm 1. The country is not bothered by the fact that the subsidy is financed out of taxes paid by the entire citizenry, and therefore the subsidy constitutes a transfer of capital and resources from the citizens to the owners of a single firm. A possible justification for this is that some or all of the country's citizens will also benefit indirectly from the increase in the firm's production volume (from $q_1^* = \frac{4}{3}$ to $q_1^{**} = \frac{4}{2}$) and from the firm's increased profits, through the creation of additional jobs, or through taxes that the state will impose on the firm along with granting the subsidy (such as property taxes that do not depend on the volume of production).[4]

At the same time, an increase in the profits of firm 1 in the first country comes at the expense of the profits of firm 2 in the second country, if the latter is not rich enough to finance a similar subsidy plan out of the taxes that it collects from its citizens. Sometimes, the detriment to the profits of manufacturing firms in poor third world countries resulting from the subsidy enjoyed by their competitors in wealthy countries exceeds the volume of direct aid that those wealthy countries actually provide to the poor countries, through various international organizations such as the United Nations, the World Bank or the International Monetary Fund.[5] As a result,

---

[4] In practice, governments have only limited capability of distributing the increase of commercial firms' profits among the entire population. Sometimes, the increase in the firm's profits, which relies on government support, is detrimental to the welfare of the population as a whole (except for the corporate owners themselves, of course). In the context of governmental support for firms extracting and exporting natural resources such as oil, precious stones or metals in developing countries, this phenomenon is known as "the resource curse." The government's power of distributing the wealth among the totality of the population is restricted by institutional structures in the state, the ability of interest groups to boost their relative share of the profits, given those institutional structures and the short-term incentives of the politicians. See, for example, Robinson, J. A., T. Ragnar, and T. Verdier (2006), "Political Foundations of the Resource Curse," *Journal of Development Economics* 79 (2), 447–468.

[5] Or, alternatively, as a result of lower levels of customs duties imposed by such countries on imports from wealthy countries with which they have free trade agreements, compared with higher levels of customs duties that they impose on imports from poor countries, with which they have no such agreements.

manufacturers and households in these poor countries, which can no longer subsist on what they produce, must perforce resort to products that are illegal in the wealthy countries, such as agricultural crops for the drugs trade.

20.3 Simultaneous commitment

20.3.1 Advertising

We will now return to the advertising example in section 20.2.1. What will happen if both firms try to brand their product by means of an appropriate advertising campaign? The two-stage game between them will look like this:

1. At the first stage, both firms, $i = 1, 2$, simultaneously choose their volume of advertisement. That advertisement volume entails the price increment m_i that the consumers of that firm will be prepared to pay for a product unit in excess of the price $A - q_1 - q_2$. Each company prepays the sum of $M_i = m_i q_i^{***}$ to its advertising agency, q_i^{***} being the quantity that the firm expects to produce at the second stage.
2. At the second stage, both firms simultaneously choose how many units to produce. Their profits as a function of the quantities produced are:

$$\Pi_1(q_1, q_2) = (A - q_1 - q_2 + m_1)q_1 - M_1$$
$$\Pi_1(q_1, q_2) = (A - q_1 - q_2 + m_2)q_2 - M_2$$

In this two-stage game, a subgame perfect equilibrium is found by backward induction.

The best-reply functions at the second stage are:

$$BR_1(q_2) = \frac{A - q_2 + m_1}{2}$$
$$BR_2(q_1) = \frac{A - q_1 + m_2}{2}$$

and at a Nash equilibrium of this subgame each of the firms will produce:

$$q_1^{***} = \frac{A + 2m_1 - m_2}{3}$$
$$q_2^{***} = \frac{A + 2m_2 - m_1}{3}$$

with the profits to the firms being:

$$\Pi_1\left(q_1^{***}, q_2^{***}\right) = (A - q_1^{***} - q_2^{***} + m_1)q_1^{***} - m_1 q_1^{***}$$

$$\Pi_2\left(q_1^{***}, q_2^{***}\right) = (A - q_1^{***} - q_2^{***} + m_1)q_2^{***} - m_2 q_2^{***}$$

Substituting q_1^{***}, q_2^{***} in the profit functions will lead to a description of the profit of each firm as a function of m_1, m_2:

$$\Pi_1(m_1, m_2) = (A - q_1^{***} - q_2^{***} + m_1)q_1^{***} - m_1 q_1^{***}$$

$$= \left(A - \frac{A+2m_1 - m_2}{3} - \frac{A+2m_2 - m_1}{3} + m_1\right)\frac{A+2m_1 - m_2}{3} - m_1\frac{A+2m_1 - m_2}{3}$$

$$= \left(A - \frac{A + 2m_1 - m_2}{3} - \frac{A + 2m_2 - m_1}{3}\right)\frac{A + 2m_1 - m_2}{3}$$

$$\Pi_2(m_1, m_2) = (A - q_1^{***} - q_2^{***} + m_2)q_1^{***} - m_2 q_1^{***}$$

$$= \left(A - \frac{A+2m_2 - m_1}{3} - \frac{A+2m_1 - m_2}{3} + m_2\right)\frac{A+2m_2 - m_1}{3} - m_2\frac{A+2m_2 - m_1}{3}$$

$$= \left(A - \frac{A + 2m_2 - m_1}{3} - \frac{A + 2m_1 - m_2}{3}\right)\frac{A + 2m_2 - m_1}{3}$$

In this way, we have "folded" the tree backwards: we have found the payoffs to each firm as a function of their choices m_1, m_2 at the first stage.

In the game that was obtained at the post-folding stage, the best-reply functions are:

$$BR_1(m_2) = \frac{A - m_2}{4}$$

$$BR_2(m_1) = \frac{A - m_1}{4}$$

(verify this!) and at a Nash equilibrium the firms choose:

$$m_1^{***} = m_2^{***} = \frac{A}{5}$$

As a result, at the second stage of the game, the firms produce:

$$q_1^{***} = \frac{A + 2m_1^{***} - m_2^{***}}{3} = \frac{A + 2 \times \frac{A}{5} - \frac{A}{5}}{3} = \frac{2A}{5}$$

$$q_2^{***} = \frac{A + 2m_2^{***} - m_1^{***}}{3} = \frac{A + 2 \times \frac{A}{5} - \frac{A}{5}}{3} = \frac{2A}{5}$$

These quantities are larger than the quantities $q_1^* = q_2^* = \frac{4}{3}$ that the firms would produce at a Cournot equilibrium. As a result, their profit declines from:

$$\Pi_i^{\text{Cournot}} = \left(A - \frac{A}{3} - \frac{A}{3}\right)\frac{A}{3} = \frac{A^2}{9}$$

at the Cournot equilibrium to:

$$\Pi_i^{\text{Advertisement}} = \left(A - \frac{2A}{3} - \frac{2A}{3}\right)\frac{2A}{3} = \frac{2A^2}{25}$$

at the equilibrium in the current model.

Why did the advertising competition ultimately result in a decrease in the firms' profits? As we can see in Figure 20.8, branding caused each of the firms to be more aggressive in its reactions (the reaction curve of each firm "shifted outwards" compared with its reaction curve in the game without advertising). As a result, at the intersection point of the reaction curves – at the equilibrium $q_1^{***} = q_2^{***} = \frac{2A}{5}$ – the quantities produced are higher than those produced at the Cournot equilibrium $q_1^* = q_2^* = \frac{4}{3}$. According to our analysis in Chapter 8, even the profile of quantities at the Cournot equilibrium is not efficient from the point of view of the two firms: were they able to commit themselves to a cartel agreement, in which the total quantity that they produce is only $\frac{4}{2}$ (for example, a symmetric agreement in which each of

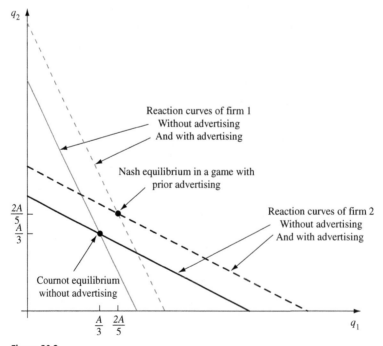

Figure 20.8

them produces $\frac{4}{4}$), their total profits would then be maximal. The transition from a hypothetical agreement of this sort to a Cournot equilibrium involves a loss to the firms, and a further increase of the quantities that each firm produces, from $\frac{4}{3}$ to $\frac{24}{5}$, as a result of the fiercer competition between them in the additional dimension of branding, therefore leads to a further loss. Accordingly, if the two firms were able to bind themselves ahead of time to an agreement that would prevent them from advertising, both would profit thereby.

20.3.2   Subsidies and quotas in international trade

In the example in section 20.2.3, we saw how the model by means of which we described a prior investment in advertising can also describe governmental investment in a subsidy. Therefore, if we apply this model for a case in which two different governments simultaneously subsidize the firms operating in their respective domains, the result will be worse for both firms (and therefore also for both countries) compared with a situation in which both countries jointly refrain from the support policy.

Out of this understanding countries worldwide have for many years been exerting themselves to reach multinational agreements, whereby they undertake to reduce subsidies of this kind, or to refrain from them altogether, and also to reduce or to refrain from imposing customs duties on goods that they import from competing countries that are signatories to such agreements. A significant proportion of such agreements gets tabled for discussion by the WTO, the organization founded in 1995 to replace the General Agreement of Tariffs and Trade (GATT), which was the precedent trade agreements mechanism. Most countries belong to the WTO and at the time of writing[6] some sixty trade agreements that are binding upon organization members have been signed under its auspices.

The analysis in this chapter casts light on the difficulty inherent in forming agreements of this type: if all the countries that are party to the agreement do indeed refrain from imposing customs duties and providing subsidies, the analysis in section 20.2.3 shows that it thereupon becomes in the interest of each country to impose customs duties and to provide subsidies unilaterally. Therefore, the trade agreements must also define penalties and economic sanctions to be imposed on countries breaching the agreement. Such penalties must be severe enough to actually deter the parties from breaching the agreement. Likewise, the imposition of sanctions on a country that has violated the agreement must be "cheap enough" for the other parties, so that they will have a sufficient incentive to impose the sanctions in case of need, and not to waive them *post factum*. Accordingly, the WTO has an

---

[6] 2010.

arbitration mechanism for settling differences of opinion. This body is also empowered to impose, if necessary, economic sanctions against countries being in breach of the agreements.

No wonder, then, that agreements for the promotion of international trade are signed only gradually, following discussions lasting several years. Each agreement binds the parties thereto to relatively small steps and not to far-reaching commitments that they will find it well worth their while to violate. The strategic interaction between the partners therefore has attributes of a repeated game – each additional round of discussions resembles the precedent rounds. We will address the topic of repeated games in Chapters 23 and 24.

21

Backward induction: limitations and difficulties

In Chapter 19, we demonstrated how to find perfect equilibrium by backward induction in games with a finite number of nodes, in which a unique player plays at each node. We saw how this solution concept excludes Nash equilibria that rely on non-credible threats. In Chapter 20, we saw how strategic behavior that embodies commitment can be reflected in subgame perfect equilibria found by backward induction.

At the same time, even when backward induction leads us to find a unique subgame perfect equilibrium, there are instances in which this equilibrium is not consistent with players' actual real-life behavior, nor with our intuition concerning "reasonable" or "fore-seeable" behavior of players in the strategic situation at hand. In this chapter, we will present two key examples illustrating the limitations of this solution concept: the "ultima-tum game" and the "centipede game." We will analyze the reasons for the limitations that these games illustrate.

21.1　The ultimatum game

This is a very simply structured two-player game. Player 1 gets an amount X of money. She must offer part of it, Y, to player 2. If player 2 accepts the offer, the transaction takes place: player 1 gets the payoff $X - Y$ and player 2 gets the payoff Y. If, however, player 2 refuses the offer, both players get the payoff 0.

Question 21.1

Assume, for the sake of simplicity, that the sums of money in the game are denominated in a currency that has a minimal value unit. Thus, if the dollar is the currency in the game, the offer Y must be quoted in whole cents (player 1 cannot offer player 2 half a cent, for example). Find all the subgame perfect equilibria in the ultimatum game.

Answer

In this game there is a finite number of nodes (since there is a finite number of offers Y that player 1 can propose – offers which are smaller than X that are couched in whole cents), and a unique player plays at each node. (Player 1 acts at the root of the game, making the offer $Y \in [0,X]$ in whole cents; after every possible such offer, player 2 must decide whether to accept or reject the offer.) Therefore, all the subgame perfect equilibria of this game can be found by means of backward induction.

How, then, will player 2 act following each offer Y by player 1?

A. If $Y > 0$, player 2 will find it worth her while to accept the offer, since refusal will entail a payoff of 0.
B. If $Y = 0$, player 2 will be indifferent between rejecting and accepting the offer, since in either case the payoff she gets will be 0. Thus, according to the definition of the backward induction process, the choice of any one of these actions is possible and will lead to a different subgame perfect equilibrium.

What is the optimal action that player 1 can take, given each of the possibilities in B?

B1. If player 2 rejects the offer $Y = 0$, the optimal action of player 1 is to offer player 2 a single cent. This is the minimal amount that player 2 will agree to accept, and this amount will maximize the amount $X - Y$ that will remain in the hands of player 1.
B2. If player 2 accepts the offer $Y = 0$, the optimal action for player 1 is to propose to player 2 the offer $Y = 0$. Since player 2 does not reject this offer, which will leave player 1 with the entire amount X, this is player 1's optimal move.

Thus we have obtained two subgame perfect equilibria:

1. In the first equilibrium, player 1 will offer player 2 a single cent and player 2 will accept the offer.
2. In the second equilibrium, player 1 will propose that player 2 accept an offer of nothing and player 2 will accept the offer.

The two equilibria closely resemble one another; in both of them, the entire amount X, or almost all of it, remains in the hands of player 1.

How would you play this game? In the role of player 1, what portion of the amount would you offer player 2? And in the role of player 2, which offers would you accept and which would you reject? Think about this before going on with your reading.

21.1.1　The ultimatum game in laboratory experiments

The behavior of the players in the ultimatum game has been examined in a large number of laboratory experiments and in a wide range of settings – different amounts of money, different countries, and under different conditions: a one-shot or an iterative encounter, a *tête-à-tête* or an anonymous encounter, etc. Despite the differences arising from the varied character of the experiments, the results in all cases were significantly different from behavior at a subgame perfect equilibrium. In the experiments, the great majority of participants in the role of the proposer (player 1) offer the other player an amount Y in the range of between 20 percent and 50 percent of the amount X, and the participants in the role of the responder (player 2) are prepared to accept only offers that are not below a threshold that does in fact lie within this range.[1]

It appears, therefore, that the monetary payoffs in the ultimatum game constitute just one dimension in the players' preferences, which are influenced by additional dimensions as well. A "highly unequal" distribution may seem unfair to player 2, and therefore she may prefer to waive any monetary payoff in order to refrain from consenting to a distribution that she perceives as unfairly discriminating against her. The threshold at which a distribution becomes "unfairly discriminatory" is, of course, subjective; it also depends on the absolute size of the amount X that is available for distribution, as well as on general norms prevailing in the social frameworks to which the player participating in the experiment belongs.

Correspondingly, certain aspects of fairness may also be important to player 1, and she may be motivated by some degree of altruism toward player 2, even if the encounter in the experiment is anonymous. Alternatively, even if player 1 is only interested in her monetary payoff in the experiment, but believes that player 2 is more likely to reject an offer Y which is below a certain threshold located in the range of 20–50 percent of X, player 1 will indeed wish to make an offer Y that lies within that range. The more generous the offer Y of player 1, the greater the probability $P(Y)$ that player 2 will accept it; at the same time, however, the balance $X - Y$ remaining in the hands of player 1 will also decrease. The expected payoff of player 1 will then be:

$$P(Y) \times (X - Y) \tag{21.1}$$

In some experiments it was found that the most frequent offer made by participants in the role of player 1 was indeed the one that maximized the expected payoff (21.1), given the probability distribution P for the rejection of offers by the population of participants in the role of player 2 in the experiment.

This explanation of the behavior of the proposers (the participants in the role of player 1) still begs the question of why most of the responders (the participants in the role of player 2) insist on a minimal share Y expressing a certain degree of "fairness."

---

[1] A detailed review of these experiments may be found in: Camerer, C. F. (2003), *Behavioral Game Theory – Experiments in Strategic Interaction*, Princeton University Press.

In the appendix to this chapter, we will propose a theoretical explanation for this phenomenon, based on the concept of stochastic stability.

There is another possible explanation for the patently manifest difference between the game-theoretic prediction and the behavior of the participants in the experiments. The situation of a one-shot experiment is largely artificial. In real life, people meet again and again with the same friends, family members, and work or business colleagues. Therefore, these encounters bear a recurrent character that can better be described by means of a model of repeated games, which we shall explore in Chapters 23 and 24. Were the ultimatum game to be repeated a number of times for which no bound had been imposed, player 2 might find it reasonable to create herself a reputation for a measure of toughness, i.e. insistence on a certain threshold of whatever minimal share of the pie she is not prepared to forgo. Such insistence is liable to cause player 2 a loss in the initial rounds of the game, but at the same time it can guarantee her a strictly positive slice of the pie in the long term, when player 1, if she wishes to avoid consigning the entire pie to perdition, learns to get used to player 2's insistence.

Alternatively, it is entirely likely that the behavior of the participants in the experiments reflects "rules of thumb" whereby they act in real life, rules that constitute part of the equilibrium behavior in a repeated game that goes beyond the confines of a one-shot encounter and reflect the norms and the conventions of the social frameworks to which the participants belong. These rules are not necessarily optimal in specific situations, such as the experiment we have described; but under the assumption that people do indeed resort to the use of rules of thumb, in order to be able to respond rapidly in the series of social encounters in which they participate even without being able to dedicate any in-depth thinking to each of them, the rule of thumb "insistence on fair distribution" may certainly be an optimal decision-making rule – the sort that constitutes part of an equilibrium in that society.

21.1.2 The ultimatum game in anthropological studies

Instructive examples of human behavior in the ultimatum game can be found in a series of experiments of this game conducted on small, relatively isolated tribes in Africa, Mongolia, Pacific islands and South America.[2] These experiments are especially instructive since they illustrate modes of thinking about social reality that are not entirely foreign to us, yet at the same time express norms and perceptions

---

[2] Henrich, J., R. Boyd, S. Bowles, C. Camerer, E. Fehr, and H. Gintis (eds.) (2004), *Foundations of Human Sociality: Economic Experiments and Ethnographic Evidence from Fifteen Small-scale Societies*, Oxford University Press.

Henrich, J., R. McElreath, A. Barr, J. Ensminger, C. Barrett, A. Bolyanatz, J. C. Cardenas, M. Gurven, E. Gwako, N. Henrich, C. Lesorogol, F. Marlowe, D. Tracer, and J. Ziker (2006), "Costly Punishment Across Human Societies," *Science* 312, 1767–1770.

the relative weight of which in western society is smaller than in those small-scale societies.

Two key findings of these experiments are worth mentioning:

1. In societies characterized by a large measure of isolation and segregation, in which the unique social unit is the family, experimenters observed behavior that is closer to the game-theoretic solution: typical offers were lower and preparedness to accept low offers was higher than in societies characterized by ramified social connections. For example, the Machiguenga in Peru live in small self-sufficient villages subsisting on hunting, gathering, and farming. Every such village has one unique extended family, and the language of the Machiguenga does not assign express names to anyone outside the family. In this society, the typical offer in the ultimatum game experiment was at a level of only 15 percent of the total X (with an average of 26 percent) and only one offer out of twenty-one was rejected.

2. In small societies characterized by cooperation among members of different families in the same village, in a "labor market" which permits compensation being paid for labor in the form of money and goods, or in trade between different villages that share a common language, two phenomena were noted that were not found at all in experiments in western societies: some of the offers were "supremely generous," standing at more than 50 percent of the overall amount X, and a large fraction of these offers was rejected by the responders. For example, in the Lamalera society of whale-hunters that we described in Chapter 9, almost all the offers were higher than or equal to 50 percent of X, with the average offer standing at 56 percent. (In this society, the goods that were on offer in the experiment for distribution were packets of cigarettes – a rare and highly desirable commodity, which also serves for barter trade.) In the Sursurunga society in Papua New Guinea, the average offer was 51 percent, but most of the offers exceeding 50 percent were rejected. It would seem that in these societies, generous gifts (of hunks of whale meat from the catch, for example) are a demonstration of patronage and power, and the recipient, by accepting them, commits to some future consideration, in the form of material or other goods. Therefore, the responders sometimes prefer to refuse gifts of this type.

These findings illustrate the extent of correlation between cultural attributes of trade and barter and the norms of sharing and fairness. The assumption whereby economic efficiency is achieved even when every individual pursues his private interest, and the discourse emphasizing material profits in the business world, disregard the fact that fair play is a deeply rooted value in societies based on a free market economy.[3]

---

[3] See also Cohen, R. (1997), *Negotiating Across Cultures: International Communication in an Interdependent World*, City: United States Institute of Peace Press.

21.2   The centipede game

The game tree of the centipede game[4] is described in Figure 21.1. In this game, players 1 and 2 take turns and each player can decide whether to quit or to continue. If the player decides to quit, the game ends. If the player chooses to continue, the other player gets a chance to make a similar choice – to quit or to continue. The game ends, in any event, after a large and predetermined number of such game rounds (i.e. in the last game round, the game ends even if the player then playing chooses to continue). In the example shown in Figure 21.1, the game ends in any event in the fifth game round, but a game tree might similarly have been described, with as large a finite number of game rounds as we might like. Every branch of the tree that describes a player's choice to "quit" is described in the figure by means of a "leg" – hence the name of the game.

A player choosing to quit precipitates, as explained, the termination of the game and guarantees herself the payoff appearing next to the appropriate leaf in the figure (the top payoff appearing next to the leaf pertains to player 1 and the bottom payoff pertains to player 2). If the player chooses to continue, she will get a much higher payoff on condition that her rival, who is next to play, likewise chooses to continue, but if the rival chooses to quit there and then, the player will suffer a small loss compared with the payoff that she could have guaranteed herself were she to have quit.

This is how matters proceed until the last round of the game. If the player playing in the last game round chooses to continue, she will occasion herself a small loss compared with the payoff she would get by choosing to quit. Therefore, if we solve the game by backward induction, we will find that in the last game round (node E in the game shown in Figure 21.1), the player playing there (player 1 in the game in the figure) will prefer to quit rather than to continue. Once the tree is folded back following that choice, it transpires that the player playing in the penultimate round (player 2 at node D in the game in the figure) will also prefer to quit rather than

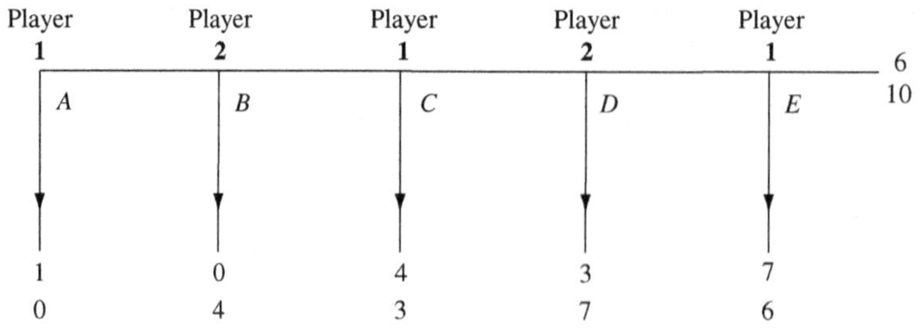

Figure 21.1

---

[4] A game of this type was first presented by Rosenthal, R. W. (1981), "Games of Perfect Information, Predatory Pricing, and the Chain Store Paradox," *Journal of Economic Theory* 25, 92–100.

continue. Similarly, these considerations will lead us to the conclusion that when folding the game tree by backward induction, each of the players will choose to quit at each node of the game. In particular, the game has a unique subgame perfect equilibrium, at which the first player quits immediately, and ends the game with low payoffs to both players.

This equilibrium is non-intuitive. If player 1 deviates from this equilibrium and continues at node A instead of quitting, what conclusion should player 2 derive from that move? Is it not likely that at node B player 2 will believe that there is a high probability that player 1 will continue for at least one more round, at node C? Under this belief, player 2 will likewise wish to continue. But if this is the case, then it is indeed worthwhile for player 1 to continue at the beginning of the game, at node A: thus she may cause player 2 to continue at node B, and as a result player 1's payoff will in any event be higher than if she had quit at the beginning of the game and the game had terminated there and then.

This conclusion may even more strongly reinforce the belief of player 2 at node B that if player 1 continued once at node A, it is quite likely that she will continue for at least one more round, at node C. Initially, player 2 at node B might have suspected that the fact that player 1 chose to continue at node A was rooted, quite simply, in an error on the part of player 1 – an error that she will not necessarily repeat at node C. But on second thoughts, the strategic situation in which player 1 finds herself at node C resembles the one that she faced at node A. And if, as we concluded in the preceding paragraph, there exists a set of considerations – rather than an error – that caused player 1 to want to continue at node A, then a similar set of considerations may cause player 1 to want to continue at node C, too. Under the assumption that player 1 is acting in accordance with such a set of considerations, player 2 will find it worth her while to continue at node B. This conclusion may even more emphatically confirm player 1 in her belief that it is worth her while to continue at node A.

In order to sharpen this intuition, we will now imagine that there were 100 "legs" in the game rather than just five as in the example in the figure. We will further assume that after every pair of "continue" moves, the payoffs to the players double in size, rather than merely increasing by a constant.[5] We would then obtain a game that could be described as follows.

There is a pile of coins in front of each player. Each player in turn can terminate the game by raking in the entire pile for herself, and in such a case, the other player, too, rakes in her pile for herself. Alternatively, the player may decide to continue with the game. In this case, one coin is removed from the pile in front of her, but the pile in front of her co-player gets doubled in size. The game continues in this way for

---

[5] In the game in Figure 21.1, this constant is 3: if player 1 chooses to quit at node C, the payoffs to the players are higher by 3 than the payoffs they would get if player 1 chose to quit at node A; and if player 1 quits at node E, the payoffs to the players increase again by 3.

at most 100 rounds in which the players choose alternately whether to terminate the game or to continue it (in the event that the game has not previously terminated). In the last round, the game ends even if the player currently playing chooses to "continue" (in such a case, a coin is removed from the pile in front of her, the pile in front of her co-player is doubled in size, and then the game ends with each player winning the pile in front of her).

In this game, the payoffs that the players can win if they choose to "continue" a large number of times are legendary and may approach an order of magnitude of 2^{100} toward the end of the game. In a strategic situation of this kind, it is hard to imagine that the two players will not choose to "continue" a large number of times: it seems probable that each player's chance of raking in an enormous future profit if her co-player likewise chooses to continue, as against relinquishing the single coin that she needs to jeopardize in order to do so, is likely to prompt the player to continue even if she has not worked out any express theory concerning the reasons that might bring her co-player to continue after her. Moreover, if player 2 believes that her co-player thinks along similar lines, and, like herself, may be expected to continue in her wake on the strength of her hope of pocketing tremendous profits, even this belief on the part of player 1 in and of itself suffices to confirm the choice of player 1 to continue with the game. Likewise, such considerations obviously appear all the stronger and more convincing as the number of rounds remaining until the end of the game is greater.

Nevertheless, an intuitive set of considerations of this kind is excluded from the backward induction process. What is the reason for this exclusion? What underlying element of the backward induction process clashes with the intuitive (albeit informal!) analysis that we have conducted?

Backward induction retains only strategies which are consistent with the assumption that the players share common knowledge that all of them are rational after any possible history of the game, including game histories which are not, themselves, consistent with that assumption. Expressly, assume that the backward induction process is uniquely defined in a game, such as in the centipede game. In such a case, backward induction is based on the following assumption, which we will denote by (*):

(*) At any stage of the game, there is common knowledge among the players that **if and when** player i's turn arrives to play at a node n which leads only to leaves, player i will choose the optimal action available to her at node n (the one that will give her the highest payoff) even if reaching this node ultimately transpires to be counterfactual, given the operation plan of player i herself, as defined through the backward induction process.

Thus, in the assumption (*) the expression "if and when" is of key importance. In practice, the backward induction process defines a unique path in the game, from the root to one of the leaves. The backward induction process is based on the assumption

(*) prevailing at every stage of the game and in any hypothetical development of the game, particularly at nodes that are located on paths that are different from the backward induction path.

This is a problematic assumption. If the assumption (*) by itself defines a unique path along the game tree, it is not clear what might confirm the assumption (*) along other paths. If one of the players deviates from the operation plan defined by (*), why should the other players continue to believe that that player will act, later on in the game, in accordance with the operation plan defined for her by backward induction? If the player's actions have already proved that the assumption (*) was not valid for her at one stage of the game, what will cause the other players to believe that (*) will nevertheless continue to be valid at all the following stages of the game?

21.2.1   The centipede game in laboratory experiments

As we have seen, the problematic character of the assumption (*) above is clearly expressed in the centipede game. Sure enough, in laboratory experiments of lengthy centipede games, a significant proportion of the participants choose to continue in the first game rounds. It would seem that experiment participants hold the belief that their co-players are inclined to continue in the first game rounds – a belief that is in fact confirmed in practice, and confirms the decision to continue at the beginning of the game.

A number of models may be proposed that provide an express basis for confirming the belief that players are inclined – with a high probability – to continue at the initial stages of the game and that this probability decreases as the game progresses. All these models are based on one deviation or another from the assumption concerning common knowledge of rationality following any possible history of the game, but still assume that both players are by and large rational.

According to one of these models, the Quantal Response Equilibrium, the higher the utility to be derived from a particular action, the higher will be a player's probability of choosing that action; but she chooses, with a small probability, also strategies that are not optimal; her chances of "erring" and choosing an inferior strategy decrease with the extent that such strategy occasions her a greater loss compared with her payoff from choosing the optimal strategy. Moreover, there is common knowledge among the players as to how the probability of making a mistake gradually decreases along with the damage that the error occasions; and the players take this into account when calculating their best reply. McKelvey and Palfrey (1998) showed how this model is consistent with the behavior of participants in certain experiments of the centipede game, as well as in other games.[6]

---

[6] McKelvey, R. D. and T. R. Palfrey (1998), "Quantal Response Equilibria for Extensive Form Games," *Experimental Economics* 1, 9–41.

Comprehension check: the chain-store paradox[7]

The long-standing Safe-Mart supermarket chain has branches in twenty different communities in Baledonia, and each branch yields it a profit at a level of 10. In each such community, there is a local businesswoman who intends to open an additional supermarket in that community. The cost of setting up the supermarket is 2. If the businesswoman realizes her intention, the profits will be divided between the two supermarkets in the community (a profit of 5 to the Safe-Mart outlet and a profit of 5 to the new supermarket; net of set-up costs, the businesswoman's profit will be 3) unless Safe-Mart launches a price war, and announces discounts and sales specials at its outlet. These moves will force the new supermarket to reduce prices, and the result will be a profit of 1 for each of the supermarkets in the community (and net of set-up costs, the businesswoman's profit will be negative, standing at −1).

1. Sketch the game tree between Safe-Mart and the businesswoman in each community. Assume that the businesswoman acts first and decides whether to open the competing supermarket in the community. If the supermarket is opened, Safe-Mart must decide whether to launch a price war or to come to terms with the advent of the competitor, without going to war. Find a subgame perfect equilibrium in this game using backward induction.

2. Assume that the businesswomen in the various communities do not intend to open up the new supermarkets simultaneously: the businesswoman in community A is the first to decide whether to open her supermarket; the businesswoman in community B decides whether to open the supermarket in her community only after learning of the developments in community A, and particularly the reaction of Safe-Mart in community A if the new supermarket is launched there; the businesswoman in community C acts only after becoming informed of developments in communities A and B; and so on. Describe the game tree between Safe-Mart and the businesswomen. Sketch the game tree in the event that there are only two (and not twenty) communities and find, in that tree, a subgame perfect equilibrium. Find the subgame perfect equilibrium in the game as a whole (with twenty communities).

3. Safe-Mart has threatened to launch a price war in any community in which a new supermarket is launched. Is the threat a credible one? Explain your answer.

4. Assume that new supermarkets were opened in the first fourteen communities, and in all those communities Safe-Mart made good on its threat to launch a price war. How would you act in place of the businesswoman in the fifteenth community? Would you open the supermarket?

[7] The example is based on Selten, R. (1978), "The Chain Store Paradox," *Theory and Decision* 9, 127–159; Rosenthal, R. W. (1981), "Games of Perfect Information, Predatory Pricing and the Chain Store Paradox," *Journal of Economic Theory* 25, 92–100.

Appendix: Fair divisions and stochastic stability

Peyton Young proposed an explanation for the fact that norms of "fair" division are more frequent than norms of distribution that strongly tend in favor of one of the parties.[8] This explanation is based on the concept of **stochastic stability**. The full development of this concept lies beyond the scope of this book, but we can nonetheless provide an explanation, at this point, of the basic intuition underlying the formal analysis in the case of the present example.

This explanation is based on the assumption that a social norm of distribution in which the proposer receives $X - Y$ and the responder receives Y materializes by virtue of the fact that, in practice, most proposers do indeed offer Y, and most of the time the offer is accepted by the responders. On every specific occasion when a proposer is undecided as to what amount to offer, she examines a small number of similar instances with which she is familiar from the recent past and from her close environment. She assumes that the distribution of the behavior P of the responders in these cases also characterizes the probability with which the particular responder confronting her will accept or reject the various offers, and chooses an offer Y which will maximize her expected payoff (expression (21.1) above). Likewise, the responder examines a small number of similar instances with which she is familiar from the recent past and from her immediate environment, and assumes that the distribution of the proposers' offers in these instances defines the probability $Q(Y)$ with which the particular proposer confronting her will offer her an amount either larger than or equal to Y. On the basis of this information, the responder chooses ahead of time a minimal offer, one that will maximize her expected payoff:

$$Q(Y) \times Y \tag{21.2}$$

and to which she will respond affirmatively.

From time to time, however, the proposing player, in an erroneous departure from the norm, offers the responder an amount that is slightly lower than the one the responder expects. Likewise, from time to time, the responding player erroneously departs from the norm, and insists on an amount slightly larger than the norm dictates. In general, such departures simply result in a refusal and a payoff of 0 to both parties. Rarely, however, such an accumulation of errors of this type does take place.

An accumulation of errors on the part of the responders will cause the proposers to believe that there has been a significant erosion of the probability $P(Y)$ that the offer Y that they had been offering customarily hitherto will continue to be accepted in the

[8] Young, P. (1998), *Individual Strategy and Social Structure – An Evolutionary Theory of Institutions*, Princeton University Press. See Chapter 8 for the model described here.

future as well, and thence they conclude that in order to maximize their expected payoff (21.1) it is worth their while to slightly increase their offer. The social norm is thus modified, and in the new situation the proposers make it their practice to put forward an offer Y' which is higher than the offer Y that prevailed in the previous norm. Similarly, a sufficient agglomeration of errors on the part of the proposers will lead the responders to believe that henceforth it will be worth their while (in order to maximize their expected payoff (21.2)) to insist only on a smaller slice of the pie.

Thus, any norm of division may ultimately be modified in this way. But even so, norms are distinguishable from one another in terms of the number of errors required in order to change them. The larger this number of errors, the more robust we expect the norm to be, and the longer we expect it to survive in society.

What norms of division, then, are more robust, and what norms are less robust? To keep things simple, assume that $X = 10$ and the offer Y is always quoted in whole units. If the prevailing norm is "to offer Y," but in recent instances in which the proposer was present a proportion α of the responders remained erroneously obstinate and refused any offer smaller than $Y + 1$, then the proposer believes that:

- if she proceeds in accordance with the norm and offers Y, her expected payoff will be $(1 - \alpha)(10 - Y)$;
- if she departs from the norm and makes a more generous offer, at the level of $Y + 1$, then her offer will certainly be accepted. In such case, her payoff will be $10 - (Y + 1)$.

Therefore, the proposer departs from the existing norm and offers $Y + 1$ if and only if:

$$10 - (Y + 1) > (1 - \alpha)(10 - Y)$$

i.e. if and only if:

$$\alpha > \frac{1}{10 - Y}$$

Thus, the larger the share Y of the responder to begin with in the division in accordance with the existing norm, the larger the portion α of the responders that must deviate from the norm in order to bring about a change of the norm from "offer Y" to "offer $Y + 1$."

Similarly, if the customary norm is "offer Y," but in the most recent instances that the responder witnessed, portion β of the proposers mistakenly offered $Y - 1$, then the proposer believes that:

- if she insists on receiving at least Y, her expected payoff will be $(1 - \beta)Y$;
- if she agrees to accept also an offer at the level of $Y - 1$, she will certainly receive that amount.

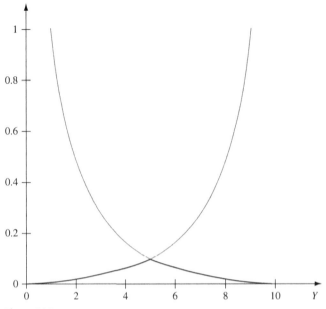

Figure 21.2

Therefore, the responder deviates from the existing norm and agrees to accept $Y-1$ if and only if:

$$Y - 1 > (1 - \beta)Y$$

i.e. if and only if:

$$\beta > \frac{1}{Y}$$

Therefore, the minimal proportion of errors in a population of proposers or responders that is required in order to modify the norm "offer Y" is the minimum of $\frac{1}{10-Y}$ and $\frac{1}{Y}$, whose graphs are depicted in Figure 21.2, and whose minimum is bold with a thick line. The larger $\min\{\frac{1}{10-Y}, \frac{1}{Y}\}$ is, the more robust is the norm "offer Y," since a rarer accumulation of errors is required in order for the proposers or the responders to wish to deviate from this norm.

From the graph of the function $\min\{\frac{1}{10-Y}, \frac{1}{Y}\}$ (the thick line in Figure 21.2) we learn that the more egalitarian the norm Y is, the more robust it is. The most robust norm is the norm at which the pie is shared equally between the proposer and the responder, and each of them gets the same amount, at the level 5.

22

Moves of nature

So far, we have dealt with extensive form games, in which a given action profile by the players at a particular node always and unequivocally defines the next node to which this action profile leads. However, many strategic situations exist in which the development of the game does not depend solely on the actions of the players, and a certain randomness prevails over which the players have no control – either severally or jointly.

This randomness may be modeled with the aid of *moves of nature* at a *chance node*. This is a node on the game tree from which a number of branches divide; however, as distinct from nodes of the type we have dealt with hitherto, there are, at this node, no players who have to choose between the branches. Instead, there is a predefined probability at which each of the branches will be chosen. A node of this type may also be thought of as a node at which an imaginary player – "nature" – chooses how to act. Here, however, the probability of nature's choice of each branch is given beforehand and is not a result of a conscious and mediated, intelligent choice. The "choice" of nature differs from the choices of the other players in that it is random and is not restricted to a definite choice of one of the branches.

When moves of nature are part of the game tree, the players' strategies do not determine one unique path on the tree that leads to a particular leaf in a deterministic fashion. At every chance node, the game path splits into a number of possible continuations, in accordance with the probabilities dictated by the move of nature at that node; if the game has a number of chance nodes, the results of the lotteries at the various nodes are independent of one another. As a result, the players' strategies determine a probability distribution over the leaves on the tree.

In the following sections we will analyze several extensive form games involving moves of nature.

22.1   The ultimatum game with a random responder type

In our discussion of the ultimatum game in the preceding chapter (section 21.1), we found that in this game there are only two subgame perfect equilibria, in both of which player 1 ("the proposer") invites player 2 ("the responder") to content herself with a zero or minimal slice of the pie, and player 2 indeed accepts this offer. However, in experiments of the game, a large proportion of responders refused

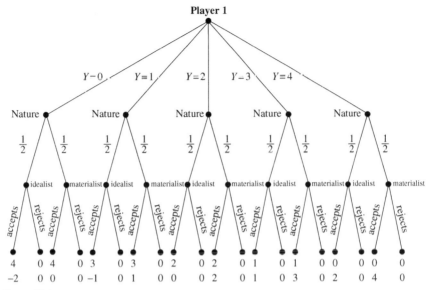

Figure 22.1

offers that they deemed unfair and which were much smaller than half the pie. For these responders, the monetary payoff does not reflect their preferences, and they "suffer" when the distribution is perceived by them to be unfair.

Assume, therefore, that after the proposer has presented her offer of how to share out a pie consisting of $X = 4$ slices, with Y going to the responder and $4 - Y$ to the proposer, the type of the responder is randomly chosen: with a probably of $\frac{1}{2}$ the responder is "materialistic" – the monetary payoff that she receives represents her preferences, and therefore she accepts any offer $Y \geq 0$; while with the complementary probability, the responder is an "idealist" who is offended if the offer Y is less than 2. For the "idealist" responder, the utility, therefore, is $Y - 2$ and she therefore accepts only offers of $Y \geq 2$.

Figure 22.1 describes the game tree. Player 1 can make one out of five possible offers: $Y = 0, 1, \ldots, 4$. Consecutively, nature "draws at random" the type of player 2 – either "materialist" or "idealist." This type defines the payoffs of player 2 following each action she takes (acceptance or rejection of the offer). The payoffs to the players are recorded alongside the leaves – the top payoff to player 1 and the bottom payoff to player 2.

In Figure 22.2 arrows denote an optimal strategy of player 2. But even if player 1 knows that this is the strategy that player 2 will adopt, she still cannot know for sure at what leaf the game will end, given any possible strategy of hers. This is because after she chooses her action (the offer Y to player 2), she still cannot know what type of player 2 she is facing. For any proposal Y that player 1 may choose, there are two possible leaves on the tree at which the game may end, and each of those leaves has a probability of $\frac{1}{2}$.

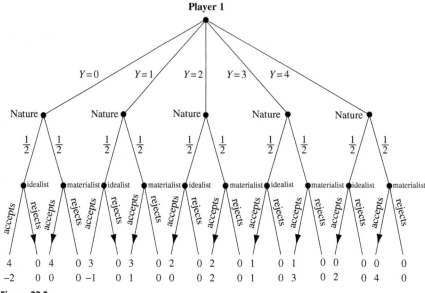

Figure 22.2

For example, if player 1 chooses the offer $Y = 1$, the game can end at a leaf at which player 2 (being an "idealist") refuses to accept the offer, with payoffs of 0 to both players, or at a leaf at which player 2 (being a "materialist") accepts the offer, with a payoff of 3 to player 1 and a payoff of 1 to player 2.

In a general extensive form game with moves of nature, the strategy profile $x = (x_j)_{j \in I} \in X$ of the players $j \in I$ determines the probability $p^\ell(x)$ that the game will end at leaf ℓ, with payoffs of $\pi^\ell = (\pi_i^\ell)_{i \in I} \in \mathbb{R}^I$ to the players. Every player $i \in I$ wishes to maximize her expected payoff:

$$U_i(x) = \sum_{\substack{\text{The leaves } \ell \\ \text{of the game}}} p^\ell(x)\pi_i^\ell$$

Therefore, the strategy profile $x^* = (x_j^*)_{j \in I} \in X$ of the players is a Nash equilibrium if for every player $i \in I$ and for every strategy x_i' of hers it is the case that:

$$U_i\left((x_j^*)_{j \in I}\right) \geq U_i\left((x_i', x_{-i}^*)\right)$$

It will be recalled that the strategy profile $x^* = (x_j^*)_{j \in I} \in X$ of the players is a subgame perfect equilibrium if it induces a Nash equilibrium in every subgame.

In the present example, we have already denoted with arrows the optimal strategy of player 2. Now, using backward induction, we will be able to find the optimal strategy of player 1. If player 1 chooses the strategy $Y = 2$, she will guarantee herself a payoff of 2 because both types of player 2 will accept her offer. Therefore it is not worth her while to make a higher offer $Y > 2$; such an offer will likewise certainly be accepted, but will yield player 1 a lower payoff. However, if player 1 makes an offer $Y > 2$, it will be accepted only by the materialist type and the probability of that is only $\frac{1}{2}$.

- The offer $Y = 2$ will yield her, therefore, a payoff of 3 with a probability of $\frac{1}{2}$, and the expected payoff in this case will be $1\frac{1}{2}$, which is less than the payoff 2 that is guaranteed by the offer $Y = 2$.
- The offer $Y = 0$ will yield player 1 a payoff of 4 with a probability of $\frac{1}{2}$, and the expected payoff from this offer is therefore 2. This expected payoff is equal to the payoff that is guaranteed by the offer $Y = 2$.

Thus we have found two subgame perfect equilibria in the game – in one of which player 1 offers $Y = 2$, while in the other player 1 offers $Y = 0$.

> ### Comprehension check: patent development race
>
> Describe the game outlined in the example in section 7.3 (pp. 108ff.) as an extensive form game: two competing firms simultaneously decide what quantity of resources to invest in the research and development of a patent. Once firm i ($i = 1, 2$) has elected to invest x_i million dollars, a move of nature determines the identity of the winner: the winner is firm 1 with probability $\frac{x_1}{x_1+x_2}$, whereas firm 2 wins the patent with the complementary probability $\frac{x_2}{x_1+x_2}$. (If neither firm makes any investment in research and development, neither of them wins the patent.) Winning the patent race yields a payoff in the amount of $V = 9$ million dollars for the winner. Each firm maximizes its expected profit.
>
> Draw the game tree for the case in which each firm, $i = 1, 2$, has only two possible levels of investment: either $x_i = 0$ or $x_i = \frac{9}{4}$.

22.2 Brinkmanship

In Chapter 11, we discussed the different meanings of the term "mixed strategy." We saw that this term is especially problematic in a one-shot, non-recurrent strategic situation between two players. This is the context in which a random choice by lottery appears, at first sight, to be unreasonable: in order for a player to want to hold a lottery between two alternatives, she must be indifferent between those alternatives at the time she conducts the lottery. But when that is the situation, what will cause her to actually implement the alternative that came up in the lottery, rather than the other alternative? And if she can in fact always change her mind and disregard the outcome of the lottery, why should she bother to draw lots in the first place?

The picture changes if the player has some way of committing to the lottery being conducted and to her abiding by the result. Such commitment is created in the case that the player is able to appoint an agent who will conduct the lottery and implement the result in her stead.

Such a delegation mechanism exists when the player is not a single individual but the management of an organization: a commercial firm, a labor union, a political party, a nation-state. The decisions taken by the organization's management are put into effect by means of some executive arm of the organization, and in most cases via a long hierarchical chain. The directives proceeding from the organization's management are necessarily general and succinct. The executive arm of the organization is empowered to interpret the management's directives and to adjust them to the concrete reality it is facing. In practice, such interpretation is not, in 100 percent of cases, precisely aligned with the intention of the management. In some cases, the executive arm will act other than in accordance with management's intentions, leaving management neither sufficient time nor means of control to arrest the march of events. Therefore, the management's instructions to the executive arm – especially when they deviate from the ordinary routine of activity – necessarily endow the organization's action with a probabilistic nature. The action that the organization will ultimately take will be characterized by a degree of randomness.

Therefore, to confide execution to the agent is like choosing an action following which a **move of nature** takes place, over whose random outcome the player has no control. Thus, activating a delegation mechanism by the player may create a calculated risk, borne by both players and in particular by the rival player. If the rival views such risk as undesirable, that rival will want to choose an action that will forestall or reduce the risk. This action may be deemed as highly desirable by the player who initiated the calculated risk. If, however, the rival could have known the lottery results ahead of time, she may have wanted to choose a completely different action (as a function of the result of the lottery), an action that is by no means desirable for the first player. In such a case, the very fact that the risk has been created – by irrevocably empowering an agent to conduct the lottery – may lead the rival to behave in a way that is seen as desirable by the player who has initiated the risk.

The player who creates the calculated risk is not indifferent between the results of the lottery. If the risk materializes, the player herself, and not only her rival, could suffer severe damage. Therefore, the strategy of deliberately creating a calculated risk of this sort is designated **brinkmanship**. If to refrain from incurring a risk will lead the rival to make a move that is highly undesirable for the player, then that player may prefer to initiate that calculated risk even if she herself is very much afraid of the possibility that the risk will materialize.

The Cuban missile crisis was a classic example of brinkmanship policy.

22.2.1   The Cuban missile crisis[1]

In the summer and fall of 1962, the Soviets started constructing launching pads in Cuba for forty medium-range nuclear missiles that could potentially hit most major population hubs and military facilities in the United States. This was the first time the Soviet Union had tried to position nuclear missiles outside its own borders. At that time it had, in its own territory, less than twenty intercontinental ballistic missiles able to hit the United States, perhaps 2 or 3 of them operational. Positioning missiles in Cuba, therefore, was liable to represent a substantial upgrade from the viewpoint of the Soviet Union, despite the fact that it would do nothing to breach US supremacy in the nuclear balance. Accordingly, the positioning of missiles in Cuba would have become a deterrent against any potential invasion by the United States and an important precedent in favor of the Soviet Union in the inter-bloc struggle over areas of influence in the world.

Discovery of the launching sites build-up in Cuba came by means of the decoding of aerial photographs taken in reconnaissance sorties made by a US U-2 spy plane on October 14–15, 1962. President Kennedy was shown the photographs on October 16. Kennedy promptly convened an *ad hoc* advisory committee, which would later become known as the ExComm, and which accompanied him throughout the decision-making process in the crisis.

From the outset, the committee considered two principal alternatives: to launch a military attack against Cuba, or to refrain from such attack. To refrain from attacking would prevent a military conflagration, but would enable the Soviet Union to consolidate its new tier of nuclear capability in Cuba – an outcome the committee members deemed unacceptable. A military attack on Cuba could bring about the destruction of the missile infrastructure already in place, but carried a significant latent threat of a nuclear flare-up between the two powers. Underlining this risk was the CIA's intelligence assessment that some of the missiles in Cuba were already operational. Even so, the committee reviewed a number of possible sub-alternatives concerning the scope of the attack – from attacking the missile sites only, through a broader aerial assault, which would also include targeting Cuban and Soviet military aircraft in Cuba, to an all-inclusive ground invasion of Cuba.

At the end of its first day of deliberations, the ExComm initially tabled yet another possible course of action, that of imposing a naval blockade on Cuba while

---

[1] The course of events in this example and some of the conceptual ideas are based on Dixit, A. and S. Skeath (1999), *Games of Strategy*, New York: W.W. Norton & Company, Chapter 13, which, in turn, is based on an extensive collection of primary and secondary sources. However, the analysis given here in game-theoretic terms differs from the analysis in Dixit and Skeath's book, where readers interested in the topic are invited to follow a fascinating discussion and an analysis of several alternative models to that historical situation. The Cuban missile crisis has, of course, been accorded an extensive treatment in the international relations literature, sometimes using analytical tools from game theory, as well as from other fields.

demanding that the Soviet Union dismantle and withdraw the missile array. While the blockade, in and of itself, could of course prevent the missile array in Cuba from being completed, it could not neutralize the operational missiles already positioned there. Thus, at first glance, there was no categorical difference between the strategy of refraining from attack and the strategy of imposing a naval blockade. This, however, was the alternative that was gradually garnering ever increasing support on the part of the committee members. On October 20, it had the support of eleven committee members, compared with six who supported a military assault on Cuba. President Kennedy adopted the majority view, and in his televised address of October 22, announced the imposition of the naval blockade.

The blockade actually went into effect commencing October 24, but was not executed impartially: naval vessels carrying civilian freights were permitted to continue unmolested *en route* for Cuba, or were subjected to a token delay only. The Soviet Union, looking for a peaceful way out of the crisis, took the mild form of the blockade to mean that it had time enough to wrest itself certain advantages from the crisis.

The ExComm and the President, realizing that time was not working in the United States' favor, decided to escalate their reaction. On October 27, the US Air Force had to hand full-fledged operational plans for a broad-gauge aerial attack on Cuba on the 29–30th of that month. At the same time, President Kennedy wrote a strongly worded letter to Soviet President Khrushchev, which was handed to the Soviet ambassador in Washington. Kennedy's proposal in this letter was that in return for the withdrawal of the Soviet missiles (as well as Soviet bombers) from Cuba, the United States would refrain from attacking; also, a few months later, the United States would withdraw US missiles previously positioned in Turkey, provided that the Soviets kept mum about the link between the Cuban crisis and such missile withdrawal.[2] Kennedy's letter required his Soviet counterpart to respond within 12–24 hours, on pain of "drastic consequences."

The following day, Soviet radio broadcast the wording of Khrushchev's response to Kennedy, announcing that the construction of the missile array in Cuba would be suspended forthwith, and that the missiles already positioned there would be dismantled and sent back to the Soviet Union. Kennedy promptly replied that he welcomed the Russians' decision. The announcement was broadcast in a radio communiqué on Voice of America.

However, this did not completely put an end to the missile crisis. The US Joint Chief of Staff remained doubtful that the Soviets intended to keep their word, and continued to speak out in favor of an air strike. In fact, construction on the missile

---

[2] The United States was in any event planning to withdraw, before long, the missiles it had positioned in Turkey, which were of an outdated model.

sites in Cuba did continue for a few more days, withdrawal of the missiles actually commencing only on November 20.

How are we to understand the strategy of imposing a naval blockade in game-theoretic terms? What essential difference is there between imposing such a blockade and refraining from attack (while resting content with mere demands and threats)? What was the secret of its success?

The imposition of the blockade does not nullify the threat of the missiles already positioned in Cuba. But the minute the order is handed down by the political leadership to the military forces to alter the status quo in the field, a certain risk of military escalation comes into being, over whose development the political leadership does not have full control.

Indeed, following imposition of the blockade, the Soviet Union ordered the commander of its forces in Cuba to prepare his troops, and to use all the means at his disposal – other than nuclear weaponry – to confront an American attack. In fact, the Soviet Union twice prepared orders – which, however, it cancelled before sending – permitting the commander of the troops in Cuba to use tactical nuclear weapons in case of a US invasion. On October 27, the Soviet forces downed an American U-2 spy plane that was on an aerial photography mission in Cuba, and opened fire on other US reconnaissance planes. The local commanding officer in Cuba evidently interpreted the orders he got from Moscow as permitting him greater freedom of action than intended by the Soviet leadership, which was not looking for military escalation at that stage.

On the American side, too, there were plenty of communication short-circuits between the political and military levels. The US navy had a ready-made contingency plan for imposing a naval blockade. The political echelon demanded that the navy formulate a slightly less harsh version of this plan, and, in particular, one that would more closely encircle Cuba with a blockade, in order to allow the Soviet Union more time to consider its moves. Notwithstanding these directives, the actual blockade hewed close, in outline, to the navy's original plan. Concurrently, the American Air Force, too, failed to display the maximal degree of caution called for by the political echelon. A U-2 spy plane "mistakenly" entered Soviet airspace; General Curtis Lemay, without the knowledge or permission of President Kennedy, ordered the US nuclear bombers to fly closer than usual to Soviet airspace, where they could be detected by Soviet radar. The Soviet forces, fortunately, kept their cool, contenting themselves with having President Khrushchev register a protest with President Kennedy.[3]

---

[3] General Lemay, who was known for his radical views and his blunt behavior, was probably the inspiration for the character of General Jack D. Ripper in director Stanley Kubrick's movie *Dr. Strangelove*. In this biting satire, the General, off his own bat, orders a nuclear bomber squadron to launch an offensive against the Soviet Union.

Thus, the United States' imposition of the naval blockade can be understood as leading to a move of nature. In the lottery of this move of nature, there is a high probability p that the blockade will lead the US to nothing but refraining from attacking Cuba. In the small complementary probability, $1 - p$, matters are liable to get out of control: misunderstandings and local initiatives by military commanders in the field are liable to lead to a military escalation, which will ultimately force the United States to attack the nuclear missiles, and could consequently develop into an inter-bloc nuclear war.

Neither of the two adversaries has any interest whatsoever in the second possibility. But when the US president decides to impose a blockade, he commits himself to the risk inhering in the move of nature. From that moment onward, he is no longer able to completely control how matters will evolve in the field, and cannot completely prevent all possibility of nuclear escalation.

What President Kennedy was counting on was that, given this move of nature, President Khrushchev would prefer to withdraw the missiles from Cuba, and thereby yield the annulment of the nuclear threat. In fact, Kennedy's acts gradually and carefully augmented the risk $1 - p$ of the conflagration that Khrushchev feared. At the time the naval blockade was declared on October 22, this risk was very slight. The risk increased somewhat at the time the naval blockade was actually (albeit moderately) imposed on October 24. Finally, the risk $1 - p$ increased even more on October 27, when Kennedy sent Khrushchev a sharply worded ultimatum with an imminent expiration date, while at the same time preparing detailed plans for an aerial offensive. This was the stage at which the risk $1 - p$ appeared serious enough to Khrushchev for him to prefer to retreat from his aggressive plans. See Figure 22.3.

22.3   Nuisance suits

Law and economics is a field in which the use of game theory is becoming increasingly widespread. The legal arena is a focal point for strategic fencing between plaintiffs and defendants through the attorneys representing them, and game theory is therefore a natural tool for modeling such strategic interaction.

The outcome of the swordplay, which is determined by the judges (or the jury), is of course influenced, but not unequivocally determined, by the behavior of the parties: different judges will rule differently, since they may place different interpretations on laws and precedents, depending on their experience, judgment, and philosophy. Therefore, from the litigants' point of view, going to court is something of a lottery, the prospects of which may perhaps be estimated ahead of time; yet the results cannot be predicted with certainty. Attempts at out-of-court settlement and negotiation between the parties are thus carried out under the shadow of this lottery, which takes

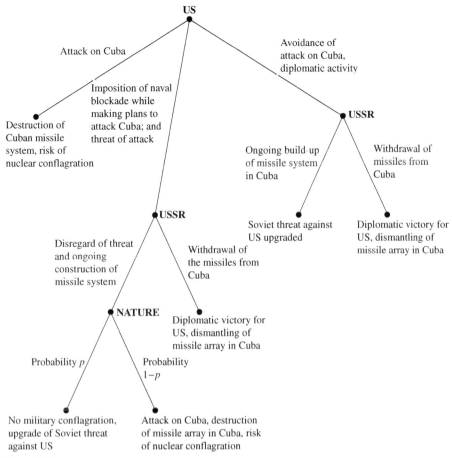

Figure 22.3

place if and when such attempts fail. For both parties, of course, going to court involves substantial costs – lawyers' fees, payment to expert witnesses, and so forth.

People sometimes take advantage of this fact to bring **nuisance suits**. A plaintiff may file a claim for compensation even when he is aware that his chances of winning the court case are slight. He expects the defendant to agree to settle out of court for an amount of compensation which, while smaller than that specified in the lawsuit, is still a non-negligible amount of money. He does so knowing that the defendant will agree to pay, in such settlement, any amount that is less than the expenses the defendant expects to be forced to disburse in the court case, even if the defendant ultimately wins it.

We will now outline a model describing this strategic situation.[4] The figures and the names appearing in this example are, of course, for purposes of illustration only.

---

[4] Based on Rosenberg, D. and S. Shavell (1985), "A Model in which Suits are Brought for their Nuisance Value," *International Review of Law and Economics* 5, 3–13.

Adam can sue Eve for compensation in the amount of $100,000, while at the same time inviting her to settle out of court by paying $5,000 compensation. If the case does in fact come up before a judge, each of the litigants will have to bear costs of $10,000. Adam has a mere 1 percent probability of winning, and both parties are aware of this fact. In addition, in order to file the action, Adam must pay a court fee of $1,000. Thus, the strategic interaction between the parties is described by the game tree in Figure 22.4.

If Eve consents to the compromise proposal, she loses $5,000 while Adam makes a $4,000 profit ($5,000 net of $1,000 court fee). If she refuses the compromise offer and loses in court, she loses $110,000 ($100,000 compensation, plus her $10,000 court costs), while Adam makes a profit of $89,000 ($100,000, net of $1,000 fee and $10,000 court costs); and if Adam loses the case, he loses $11,000 (fee + court costs), while Eve loses $10,000 (court costs).[5]

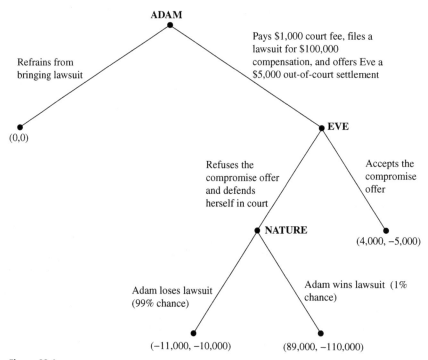

Figure 22.4

---

[5] Under British law, the legal costs of either party may depend on the outcome of the trial, since the judge may order the losing party to pay the winning party's costs. But even in that case, the winning party does not usually get full compensation for the time and mental effort invested in the conduct of the trial. Therefore, the assumption that the conduct of the trial entails expenses for both the plaintiff and the defendant is realistic. In any event, the precise amount of these costs does not affect insights in the present example. Under US law, either party disburses his or her own costs – as we have assumed in the present numerical example.

Question 22.1	Find a subgame perfect equilibrium in the game, assuming that Adam and Eve both maximize their expected payoff.
Answer	If the matter goes to court, Adam's expected payoff is:

$$99\% \times (-11,000) + 1\% \times (89,000) = -10,000$$

(The expected compensation that will be awarded in his favor is $1,000 = 1\% \times 100,000$, which offsets the court fee; in addition, he must strictly bear court costs of $10,000.)

Eve's expected payoff is:

$$99\% \times (-10,000) + 1\% \times (-110,000) = -11,000$$

Therefore, if Adam brings action, Eve will prefer to settle and pay him out-of-court compensation of $5,000. In this case, the payoff to Adam will be $4,000, which is greater than the payoff of 0 that he will get if he does not take action. Therefore, Adam will sue Eve at a subgame perfect equilibrium, and Eve will accept the compromise offer.

How does Adam manage to extort from Eve, in a compromise agreement, compensation in excess of the expected compensation she would pay him if a court case took place? The answer is that filing an action serves Adam as a **commitment device**. Adam commits himself to conduct an inefficient and non-worthwhile court case, the (expected) outcome of which is worse for both Eve and himself, in the event that Eve does not agree to his compromise offer.[6] Eve does not have a similar commitment device at her disposal in the currently prevailing legal system.

Judicial literature has proposed a number of mechanisms that could correct this state of affairs. According to one such proposal[7] the defending party in a lawsuit for compensation may oblige the court not to approve any compromise agreement that is signed out of court. In general, the court's approval is in fact needed for such compromise agreement to be accorded the force of a verdict and bring about the closure of the action file. What will happen if and when the defendant's right to bar the court from approving compromise agreements, when the defendant so requests, is anchored in law? The game tree will look like the one shown in Figure 22.5.

---

[6] The assumption inhering in the description of the game is that once he has filed the action, Adam must conduct the trial and bear its costs if Eve does not consent to a compromise offer but rather defends herself in court.

[7] Rosenberg, D. and S. Shavell (2006), "A Solution to the Problem of Nuisance Suits: The Option to Have the Court Bar Settlement," *International Review of Law and Economics* 26, 42–51.

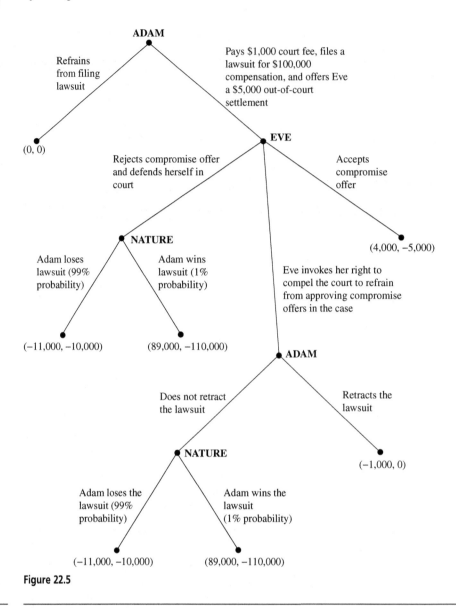

ADAM

Refrains
from filing
lawsuit

Pays $1,000 court fee, files a
lawsuit for $100,000
compensation, and offers Eve
a $5,000 out-of-court
settlement

(0, 0)

EVE

Rejects compromise offer
and defends herself in
court

Accepts
compromise
offer

(4,000, −5,000)

NATURE

Adam loses
lawsuit (99%
probability)

Adam wins
lawsuit (1%
probability)

Eve invokes her right to
compel the court to refrain
from approving compromise
offers in the case

(−11,000, −10,000)   (89,000, −110,000)

ADAM

Does not retract
the lawsuit

Retracts the
lawsuit

(−1,000, 0)

NATURE

Adam loses the
lawsuit (99%
probability)

Adam wins the
lawsuit
(1% probability)

(−11,000, −10,000)   (89,000, −110,000)

Figure 22.5

Question 22.2

Find a subgame perfect equilibrium in this game.

Answer

If Eve invokes her right to bar the court from approving an out-of-court settlement, Adam will prefer to withdraw the action, and to absorb the $1,000 court fee he has paid. This is because the alternative of continuing the court case will occasion him expected damage of $10,000 – as we calculated in the answer to Question 22.1.

If Adam withdraws the court case, Eve will suffer no damage. Therefore, on expectation of this reaction on Adam's part, Eve will in fact prefer to bar the court from approving a compromise agreement. This is because she will sustain losses under both the other alternatives available to her: a compromise will cause her a loss of $5,000, while filing a defense and going on with the court case will cause her an expected loss of $11,000, as we calculated in the preceding question.

Having cottoned on to this state of affairs from the outset, Adam refrains, from the very beginning of the game, from bringing action. This is because he realizes that filing action will cause Eve to bar the court from approving the compromise agreement, and as a result he will have to withdraw the action after already having paid the court fee.

The subgame perfect equilibrium that we have found is denoted with arrows in Figure 22.6.

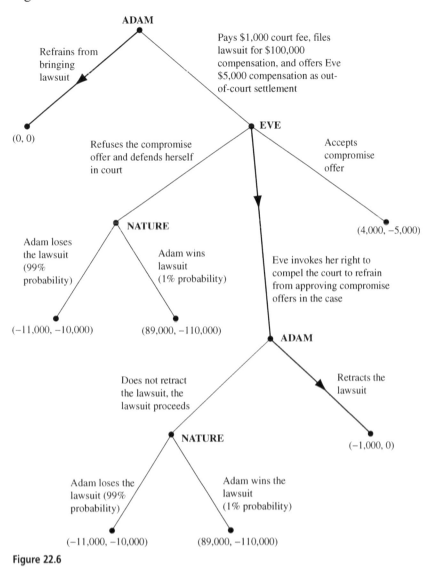

Figure 22.6

Thus, the proposed mechanism will indeed lead the plaintiff to refrain from bringing an action if his expected profit from a court case on such action is negative. The mechanism permits the defendant to "burn down the bridges" enabling a retreat to a compromise solution, and commits her to fight for her position in court. This fight is of course not worthwhile from the point of view of the defendant, but the credible "bridge-burning" threat leads the plaintiff to waive his unjustified action in advance.

But will this mechanism prevent the plaintiff from suing the defendant for damages when his expected profit from conducting his action is positive?

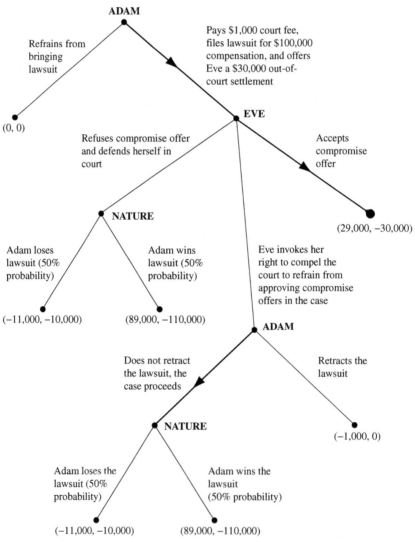

Figure 22.7

Question 22.3

Repeat Question 22.2 under the assumption that Adam has a 50 percent chance of winning the case, and that he proposes that Eve compensate him to the tune of $30,000 in an out-of-court settlement agreement.

Answer

If the court case takes place, Eve's expected loss is $60,000 (expected compensation of $50,000 = 50% × 100,000 plus $10,000 costs of conducting the court case), and Adam's expected profit is $39,000 (the expected compensation is $50,000 = 50% × 100,000, and from that amount, a sum total of $11,000 is to be deducted, representing court fee and costs). Therefore, Eve knows that even if she bars the court from approving the compromise agreement, Adam will not withdraw the action[8] and she will agree to the compromise offer from the outset. Under this compromise proposal, she will pay only $30,000 and will avoid a higher expected loss of $60,000, which she will sustain if the court case takes place. The subgame perfect equilibrium is described by arrows in Figure 22.7. Thus, under the proposed mechanism, the plaintiff will not refrain from filing actions he deems justified, i.e. those which will yield him a positive expected profit if he goes to trial.[9]

This property of the mechanism is of especial importance: it causes the parties' behavior *vis-à-vis* the confrontation to be efficient without the court needing to invest any effort in investigating the details of the case. The parties have in their possession the best information concerning the chances of winning by each side – information which is not, initially, in the hands of the legal authorities. The mechanism creates an incentive for both parties to proceed, of their own free will, in accordance with the intention of the legislators.

Thus, at equilibrium, the parties will not in any event approach the court, and in case of a justified action they will decide to compromise. This assumes that they share the same perspective of each side's chances of success at trial. When their expectations of success do not coincide, and at least one of the parties is overly optimistic as to the prospects of his or her success, a situation could well come about in which the action does ultimately come up for review in court. A broad-gauge discussion is in fact taking place in judicial and economic literature concerning situations in which the players' beliefs differ. However, in analyzing such a state of affairs, we need models of strategic interaction with private information that is not symmetrically imparted to the two players. This topic is beyond the scope of the current book.

---

[8] In fact, Adam will not withdraw the action as long as his expected profit exceeds – $1,000, i.e. the cost of the court fee.

[9] As stated in the preceding note, the mechanism will not, even so, cause the plaintiff to refrain from filing "slightly unjustified" actions, the expected profit from which – if the trial takes place – will exceed the loss occasioned him by paying the court fee.

PART VII

Repeated games

A repeated game is an extensive form game with an infinite horizon, in which the same normal form game is played again and again indefinitely. While the game repeats itself irrespective of the history of play, the players' strategies may very well depend on the history of play. Along each infinite history of repetitions of the game, the payoff to each player is the discounted sum of her stage payoffs, with some discount factor between 0 and 1. The discounting is interpreted as either (1) the extent to which players prefer current payments over future ones, or (2) the probability that the game will not be halted but will actually continue into the future, or (3) as resulting from a monetary interest rate applying to saving of accumulated payments or to loans on account of future payments.

In Chapter 23 we study the infinitely repeated Prisoner's Dilemma. Despite the fact that defection is a dominant strategy in the one-shot game, we show that the infinitely repeated Prisoner's Dilemma has subgame perfect equilibrium strategies in which the players cooperate in all or at least some of the rounds. Such equilibrium strategies call the players to cooperate, and involve a threat of a "punishment phase" of defection for several rounds by the player who suffered from the initial unexpected defection if and when unexpected defection has indeed occurred. At equilibrium, the punishment phase is long enough so as to foreshadow the short-term gains that the defector could potentially achieve by surprising his opponent, and hence no unexpected defection actually occurs on the equilibrium path. The higher the discount rate, the shorter the punishment phase (from which the punisher might suffer as well) needed to induce the equilibrium cooperation.

Overall, the "folk theorem" states that the average payoffs achievable for a player at subgame perfect equilibria of the repeated game are those that are both feasible (i.e. they are some average of the player's payoffs in the stage game matrix) and individually rational (i.e. above or equal to the payoff the player can guarantee by playing his security strategy). In the Prisoner's Dilemma and in many other repeated games, the folk theorem thus implies that there is a large host of subgame perfect equilibria, with many different degrees of cooperation. Hence, the concept of subgame perfect equilibrium has less predictive power than in games with a finite horizon, but it is compatible with a positive extent of cooperation in the Prisoner's Dilemma. Such cooperation is ruled out at equilibrium in the one-shot or the finitely repeated Prisoner's Dilemma, but it is nevertheless actually observed in laboratory experiments of the repeated Prisoner's Dilemma.

The large multiplicity of equilibria in the infinitely repeated game begs the question whether some plausible refinement could narrow down the set of equilibria and provide a tighter set of predictions. One such refinement is renegotiation proofness, which requires that at equilibrium, after no history of play, would the players be unanimous that they would like to "renegotiate" the prescribed continuation strategies and rather play what their equilibrium strategies prescribe after a *different* history. We show that renegotiation proofness indeed rules out some of the equilibrium strategy profiles in the infinitely repeated Prisoner's Dilemma, while leaving out a strict subset of equilibrium profiles which satisfies this additional criterion.

Chapter 24 provides further applications of repeated games. Efficiency wages are higher than the industry standard, aimed at incentivizing the worker to exert effort at work, based on the fact that the negative shock due to shirking followed by losing the job becomes larger. The tradeoff between the short-term gain and the long-run loss is analyzed so as to determine the minimal level of efficiency wages which would induce effort. A variant of this example deals with the analysis of a historical episode of royalties paid by merchants to their agents in two different trading systems in the Mediterranean Sea in the twelfth century.

An additional example deals with the strategies needed to sustain a stable cartel in a repeated oligopoly model. If the discount value of the competing firms is relatively low (i.e. if they put a lot of emphasis on current and near-future profits), they might not be able to sustain the most efficient behavior on their part, which would be to behave as if they were one big monopoly that distributes the monopolistic profits among the cartel members. The analysis provides the connection between the degree of impatience, as expressed by the discount factor, and the maximal profits that can be sustained at a subgame perfect equilibrium of the repeated game.

The chapter concludes with the alternating-offers bargaining model, in which the parties bargaining over the division of a pie make offers and counter-offers to each other, in between which the value of the pie for them shrinks to their discounting. At the unique subgame perfect equilibrium of the game the first offer to be made is accepted immediately, with a division in which there is a small advantage to the proposer. This advantage increases the more patient the proposer is and the less patient is the responder. The fact that in real life immediate agreement in bargaining is the exception rather than the rule suggests that additional factors play a role, such as asymmetric information or biased judgments.

23 The repeated Prisoner's Dilemma

So far, we have dealt with extensive form games in which all the paths had a finite length. Recall, however, that in Chapter 18 we also defined game trees with infinite paths. Such paths do not end with a leaf at which payoffs to the players are specified. Rather, payoffs are defined for each of the players for the entirety of each such an infinite path.

Despite the existence of such infinite paths, the concept of a strategy continues to be well defined: a player's strategy is her strategy plan, describing how she will act if and when her turn comes to play at each of the nodes at which she is one of the active players. The concept of Nash equilibrium likewise remains well defined: a profile of the players' strategies is a Nash equilibrium if the strategy of each player is a best reply, from her point of view, to the strategies of the other players.

As usual, a subgame commencing at a particular node is defined by a subtree for which that node serves as a root. Therefore, the concept of a subgame perfect equilibrium remains well defined: the strategy profile of the players is a subgame perfect equilibrium if the strategies induced by them in each subgame constitute a Nash equilibrium in that subgame. However, unlike for games with finite paths, when there are infinite paths in the game tree, a subgame perfect equilibrium cannot be found by backward induction. This is because an infinite path cannot be "folded" backwards, from the leaf to the root, since an infinite path does not have a leaf from which the "folding" can start. Accordingly, we must adopt other methods in order to find a subgame perfect equilibrium in a game with infinite paths.

23.1 Repeated games

An important class of games with an infinite horizon is that of repeated games. In a **repeated game** the players play a strategic form game over and over again. For example, in the repeated Prisoner's Dilemma, the players play the Prisoner's Dilemma repeatedly.

The players may, of course, play differently in different rounds of the game: they may cooperate in some game rounds and behave selfishly in others. In particular, the strategy of each player in a repeated game may depend on the history of the game prior to that phase: the strategy of a player in round n of the game determines how she will act, depending on the actions of her rivals and her own actions in the first $n - 1$ rounds of the game. For example, in the repeated Prisoner's Dilemma, a player's possible strategy might be:

> "Cooperate in the first round; and in each of the following rounds cooperate if and only if your rival has cooperated an even number of times prior to that round, while you yourself have cooperated an odd number of times."

In order to distinguish between the notion of a strategy in a repeated game and that of a strategy in a one-shot game, we will henceforth call a strategy $x_i \in X_i$ of player $i \in I$ in the one-shot game an **action**, while reserving the term **strategy** for the entire repeated game.

Definition   A player's strategy in a repeated game defines, for every round n of the game $(n = 1, 2, ...)$, the action which that player will take as a function of the actions taken by all the players in the preceding game rounds.

Formally, the history h_n of length n is composed of n action profiles of the players – the action profile $(x_i^k)_{i \in I}$ for every game round $k = 1, ..., n$.

We will denote by H_n the set of histories of length n for $n = 1, 2 ...,$

$$H_n = X^n = (\Pi_{i \in I} X_i)^n$$

where $X = \Pi_{i \in I} X_i$ is the set of action profiles of the players in the one-shot game.

For $n = 0$ there exists one (vacuous) history h_0, in which no actions have yet been played, and therefore the set of histories of zero length consists of a single history:

$$H_0 = X^0 = \{h_0\}$$

We will denote by $H = \bigcup_{n=0}^{\infty} H_n$ the set of all histories of all possible lengths $n = 0, 1, 2 ...$

A strategy σ_i of player $i \in I$ is a function:

$$\sigma_i : H \to X_i$$

that defines the action that the player will take after each such history.

To complete the description of the game, we must describe the payoffs to the players as a function of their strategies. In other words, we must define how to sum up the players' payoffs throughout the game rounds, for each infinite history of rounds of the game.

To that end we must sum up an infinite series of payoffs – one payoff from every game round. There are several ways of defining a convergent summation of this kind. We will focus on the case of the **discounted sum**:

- We first multiply the payoffs in round n by δ^{n-1} for a given discount factor $\delta \in (0,1)$: if the payoff of player i in round n is $\pi_{i,n}$, then her discounted payoff is $\delta^{n-1}\pi_{i,n}$.
- We add up the discounted payoffs: the payoff of player i in the infinite repeated game is:

$$\pi_i = \sum_{n=1}^{\infty} \delta^{n-1}\pi_{i,n}$$

Discounted summation is consistent with a number of potential alternative interpretations:

1. The player has a time preference by which she ascribes the greatest importance to the payoff in the first round (which gets multiplied by $\delta^0 = 1$); she ascribes less importance to the payoff in the second round, and therefore that payoff is multiplied by the factor $\delta < 1$; to the payoff in the third round, which is multiplied by δ^2, she ascribes even less importance; and so forth. The more remote the game round, the smaller the factor by which the payoff in that round is multiplied.

   As δ increases and tends to 1, the more patient the player becomes: she ascribes to the payoff in the next round almost the same weight as she ascribes to the payoff in the current round. And vice versa: as δ decreases and tends to 0, the player becomes increasingly impatient – she ascribes a much greater weight to the payoff in the current round than she ascribes to the payoff in the next round.

Another possible interpretation is as follows:

2. There exists a probability $1 - \delta$ that the strategic encounter will end after the first game round and no further game rounds will take place. Similarly, if n rounds of the game have already taken place, there is a probability $1 - \delta$ that the round n is the last game round. Thus:
   - the probability that the first game round will take place is $p_1 = 1$;
   - the probability that the second game round will take place is only $p_2 = \delta$;
   - the third game round will take place only in the case that the strategic encounter did not end after the first game round (a probability of δ) and also that the strategic encounter did not end after the second round (a probability of δ). Therefore, the probability that the third game round will take place is $p_3 = \delta^2$.

And so on: the probability that round n of the game will take place is $p_n = \delta^{n-1}$.

Therefore, the player's expected payoff is $\pi_i = \sum_{n=1}^{\infty} \delta^{n-1}\pi_{i,n}$. This is the payoff that represents the player's preferences, assuming that she maximizes her expected payoff.

A third possible interpretation is the following:

3. The payoffs in the various game rounds are monetary payoffs. The player can save her money in a bank from one round to the next, or borrow money from the bank against future payoffs she is due to receive. Assume that the savings and the loan from one period to the next bear interest at the rate $r > 0$: for every dollar that the player saves over the period of a particular game round, she will receive $1 + r$ dollars in the next period, $(1 + r)^2$ dollars after two savings periods, and so forth $- (1 + r)^k$ dollars after k periods. Similarly, if the player borrows a dollar from the bank in a particular period, then after k periods she must repay $(1 + r)^k$ dollars to the bank.

Therefore, if the player is prepared for her loan repayment in the second period to be in the amount of one dollar, she can borrow $\frac{1}{1+r}$ dollars from the bank in the first round; if she is prepared for her repayment in the third round to be in the amount of one dollar, she can borrow only $\frac{1}{(1+r)^2}$ in the first round; and so forth. If the loan is repaid only in round n, then against every dollar that is repaid, the player can borrow only $\frac{1}{(1+r)^{n-1}}$ dollars in the first round.

Thus, if we denote by $\delta = \frac{1}{1+r}$, the sum $\pi_i = \sum_{n=1}^{\infty} \delta^{n-1} \pi_{i,n}$ describes net present value (NPV) of the player's payoffs, in terms of the first round. This is the amount in dollars that will be available to her in the first round if she borrows the maximum possible amount from the bank and uses her payoffs in all the subsequent rounds of the game in order to repay the loan.

Frequently, we will find it more convenient to discuss the player's average payoff $\bar{\pi}_i$. If the player receives the payoffs $\pi_{i,n}$ in rounds $n = 1,2 \dots$ of the game, such that her total payoff amounts to $\pi_i = \sum_{n=1}^{\infty} \delta^{n-1} \pi_{i,n}$, then the player's average payoff $\bar{\pi}_i$ is the payoff she must obtain in every round of the game in order for her total payoff to be π_i.

The nexus between the total payoff and the average payoff is simple: if the player were to obtain a payoff of $\bar{\pi}_i$ in every round of the game, then her overall payoff would be:[1]

---

[1] The sum of a geometric series of m terms, it will be recalled, is:

$$\sum_{n-1}^{m} \delta^{n-1} = \frac{1 - \delta^m}{1 - \delta}$$

When $m \to \infty$, we obtain the infinite geometric series, the sum of which is:

$$\sum_{n-1}^{\infty} \delta^{n-1} = \frac{1}{1 - \delta}$$

assuming that $0 < \delta < 1$.

$$\sum_{n=1}^{\infty} \delta^{n-1}\overline{\pi}_i = \frac{\overline{\pi}_i}{1-\delta}$$

Therefore, in order for this total payoff to be equal to π_i,

$$\frac{\overline{\pi}_i}{1-\delta} = \pi_i$$

it must be the case that:

$$\overline{\pi}_i = (1-\delta)\pi_i = (1-\delta)\sum_{n=1}^{\infty} \delta^{n-1}\pi_{i,n}$$

23.2 The repeated Prisoner's Dilemma

Question 23.1 Two players play the Prisoner's Dilemma game again and again, with the following payoffs:

Player 2

		C	D
Player 1	C	2, 2	0, 3
	D	3, 0	1, 1

What are the players' average payoffs if:

A. They cooperate (play C) in all rounds of the game?

B. They cooperate in the first ten rounds of the game and then no longer cooperate (play D)?

C. They cooperate in all even rounds of the game and do not cooperate in odd rounds of the game?

D. The first player cooperates only in the first game round and the second player does not cooperate at all?

Answer A. The payoff of each player in each round is $\pi_{i,n} = 2$. Therefore, the average payoff of each player is:

$$\bar{\pi}_i = (1-\delta)\sum_{n=1}^{\infty}\delta^{n-1}\pi_{i,n} = 2(1-\delta)\sum_{n=1}^{\infty}\delta^{n-1} = 2(1-\delta)\times\frac{1}{1-\delta} = 2$$

B. In the first ten rounds of the game, the payoff of each player is 2, and in other rounds, the payoff of each player is 1. Therefore, the average payoff of each player is:

$$\bar{\pi}_i = 2(1-\delta)\sum_{n=1}^{10}\delta^{n-1} + (1-\delta)\sum_{n=11}^{10}\delta^{n-1}$$

$$= 2(1-\delta)\frac{1-\delta^{10}}{1-\delta} + (1-\delta)\frac{\delta^{10}}{1-\delta} = 2 - \delta^{10}$$

C. The payoffs of each player are 2 in the even game rounds $n = 2k(k = 1, 2, \ldots)$; in the odd game rounds $n = 2k - 1(k = 1, 2, \ldots)$, the payoff of each player is 1. On average:

$$\bar{\pi}_i = 2(1-\delta)\sum_{k=1}^{\infty}\delta^{2k-1} + (1-\delta)\sum_{k=1}^{\infty}\delta^{(2k-1)-1}$$

$$= 2(1-\delta)\frac{\delta}{1-\delta^2} + (1-\delta)\frac{1}{1-\delta^2} = \frac{2\delta+1}{1+\delta}$$

D. The first player has a payoff of 0 in the first round and a payoff of 1 in the other rounds of the game. Therefore, her average payoff is:

$$\bar{\pi}_i = 0 + (1+\delta)\sum_{n=2}^{\infty}\delta^{n-1} = (1-\delta)\frac{\delta}{1-\delta} = \delta$$

The second player has a payoff of 3 in the first round and a payoff of 1 in the other rounds of the game. Therefore her average payoff is:

$$\bar{\pi}_2 = 3(1-\delta) + (1-\delta)\sum_{n=2}^{\infty}\delta^{n-1} = 3(1-\delta) + (1-\delta)\frac{\delta}{1-\delta} = 3 - 2\delta$$

Why are repeated games with an infinite horizon especially interesting? Is it the case that in recurrent strategic situations with an unlimited horizon there exist preferable equilibria, with average payoffs that the players cannot obtain in the one-shot game?

This is indeed the case, and that is the central source of interest in repeated games, as we will now demonstrate.

Question 23.2

The grim-trigger strategy

In the repeated Prisoner's Dilemma, the "grim-trigger strategy" is defined as follows:

1. Cooperate (play C) in the first game round.
2. In each of the following game rounds: cooperate (play C) if the two players cooperated in all the preceding game rounds; otherwise, defect (play D).

Show that when the players are patient enough, i.e. when δ is large and sufficiently close to 1, adoption of the grim-trigger strategy by both players constitutes a subgame perfect equilibrium.

Answer

When both players adopt the grim-trigger strategy, they cooperate throughout all rounds of the game. Therefore, the average payoff of each of them is:

$$\bar{\pi}_i = (1 - \delta) \sum_{n=1}^{\infty} 2\delta^{n-1} = 2$$

What will happen if player 1, for example, deviates from this strategy and plays D in the first game round, while player 2 adheres to the grim-trigger strategy? In the first round, player 2 will play C and player 1 will therefore enjoy a payoff of 3. But as a result of player 1 playing D, player 2 will play D in the second round and onwards. Player 1's best reply to this is likewise to play D commencing from the second round and thereafter, and as a result, her payoff will be 1 in all of those game rounds. This is in contrast to the payoff of 2 that she could have enjoyed had she not deviated from the grim-trigger strategy.

In other words, given the fact that player 2 adopts the grim-trigger strategy, if player 1 chooses to play D in the first round, it will be worth her while to play D in all the other game rounds, too. Therefore, player 1's deviation from the grim-trigger strategy to some other strategy σ_i, which is different from the grim-trigger strategy in the first round, can be worthwhile for player 1 only if deviation to a strategy of "always D" is worth her while. Compared with the grim-trigger strategy, by using the "always D" strategy, player 1 obtains a higher payoff (3 instead of 2) in the first game round, but at the cost of obtaining a lower payoff (1 instead of 2) in all the following game rounds.

Is this deviation worthwhile for player 1? Does the higher immediate payoff compensate for the loss in all the following rounds? The answer, of course, depends on how patient the player is – how willing she is to waive immediate gains in order to protect herself from long-term damage. The discount factor δ

expresses this aspect: as δ increases in size and tends to 1, so, too, does the player's patience increase.

Formally, when player 2 adopts a grim-trigger strategy, the strategy of "always play D" will yield player 1 an average payoff of:

$$\pi_1' = 3(1 - \delta) + (1 - \delta) \sum_{n=2}^{\infty} \delta^{n-1} = 3(1 - \delta) + (1 - \delta)\frac{\delta}{1 - \delta} = 3 - 2\delta$$

Is this average payoff higher than the average payoff:

$$\pi_1 = 2(1 - \delta) \sum_{n=1}^{\infty} \delta^{n-1} = 2$$

that the grim-trigger strategy yields player 1? The answer is that:

$$\pi_1' = 3 - 2\delta > 2 = \pi_1$$

if and only if:

$$\delta < \frac{1}{2}$$

Thus, only if player 1 is very impatient and is prepared, in order to increase her payoff by $\frac{1}{2}$ in the current round, to waive the incremental payoff of 1 in the following round, then the grim-trigger strategy does not constitute a best reply from her point of view when player 2 adopts the grim-trigger strategy. On the other hand, if $\delta \geq \frac{1}{2}$, then we have found that it is not profitable for player 1 to deviate from the grim-trigger strategy in the first game round.

Assume, therefore, that the players are sufficiently patient, $\delta \geq \frac{1}{2}$. Is it worthwhile for player 1 to deviate from the grim-trigger strategy in a subsequent round but not in the first round? That is, is it worthwhile for player 1 to adopt a strategy that is identical to the grim-trigger strategy over a finite number of rounds $\ell = 1, 2 \ldots k - 1$ but differs from it in round k (and possibly also in additional rounds)?

The answer to this question can easily be seen to be negative. Assume that player 1 mulls the idea of deviating from the grim-trigger strategy in round k. In other words, with the two players having cooperated in the first $k - 1$ rounds, player 1 asks herself whether it is worth her while to play D instead of C in round k. In the subgame commencing in round k, player 2's strategy is the grim-trigger strategy: she will continue to cooperate as long as both players cooperate. Therefore, as we have seen, deviation from the grim-trigger strategy on the part of player 1 will reduce her average payoff in this subgame from 2 to $3 - 2\delta$. This is assuming that player 1 plays D commencing from round k and thereafter, which is in fact the optimal deviation for player 1 *assuming* she deviates from the grim-trigger strategy in round k. Hence, the average payoff of player 1 over the entire repeated game will diminish: the payoffs to player 1 from the first $k - 1$ rounds will in any event aggregate to:

$$2 \times \sum_{n=1}^{k-1} \delta^{n-1} = 2 \times \frac{1 - \delta^{k-1}}{1 - \delta}$$

but the average payoff will decrease in the subgame from round k onwards.

We have thus completed the proof that when $\delta \geq \frac{1}{2}$, the grim-trigger strategy is a best reply of player 1 as against the grim-trigger strategy on the part of player 2. Similarly, the grim-trigger strategy is a best reply of player 2 when player 1 adopts the grim-trigger strategy. Hence, the grim-trigger strategies profile is a Nash equilibrium in the repeated game.

Does the grim-trigger strategies profile constitute also a subgame perfect equilibrium? In order to prove this, we must verify that when a particular player adopts the grim-trigger strategy, this strategy is optimal for the other player also in subgames that these players will never get to play, i.e. even after game histories that are excluded by the grim-trigger strategy profile itself.

If both players choose the grim-trigger strategy, they will play C in all rounds of the game. We have already verified that after every finite number of game rounds in which both players played only C, the grim-trigger strategy continues to be optimal against the grim-trigger strategy adopted by the rival. But what about the histories of a game that the players will not actually play, i.e. game histories (with a finite number of rounds) in the course of which at least one of the players played D at least once?

Following such a game history, the grim-trigger strategy dictates playing only D in all subsequent rounds. As against this play pattern, the best reply for the other player is likewise to play D in all the subsequent game rounds. Therefore, if one of the players adopts the grim-trigger strategy and plays D in all the rounds of this subgame, then the grim-trigger strategy is indeed optimal for the other player, since it dictates that she play D constantly as well.

In Question 23.2 we found a subgame perfect equilibrium at which patient players ($\delta \geq \frac{1}{2}$) cooperate (play C) at equilibrium throughout all rounds of the repeated Prisoner's Dilemma game, despite the fact that defection (the choice of D) in any game round in and of itself is a dominant action. In every round, the players cooperate and refrain from pocketing a momentary profit (which they could obtain by deviating from C to D). They do so in order not to curtail further cooperation and the profits it will yield.

However, the grim-trigger strategy in Question 23.2 – even though it leads to cooperation at equilibrium – imposes a heavy loss on the "grim-trigger" player if and when she is called upon to make good her threat of forever playing D, even after a one-shot "slip-up" in which her rival played D. Does a "slip-up" of this kind, which in real life may take place even as a result of error and not necessarily by deliberate choice, indeed warrant such severe punishment – for both the "erring" player and her rival? Are there no subgame perfect equilibrium strategies at which the punishment for deviating from the equilibrium strategy is less severe?

Question 23.3

Limited retaliation

In the repeated Prisoner's Dilemma, define the limited retaliation strategy as follows:

1. Cooperate (play C) in the first game round.
2. In round $n + 1$ proceed as follows:
   A. If in round n both players played C, play C in round $n + 1$.
   B. If in round n at least one of the players played D, play D continuously over the k rounds $n + 1$, ..., $n + k$, and in round $n + k + 1$ play C. Follow Rule 2 again only for round $n + k + 2$.[2]

If and when the player acts in accordance with Rule 2B, we say that the game is "at the punishment phase." For every number k of punishment rounds defined by Rule 2B, find the minimal discount factor δ_k for which the adoption of the limited retaliation strategy of length k by both players constitutes a subgame perfect equilibrium.

Answer

When both players adopt the limited retaliation strategy, they play C throughout all rounds of the game, and their average payoff is 2.

What will happen if, from the very first round, player 1 deviates from this strategy and plays D? According to Rule 2B, player 2 will play D over the k rounds 2, ..., $k + 1$, and her later behavior does not depend on the behavior of player 1 over those k rounds.[3] Therefore, over the k rounds 2, ..., $k + 1$, the optimum from the point of view of player 1 is to play D: the choice of D in these rounds is a dominant action and does not affect the later behavior of player 2.

---

[2] Meaning that even if in the rounds $n + 1$, ..., $n + k$ at least one of the players plays D (which, indeed, is what you should do!), do not follow Rule 2B in those rounds, and do not start to make a recount of the k rounds in which you play D. Likewise, even if in some of the rounds $n + 1$, ..., $n + k$ you got confused and played C, continue to adhere to the plan and play D in the remaining rounds up to and including round $n + k$, and in round $n + k + 1$ play C. (In particular, even if, under such "confusion," both players simultaneously played C in one of the rounds $n + 1$, ..., $n + k$, do not follow Rule 2A in the succeeding round.)

[3] Player 2 will play C again in round $k + 2$, and her subsequent behavior, from round $k + 3$ and thereafter, will be determined (according to Rule 2) solely on the basis of player 1's behavior in round $k + 1$ and onwards.

Thus, even if player 1 deviates from the limited retaliation strategy already in the first round and plays D instead of C, she will in fact increase her payoff in the first round from 2 to 3, but will be unable to obtain a payoff higher than 1 during the k rounds 2, ..., $k + 1$ – the payoff obtained when she plays D in those rounds. As a result of this deviation, her payoff in the first $k + 1$ rounds will change from:

$$\pi_{1, k+1} = \sum_{n=1}^{k+1} 2\delta^{n-1} = \frac{2 - 2\delta^{k+1}}{1 - \delta}$$

to:

$$\pi'_{1, k+1} = 3 + \sum_{n=2}^{k+1} \delta^{n-1} = 3 + \frac{\delta(1 - \delta^k)}{1 - \delta} = \frac{3 - 2\delta - \delta^{k+1}}{1 - \delta}$$

Therefore, from the point of view of the first $k + 1$ rounds, the deviation is suboptimal if and only if:

$$\pi_{1, k+1} \geq \pi'_{k+1}$$

i.e. if and only if:

$$2\delta \geq 1 + \delta^{k+1}$$

(Verify this!) If $k = 1$, i.e. if the punishment phase lasts only one round, then this inequality is not satisfied for any $\delta < 1$; if $k = 2$, i.e. the punishment phase lasts two rounds, then this inequality is satisfied for every:

$$\delta \geq \delta_2 = 0.618$$

If $k = 3$, i.e. if the punishment phase lasts three rounds, then this inequality is satisfied for every:

$$\delta \geq \delta_3 = 0.544$$

The longer the punishment phase k becomes, the broader is the domain of values of δ for which the inequality is satisfied, since the threshold value δ_k gradually decreases, tending to $\frac{1}{2}$.

Thus, if the duration of the punishment phase is k and $\delta \geq \delta_k$, player 1 cannot increase her payoff from the first $k + 1$ rounds if she deviates from the limited retaliation strategy in the first round. Similarly, if she deviates from that strategy in any other round n in which player 2 plays C, then she will reduce her payoff from the rounds $k + 1, n, n + 1, ..., n + k + 1$; however, if player 1 deviates from the limited retaliation strategy when player 2 punishes her, i.e. if round n is one of the rounds in which player 2 plays D in order to punish player 1, and player 1 plays C instead of D, player 1 will lose by it in round n itself, and will not profit by it in the future since the behavior of player 1 in the punishment phase has no effect on the future behavior of player 2.

Hence, whether or not player 1 or player 2 has already deviated from the limited retaliation strategy of length k prior to round n, player 1 cannot profit from a deviation from this strategy in round n. This is assuming that player 2 adopts this strategy, and $\delta \geq \delta_k$.

This completes our demonstration of the fact that when $\delta \geq \delta_k$, the limited retaliation strategy of length k is a best reply to the k-long retaliation strategy in any subgame, and hence the profile of these strategies is a subgame perfect equilibrium.

We have seen, therefore, that when the players are fairly patient ($\delta \geq 0.618$), even a threat of a short punishment phase ($k = 2$) suffices to cause them to cooperate throughout the game rounds.[4] The more impatient the players are (smaller δ and tending to $\frac{1}{2}$), the longer the punishment phase needed in order for there to exist a subgame perfect equilibrium at which the players constantly cooperate. When $\delta = \frac{1}{2}$, only if the punishment phase is infinite, and the players adopt the grim-trigger strategy, does constant cooperation take place at equilibrium. If the players are even less patient and $\delta < \frac{1}{2}$, there is no equilibrium at which the players cooperate throughout all the game rounds.

Is the infinite horizon of the game essential for obtaining cooperation? This issue is addressed next.

Question 23.4

The finitely repeated Prisoner's Dilemma

If the number of game rounds of the Prisoner's Dilemma were finite and known beforehand, would an equilibrium exist at which the players cooperate through all or some of the rounds of the game?

Answer

The answer is negative. If the game has a finite number n of rounds, it can be solved by backward induction. In the last game round, the action D is a dominant action. Whether the players decline, in whole or in part, to cooperate in the first $n - 1$ rounds, they understand that in the last round of the game they have nothing to lose

---

[4] But an even shorter punishment phase, $k = 1$, does not suffice for this purpose even if δ is arbitrarily close to (albeit strictly smaller than) 1, i.e. even if the players are very patient indeed.

from choosing D: absent any succeeding game round, they cannot be punished for an action that is injurious to their rival. Therefore, at a subgame perfect equilibrium, both players will play D in the final round of the game.

How will the players act in the penultimate round? Both players realize that in the final game round they are going to play D regardless of the game history. Player 1, for example, cannot guarantee her rival a future reward if the latter chooses C in the penultimate round, since both players are aware that such a "guarantee" is not credible: as we have seen, in any event player 1 is about to play D in the last round. Therefore, seeing that neither "reward" nor "punishment" can be guaranteed, in the penultimate round each player will choose her dominant action, which is D.

Similarly, under the inductive assumption that the players will play D in the final k rounds of the game, then in round number $k + 1$ before the end, the players do not possess any credible capability of guaranteeing one another any future reward or punishment. Thus we have shown, by using backward induction, that the players will choose D in all rounds of the game.

Question 23.4 illustrates how the infinite horizon of the repeated game is essential in order to guarantee reaction options – the bestowing of "reward" or "punishment" – at every phase of the game, and thus to allow for an equilibrium at which the players cooperate throughout all rounds of the game.

Nevertheless, when the number of rounds is finite but very large, the unique subgame perfect equilibrium we found, at which the two players refrain from cooperating, does not appear to be particularly intuitive. In practice, a player may play C several times in the first phases of the game, in order to signal to her rival that she is interested in cooperating. Such signaling does not precisely define the duration of the cooperation that the player intends. Thus, if the rival responds to such an "invitation," the players may benefit from the fruits of the cooperation over a lengthy period of time. The cooperation term will come to an end toward the end of the game, when one of the players senses that the logic underlying backward induction becomes more prevalent than the tacit understanding between the players concerning their wish to cooperate. Alternatively, if the rival does not initially respond to the player's "signal," then that player will very soon stop signaling and will suffer the losses only in a short and limited number of rounds.

Similarly, if, in fact, a long period of cooperation does take place, and while it is in effect one of the players tries to "cheat" and make a one-shot gain by playing D, the other player can "punish" her by playing D over a limited number of rounds, and not necessarily through to the end of the game.

23.2.1   The repeated Prisoner's Dilemma in laboratory experiments

Such behavior on the part of players in a game with a finite but very large number of rounds has in fact been observed in laboratory experiments. In one such experiment the Prisoner's Dilemma was played 100 times by a pair of players.[5] They cooperated in sixty out of the last eighty-nine rounds of the game, and in most of the rounds in which a player suddenly stopped cooperating, his rival punished him by choosing D for a period of not more than four rounds.

A deviation of this type from the unique subgame perfect equilibrium thus possesses an intrinsic logic of its own. In particular, the problems we discussed in Chapter 21 in connection with the centipede game are relevant also in the present case. If one of the players believes that her rival will choose D throughout the entire game, but the rival, on the contrary, chooses C at the start of the game, then the player must work out an alternative theory concerning the rival's anticipated behavior in the course of the game. Once the rival has already shown at the beginning of the game that her behavior is not consistent with the backward induction outcome, there is no longer any basis for assuming that the rival will necessarily use backward induction as the game proceeds.

In this situation, a large number of reasonable theories might be induced concerning the rival's behavior further along in the game, such as, for example, the one we have described above. Does some simple rule of behavior exist that will guarantee a high payoff *vis-à-vis* a diverse range of behaviors of this kind? Robert Axelrod examined this question.[6] He invited economists, mathematicians, psychologists, and sociologists to send him a software program encoding a strategy for a 200-round Prisoner's Dilemma, where the payoffs in each round were:

		Player 2	
		C	D
Player 1	C	3, 3	0, 5
	D	5, 0	1, 1

Fourteen different strategies were submitted to Axelrod. Of these, he put each pair of strategies into play five times (of the 200-round repeated game), one against the other. Also, every strategy that was submitted was made to confront a strategy that chose to play C or D randomly in every round (with equal probabilities), with no interdependence between the rounds.

[5] Flood, M. M. (1958–1959), "Some Experimental Games," *Management Science* 5, 5–26.
[6] Axelrod, R. (1984), *The Evolution of Cooperation*, New York: Basic Books.

The strategy that won the highest payoff in Axelrod's competition was the **tit-for-tat** strategy, which is defined as follows:

1. Play C in the first game round.
2. Commencing from the second round, play the action that your rival adopted in the preceding round.

This is a strategy in which the player "signals" her wish to cooperate by choosing C. The player "punishes" her rival by choosing D whenever the rival fails to cooperate. Also, the strategy reverts to the format of cooperation only after such a "punishment" round in which the rival "bows her head" and "pays her dues" by playing C.

After Axelrod published the results of the first contest, he asked for more strategies to be submitted, but this time to a contest in which the number of rounds in each encounter of a pair of strategies would be randomly determined in the course of the encounter. Sixty-two additional strategies were submitted to the second contest, and this time, too, the tit-for-tat strategy was the winner, gaining the highest average payoff.

23.3   Partial cooperation

We will now reprise the discussion of the Prisoner's Dilemma when repeated over an infinite number of rounds. So far we have focused on strategies that lead to cooperation among the players in this game. But do all equilibrium strategies lead to enduring cooperation?

Certainly not. If one of the players chooses the "always play D" strategy, then her rival, too, will find it worthwhile to choose that very same strategy. The strategy profile "always play D" is a subgame perfect equilibrium for every $\delta \in (0,1)$. In this equilibrium, the players obtain the payoff 1 in every round, and therefore this is also their average payoff.

The game has many more equilibria. Consider, for example, the strategy defined by the following pair of rules:

A. Play C in odd rounds and D in even rounds.
B. If one of the players deviates from Rule A, play D in all subsequent rounds.

In this strategy, the "punishment phase" that is defined by Rule B resembles the one in the grim-trigger strategy – punishment is unlimited in time. But as distinct from the grim-trigger strategy, here the players cooperate only in some of the rounds.

If player 2 adopts this strategy, is it worthwhile for player 1 to adopt it, too? Is the strategy in fact a best reply for player 1, or would she be well advised to deviate from it?

It is clearly suboptimal for player 1 to deviate from this strategy in an even round – she will suffer a loss in that round (a payoff of 0 instead of 1) and will cause player 2 to refrain from cooperating in all the subsequent rounds.

Is it worth player 1's while to deviate from this strategy in the first round? If she does not deviate from it, her average payoff will be:

$$(1 - \delta) \sum_{k=1}^{\infty} 2\delta^{(2k-1)-1} + (1 - \delta) \sum_{k=1}^{\infty} \delta^{2k-1}$$

$$= \frac{2(1 - \delta)}{1 - \delta^2} + \frac{\delta(1 - \delta)}{1 - \delta^2} = \frac{2 + \delta}{1 + \delta}$$

If, however, she does deviate from it in the first round and plays C instead of D, then in this round she will obtain 3 instead of 2; but as a result of this deviation, player 2 will play D in round 2 and thereafter, and accordingly, the highest payoff that player 1 will be able to guarantee herself in any such round is only 1 – if player 2 indeed plays D in those rounds. Her average payoff will then be:

$$3(1 - \delta) + (1 - \delta) \sum_{n=2}^{\infty} \delta^{n-1} = 3 - 2\delta$$

Therefore, such deviation is suboptimal for player 1 if and only if:

$$\frac{2 + \delta}{1 + \delta} \geq 3 - 2\delta$$

i.e. if and only if:

$$\delta \geq \frac{\sqrt{2}}{2} = 0.707$$

Comprehension check

Complete the proof that the strategy profile of "partial cooperation" constitutes a subgame perfect equilibrium when $\delta \geq \frac{\sqrt{2}}{2}$. (Hint: use arguments similar to those in the solution to Question 23.2.)

Question 23.5

Explain, qualitatively, why the grim-trigger strategy profile (Question 23.2) is a subgame perfect equilibrium for a broader range of discount factors, $\delta \geq \frac{1}{2}$, than the range $\delta \geq \frac{\sqrt{2}}{2}$ for which the strategy profile "partial cooperation" is a subgame perfect equilibrium.

Answer

The discount factor measures the degree of the players' patience, i.e. to what extent they are prepared to sacrifice part of their present payoff in order to guarantee a higher future payoff. The higher the discount factor, the more patient are the players.

The strategy profile "partial cooperation" guarantees a lower future payoff than is guaranteed by the grim-trigger strategy profile. This is because the grim-trigger strategy profile guarantees cooperation in all future rounds of the game, while the "partial cooperation" strategy profile guarantees cooperation solely in the odd rounds of the game. Therefore, with an average extent of patience, $\frac{1}{2} \leq \delta < \frac{\sqrt{2}}{2}$, in return for the increase of the present payoff from 2 to 3 (the increase that the player can achieve by playing D instead of C in the present round), the player is prepared to relinquish the relatively small future incremental payoff that she will obtain if both players adhere to "partial cooperation" (the increment in excess of the payoff of 1 that she can always guarantee herself by always playing D), but she is not prepared to waive the higher future increment payoff that is guaranteed by the grim-trigger strategy profile, yielding constant cooperation.

On the other hand, a player endowed with greater patience $\delta \geq \frac{\sqrt{2}}{2}$ is not prepared to forgo the future increment payoff even when it derives solely from partial cooperation (in the strategies we have defined here). In this case, each of the two strategy profiles constitutes a subgame perfect equilibrium.

23.4   ## The one-deviation principle in repeated games

When we examined, in the examples reviewed so far, whether it is worth a player's while to deviate from her strategy following a particular history (given her rival's strategy), it was easy for us to find the optimal strategy for that player subsequent to such deviation. But in more complicated examples this is not necessarily the case. After a player has once deviated from her strategy, it may be worth her while to keep deviating from it in numerous rounds as the game progresses, perhaps even an infinite number of times. Checking out all these possibilities is complicated and could hinder verification of whether the first deviation was worthwhile.

This is where the one-deviation principle in repeated games comes to our aid.

Theorem 23.1

If there is no subgame at which a player can strictly improve her payoff by deviating from her strategy at the beginning of the subgame only, then no complex deviation, that involves a deviation in a finite or infinite number of rounds, can improve her payoff in any subgame.

Proof

The proof is by contradiction. Assume for the moment that the conclusion of the theorem is false, and that there exists a subgame that commenced at round n' following a particular game history $h^{n'}$, in which a complicated deviation σ'_i by player i from her original strategy, σ_i, improves her payoff in that subgame (given the strategy profile σ_{-i} of the other player or players). We will now show how this implies that the premise of the claim is false: we will find another deviation, σ'', which differs from σ_i only at the beginning of another particular subgame, commencing after $n'' \geq n'$ rounds, and which improves the player's payoff in that subgame. The existence of the deviation σ'' contradicts the premise that there is no subgame in which the player can improve her payoff by means of deviating from σ_i solely at the start of that subgame.

We will construct the deviation σ''_i in two stages:

1. We will denote by $g > 0$ the improvement in the payoff of player i in the subgame commencing after the history $h^{n'}$ as a result of her deviating from σ_i to σ'_i.

    Likewise, we will denote by $M \geq 0$ the maximum possible improvement in the payoff of player i in each individual game round. (M is the difference between the player's highest and lowest payoff in the payoff matrix.)

    Due to the discounting of future payoffs, the improvements in payoff to the player in the game rounds taking place in the distant future make a small contribution to the overall improvement g. The increase in payoffs due to the deviation from σ_i to σ'_i in the rounds succeeding the round t after the beginning of the subgame contribute to a small improvement in the overall payoff in the subgame, an improvement that does not exceed:

$$\sum_{k=t}^{\infty} M\delta^{k-1} = \frac{M\delta^{t-1}}{1-\delta} \xrightarrow[t\to\infty]{} 0$$

In particular, there exists a sufficiently remote game round t_0 for which:

$$\sum_{k=t_0}^{\infty} M\delta^{k-1} = \frac{M\delta^{t_0-1}}{1-\delta} < \frac{g}{2}$$

Therefore, if we replace σ_i' by the original strategy σ_i commencing from round t_0 onwards, we will obtain the strategy $\hat{\sigma}_i'$ which is different from the original strategy σ_i only in the game rounds $1,\dots,t_0-1$, which still brings about an improvement (of at least $\frac{g}{2}$) in player i's payoff in the subgame commencing after the history $h^{n'}$.

2. We will denote by $n'' < t_0$ the remotest round in which the deviation from σ_i to $\hat{\sigma}_i'$ leads to some improvement in the payoff of player i in the subgame commencing after the history $h^{n'},$[7] and we will denote by $h^{n''}$ a history of length n'' following which the deviation from σ_i to $\hat{\sigma}_i'$ leads to such an improvement. If we change $\hat{\sigma}_i'$ by restoring the original strategy σ_i commencing from the round $n'' + 1$ onwards, we will obtain a strategy σ_i'' that is different from σ_i only in the first n'' rounds, and in which the deviation in round n'' from σ_i to σ'' improves the payoff of player i in the subgame commencing after the history $h^{n''}$. In this subgame, the deviation from σ_i to σ'' takes place only at the start of the subgame, contrary to the premise of the theorem that there exists no subgame in which a deviation from σ_i only at the beginning of which improves the player's payoff in the subgame.

QED

As stated, the principle of the one deviation makes it easier for us to verify that a given strategy profile is a subgame perfect equilibrium: in order to do so, it suffices to verify that in each subgame no deviation by a player at the beginning of the subgame will improve her payoff in the subgame, and there is no need to examine whether the payoff to the player in the subgame can improve as a result of more complicated deviations on the part of the player in the subgame – deviations that involve changes in numerous game rounds.

23.5 Equilibrium payoffs

So far we have found a number of subgame perfect equilibria in which the players cooperate throughout all rounds of the game: the equilibrium with the grim-trigger strategies, and the equilibria with strategies in which the punishment phase is limited to various lengths of time. All these equilibria guarantee the players the same average payoff, at the level of 2. Likewise, we have also found equilibria with no cooperation at all, at which the average payoff, at the level of 1, is much lower, and also equilibria with partial cooperation, at which the average payoff per player, $\frac{2+\delta}{1+\delta}$, falls somewhere between these two extremes.

What additional average payoffs can result in subgame perfect equilibria of the repeated Prisoner's Dilemma? Obviously, such average equilibrium payoffs must meet two conditions:

---

[7] While the other players adhere to their original strategies σ_{-i}.

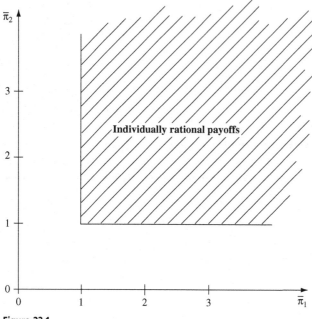

Figure 23.1

1. **Individual rationality**: if a player plays D throughout all rounds of the game, she can guarantee herself a payoff at a level of at least 1 in every game round, and, accordingly, an average payoff $\bar{\pi}_i$ of at least 1 in the entire game. Therefore, at any subgame perfect equilibrium, the average payoff of any player must be at least 1: if a particular strategy profile yields the player an average payoff lower than 1, then a deviation by the player to the strategy "always play D" will increase her payoff, and hence the original strategy profile is not a Nash equilibrium (and certainly not a subgame perfect equilibrium). See Figure 23.1.

    Note that 1 is indeed the highest average payoff that a player can guarantee herself in the game: if, in a particular game round, the player chooses C instead of D, while her rival plays D in all rounds of the game, the player's average payoff will be lower than 1.[8]

2. **Feasibility**: the average payoff profile of the players must be a result of a pair of strategies that they adopt. In the case of the Prisoner's Dilemma, these average payoff profiles are bounded within the parallelogram whose nodes are the four payoffs appearing in the game matrix. See Figure 23.2.

Why?

---

[8] In other words, "always play D" is a security strategy (a maxmin strategy – see Chapter 12) of the player. This is the strategy that yields the player the highest payoff under the assumption that her rival will always act in such a way as to minimize this payoff. (In the case of the Prisoner's Dilemma, the rival can do this by playing D in every round.)

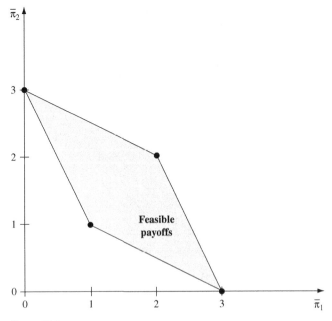

Figure 23.2

A. If the players play the profile (C, C) throughout the game, their average payoffs will be $(2, 2)$.

B. If the players play the profile (C, D) throughout the game, their average payoffs will be $(0, 3)$.

C. If the players play the profile (D, C) throughout the game, their average payoffs will be $(3, 0)$.

D. If the players play the profile (D, D) throughout the game, their average payoffs will be $(1, 1)$.

Any strategy profile of the players (*including* a strategy profile that is an equilibrium) defines, in particular, how the game will actually evolve – at what rounds the combination (C, C) will be played, and likewise at what rounds each of the other combinations (C, D), (D, C) and (D, D) will be played. The frequency and timing of play of each combination define a weighted average of the corresponding payoffs $(2, 2)$, $(0, 3)$, $(3, 0)$, and $(1, 1)$.

Altogether, these two conditions – individual rationality and feasibility, taken in tandem – define the domain in which all the average equilibrium payoffs of the repeated Prisoner's Dilemma are to be found. In Figure 23.3, the domain in which the individually rational average payoff profiles are to be found is denoted with diagonal shading, and the domain in which the feasible average payoff profiles are found appears in gray. The average equilibrium payoffs are therefore to be found at the intersection of these two domains.

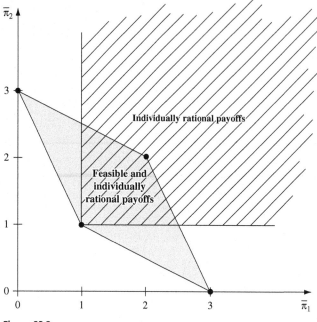

Figure 23.3

Is the converse also true? That is, can every combination of average payoffs that is both individually rational and feasible be obtained at a subgame perfect equilibrium of the Prisoner's Dilemma? As we have already seen, the answer depends *inter alia* on the discount factor δ. We have seen that the strategy profile "always play D" is a subgame perfect equilibrium for every $\delta > 0$, with an average payoff of 1 to each player. The grim-trigger strategy profile, meanwhile, which yields an average payoff of 2 to each player, is a subgame perfect equilibrium only for $\delta \geq \frac{1}{2}$.

Accordingly, we will want to know for which pairs of numbers $(\overline{\pi}_1, \overline{\pi}_2)$ there **exist** discount factors δ for which $(\overline{\pi}_1, \overline{\pi}_2)$ is the combination of average payoffs at **some** subgame perfect equilibrium. The next important theorem answers this question.

Theorem 23.2: The folk theorem for the repeated Prisoner's Dilemma

For any average payoff profile that is both individually rational and feasible in the repeated Prisoner's Dilemma there exists a minimal discount factor $\delta^* < 1$, such that for every discount factor $\delta^* \leq \delta < 1$, there exists a subgame perfect equilibrium of the repeated Prisoner's Dilemma that leads to this average payoff profile.

The origin of the name "the folk theorem" can be traced to the fact that theorems of this kind were accepted as valid among game theorists from the initiation of the study of repeated games, even though the formal proofs were presented only later.

Since (D,D) is a Nash equilibrium of the Prisoner's Dilemma, Theorem 23.2 is a corollary from the following "folk theorem."[9]

Theorem 23.3: Friedman's folk theorem (1971)[10]

Consider a game with a finite number of actions per player $i \in I$ and let $(a_i^*)_{i \in I}$ be a Nash equilibrium in which the players' payoffs are $(r_i^*)_{i \in I}$. If $q_i \geq r_i^*$ for every $i \in I$, and $(q_i)_{i \in I}$ is a feasible payoff profile in the game (i.e. a weighted average of the payoff profiles in the game matrix), then there exists a minimal discount factor δ^*, such that for every discount factor $\delta^* \leq \delta < 1$ there exists a subgame perfect equilibrium of the repeated game in which the average payoff profile is $(q_i)_{i \in I}$.

Thus, in the repeated Prisoner's Dilemma, there is a continuum of payoff profiles that can be obtained at a subgame perfect equilibrium. Therefore, this solution concept does not allow for any unequivocal prediction of the behavior of rational players. Ongoing cooperation is consistent with such rational behavior, but many other behavioral profiles are equally rational.

23.6 Renegotiation proofness

Can additional restrictions be imposed on the solution concept so as to narrow down the range of possible outcomes of the repeated game? One proposal in this spirit is **renegotiation proofness**.[11] Underlying the proposal is the following idea. On the one hand, a repeated game has a recursive structure, one that repeats itself every subgame: after every initial history, it is structurally identical to the game as a whole. Nevertheless, the players' strategies dictate different behavior in every subgame, in accordance with its precedent history. These different behaviors may

---

[9] More general "folk theorems" concerning the average payoff profiles at subgame perfect equilibria were proven by Aumann, R. J. and L. S. Shapley (1994), "Long-term Competition – A Game-theoretic Analysis," in N. Megiddo (ed.), *Essays in Game Theory in Honor of Michael Maschler*, New York: Springer-Verlag, pp. 395–409; Rubinstein, A. (1979), "Equilibrium in Supergames with the Overtaking Criterion," *Journal of Economic Theory* 21, 1–9; Rubinstein, A. (1994), "Equilibrium in Supergames," in N. Megiddo (ed.), *Essays in Game Theory in Honor of Michael Maschler*, New York: Springer-Verlag, pp. 17–27. (These results by Rubinstein and Aumann and Shapley were proven concurrently during the mid-1970s.) Fudenberg, D. and E. S. Maskin (1986), "The Folk Theorem in Repeated Games with Discounting or with Incomplete Information," *Econometrica* 54, 533–554; Fudenberg, D. and E. S. Maskin (1991), "On the Dispensability of Public Randomization in Discounted Repeated Games," *Journal of Economic Theory* 53, 428–438.

[10] Friedman, J. (1971), "A Non-cooperative Equilibrium for Supergames," *Review of Economic Studies* 38, 1–12.

[11] Farrell, J. and E. Maskin (1989), "Renegotiation in Repeated Games," *Games and Economic Behavior* 1, 327–360.

be thought of as **conventions** or **behavioral norms**. At the beginning of each subgame the players have an opportunity to muse on the behavioral norm on which they intend to base the game subsequently.

In a subgame perfect equilibrium, every player wishes to adhere to the behavioral norm dictated by the game history, under the assumption that the other players will do the same. But a situation can well be imagined in which all the players get together to reconsider whether this behavioral norm is in fact worth their while. If they find, in the set of norms with which they are acquainted, a different behavioral norm that is perceived by all to be preferable to the norm that they were about to play, they will prefer to adopt this alternative convention.

Formally, assume that the players' strategies in the game as a whole are $(\sigma_i)_{i \in I}$. Following a game history $h'_{n'}$, the players can ask themselves whether they would henceforth prefer to play the strategy profile that they would play if the game history were h_n rather than $h'_{n'}$. What is this alternative strategy profile? In the subgame commencing after the history h_n, the strategy profile $(\sigma_i)_{i \in I}$ of the players dictates that they play the strategy $(\sigma_i^{h_n})_{i \in I}$, which is defined by:

$$\sigma_i^{h_n}(h_k) = \sigma_i(h_n \circ h_k)$$

In other words, in the subgame commencing after h_n, the strategy $\sigma_i^{h_n}$ dictates that player i play, after the history h_k, the action that the strategy σ_i of the game as a whole dictates that she play after the history $h_n \circ h_k$ – the history that commences at h_n and concatenated with h_k.[12]

The strategy $\sigma_i^{h_n}$ is called the strategy of player i induced by the strategy σ_i in the subgame commencing after the history h_n.

Definition　We say that the strategy profile $(\sigma_i)_{i \in I}$ of the players in the repeated game is **(weakly) renegotiation-proof** if the following two conditions are satisfied:

1. The strategy profile σ_i constitutes a subgame perfect equilibrium.
2. There is no history h'_n, such that in the subgame commencing after h'_n all the players would prefer to play the profile strategy $(\sigma_i^{h_n})_{i \in I}$ which is induced by their strategies σ_i in some subgame commencing after some other history h_n.

The renegotiation proofness that this solution concept defines is indeed "weak," since the solution concept permits the players to "discuss" at the beginning of every subgame only strategy profiles that they "know," i.e. strategy profiles that they could play in some subgame given their strategies as initially defined for the repeated game

---

[12] The history h_k may, in particular, be the vacuous history h_0. In such case, $h_n \circ h_0 = h_n$.

as a whole (and therefore, in particular, for each of its subgames). The solution concept does not permit the players to discuss other strategy profiles, i.e. "behavioral norms" that do not belong to the inventory of behaviors agreed upon among the players and which appear across the various subgames.[13]

Question 23.6

Are the equilibria that we have examined so far in the repeated Prisoner's Dilemma renegotiation-proof?

Answer

The equilibrium with the strategies "always play D" for every player is indeed renegotiation-proof: in every subgame, i.e. following any possible history of the game – even if in some of the rounds one or two players "erroneously" cooperated – the players' strategies always dictate to them the same behavioral convention: "play D for ever more." Therefore, the players do not know any other behavioral conventions at all, and according to the solution concept of weak renegotiation proofness, their arsenal of conventions does not contain any behavioral convention that is preferable for both of them over the one that they are about to adopt. Hence, the equilibria with the strategies "always play D" are indeed (weakly) renegotiation-proof.

But what about the equilibria at which the players cooperate, in whole or in part? All the equilibria of this type that we have dealt with so far included a – longer or shorter – "punishment phase" from which both players suffered, even when only one of them had deviated from the pre-agreed cooperation format. Therefore, if and when the players reach the phase at which they are supposed to both play D for several rounds, and if they are given the option of "reconsidering" whether in fact to materialize the punishment phase or whether, alternatively, to revert promptly to the cooperation format, then they will, of course, prefer the second option. Therefore, these equilibria are not (weakly) renegotiation-proof.

Does there exist, in the repeated Prisoner's Dilemma, an equilibrium at which the players cooperate throughout all the game rounds, and which is renegotiation-proof? At such an equilibrium, not only must the deviant player be punished, the punishing player must herself emerge uninjured by the imposition of the punishment. Such a state of affairs is possible if the punished player plays C while the punishing player plays D, so that the punishing player enjoys a particularly high payoff (at a level of 3) during the punishment phase. Thus, if the punishing player is to benefit from

---

[13] The game theory literature suggests also other definitions of renegotiation proofness, which "permit" the players to discuss also strategy profiles that do not appear in any subgame of the strategy profile of the game as a whole. See, for example, Abreu, D., D. Pearce, and E. Stacchetti (1993), "Renegotiation and Symmetry in Repeated Games," *Journal of Economic Theory* 60, 217–240.

the imposition of the punishment, she will not consent to waive it and revert immediately to the cooperation format, even if the players "reconsider" the continuation of the game before the punishment phase.

We will now examine the following **make-up strategy** in the repeated Prisoner's Dilemma:

1. Play C in the first round.
2. In each of the following rounds:
   A. If in the previous round you played C and your rival played D, play D as long as the rival continues to play D, and revert to playing C only after a round in which she played C and you played D. (Consequently, resume acting in accordance with Rule 2.)
   B. Otherwise, play C.

Question 23.7

Show that when $\delta \geq \frac{1}{2}$, the make-up strategy profile is a (weakly) renegotiation-proof equilibrium.[14] (Hint: use the one-deviation principle.)

Answer

Three types of subgames exist under the make-up strategy profile:

(1) Subgames in which both players are supposed to cooperate (at the beginning of the game, after a round of cooperation, or after a round in which both players played D and which was not part of the punishment phase 2A).
(2) Subgames at the beginning of which player 1 is supposed "to punish" player 2 (because in one round or several rounds previously player 2 played D, and has since not played C). At the beginning of such a subgame, player 1 is supposed to play D and player 2 is supposed to play C.
(3) In subgames at the beginning of which player 2 is due to "punish" player 1. At the beginning of a such a subgame, player 2 is supposed to play D and player 1 is supposed to play C.

In every subgame of the type (1) that begins with cooperation on the part of both players, the players continue to cooperate when both adopt the make-up strategy, and therefore the average payoff of each of them is 2, and the overall payoff in the subgame is $\frac{2}{1-\delta}$.

Assume that one of the players deviates from Rule (1), or alternatively from Rule 2B in the make-up strategy only in round n – the deviation consisting of playing D instead of C, and getting a payoff of 3 instead of 2 – but later in the game reverts to the make-up strategy: in round $n + 1$ she "bows her head" for the duration of one round, in

---

[14] This exercise is based on Van Damme, E. (1989), "Renegotiation-Proof Equilibria in Repeated Prisoner's Dilemma," *Journal of Economic Theory* 47, 206–217.

which her rival chooses D while she plays C and gets a payoff of 0, and in round $n + 2$ and onwards, both players revert to the format of cooperation with a payoff of 2 to each of them. In this subgame the payoff of the player who deviated in round n is:

$$3 + 0 + \sum_{k=3}^{\infty} 2\delta^{k-1} = 3 + \frac{2\delta^2}{1 - \delta} = \frac{3 - 3\delta + 2\delta^2}{1 - \delta}$$

For $\delta \geq \frac{1}{2}$, this payoff is smaller than or equal to the payoff $\frac{2}{1-\delta}$ that she would obtain in the subgame if she did not deviate.

The subgame following such a deviation (which commences in round $n + 1$) is of the type (2) or (3), according to the identity of the "punishing" player. The payoff to the punishing player is:

$$3 + \sum_{k=2}^{\infty} 2\delta^{k-1} = 3 + \frac{2\delta}{1 - \delta} = \frac{3 - \delta}{1 - \delta}$$

which is higher than the payoff $\frac{2}{1-\delta}$ that she would obtain if she did not punish.

For the player being punished it is indeed worthwhile to "bow her head" and play C at the beginning of this subgame. Her payoff in the subgame is:

$$0 + \sum_{k=2}^{\infty} 2\delta^{k-1} = \frac{2\delta}{1 - \delta}$$

If she were to "insist" on playing D, but in the next round would revert to the make-up strategy, then she would "bow her head" in the next round (i.e. play C while her rival plays D), and only after that the players would revert to a format of cooperation. Her payoff in the subgame would then be:

$$1 + 0 + \sum_{k=3}^{\infty} 2\delta^{k-1} = 1 + \frac{2\delta^2}{1 - \delta} = \frac{1 - \delta + 2\delta^2}{1 - \delta}$$

For $\delta \geq \frac{1}{2}$, this payoff does not exceed the payoff $\frac{2\delta}{1-\delta}$ that she would obtain in this subgame if she did not deviate.

To sum up, when $\delta \geq \frac{1}{2}$, under the make-up strategy profile it is the case that:

1. In subgames of the first type, in which the two players are supposed to cooperate, the payoff of each player in the subgame is $\frac{2}{1-\delta}$, and neither one of the players can improve her payoff if she deviates and plays D instead of C at the beginning of the subgame.

2. In subgames of the second type, at the beginning of which player 1 is supposed to punish player 2, player 1 is supposed to play D and player 2 is supposed to play C at the beginning of the subgame. Their payoffs in the subgame are $\frac{3-\delta}{1-\delta}$ to player 1 and $\frac{2\delta}{1-\delta}$ to player 2. Neither player can improve her payoff in the subgame by deviating from the make-up strategy at the start of the subgame.

3. In subgames of the third kind, at the beginning of which player 2 is supposed to punish player 1, player 2 is supposed to play D and player 1 is supposed to play C at the beginning of the subgame. Their payoffs in the subgame are $\frac{3-\delta}{1-\delta}$ to player 2 and $\frac{2\delta}{1-\delta}$ to player 1. Neither player can improve her payoff in the subgame by deviating from the make-up strategy at the beginning of the subgame.

Two conclusions may hence be drawn:

A. According to the one-deviation principle, the make-up strategy profile constitutes a subgame perfect equilibrium.

B. Since

$$\frac{2\delta}{1-\delta} < \frac{2}{1-\delta} < \frac{3-\delta}{1-\delta}$$

There is no subgame at the beginning of which both players will be interested to replace the equilibrium strategy profile which they are about to play by the equilibrium profile that they play in one of the other subgames:

- If in a subgame of type (1) they switch to playing the equilibrium of the subgames of type (2), then player 2 will lose by it; and if they switch to playing the equilibrium of the subgames (3), player 1 will lose by it.
- If in a subgame of the type (2) they switch to playing the equilibrium of subgames of the type (1) or the equilibrium of the subgames of the type (3), then player 1 will lose by it.
- If in a subgame of the type (3) they switch to playing the equilibrium of the subgame of the type (1) or the equilibrium of the subgames of the type (2), then player 2 will lose by it.

Hence we deduce that the make-up strategy profile constitutes a (weakly) renegotiation-proof equilibrium.

In the repeated Prisoner's Dilemma we have succeeded in finding a (weakly) renegotiation-proof equilibrium at which the players cooperate continuously throughout all the rounds of the game, for the same range of discount factors – $\delta \geq \frac{1}{2}$ – for which we found a subgame perfect equilibrium of cooperation (the equilibrium with the grim-trigger strategies). The additional requirement of renegotiation proofness did not, in this case, narrow down the scope of discount factors allowing for persistent cooperation. But Farrell and Maskin (1989) showed that many other games exist in which the requirement of renegotiation proofness strictly limits the range of payoffs that the players can obtain at equilibrium in the repeated game.

Games with an unbounded horizon: additional models and results

In the preceding chapter, we discussed the repeated Prisoner's Dilemma. In this game, the extent to which a player can "punish" or "reward" her rival in any round is fixed and predetermined. What happens in repeated games in which this extent is modifiable? How does this affect the set of equilibria in the game? We will examine this question in the following example.

Efficiency wages

According to the competitive economics model, in a perfect and frictionless market there should be no unemployment: if the supply of labor is greater than the demand for labor on the part of employers, workers will be prepared to work even at a lower wage – a wage at which employers will find it profitable to hire additional hands. The process of decrease in salaries will continue until the demand for employees equals the supply of labor.

In practice, however, even in competitive markets such as that of the United States, unemployment levels typically do not fall below 4–5 percent. One possible reason for such unemployment is the process of job search on the part of the unemployed, and the search for workers by potential employers. We discussed the modeling of job search and unemployment in Chapter 9.

We will now turn to examine another possible cause for the existence of a minimal level of unemployment, one that is related to the ongoing and repeated interaction between employers and employees.[1]

When an employee does not invest sufficient effort into the work process, he injures the employer, since the employer has perforce to pay the employee at least one wage before firing him; the employer may also lose the investment she made in training the employee. Therefore, if the cooperation between employer and

---

[1] This model is based on ideas presented in Shapiro, C. and J. E. Stiglitz (1984), "Equilibrium Unemployment as a Worker Discipline Device," *American Economic Review* 74, 433–444. The model in the article is formulated in continuous time, whereas in our case, the model presents some of the ideas of the original model in explicit terms of strategic interaction in a repeated game with discrete game rounds.

employee were to be short-lived, there would come about, under such circumstances, a severe problem of incentives between the **principal** (the employer) and the **agent** (the employee performing the task for her): the employer would estimate that even after the employee had been trained for the job, he would not invest the effort required of him in that role. In such a situation, the employer would not have hired the employee in the first place, and the business would not be sustainable. In the economic literature, this problem is called the **hold-up problem** between the principal and the agent, and how to cope with it is one of the topics addressed in economics by **contract theory**.

When the relationship between the employer and the employee is expected to be long-lasting, an opportunity for overcoming this problem may present itself. Were the employee sure that upon being fired he could promptly find new work, he would have no incentive to exert effort on the job and prevent the dismissal.[2] But when the employee is aware that if he is fired he will join the ranks of the unemployed, and can find new work only after a period of several months without any pay packet, he will have an incentive to invest effort in his work.

Such an incentive will indeed exist provided that the wage that the employee receives not only compensates him directly for the effort he invests in the course of his work but also includes an increment that is high enough for the employee not to want to find himself dismissed and devoid also of this increment for as long as he is unemployed. A wage that includes such an increment is called **an efficiency wage**. The term derives from the fact that the increment is designed to cause the employee to exert himself and work efficiently.

We will therefore assume that the employee's discount factor is $\delta < 1$, and that e is his "cost of effort": in respect of any particular month, in and of itself, the employee would prefer not to exert himself at work in consideration of a wage smaller than e, and would be prepared to make an effort only in consideration of a wage greater than or equal to e. The employee is indifferent between making an effort and obtaining a wage at exactly the level e, and not making an effort and relinquishing the wage.

If the employee's monthly wage is w, then the difference $w - e$ is the net utility to the employee from his work in a given month when he makes an effort. If he makes no effort and even so gets the wage w, his utility is w. If he makes no effort whatsoever and gets no wage, his utility is 0.

Thus, the (discounted) utility V_1 to the employee when he exerts himself at work is:

$$V_1 = (w - e) \sum_{k=1}^{\infty} \delta^{k-1} = \frac{w - e}{1 - \delta}$$

---

[2] There are, of course, additional factors that could cause the employee to want to exert himself on the job, such as the wish to cope with workplace challenges, to gain experience, and so forth. The present model ignores these additional factors.

What, by contrast, is the utility V_0 of an employee who never makes any effort while working for an employer, and is always fired after just one month's work, following which he is unemployed for m months? This employee is gainfully employed only once in $m+1$ months, but in every month in which he works his utility is w, since he invests no effort in his work. Altogether, this utility is:

$$V_0 = w \sum_{k=0}^{\infty} \delta^{(m+1)k} = \frac{w}{1 - \delta^{m+1}}$$

For the employee to want to invest an effort while on the job, it must be the case that:

$$V_1 = \frac{w - e}{1 - \delta} \geq V_0 = \frac{w}{1 - \delta^{m+1}}$$

i.e.:

$$w \geq e \frac{1 - \delta^{m+1}}{\delta - \delta^{m+1}}$$

As we anticipated, the minimal wage:

$$w_1 = e \frac{1 - \delta^{m+1}}{\delta - \delta^{m+1}} > e$$

that the employer must pay in order for the employee to wish to invest an effort is greater than the minimal compensation e required in order to cause the employee to invest an effort in a single month. The wage must also cause the employee to overcome the temptation to obtain a utility of w_1 in lieu of $w_1 - e$ in the current month, under the threat of losing his job next month. The less patience the employee has, i.e. the smaller δ is, the higher this minimal wage w_1 must be, since then the temptation to earn w_1 instantly (without any effort) becomes greater. On the other hand, the greater the anticipated number of months of unemployment m, the more painful the threat of dismissal, and the minimal wage w_1 that will cause the employee to exert himself diminishes. (Verify these claims using the above equation.)

Assume that every employer has a positive profit even if he pays every employee the wage w_1 and each of the employees exerts himself, but the employer will lose money from having on the payroll an employee who makes no effort – even if the wage that he pays the employee is very small. We will now show that there is a subgame perfect equilibrium at which every employee is prepared to make an effort at work only at a wage of at least w_1, while every employer who is seeking staff offers work to unemployed persons coming to her for a job at a monthly wage of w_1, and does not fire them as long as they invest an effort in work.[3]

---

[3] At this equilibrium, the employees are never dismissed from their jobs, and therefore we are implicitly assuming here that the unemployed persons in the economy are young people who have only just joined the

Any employer may deviate from her strategy at the beginning of any month. Such deviation may find expression in the offer of a monthly wage that is higher or lower than w_1. Under the above assumptions such a deviation is suboptimal: since the employee will exert himself even at a salary of w_1, the employer will make less of a profit if she offers the employee a wage that is higher than w_1; and if the employer hires the employee at a wage that is lower than w_1, the employee will not make any effort, and will occasion the employer a loss during every month in which he is employed.

Is it worth the employee's while to deviate from his strategy? Any employee can deviate from his strategy only in months in which he is employed. The subgame commencing in such a period has precisely the same structure as the game as a whole. Therefore, according to the one-deviation principle, it suffices to ascertain that the employee:

A. will not prefer not to shirk if his monthly wage w is at least w_1, and also
B. will not prefer to make an effort if his monthly wage w is less than w_1

under the assumption that in the future, he will revert to his original strategy (to make an effort in any period in which he is employed as long as his monthly wage is at least w_1), and that any offer of work that he receives in the future will be at a monthly wage of w_1.

We will now examine these two possible deviations.

1. If the employee shirks despite the fact that $w \geq w_1$, his discounted payoff will be:

$$w + (w_1 - e) \sum_{k=m+2}^{\infty} \delta^{k-1} = w + \delta^{m+1} \frac{w_1 - e}{1 - \delta}$$

Why? In the first month he will enjoy a wage of w without making any effort, as a result of which he will be fired and will become unemployed for a period of m months; and in the month $m + 2$, a subgame will commence in which an employer hires him to work at a wage of w_1 and the employee constantly exerts himself and is therefore not dismissed. However, if he adheres to his original strategy and regularly makes an effort with the first employer, he will not be dismissed and his discounted payoff will be:

job-seekers market, and every such individual ultimately finds work after m months of searching – either with an existing employer who is expanding the scope of her business activity, or with a new employer who has begun operating in the market. In the original article, Shapiro and Stiglitz (1984) assumed that employers are sometimes constrained to dismiss employees who have made an effort at work due to the downsizing of their business activity, or because they cannot directly supervise the level of effort of each employee, but merely his output; and they therefore dismiss an employee with a low output even when the low output derives from causes that are beyond the employee's control. Under these assumptions, employees are fired from their jobs and are hired by other employers after a certain period of time even when the number of employers and employees in the economy remains unchanged.

$$(w - e) \sum_{k=1}^{\infty} \delta^{k-1} = \frac{w - e}{1 - \delta}$$

This payoff is in fact higher, since:

$$(w - e) \sum_{k=1}^{\infty} \delta^{k-1} = (w - e) \sum_{k=1}^{m+1} \delta^{k-1} + (w - e) \sum_{k=m+2}^{\infty} \delta^{k-1}$$

$$= (1 - \delta^{m+1}) \frac{w - e}{1 - \delta} + \delta^{m+1} \frac{w - e}{1 - \delta} \geq (1 - \delta^{m+1}) \frac{w - e}{1 - \delta} + \delta^{m+1} \frac{w_1 - e}{1 - \delta}$$

$$= (1 - \delta^{m+1}) \frac{w - w_1 \frac{\delta - \delta^{m+1}}{1 - \delta^{m+1}}}{1 - \delta} + \delta^{m+1} \frac{w_1 - e}{1 - \delta}$$

$$\geq (1 - \delta^{m+1}) \frac{w - w \frac{\delta - \delta^{m+1}}{1 - \delta^{m+1}}}{1 - \delta} + \delta^{m+1} \frac{w_1 - e}{1 - \delta} = w + \delta^{m+1} \frac{w_1 - e}{1 - \delta}$$

2. If the employee makes an effort even when the wage w paid to him is smaller than w_1, he will not be dismissed. Under the assumption that neither the employer nor the employee will later deviate from their original strategies, the employer will offer the employee a monthly wage of w_1 commencing from the following month, and the employee will regularly invest an effort. Therefore, the employee's total payoff will be:

$$w - e + (w_1 - e) \sum_{k=2}^{\infty} \delta^{k-1} = w - e + \frac{\delta(w_1 - e)}{1 - \delta}$$

In contrast, if the employee adheres to his original strategy, he will shirk when $w < w_1$, will be fired after one month of work, and after m months of unemployment will find a new job at a monthly wage of w_1, at which he will constantly exert effort. His overall payoff will therefore be:

$$w + (w_1 - e) \sum_{k=m+2}^{\infty} \delta^{k-1} = w + \frac{\delta^{m+1}(w_1 - e)}{1 - \delta}$$

These two payoffs are equal:

$$w + \frac{\delta^{m+1}(w_1 - e)}{1 - \delta} = \left[w - e + \frac{\delta(w_1 - e)}{1 - \delta} \right] + e - \frac{(\delta - \delta^{m+1})(w_1 - e)}{1 - \delta}$$

$$= \left[w - e + \frac{\delta(w_1 - e)}{1 - \delta} \right] + e - \frac{(\delta - \delta^{m+1})\left(e \frac{1 - \delta^{m+1}}{\delta - \delta^{m+1}} - e \right)}{1 - \delta}$$

$$= \left[w - e + \frac{\delta(w_1 - e)}{1 - \delta} \right] + e - e = w - e + \frac{\delta(w_1 - e)}{1 - \delta}$$

Therefore the employee will not profit if he deviates from his strategy, according to which he makes no effort when his wage w is less than w_1.

Maghrebi merchants and Genoese merchants in the eleventh and twelfth centuries[4]

Two groups of merchants operated in the Mediterranean Basin in the eleventh and twelfth centuries – one from Genoa, Italy and the other from the Maghreb in North Africa. The Maghrebi merchants were Jews who had migrated to North Africa from Iraq, and were interconnected by family ties. When a Maghrebi merchant needed an overseas agent to handle the sale and distribution of merchandise he had shipped there, he would always approach another Maghrebi merchant to serve as his agent. If satisfied with the agent's work, he would continue to employ that same agent whenever shipping merchandise to that destination. However, if the agent committed a breach of trust the merchant would not only cease to employ him but would also spread word of the malfeasance among the Maghrebi merchant community. As a result, no other Maghrebi merchant would hire the defaulting agent.

The Genoese merchants operated differently. When a Genoese merchant was pleased with the services of an overseas agent he had hired, he would continue to employ him. If, however, the agent committed a breach of trust, the merchant would forgo his services but without troubling himself to spread word of the malfeasance among his fellow merchants of Genoa. As a result, the agent, without a stain to his name, would rejoin the pool of potential agents to be hired by the Genoese merchants.

Assume, for the sake of simplicity, that the agent's wage, w, was calculated as a fraction of the value of the merchandise W that was shipped out to be sold, and that a dishonest agent would pocket the entire consideration W, instead of contenting himself with the agreed payment of w. If the merchant who had hired him was Genoese, that agent would be forced to wait m trading rounds until being asked to serve again as agent for some merchant from Genoa. If the merchant who had hired the defaulting agent was a Maghrebi, that agent would never find employment again.

A. Find a subgame perfect equilibrium in the repeated game between the Maghrebi merchants and their agents, and between the Genoese merchants and their agents. In every such game, the merchant must offer the agent a consideration of $w > 0$, and when the merchandise reaches the agent he must decide whether or not to defraud the merchant. Assume that the discount factor is δ. In which set of merchants is the consideration to the agent w the higher? Explain why.

---

[4] The model in this question is a highly simplified version of the model in Greif, A. (1994), "Cultural Beliefs and the Organization of Society: A Historical and Theoretical Reflection on Collectivist and Individualist Societies," *Journal of Political Economy* 102, 912–950.

This was a ground-breaking study in game theory as an analytic tool in economic history. Such analyses in economic history are henceforth called "analytic narratives." See also the review Greif, A. (2002), "Economic History and Game Theory," in R. J. Aumann and S. Hart (eds.), *Handbook of Game Theory with Economic Applications*, Volume 3, Amsterdam: North-Holland. pp. 1989–2024.

B. In the twelfth century, the volume of trade in the Mediterranean expanded. The Maghrebi merchants sent members of their families to migrate to potential trading destinations and continued to employ them as agents, but now had the opportunity also to hire non-Maghrebi individuals as agents. The Genoese merchants did not migrate to the trading destinations; they, too, encountered the opportunity to hire agents they had not engaged in the past, and in particular they encountered the opportunity to hire Maghrebi merchants as agents.

Was it worthwhile for the Maghrebi merchants to hire the services of non-Maghrebi agents? Was it worthwhile for the Genoese merchants to hire the services of the Maghrebis as agents? Try to answer these questions on the basis of the model in section A. Which method of trading could be expected, in your opinion, to prove durable over time – that of the Genoese merchants or that of the Maghrebi merchants? Explain your argument.

Answer   A. If an agent of a Genoese merchant or a Maghrebi merchant is not guilty of theft, he is engaged continuously by the merchant, and his overall payoff is:

$$w \sum_{k=1}^{\infty} \delta^{k-1} = \frac{w}{1 - \delta}$$

If an agent of a Genoese merchant acts dishonestly whenever he is hired, he finds himself being hired only once in $m + 1$ trading rounds: after each instance of dishonesty he is fired by the merchant, and is rehired, by another merchant, only after m trading rounds. Nevertheless, his profit in each instance of dishonesty is W, such that his total discounted payoff is:

$$W \sum_{k=0}^{\infty} \delta^{(m+1)k} = \frac{W}{1 - \delta^{m+1}}$$

The position of a dishonest Maghrebi agent is even worse – he gets a payoff of W the first time, but afterwards no Maghrebi merchant will ever hire him again. Therefore, W is his entire payoff.

Thus, the payoff of an honest agent working for a Genoese merchant is at least that of a dishonest agent if and only if:

$$\frac{w}{1 - \delta} \geq \frac{W}{1 - \delta^{m+1}}$$

i.e. if and only if:

$$w \geq w_G \equiv \frac{1 - \delta}{1 - \delta^{m+1}} W$$

Therefore, a subgame perfect equilibrium exists in the game between the Genoese merchants and their agents, at which the merchants offer every agent the payoff w_G, and the agents do not commit malfeasance. (Prove this, using the arguments we developed in the model of the efficiency wage: in particular, use the one-deviation principle.)

On the other hand, the payoff of an honest Maghrebi agent in the service of a Maghrebi merchant is at least the payoff of a dishonest agent if and only if:

$$\frac{w}{1-\delta} \geq W$$

i.e. if and only if:

$$w \geq w_M \equiv (1-\delta) W$$

Therefore, there exists a subgame perfect equilibrium at which the Maghrebi merchants offer their agents the payoff w_M, and the latter do not commit malfeasance. (Prove this!)

We see that $w_G > w_M$: in order for an agent of a Genoese merchant not to act dishonestly, he must be paid more than the agent of the Maghrebi merchant. This is because the "punishment" for dishonesty is less severe in the case of the Genoese merchant's agent. This punishment consists of unemployment for the duration of m trading rounds, compared with permanent outcast status in the case of the Maghrebi agent. In other words, the Maghrebi agent has more to lose if he commits malfeasance, and therefore even the lower payoff of w_M will suffice to cause him to refrain doing so.

B. With the expansion of trade, Maghrebi agents may be happy to serve as agents for Genoese merchants and receive a commission of w_G which is higher than the commission they get from the Maghrebi merchants. Yet agents who have worked for Maghrebi merchants are unlikely to content themselves with the commission of w_M that the Maghrebi merchant customarily pays. The Maghrebi merchants, therefore, will probably continue to hire Maghrebi agents only – as, indeed, actually was the case. But if Genoese merchants, too, start using the services of those Maghrebi agents, the latter may, ultimately, switch to working primarily in the service of the Genoese merchants. In the long run, this turn of events is liable to topple the trading method of the Maghrebi merchants.

In the historic case at hand the Maghrebi merchant community ceased to exist as such for a different reason: at the end of the twelfth century, the ruler of Egypt outlawed trading by the Maghrebi merchants, whereupon they were assimilated into the Jewish communities in their places of domicile.

The two examples cited above illustrate the connection between the duration of the punishment phase at equilibrium and its intensity in games in which the player being punished has two available actions. The lower the intensity of the possible punishment in the game, the longer the punishment phase that is required at equilibrium.

What happens in repeated games in which each player has more than two possible actions in each game round? In such games, a substitution may prevail between the duration of the punishment phase and the intensity thereof, a substitution that finds expression at various equilibria of the same game. In order to guarantee cooperation over time, the player must threaten his rival with a long punishment phase when the intensity of the punishment is low; but if the player threatens to punish his rival with an action that will cause him the most severe possible damage, then the rival will prefer to continue to cooperate even if the threatened punishment phase is relatively short. We will demonstrate this now.

24.2   Stable cartel[5]

In Chapter 8 we presented the Cournot model of quantity competition between two manufacturers who must simultaneously choose the quantities q_1, q_2 that they produce. If the overall quantity that is to be produced is $Q = q_1 + q_2$, then the manufacturers will have to sell each product unit at a price $P = A - Q$ in order for there to be a demand for all of the Q units that are to be produced.[6] Assuming production costs to be negligible, the manufacturers' profit will be:

$$\Pi_1(q_1, q_2) = Pq_1 = (A - q_1 - q_2)q_1$$
$$\Pi_1(q_1, q_2) = Pq_2 = (A - q_1 - q_2)q_2$$

At a Nash equilibrium of the Cournot model, each manufacturer will produce:

$$q^C = \frac{A}{3}$$

and the profit of each manufacturer will be:

$$\Pi^C \equiv \Pi_1(q^C, q^C) = \Pi_2(q^C, q^C) = \left(A - \frac{A}{3} - \frac{A}{3}\right)\frac{A}{3} = \frac{A^2}{9}$$

In order to maximize their total profits $PQ = (A - Q)Q$, the manufacturers had to join forces and jointly produce the quantity $Q^M = \frac{A}{2}$ (this is the quantity that a manufacturer would produce if it were a monopoly, i.e. if it were the sole manufacturer in

[5] This example is based on the example in Gibbons, R. (1992), *Game Theory for Applied Economists*, Princeton University Press, section 2.3.C.
[6] A is a parameter of the demand function in this sector.

the sector producing the commodity). In order to share the profit equally between the two, each manufacturer would then have to produce only $q^M = \frac{A}{4}$ and its profit would increase to:

$$\Pi^M \equiv \Pi_1(q^M, q^M) = \Pi_2(q^M, q^M) = \left(A - \frac{A}{4} - \frac{A}{4}\right)\frac{A}{4} = \frac{A^2}{8}$$

An alliance agreement of this kind is called a **cartel**. According to our analysis in Chapter 8, a cartel agreement is not a self-enforcing stable agreement; it does not constitute a Nash equilibrium in the game. This is because if firm 1, for example, produces the quantity q^M, firm 2's best reply is to produce:

$$q' \equiv BR_2(q^M) = \frac{A - q^M}{2} = \frac{A - \frac{A}{4}}{2} = \frac{3A}{8}$$

This quantity profile will yield player 2 the profit:

$$\Pi' \equiv \Pi_2\left(\frac{A}{4}, \frac{3A}{8}\right) = \left(A - \frac{A}{4} - \frac{3A}{8}\right)\frac{3A}{8} = \frac{9A^2}{64} > \Pi^M$$

But what happens if the game between the manufacturers is repeated numerous times? Consider, for instance, the following repeated-game strategy of a manufacturer, which we will designate the **Cournot-cartel strategy**:

1. Produce q^M in the first round.
2. In each of the following rounds:
   A. If you or your rival produced more than q^M in the preceding round, produce q^C for the duration of ℓ rounds, and in the round $\ell + 1$ again produce q^M. Follow Rule 2 again only in the succeeding round.
   B. Otherwise, produce q^M.

Question 24.2

What is the minimal punishment phase ℓ for which there exists a subgame perfect equilibrium at which both manufacturers use the Cournot-cartel strategy, when their discount factor is δ?

Answer

According to the one-deviation principle, in order to verify that the Cournot-cartel strategy profile is a subgame perfect equilibrium, it suffices to verify that a manufacturer cannot improve its average profit by deviating in a unique game round.

There are two types of histories following which a manufacturer may consider deviating from this strategy:

(1) A history following which both manufacturers are supposed to produce q^M. (Every history ending at the round in which each of the manufacturers produced

q^M or less is such a history; likewise, a history in which the "punishment phase" ended is such a history.)

(2) A history following which both manufacturers are meant to produce q^C (i.e. a history leading to a "punishment phase").

We will therefore examine, for each of these two types of histories, on what conditions deviation by a manufacturer will be suboptimal for it.

It is obviously not worthwhile for a manufacturer to deviate following a type (2) history: in every round of the punishment phase, the rival manufacturer plays q^C and therefore q^C is a best reply in any such round in its own right. Moreover, the manufacturer's behavior during the phase in which its rival "punishes" it does not affect the rival's conduct after the punishment phase ends. Therefore, the manufacturer bearing the punishment cannot profit if it deviates from its strategy in a round in which its rival is "punishing" it.

What will happen if a manufacturer deviates following a type (1) history? It can make at most a profit of Π' for the duration of one round; in each of the next ℓ rounds it will earn Π^C; and commencing from round $\ell + 2$ both manufacturers will produce q^M, such that the manufacturer will earn Π^M in every round. Barring any deviation, the manufacturers produce q^M in each round, with a profit of Π^M in every round for each one of them. Therefore, such a deviation affects the profit only in the first $\ell + 1$ rounds of the subgame, and is suboptimal if and only if:

$$\Pi' + \Pi^C \sum_{k=2}^{\ell+1} \delta^{k-1} \le \Pi^M \sum_{k=1}^{\ell+1} \delta^{k-1}$$

i.e. if and only if:

$$\frac{9A^2}{64} + \frac{A^2}{9} \frac{\delta - \delta^{\ell+1}}{1 - \delta} \le \frac{A^2}{8} \frac{1 - \delta^{\ell+1}}{1 - \delta}$$

i.e.:

$$\ell \ge \ell^* \equiv \frac{\ln \frac{17\delta - 9}{8\delta}}{\ln \delta}$$

The graph of ℓ^* (as function of δ) appears in Figure 24.1.

ℓ^* is defined only for $\delta > \frac{9}{17}$. That is to say, only when $\delta > \frac{9}{17}$ does there exist a finite punishment phase ℓ for which the Cournot-cartel strategy profile is a subgame perfect equilibrium. For $\delta = \frac{9}{17}$, the requisite punishment phase is infinite, i.e. following every deviation by a manufacturer from its strategy (in the direction of producing a quantity greater than q^M), the manufacturers must forever produce at equilibrium the quantity profile (q^C, q^C) in every round.

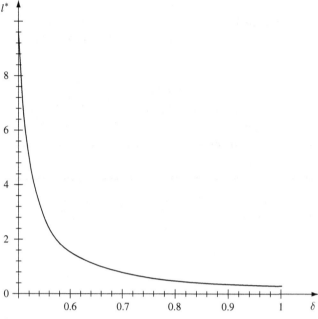

Figure 24.1

In the domain $\delta > \frac{9}{17}$, the expression $\ell^* = \frac{\ln\frac{17\delta-9}{8\delta}}{\ln\delta}$, the graph of which appears in Figure 24.1, is a decreasing function of δ: for a given δ, the minimal number of punishment rounds is $\lceil \ell^* \rceil$, i.e. the smallest integer that is greater than or equal to ℓ^*.

When the manufacturers are even more impatient and $\delta < \frac{9}{17}$,[7] there is no equilibrium at which they jointly produce the quantity $q^M = \frac{4}{4}$ which results in the maximization of their total profits, even if a deviation from that quantity would cause them forever to produce the quantity $q^C = \frac{4}{3}$, with smaller profits for both of them. This is because when $\delta < \frac{9}{17}$, the manufacturers cannot withstand the temptation, and not even the threat of any future prospect of cooperation being eliminated will deter them from trying to derive a one-shot profit at the rival's expense, by producing $q' = \frac{34}{8}$ in lieu of q^M. The problem derives from the fact that the discounted profit from such a deviation is relatively large when $\delta < \frac{9}{17}$.

If, from the outset, however, the manufacturers band together partially, producing, again and again, a quantity q^* which is greater than q^M (and smaller than q^C), then the

---

[7] This is the situation, for example, if the manager of each of the manufacturing firms does not intend to remain in office for very long, and therefore ascribes great importance to the firm's profits in the short term – profits that can boost the size of the bonus he gets in addition to his salary.

profit that each manufacturer can derive from a deviation from q^* (by producing a greater quantity, which is a best reply to the quantity q^* that the rival produces) likewise decreases. The larger q^* is, the less the temptation to deviate from it, and therefore the less the motivation of each manufacturer to derive a one-shot profit from such deviation and thereby frustrate the chance of future cooperation.

What is the smallest quantity q^* that can be produced by each manufacturer at an equilibrium in which the "punishment" for deviating from q^* is for both manufacturers forever to produce the quantity q^C? In other words, what is the (symmetric) equilibrium of this type that is the most efficient from the point of view of the manufacturers?

At this equilibrium, the profit of each manufacturer in each round is:

$$\Pi^* = (A - q^* - q^*)q^* = (A - 2q^*)q^*$$

When the rival produces q^*, however, the manufacturer's best reply (in the one-shot game) is to produce $BR(q^*) = \frac{A-q^*}{2}$ such that the manufacturer's profit in the round in which it decides to deviate will be:

$$\Pi'' = \left(A - \frac{A - q^*}{2} - q^*\right)\frac{A - q^*}{2} = \frac{(A - q^*)^2}{4}$$

As a result, however, in each of the succeeding rounds, its profit will decrease to $\Pi^C = (A - \frac{4}{3} - \frac{4}{3})\frac{4}{3} = \frac{A^2}{9}$ (the profit when both manufacturers produce the Cournot quantity $q^C = \frac{4}{3}$).

Therefore, such a deviation is not profitable if and only if:

$$\Pi'' + \Pi^C \sum_{k=2}^{\infty} \delta^{k-1} \le \Pi^* \sum_{k=1}^{\infty} \delta^{k-1}$$

i.e. if and only if:

$$\frac{(A - q^*)^2}{4} + \frac{A^2}{9}\frac{\delta}{1 - \delta} \le \frac{(A - q^*)q^*}{1 - \delta}$$

The highest value of q^* that satisfies this inequality is:

$$q^* = \frac{9 - 5\delta}{3(9 - \delta)}A$$

In the domain $\delta \in \left[0, \frac{9}{17}\right]$, q^* is a decreasing function of δ: see Figure 24.2.

When $\delta \to 0$, q^* progressively tends toward $q^C = \frac{4}{3}$: indeed, when the manufacturers ascribe importance to the current round only, no future punishment scares them, and they play the Cournot equilibrium. On the other hand, when $\delta \to \frac{9}{17}$, q^* tends to $q^M = \frac{4}{4}$, i.e. towards full cooperation between the manufacturers.

To sum up, when $\delta < \frac{9}{17}$, the quantity q^* that the manufacturers produce again and again at this equilibrium is strictly greater than the quantity q^M, which is the one that

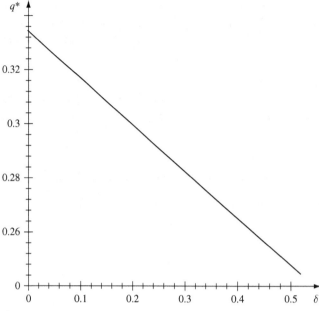

Figure 24.2

each of them must produce in order to maximize the sum of their profits. Thus, when the manufacturers have only limited patience, a certain degree of competitiveness between them persists at this equilibrium – less than at a Cournot equilibrium but more than at an efficient cartel. This happens despite the iterative character of the interaction between them: the unlimited horizon of this interaction does not suffice in order to bring them to full cooperation.

Such an equilibrium is consistent with the nature of the competition in many sectors. When a particular sector, for many years the domain of a unique manufacturer, is opened up to competition, overall output in the sector increases, while prices decrease. In other words, the competitors in the sector are unable to create and maintain among themselves a perfect cartel which will jointly produce the same low quantity that was produced in the past by the unique manufacturer in the sector. Such an agreement could have maximized the manufacturers' profits. But as we have seen, when the competitors are not strong on patience (i.e. when δ is not close to 1), they may succeed, at the equilibrium of the repeated game between them, in maintaining only partial cooperation, in which the quantities produced are higher, the price is lower, and the total profit of the manufacturers together is likewise lower.[8]

---

[8] The slide in prices, of course, which is injurious to the manufacturers, is beneficial to the consumers, and therefore the act of opening up a sector to competition may be perceived as serving the overall social interest: as a result of the heightened competition, the additional units appearing in the market are produced at a cost that is lower than the maximum price that consumers are willing to pay for them. (In the above

24.3   Sequential bargaining

Bargaining is an archetype of strategic interaction involving simultaneously aspects of both cooperation and competition. When the maximum price b that a buyer is willing to pay for a particular product exceeds the minimum price s at which the seller is prepared to sell the product, both buyer and seller will be satisfied if they reach an agreement on a sale transaction at price p between s and b. When $s < p < b$, both parties will prefer to conclude the transaction at price p than not to conclude it at all. On the other hand, the buyer will naturally prefer that the price p be as low as possible, while the seller will prefer that the price be as high as possible.

How, then, is the price determined? There are situations in which one of the parties names a price p, and all that remains to the other party is the option to choose between agreeing to conclude the transaction at the price p, or to refuse to do so. This is, for example, the situation when we enter a supermarket: each product is stamped with its price, and we must decide whether or not we wish to purchase the product at the specified price. In this state of affairs, the supermarket is actually making us a take-it-or-leave-it offer.

At a bazaar or a market, things are different. We ask the seller how much the good costs, and if the price seems too high we can go on to another stall or make the seller a counter-offer, naming a lower price. The seller, for his part, can decline our offer, or make his own counter-offer (which will usually be lower than his original offer but higher than the price we offered), and so on.

This type of bargaining is called **sequential bargaining** or **alternating-offers bargaining**, and it is prevalent not only in the market but also in bargaining between the parties to labor disputes, in legal wrangles, and in international conflicts. In such disputes, a certain interval usually elapses between the moment at which one of the parties

example, we assumed, for the sake of simplicity, that the production costs are negligible. This assumption is correct, for example, in the case of the production cost of a telephone call, when the volume of calls taking place is still smaller than the total calls that can be made with the existing telephone network infrastructure. In that situation, placing an additional telephone call may be perceived as worthwhile as long as a consumer exists in the market for whom this telephone call is strictly beneficial, and she is willing to pay a positive amount of money for it. Generally speaking, the production of an additional unit can be perceived as worthwhile from the point of view of the society as a whole, as long as there exists in the economy a consumer who is prepared to pay for this additional unit an amount that exceeds its production cost.) This notion of "efficiency" or **overall social surplus** would, in fact, be completely true to its name if the consumer purchasing this additional unit were the owner of the manufacturing firm, such that her utility from consuming the additional units would more than adequately compensate her for the decrease in profit of the firms under her ownership. But since, by and large, consumers are not the owners of the manufacturing firms, the increase of "efficiency" in the present example involves a benefit to one set of agents (the consumers) and injury to another set (the manufacturers). If the economy has no mechanism whereby those benefiting from the change compensate those who are injured by it, the notion of improvement in the *overall social surplus* reflects its literal meaning only to a limited extent.

makes an offer for settling the dispute and the time when the other party presents a counter-offer. During this interval, both parties continue to suffer from the prolongation of the dispute. During a strike, for example, the workers do not get paid, while the employer is injured by their having downed tools; when the dispute is on a war footing, both parties suffer the horrors of war as long as it persists; and so on. Therefore, with a given agreement in sight that is deemed by both parties to be preferable to the continuation of the dispute, both would prefer such agreement to be put into practice sooner rather than later.

In order to model bargaining of this type, we will examine the following game.[9] Jane and John are bargaining over how to divide a "pie" that represents the players' total surplus if they reach an agreement promptly. For example, in the case of the seller and the buyer that we described previously, the "pie" is the difference $b - s$ between the maximum price b that the buyer is willing to pay and the minimum price s at which the seller is willing to sell. Any price $p \in [s,b]$ defines the distribution of this "pie," in which the buyer gets the share $b - p$ (the difference between the maximum price b that he is willing to pay and the price he actually pays), while the seller gets the share $p - s$ (the difference between the consideration p that she actually receives and the minimum price at which she was prepared to sell). Thus the "pie" as a whole, which is the difference:

$$b - s = (b - p) + (p - s)$$

is the sum total of the profits of the buyer and the seller from the trade – the gains from trade. The bargaining over the price p between the parties determines how these gains are to be distributed among them.

For the sake of simplicity, assume that the size of the pie is 1. This means that when the pie is shared $(x, 1 - x)$ between the parties, player 1, Jane, gets the relative slice x of the pie, while player 2, John, gets the complementary relative slice $1 - x$ of the pie. How does the bargaining proceed? Player 1 is the first to go. She must offer player 2 a relative distribution of the pie, i.e. a pair of numbers $(x, 1 - x)$ in which she herself will get the share x of the pie while the second player gets the share $1 - x$. If player 2 accepts the offer, they share the pie in accordance with this offer and their payoffs are $(x, 1 - x)$, respectively. If player 2 rejects the offer, his turn comes, after a certain time interval Δ, to make player 1 a new proportionate sharing offer $(y, 1 - y)$: share y of the pie to her and share $(1 - y)$ to himself. If player 1 agrees, the pie is shared in accordance with the offer. If she rejects the offer, then after a further time interval, Δ, her turn comes to offer player 2 a new proportionate sharing $(z, 1 - z)$ of the pie. This game of alternating offers and counter-offers lasts until one of the players accepts the other's offer; if they never reach agreement, the payoff of each of them is 0.

Assume that both players have a time preference by which for every sharing agreement in which one of them gets a positive slice of the pie, they would prefer to realize the agreement sooner rather than later. This temporal preference on the part of the players is reflected in the existence of the discount factor δ: if the players arrive at the distribution agreement $(y, 1 - y)$ only in the second round (after the lapse of the time interval Δ), their payoffs are $(\delta y, \delta (1 - y))$; if they arrive at the distribution agreement $(z, 1 - z)$ in the third round (after the lapse of the time interval 2Δ), their payoffs are $(\delta^2 y, \delta^2(1 - y))$; and similarly, if they arrive at a distribution agreement $(q, 1 - q)$ in round n, their payoffs are $(\delta^{n-1} q, \delta^{n-1}(1 - q))$.

The game tree, therefore, is as shown in Figure 24.3. What subgame perfect equilibria are there in this game? The game has an unbounded horizon: a path in which the players never agree (and in which the payoff of each player is 0) is infinite, and does not end at a leaf. Therefore, the backward induction method cannot be used to find a subgame perfect equilibrium in this game, and we must adopt a different method in order to determine whether such an equilibrium exists here.

The game has a recursive structure that repeats itself: the subgame that begins in the third game round (after any combination of offers that was rejected in the first and second game rounds) is identical in structure to the game as a whole, as also to

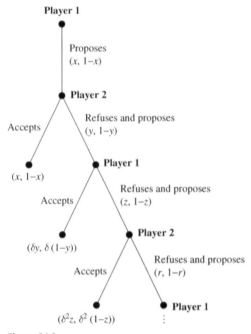

Figure 24.3

every subgame commencing at any odd round in which the proposer is player 1.[10] Similarly, all the subgames commencing in even rounds, in which the proposer is player 2, are structurally identical to one another. Accordingly, one may guess that the game has a subgame perfect equilibrium at which:

(1) Every offer (in every subgame) is always accepted.
(2) Each of the players always adopts the same strategy in every game round in which his or her turn arrives to propose a distribution of the pie, regardless of the history of the offers made (and rejected[11]) in the preceding rounds: player 1 always proposes the distribution $(x^*, 1 - x^*)$ and player 2 always proposes the distribution $(y^*, 1 - y^*)$.

If there exists a subgame perfect equilibrium with these two properties, player 1 knows that if, at the start of the game, she makes an offer that player 2 will reject, the payoff of the second player in the subgame commencing in the second round will be $\delta(1 - y^*)$. Therefore, at equilibrium with property (1), at which the offer of player 1 is accepted by player 2 as early as the first round, the slice $1 - x^*$ that is offered to player 2 must be at least the payoff that he will get in the second round:

$$1 - x^* \geq \delta(1 - y^*)$$

Since player 2 will be prepared to accept, in the first round, any slice that is not less than $\delta(1 - y^*)$, it will not be optimal from the point of view of player 1 to offer him a larger slice. Hence we infer that at such an equilibrium, an equality must obtain:

$$1 - x^* = \delta(1 - y^*)$$

Similarly, in the second round, player 2 knows that if he makes player 1 an offer that is less than δx^*, player 1 will refuse the offer (since, in the subgame commencing in the succeeding round, in which her turn to play comes again, she will offer x^* and the offer will be accepted); but player 1 has no reason to refuse, in the second round, a slice that is at least δx^*, and therefore it will be suboptimal from the point of view of player 2 to offer her a slice that is strictly greater than δx^*. Hence we deduce that at an equilibrium with property (1), at which the offer of player 2 is accepted in the second round, the following equality must obtain:

---

[10] The payoffs of each player in the subgame commencing in the third round are identical to the corresponding payoffs of the game as a whole, being multiplied by δ^2, and therefore the players' preferences in the subgame are identical to their preferences in the game as a whole. Similarly, in a subgame commencing in round $2n + 1$, in which player 1 is the proposer, the payoffs are identical to the corresponding payoffs in the game as a whole, multiplied by δ^{2n}, and therefore the players' preferences in the subgame are identical to their preferences in the game as a whole.

[11] As usual, even if, at equilibrium, all offers are accepted (and, in particular, if the offer of player 1 in the first round is accepted and the players distribute the pie without delay), the strategy of each player constitutes his or her inclusive operation plan, specifying what they will do if and when their turn arrives to play after any possible history of the game – including histories that are excluded by their own strategy or that of their rival.

$$y^* = \delta x$$

From the solution of this pair of equations we get:

$$x^* = \frac{1}{1+\delta}$$

$$y^* = \frac{\delta}{1+\delta}$$

Therefore, we conclude that there exists at most one subgame perfect equilibrium with the properties (1) and (2).

In order to check whether such an equilibrium indeed exists, we must first complete the description of the players' strategies:

- **The strategy σ_1^* of player 1:**
  - In every round in which it is your turn to propose, propose the distribution in which $x^* = \frac{1}{1+\delta}$.
  - In every round in which player 2 makes an offer, agree to every offer in which your share is at least $y^* = \delta x^* = \frac{\delta}{1+\delta}$.
- **The strategy σ_2^* of player 2:**
  - In every round in which it is your turn to propose, propose the distribution in which $y^* = \frac{\delta}{1+\delta}$.
  - In every round in which player 1 makes an offer, agree to every offer in which your share is at least $1 - x^* = \delta(1 - y^*) = \frac{\delta}{1+\delta}$.

Proposition 24.1

The strategy profile (σ_1^*, σ_2^*) is a subgame perfect equilibrium.

Proof

As explained above, we cannot use backward induction in order to examine the proposition, since the game tree has infinite paths that do not end at leaves (paths in which each of the players rejects her/his rival's offers again and again, so that the payoff to each player is 0).

How, then, are we to examine the proposition? Note that the one-deviation principle that we proved in the preceding chapter for repeated games holds good also in the present game: if no player has a subgame in which she can improve her payoff if she deviates from her strategy in a unique stage, then neither is there a larger set – finite or infinite – of stages, such that a deviation by a player in this set of stages will improve her payoff in some subgame.

In order to prove the one-deviation principle for the present game, we must show that if one of the players, $i = 1, 2$, has a strategy σ'_i that yields her a payoff higher than or equal to that yielded by the strategy σ_i in any subgame (given a strategy σ_j of the other player, $j \neq i$), and a strictly larger payoff in some subgame G, then an additional strategy σ''_i of player i can also be found, that yields her a payoff greater than or equal to the payoff from the strategy σ_i in any subgame, and being different from σ_i only at the beginning of another particular subgame G'', in which the deviation from σ_i to σ''_i strictly improves the payoff of i in G''.

The construction of σ''_i for the present game is actually identical to the construction of σ''_i in the proof of the one-deviation principle that we put forward for repeated games in the preceding chapter. Assume that there exists a stage n and a subgame G that commenced in stage n in which σ'_i improves by $g > 0$ the payoff to i compared with the payoff that strategy σ_i yields her. In this subgame G:

1. There exists a stage $n' > n$, such that the strategy $\hat{\sigma}'_i$, which is identical to σ'_i until stage $n' - 1$ and is identical to σ_i commencing from stage n and thereafter, improves by at least $\frac{g}{2} > 0$ the payoff to i compared with the payoff that the strategy σ_i yields her in that subgame G. This is because, commencing from the game stage n', the players' payoffs become smaller than $\delta^{n'}$, such that for a large enough n' (that satisfies $\delta^{n'} < \frac{g}{2}$) these payoffs will be smaller than $\frac{g}{2}$. Therefore, any change of σ'_i relative to σ_i from stage n'' and onwards – in a finite or even an infinite number of stages – cannot improve the payoff of i in the subgame G by more than $\frac{g}{2}$.
2. Since $\hat{\sigma}'_i$ differs from σ_i only in a finite number of stages, there exists a final game stage n'' for which there exists a game history $h^{n''}$ that leads to stage n'', such that thereafter, $\hat{\sigma}'_i$ strictly improves the payoff of player i in the subgame G, compared with the payoff yielded to i by the original strategy σ_i. Therefore, the strategy σ''_i, which is identical to $\hat{\sigma}'_i$ until the stage n'' and is identical to σ_i commencing from the stage $n'' + 1$ and thereafter, strictly improves the payoff of player i in the subgame G'' that commences after the history $h^{n''}$. In this subgame, σ''_i differs from σ'_i only at the beginning of the subgame.

Now that we have proved the one-deviation principle for the present game, we will use it to show that the strategy profile (σ^*_1, σ^*_2) that we have defined constitutes a subgame perfect equilibrium. According to the one-deviation principle, in order to verify that (σ^*_1, σ^*_2) is indeed a subgame perfect equilibrium, it suffices to show that there is no game stage in which a deviation by one of the players solely at that stage will strictly improve her payoff in the subgame commencing in that stage. And, indeed: at an odd stage $2n + 1$ ($n = 0,1,2 \dots$) with the strategy σ^*_1, player 1 proposes to player 2 the share $1 - x^* = \frac{\delta}{1+\delta}$. If she offers him a larger share, he will gladly accept, but the share that will then remain to player 1 will be smaller and she will lose thereby. If she offers player 2 a smaller share, he will refuse. As a result, the payoff of player 1 will decrease from $\delta^{2n}x^* = \frac{\delta^{2n}}{1+\delta}$ to a payoff of $\delta^{2n+1}y^* = \delta^{2n+1}\frac{\delta}{1+\delta} - \frac{\delta^{2n+2}}{1+\delta}$, which she will get after consenting to accept the share y^* that player 2 offers her in the succeeding stage (under the assumption that she will not deviate again from σ_1^* in the following stage).[12]

Neither can player 2 improve his payoff if he deviates from σ_2^* at an odd stage $2n + 1$. If he refuses the share x^* that player 1 offers him – a share that yields him a payoff at the level of $\delta^{2n}(1 - x^*) = \frac{\delta^{2n+1}}{1+\delta}$ – he will get exactly the same payoff, $\delta^{2n+1}(1 - y^*) = \delta^{2n+1}\left(1 - \frac{\delta}{1+\delta}\right) = \frac{\delta^{2n+1}}{1+\delta}$ in the following stage, in which player 1 gets the share y^* that he offers her.

Similarly, at an even stage $2n$ ($n = 1, 2 \dots$) with the strategy σ_2^*, player 2 offers player 1 the share $y^* = \frac{\delta}{1+\delta}$. If he offers her a greater share, she will gladly accept, but the share that will then remain to player 2 will be smaller, and he will lose thereby. If he offers player 1 a smaller share, she will refuse. As a result, the payoff of player 2 will decrease from $\delta^{2n-1}(1 - y^*) = \frac{\delta^{2n}}{1+\delta}$ to a payoff of $\delta^{2n}(1 - x^*) = \frac{\delta^{2n+2}}{1+\delta}$ which he will get after consenting to accept the share $1-x^*$ that player 1 will offer him in the following stage (under the assumption that player 2 will not deviate from σ_2^* again in the succeeding stage).

Neither can player 1 improve her payoff if she deviates from σ_1^* at an even stage $2n$. If she refuses the share y^* that player 2 offers her – a share yielding her a payoff at a level of $\delta^{2n-1}y^* = \frac{\delta^{2n}}{1+\delta}$ – she will obtain exactly the same payoff $\delta^{2n}x^* = \frac{\delta^{2n}}{1+\delta}$ in the following stage, in which player 2 will accept the share $1 - x^*$ that she offers him.

QED

At the equilibrium (σ_1^*, σ_2^*) that we found, the payoff $x^* = \frac{1}{1+\delta}$ of player 1 is greater than the payoff $1 - x^* = \frac{\delta}{1+\delta}$ of player 2. Thus, there is an advantage at this equilibrium in being in the proposer's position at the start of the game. However, the more patient the players become and $\delta \to 1$, this advantage progressively diminishes: the slice $\frac{\delta}{1+\delta}$ of player 2 approaches the size of the slice $\frac{1}{1+\delta}$ of player 1, and the sharing of the pie between the two bargaining parties gets closer to the egalitarian distribution $(\frac{1}{2}, \frac{1}{2})$.

What will happen if player 1's patience is not identical to that of player 2?

---

[12] Bear in mind that according to the one-deviation principle, we examine deviations by each player in a unique round.

Question 24.3

Find a subgame perfect equilibrium in the sequential bargaining game in the case in which the discount factor of player 1 is δ_1 and the discount factor of player 2 is δ_2.

Answer

We will again seek a subgame perfect equilibrium with properties (1) and (2), i.e. an equilibrium at which all offers are accepted, and each player has a unique offer that she/he always offers when her/his turn comes. The minimal slice $1 - x^*$ that player 2 will accept in the first stage is:

$$1 - x^* = \delta_2(1 - y^*)$$

Assume that y^* is the slice that player 2 will offer to player 1 and that she will consent to accept in the second stage; therefore, in the first stage it would indeed be suboptimal for player 1 to offer player 2 a slice larger than $\delta_2(1 - y*)$. Similarly, the minimal slice y^* that player 1 will consent to accept in the second stage is:

$$y^* = \delta_1 x^*$$

if $1 - x^*$ is the slice that she will offer player 2 and he will accept in the next stage.
    Solving this pair of equations yields:

$$x^* = \frac{1 - \delta_2}{1 - \delta_1 \delta_2}$$

$$y^* = \frac{\delta_1 (1 - \delta_2)}{1 - \delta_1 \delta_2}$$

(Verify that in the particular case in which $\delta_1 = \delta_2$, the solution of this pair of equations is identical to the one we found previously.) Therefore, the strategy profile that is a candidate for being a subgame perfect equilibrium is the one in which each player $i = 1, 2$ adopts the following strategy σ_i^*: in your turn, offer your rival j the slice $1 - \frac{1-\delta_j}{1-\delta_i\delta_j}$; when your rival makes an offer, accept any slice that is not less than $\frac{\delta_i (1-\delta_j)}{1-\delta_i \delta_j}$.

    Complete the proof that this strategy profile is a subgame perfect equilibrium. (Show that the one-deviation principle is valid in the game even in the case in which $\delta_1 \neq \delta_2$, and that there is no subgame G in which it is worthwhile for one of the players $i = 1, 2$ to deviate from σ_i^* only in the first stage of G.)

    At this equilibrium, the more patient player 2 is, i.e. the larger δ_2 is, so does player 1's payoff $x^* = \frac{1-\delta_2}{1-\delta_1 \delta_2}$ progressively diminish. (Verify this!) Likewise, the more patient player 1 is, i.e. the greater δ_1 is, so does her payoff increase. (Verify this point, too.) In any event, the payoff of player 1 remains greater than that of player 2.
    What is the reason underlying this state of affairs? Player 1's advantage derives from the fact that player 2 prefers to get a slightly smaller slice of the pie

immediately rather than a larger slice in the next stage, when he is in the proposer's position. The more patient player 2 is, the less willing he is to accept "deprivation" or "unfairness" in order to precipitate the receipt of his slice. Similarly, the more patient player 1 is, the less "deprivation" she will be ready to put up with in the second stage, and consequently, the degree to which player 2 can increase his payoff if he awaits his turn as proposer in the second stage likewise diminishes. Thus, even if player 2 is patient (δ_2 is high) but player 1 is likewise patient (δ_1 is high), player 2 cannot gain much if he refuses player 1's offer in the first stage and waits to be in the proposer's position in the second stage. Hence, the higher δ_1 is, the smaller the slice $1 - x^*$ that player 2 will agree to accept as early as the first stage, while the complementary slice x^* that player 1 rakes in increases in size.

Question 24.4   Show that the equilibrium that you found in Question 24.3 is the unique subgame perfect equilibrium in the game.

Answer[13]   As we have already noted, the game has a recursive structure: all the subgames commencing in odd game stages, in which player 1 is the proposer, are structurally identical to one another as well as being identical in terms of the players' preferences; but the payoffs in a subgame commencing in stage $2n + 1$ are multiplied by δ^{2n}. Similarly, all the subgames commencing in even game stages, in which player 1 is the proposer, are structurally identical to one another as well as being identical in terms of the players' preferences; but the payoffs in a subgame commencing in stage $2n$ are multiplied by δ^{2n-1}.

Therefore, in order to bring to a common denominator the numerical representation of the players' preferences in different subgames, we say that the players' **continuation payoffs** in a subgame commencing in stage k are the payoffs that appear in the game tree multiplied by $\delta^{-(k-1)}$.[14]

We will now denote:

$\bar{v}_i$ – the supremum[15] of all the continuation payoffs of player i in stages in which she is the proposer across all the subgame perfect equilibria of the game

---

[13] Based on Shaked, A. and J. Sutton (1984), "Involuntary Unemployment as a Perfect Equilibrium in a Bargaining Model," *Econometrica* 52, 1351–1364. The present formulation is also based on Fudenberg, D. and J. Tirole (1991), *Game Theory*, The MIT Press, section 4.4.2.

[14] In the sequel, "a player's payoff in a subgame" will hence refer to her continuation payoff in the subgame.

[15] The supremum of a set of numbers is the smallest number that is not strictly smaller than any number in the set; the infimum of a set of numbers is the largest number that is not strictly larger than any number in the set. For example, for the set of numbers in the open interval $(0,1)$, the supremum is 1 and the infimum is 0. Likewise for the set of numbers in the closed interval $[0,1]$, the supremum is 1 and the infimum is 0.

$\underline{v_i}$ – the infimum of all the continuation payoffs of player i in stages in which she is the proposer across all the subgame perfect equilibria of the game

$\overline{w_i}$ – the supremum of the continuation payoffs of player i in stages in which her rival is the proposer across all the subgame perfect equilibria of the game

$\underline{w_i}$ – the infimum of the continuation payoffs of player i in stages in which her rival is the proposer across all the subgame perfect equilibria of the game.

What connections prevail between these terms?

It is obvious that:

$$\underline{v_1} \geq 1 - \delta_2 \overline{v_2} \tag{24.1}$$

This is because player 2 knows that if he refuses an offer of player 1 in any subgame, in the subgame commencing at the game stage that follows, his payoff will not exceed $\overline{v_2}$. Therefore, at a subgame perfect equilibrium, he will not refuse any offer of player 1 that is at least as large as $\delta_2 \overline{v_2}$, and hence we deduce that the payoff of player 1 will be no smaller than $1 - \delta_2 \overline{v_2}$.

Similarly, by a role reversal between the players, we obtain:

$$\underline{v_2} \geq 1 - \delta_1 \overline{v_1} \tag{24.2}$$

Likewise, it is obvious that at a subgame perfect equilibrium, player 2 will never offer player 1 more than $\delta_1 \overline{v_1}$ and therefore:

$$\overline{w_1} \leq \delta_1 \overline{v_1} \tag{24.3}$$

In addition, we note that at a subgame perfect equilibrium, player 2 always rejects any offer in which his share is smaller than $\delta_2 \underline{v_2}$ (while the share of player 1 exceeds $1 - \delta_2 \underline{v_2}$), since in the following subgame, his payoff is at least $\underline{v_2}$. Therefore, the highest payoff $\overline{v_1}$ of player 1 satisfies:

$$\overline{v_1} \leq \max\{1 - \delta_2 \underline{v_2}, \delta_1 \overline{w_1}\} \leq \max\{1 - \delta_2 \underline{v_2}, \delta_1^2 \overline{v_1}\} \tag{24.4}$$

(The second inequality follows from inequality (24.3).)

Is it possible that $\overline{v_1} = \delta_1^2 \overline{v_1}$? Such an equality would have been possible only in case $\overline{v_1} = 0$, but this is obviously not the case since we have already found a subgame perfect equilibrium in which the payoff of player 1 is positive. Therefore from (24.4) we deduce that:

$$\overline{v_1} \leq 1 - \delta_2 \underline{v_2} \tag{24.5}$$

Similarly, by a role reversal between the players, we obtain:

$$\overline{v_2} \leq 1 - \delta_1 \underline{v_1} \tag{24.6}$$

From the inequalities (24.1) and (24.6) we deduce:

$$\underline{v}_1 \geq 1 - \delta_2 \bar{v}_2 \geq 1 - \delta_2(1 - \delta_1 \underline{v}_1) \tag{24.7}$$

and hence:

$$\underline{v}_1 \geq \frac{1 - \delta_2}{1 - \delta_1 \delta_2} \tag{24.8}$$

From the inequalities (24.5) and (24.2) we deduce:

$$\bar{v}_1 \leq 1 - \delta_2 \underline{v}_2 \leq 1 - \delta_2(1 - \delta_1 \bar{v}_1) \tag{24.9}$$

and hence:

$$\bar{v}_1 \leq \frac{1 - \delta_2}{1 - \delta_1 \delta_2} \tag{24.10}$$

Since $\underline{v}_1 \leq \bar{v}_1$, from (24.8) and (24.10) we obtain:

$$\underline{v}_1 = \bar{v}_1 = \frac{1 - \delta_2}{1 - \delta_1 \delta_2} \equiv v_1^* \tag{24.11}$$

Out of similar considerations, by a reversal of roles between the players, we get:

$$\underline{v}_2 = \bar{v}_2 = \frac{1 - \delta_1}{1 - \delta_1 \delta_2} \equiv v_2^* \tag{24.12}$$

Thus, we have shown that at every subgame perfect equilibrium, every player has the same continuation payoff in every subgame in which that player is the proposer – a payoff which is identical to that player's continuation payoff at the equilibrium we found in Question 24.3.

Does there exist another subgame perfect equilibrium (different than the one we found in Question 24.3), with different strategies but with the same continuation payoffs v_1^*, v_2^*, respectively, in each subgame? The answer is negative. In order to verify this we note, first, that at every such equilibrium the offer of each player is bound to be accepted. Why? Were the offer of player 1, for example, to be rejected at some stage, the continuation payoff of player 2 in the subgame commencing at the following stage would be v_2^*. Hence the payoff of player 1 in the subgame in which her offer was rejected would have been:

$$\delta_1 (1 - v_2^*) = \delta_1 \left(1 - \frac{1 - \delta_1}{1 - \delta_1 \delta_2} \right) = \delta_1^2 v_1^* < v_1^*$$

contrary to the fact that this payoff is v_1^*. Out of similar considerations, at such equilibrium, the offers of player 2 are likewise always accepted.

Is it possible that at such equilibrium (at which the continuation payoffs are v_1^*, v_2^* respectively, in each subgame), player i will make an offer different from that in accordance with which her slice of the pie is v_i^*? The answer is negative: if her offer were different from v_i^*, in order for her payoff in the subgame to remain v_i^*, her offer would have had to be rejected, contrary to the conclusion we reached in the preceding section.

Is it possible that at such equilibrium (at which the continuation payoffs are v_1^*, v_2^* respectively, in each subgame), the strategy of the responding player j will be different from that in the equilibrium strategy that we found – the strategy that dictates "reject any offer in which your share is less than $1 - v_i^*$ and accept any offer in which your share is greater than or equal to $1 - v_i^*$"? Here, too, the answer is negative: it is impossible that player j should reject the offer for the slice $1 - v_i^*$ that player i offers him at equilibrium, since, as we have seen, at an equilibrium of the said type no offer is rejected. Similarly, it is impossible that the strategy of player j should dictate to him to accept and content himself with some offer in which his slice is smaller than $1 - v_i^*$, since with such a strategy of player j, it would not be optimal from the point of view of player i to offer player j the slice $1 - v_i^*$.

Hence we deduce that the subgame perfect equilibrium that we found in Question 24.3 is the unique subgame equilibrium of the game.

QED

Thus, at the unique (subgame perfect) equilibrium of the sequential bargaining game, the two bargaining parties promptly reach agreement, without delay. The extent of their patience affects the distribution of the pie only through what their behavior would hypothetically be if they deviated from their equilibrium strategy. But in practice, the equilibrium path leads them to an efficient agreement, in which neither one of them suffers the damages that would be caused by a protraction of the negotiations.

In reality, by contrast, speedy and efficient negotiations are actually the exception rather than the rule. Strikes and wars are only two examples of negotiations that are carried out simultaneously with damages that both parties inflict on one another. It was the war theoretician Carl von Clausewitz who coined the famous phrase "war is the continuation of politics by other means."

What, then, is the source of this inefficiency? Why do most cases of bargaining in life not end speedily as in the model we have analyzed here? Why do the bargaining parties fail to understand what mutual interests are on the agenda, and what distribution of such interests will take place, of its own inherent stability, at equilibrium?

This question has two main types of answer.

- **Asymmetric information.** In the model it was assumed that both bargaining parties had perfect knowledge of the size of the pie. In reality, the interests of either party may be known to that party alone, and it may be only partly familiar with the interests of its rival.

For example, a buyer may know how much he is prepared to pay, at most, for a particular good, but is liable not to know what, exactly, is the minimum price at which the seller will be willing to sell it. Correspondingly, the seller may know at what minimum price she herself is prepared to sell the merchandise, but may have only partial knowledge as to the maximum price at which the buyer will be willing to purchase it. The seller may know the price range over which this maximum price may shift, or she may even have a belief concerning the **probability distribution** of the maximum price values in that range, but such partial knowledge is not equivalent to the full knowledge that we assumed in the model we analyzed.

In game theory there is a rich body of models dealing with bargaining under asymmetric information. In some of these models, postponements and delays are inevitable at equilibrium. In particular, an important result of this literature[16] determines that under fairly general conditions, when the information of either party concerning the interests of its rival is incomplete, and the parties have no common knowledge that there necessarily exists an agreement that will serve the interests of them both, no equilibrium exists at which the parties will always strike an immediate deal whenever a mutually advantageous deal indeed exists.

- **Biases in judgment.** There is an extensive literature dealing with biases in human judgment, which cause people to behave suboptimally. In the context of bargaining, the relevant biases are those that cause either party to believe that their share of the pie ought to be larger than it can actually be. These may be biases of over-optimism, causing the subject to believe that the pie as a whole is larger than it really is; a person's tendency to believe that it is logical to expect the distribution of the pie to be fair and egalitarian even if his rival is far more patient than he is;[17] a bias of the **endowment effect** type,[18] in which the seller "becomes attached" to the object in his possession and is prepared to sell it only at a price higher than its economic value to him; or a bias called the **self-serving bias,**[19] that causes each party to believe that their bargaining arguments are stronger and more firmly

[16] Myerson, R. and M. Satterthwaite (1983), "Efficient Mechanisms for Bilateral Trading," *Journal of Economic Theory* 29, 265–281.

[17] Babcock, L., G. Loewenstein, S. Issacharoff, and C. Camerer (1995), "Biased Judgments of Fairness in Bargaining," *American Economic Review* 85, 1337–1343.

[18] Kahneman, D., J. Knetch, and R. Thaler (1990), "Experimental Tests of the Endowment Effect and the Coase Theorem," *Journal of Political Economy* 98, 1325–1348.

[19] Babcock, L. and G. Loewenstein (1997), "Explaining Bargaining Impasse: The Role of Self-serving Biases," *Journal of Economic Perspectives* 11, 109–126.

founded than they really are. All these biases are liable to cause parties to adopt a tougher stance during negotiations than they otherwise would, causing the bargaining process to take longer.

The integration of such psychological aspects into game-theoretic models finds expression in a branch of game theory called **behavioral game theory**. This is yet another one of the fascinating developments of game theory in the twenty-first century.

INDEX

Printed in the United States
By Bookmasters